# After Belonging

# Áfter Bēlòngịńǧ

## The Objects, Spaces, and Territories of the Ways We Stay in Transit

Edited by Lluís Alexandre Casanovas Blanco,
Ignacio G. Galán, Carlos Mínguez Carrasco,
Alejandra Navarrete Llopis, Marina Otero Verzier

Oslo Architecture Triennale 2016
Lars Müller Publishers

# Afțēŗ Belòńģĩñg
## The Objects, Spaces, and Territories of the Ways We Stay in Transit

# Forord

Oslo arkitekturtriennale (OAT) har siden opprettelsen i 2000 utviklet seg til å bli en betydningsfull arkitekturfaglig institusjon i Norge. Hvert tredje år danner hovedstaden utgangspunktet for en serie utstillinger, konferanser og arrangementer som samler norske og internasjonale fagmiljøer og byens befolkning i relevante diskusjoner om arkitektur- og byplanfaglige spørsmål.

Oslo vokser—raskere enn mange av Europas hovedsteder. Byveksten er i stor grad migrasjonsdrevet, og bringer med seg en rekke samfunnsmessige utfordringer som bør få konsekvenser for hvordan vi planlegger og bygger i fremtiden.

Med triennalen *«Etter tilhørighet: Om å komme til—Om å komme fra»* tar årets kuratorer, After Belonging Agency, opp et tema som er relevant langt utover Norges grenser. I en tid hvor økonomien sirkulerer globalt, og gjenstander og mennesker forflytter seg mer enn noensinne er vår tilhørighet i spill. Økende migrasjon bidrar til at flere og flere befinner seg i en tilstand av permanent midlertidighet. Forskjellene mellom store grupper av mennesker øker. Vi er i ferd med å forandre måter å eie på, og hvordan vi bytter og deler ting. Forståelsen av «å være hjemme» og betydningen av eiendom og identitet er i endring.

*Etter tilhørighet* utforsker derfor hvilken tilknytning vi har til steder og fellesskap—hvor hører vi egentlig til? Hvilket forhold har vi til tingene vi eier, deler og bytter?

Med sitt hoved- og sideprogram er OAT et komplekst, men åpent arrangement som involverer en lang rekke samarbeidspartnere fra ulike fagområder og interessegrupper i samfunnet. Mange programpartnere fra inn- og utland bidrar til å løfte triennalens tema og diskusjoner ut til målgruppene.

I kjølvannet av den femte Oslotriennalen *Behind the Green Door* i 2013—der det belgiske kuratorteamet ROTOR undersøkte det forslitte begrepet bærekraft—publiserte OAT boken med samme navn. Den ga mulighet til kritisk å analysere og oppsummere arbeidet som ble lagt ned i forbindelse med triennalen. Like etter, i september 2014, var sekretariatet i gang med å forberede årets triennale med en ny kuratorutlysning. 73 team fra hele verden søkte, noe som viser den store interessen OAT vekker også internasjonalt. Grunnen er kanskje at OAT gir mulighet til å gå dypere inn i en valgt problemstilling. Denne dokumentasjons- og undersøkelsesfasener et fortrinn som skiller OAT fra andre tilsvarende begivenheter.

OAT forener de seks stifterne og medlemsorganisasjonene—Arkitektur- og designhøgskolen i Oslo (AHO), Norsk design- og arkitektursenter (DOGA), Norske arkitekters landsforbund (NAL), Nasjonalmuseet–Arkitektur, Oslo arkitektforening (OAF), og Oslo Business Region—og skaper en plattform for å samle ulike roller og kompetanse med et felles mål: Å skape et møtested for faglig utvikling, diskusjon og innflytelse.

En rekke støttespillere har kommet til det siste året, og har bidratt til at et profesjonelt sekretariat kan sørge for kontinuitet og kompetanseoverføring.

På vegne av styret i OAT vil jeg takke alle disse bidragsyterne: De åtte assosierte medlemmene—Bergen arkitekthøgskole, NTNU Fakultet for arkitektur og billedkunst, Oslo kommune Plan- og bygningsetaten, FutureBuilt, ROM for kunst og arkitektur, Norske interiørarkitekters og møbeldesigneres landsforening, Norske landskapsarkitekters forening og Arkitektbedriftene; triennalens generalpartner BARCODE; hovedsamarbeidspartnerne DARK og Kluge; samarbeidspartner Aspelin Ramm og de offentlige tilskuddsgiverne Oslo kommune, Kulturdepartementet, Utenriksdepartementet, Nordisk Kulturfond, Kulturkontakt Nord og KORO. En spesiell takk rettes også til Elise Jaffe og Jeffrey Brown for deres generøse støtte til denne boken.

Takk til årets kuratorer Lluís Alexandre Casanovas Blanco, Ignacio González Galán, Carlos Mínguez Carrasco, Alejandra Navarrete Llopis, Marina Otero Verzier for deres høye ambisjoner og utrettelige arbeid. Med *Etter tilhørighet* setter de i gang en viktig diskusjon med stor betydning for utviklingen av arkitekturfaget framover.

Til slutt vil jeg takke sekretariatet for at vårt opprinnelige mål for lengst er nådd, i det Oslo arkitekturtriennale har fått status som en av verdens mest interessante, blant et økende antall triennaler, biennaler og festivaler.

—Nina Berre, Styreleder, Oslo arkitekturtriennale

## Foreword

Since its inception in 2000, the Oslo Architecture Triennale (OAT) has evolved into a major architectural institution in Norway. Every third year, the capital serves as the venue for a series of exhibitions, conferences, and events that engage local residents and Norwegian and international professionals in meaningful and relevant discussions on architecture and urban development.

Oslo is one of Europe's fastest-growing cities. Largely driven by immigration, this urban growth brings new challenges that should influence how we plan and build for the future.

With *After Belonging: A Triennale In Residence, On Residence and the Ways We Stay in Transit,* our Chief Curators, Lluís Alexandre Casanovas Blanco, Ignacio G. Galán, Carlos Mínguez Carrasco, Alejandra Navarrete Llopis, Marina Otero Verzier (After Belonging Agency), address a topic relevant far beyond Norway's borders. At a time when the global economy allows for the unprecedented circulation of objects and people, our belonging is at stake. Ever more people find themselves in a state of permanent flux; inequalities between large groups of people are on the rise; and we are on the verge of changing the ways in which we own, exchange, and share our belongings. Our understanding of "being at home" and of property and identity is also changing.

*After Belonging* seeks to explore the attachments we feel to places and communities. Where do we actually belong? What relationship do we have with our objects?

With both its core and extended programmes, OAT engages a wide number of partners from various countries, professions, sectors, and interest groups. This approach enables the Triennale to disseminate its topics and discussions to a wide range of target groups.

Following the fifth Oslo Triennale, *Behind the Green Door,* in 2013 — where the Belgian curatorial team ROTOR explored the well-worn concept of sustainability — OAT published a book of the same name, critically analyzing and summarizing the work of the 2013 Triennale. In September 2014, the secretariat began preparing for this year's Triennale by announcing a call for curators. Seventy-three teams from all over the world applied, testifying to the great international interest in OAT. The reason is, perhaps, that OAT makes possible the investigation of a topic in great depth. This opportunity for documentation and exploration is an advantage that sets OAT apart from similar events.

OAT unites its six constituent member organizations — the Oslo School of Architecture and Design, the Norwegian Centre for Design and Architecture, the National Association of Norwegian Architects, the National Museum – Architecture, the Oslo Association of Architects, and the Oslo Business Region — to constitute a platform that brings together various forms of expertise with a common objective: creating a meeting place for professional development, discussion, and influence.

A number of new partners have joined the Triennale organization over the past year. On behalf of the OAT board I would like to thank all of these contributors: the eight associated members—the Bergen School of Architecture, the NTNU Faculty of Architecture and Fine Art, the Planning and Building Department of the Municipality of Oslo, FutureBuilt, Gallery ROM, the Norwegian Association of Interior Architects and Furniture Designers, the Norwegian Association of Landscape Architects, and Arkitektbedriftene—as well as the triennale's general sponsor BARCODE, its main sponsors DARK Architects and Kluge Law firm, and the sponsor Aspelin Ramm. I would also like to thank the Triennale's public benefactors: the Municipality of Oslo, the Norwegian Ministry of Culture, the Norwegian Ministry of Foreign Affairs, the Nordic Culture Fund, Nordic Culture Point, Public Art Norway, and Elise Jaffe and Jeffrey Brown for their generous support of this publication.

Thank you to our Chief Curators, After Belonging Agency, for their high ambitions and tireless efforts and work with the Triennale. With *After Belonging*, they are putting a pressing and important issue on the agenda, and thereby raising a discussion which will shape and influence our profession in the future.

Finally, I would like to thank the secretariat for working steadily towards the achievement of our goal: to establish the Oslo Architecture Triennale as one of the world's leading events of its kind, amidst a growing number of architecture triennales, biennales, and festivals.

— Nina Berre, Chair of the Board, Oslo Architecture Triennale

# Afțēṛ Beĺòngıňg

**Lluís Alexandre Casanovas Blanco, Ignacio G. Galán,
Carlos Mínguez Carrasco, Alejandra Navarrete Llopis,
Marina Otero Verzier**

**1** Description of scenes in the Sri-Lankan-born British singer M.I.A.'s music video "Double Bubble Trouble." "Double Bubble Trouble" is a song from the album *Matangi* (2013),written by Maya "M.I.A." Arulpragasam, Ruben Fernhout, Jerry Leembruggen, and Rypke Westra, produced by The Partysquad, and released on May 30, 2014.

**2** Alibaba Group Holding Limited, "Annual Report for the Fiscal Year ended March 31, 2016," p. 77, http://www.alibabagroup.com/en/ir/pdf/form20F_160525.pdf.

**3** https://www.instagram.com, accessed June 5, 2016.

**4** United Nations, Department of Economic and Social Affairs, Population Division, "Population Facts: Trends in International Migration, 2015," December 2015, accessed May 24, 2016, http://www.un.org/en/development/desa/population/migration/publications/populationfacts/docs/MigrationPopFacts 20154.pdf

**5** "Immigrants and Norwegian-born to immigrant parents, 1 January 2016," Statistics Norway, March 3, 2016, accessed July 1, 2016, https://www.ssb.no/en/befolkning/statistikker/innvbef/aar/2016-03-03/.

In the domestic interiors of a Brutalist council estate, new fabrication technologies coexist with laminated wood furniture, neon-colored drones, souvenirs from remote territories, faux animal prints, and leather sofas. It is mid-afternoon. Shots of colorful parrots and Capuchin monkeys interweave with scenes of teenagers who, while sitting in front of TVs displaying international channels, communicate through phones and laptops, share images with close and distant friends, and place orders online. 3-D printing alternates with hookah smoking. Jeans and leggings are combined with smiling-face-printed niqabs; hoodies, with Afropunk-patterned bomber jackets. Japanese kanji tattoos cover arms and backs. These scenes depict a weekday in Peckham, South London, the home of communities with diverse origins from all over England and from East Asia, South Asia, the Caribbean, Africa, the Middle East, and Eastern Europe.[1]

The scenes in these spaces exemplify a larger condition. In 2015, the online retailing company Alibaba shipped 12.2 billion packages to home addresses.[2] The social media platform Instagram contained 58,940,079 posts tagged #home.[3] And, at present, more than 240 million people are living in a place where they were not born.[4] In Oslo alone, the Triennale location, over 30% of the population consists of migrants.[5] At the same time, the number of tourist arrivals throughout the world—stays of less than twelve months—is over one billion.[6] In Norway, this number is almost five million, roughly the same as its stable population.[7] Contemporary spaces of residence are shaped around the circulation of goods, images, and individuals moving throughout wider territories.

Being at home has different definitions nowadays—both within domestic settings and in the spaces defined by national boundaries—under these global regimes of circulation grounded in changing geopolitical relations, the uneven developments of neoliberalism, and the expansion of media technologies. Belonging is no longer just something bound to one's own space of residence or to the territory of a nation, nor does it last an entire lifespan.

The Oslo Architecture Triennale 2016, *After Belonging*, dissects and designs the objects, spaces, and territories involved in a transforming condition of belonging. Pervasive commercial exchanges, systems of information transfer, and migratory movements have destabilized what we understand by residence, forcing us to question spatial permanence, property, and identity—a crisis of belonging. The processes of globalization have brought greater

Stills from M.I.A.'s music video "Double Bubble Trouble," 2013.

accessibility to ever-new goods, fueled alternative imaginaries, and provided access to further geographies and knowledges. And yet, not everybody circulates voluntarily, nor in the same way: circulation also promotes growing inequalities for large groups, kept in precarious states of transit.

    *After Belonging* analyzes the ways in which architecture intervenes in the construction of attachments to places and collectivities—Where does one belong?—as well as in the changing relations to the objects that are produced, owned, shared, and exchanged—How are belongings managed?

Belonging is being contemporaneously transformed at different scales and in different contexts. For example, the daily life of the middle classes around the world is being reconfigured by the economic conditions and social relations enabled by home-sharing platforms, as well as by the production of aesthetic regimes mobilized in the postings on these platforms. And yet, the universal ambitions advertised through Airbnb's motto, "Belong Anywhere," is in stark contrast to the bureaucratic realities of how such belonging is, in fact, regulated by local laws which determine the movement of the users of these home-sharing platforms between countries.[8] Moreover, flat-pack furniture companies often capitalize on the desire by users of these platforms to display a national signature in the spaces offered for rental—as is the case in Nordic countries like Denmark, where many offerings are dressed with Scandinavian design. Some commentators have recently argued that these same companies facilitate detachment from furnishing objects for transient populations,[9] while new spaces like mini-storage facilities in cities like New York continue to make possible their accumulation.

6 United Nations World Tourism Organization, *UNWTO Annual Report 2015* (Madrid: United Nations World Tourism Organization, 2016), 2, http://af.cdn.unwto.org/sites/all/files/pdf/annual_report_2015_lr.pdf/.

7 International tourism, number of arrivals in Norway in 2014: 4,855,000. Total population in Norway in 2014 5,136,886. Source: http://data.worldbank.org/indicator/ST.INT.ARVL?locations=NO/.

8 Brian Chesky, "Belong Anywhere," *Airbnb Blog*, July 16, 2014, http://blog.airbnb.com/belong-anywhere/.

9 Alison J. Clarke, professor of design history at the University of Applied Arts Vienna, cited by Sarah Amandolare in "The real reason you still shop at Ikea - and probably always will," *The Guardian*, June 26, 2016, http://www.theguardian.com/lifeandstyle/2016/jun/26/why-shop-ikea-home-decor-convenience/.

10 These fences challenge the free movement of individuals established by the Schengen Treaty. "The Schengen area and cooperation," *EUR-Lex,* last modified August 3, 2009, http://eur-lex.europa.eu/legal-content/EN/TXT/?uri=U RISERV%3A13-3020. Rana F. Sweis, "Jordan Closes Border to Syrian Refugees After Suicide Car Bomb Kills 6," *The New York Times,* June 21, 2016,http://www.nytimes.com/2016/06/22/world/middleeast/jordan-syria-attack.html?_r=0.

11 Abhishek Bhalla, "Access denied! India's High Commissioner raises questions after Delhi rejects 50% of Pakistani visa applications," *Daily Mail,* June 16, 2016, http://www.dailymail.co.uk/indiahome/article-3645543/High-Commissioner-raises-questions-India-rejects-50-Pakistani-visa-applications.html/.

12 Anne Frugé, "The opposite of Brexit: African Union launches an all-Africa passport," *The Washington Post,* July 1, 2016, https://www.washingtonpost.com/news/monkey-cage/wp/2016/07/01/the-opposite-of-brexit-african-union-launches-an-all-africa-passport/.

13 "The legality of all emirates, groups, states, and organizations, becomes null by the expansion of the khilāfah's authority and arrival of its troops to their areas." Abu Muhammad al-'Adnani al-Shami, "This Is the Promise of Allah," video transcript released by Jihadology.net / Al-Hayat Media Center, June 19, 2014, accessed July 8th, 2016, https://ia902505.us.archive.org/28/items/poa_25984/EN.pdf/.

Despite the expansion of circulatory processes affecting domestic spaces like these, current international events—including the results of the United Kingdom's European Union membership referendum; the border fences erected by European countries and in countries like Jordan as a result of the so called refugee crisis;[10] and the rejection by India of over 50% of visa applications from Pakistan since January 2016 [11]—suggest the reordering of borders, economic and political relationships, and power structures around the globe.

While these events seem to reinforce the concept of the nation-state as a geographically confined site of belonging, other phenomena support alternative arguments: progress on the development of the all-African passport will soon allow many to expand the territories they can call home; [12] and, on a darker note, the Islamic State has recently proclaimed itself to be a worldwide caliphate, with religious, political and military authority, presenting a religious inflection of the nation-state.[13] Moreover, the dissemination of information and images increasingly shared in social media builds imaginaries and shapes aspirations that continue to fuel the movement of people: the number of teenage boys migrating from Egypt—a country that is not currently indexed as suffering a civil war—after receiving images and narratives of success from friends and family members via social media, has reached unprecedented levels, to the point that some parts of the territory are almost devoid of their youth.[14]

These shifting and apparently opposed conditions (of commercial dispersion, apparent territorial stabilization, and simultaneous geopolitical re-configurations) have architectural manifestations and effects in our modes and spaces of residence and their aesthetic, technical, legal, socio-economic, and political frameworks. Addressing the architectural entanglements that lie behind these different phenomena, *After Belonging* engages with pressing challenges that are relevant for the architecture field and beyond, including, for example, the response to the huge numbers of asylum seekers currently arriving in Europe.[15] However, rather than focusing on this crisis as an isolated phenomena or responding to it without questioning its origins, this Triennale aims to locate the challenges that migration to Europe poses within a larger context from which it cannot be untangled. More broadly, *After Belonging* considers the precarious structural conditions of contemporary neoliberal regimes that have been aggravated by recent conflicts by examining how particular objects, spaces, and territories are designed and managed to produce re-articulations of belonging that are inherent in those regimes.

Belonging, as architecture, is simultaneously concerned with physical and social spaces. It addresses questions of affection, technological transformations, material transactions, and economic processes. And, at all of these levels, belonging is neither good or bad, yet it remains as a contentious concept. *After Belonging* addresses the ramifications of this concept and its relation to material manifestations at different scales, with the aim of proposing and advancing new ways of understanding architecture's transformed relation to enclosure and stability.

*After Belonging* argues that place-making and the construction of a sense of identity constitute only the most typical among other possible agendas for which architecture could be mobilized. Architecture has served over time for diverse, often opposed, ideological endeavors of belonging: it has been crucial in constructing and vindicating national identities as a symbol for liberation from colonial and imperialist forms of power, but has also supported essentialist projects. This project intends to critically inspect how architecture is articulated towards specific ends in the transformation of belonging, and aims to speculate on alternative trajectories for architectural production.

In a time defined by mobility and transit, the discussions triggered by this Triennale and contained in this volume destabilize the various definitions of the house characterized by the most canonical architectural expressions of residence and belonging, questioning the seamless construction of homeliness as a solid unity grounded in intimacy, privacy, and rootedness. Instead, these discussions consider the house as an unstable aggregate of objects, bodies, spaces, institutions, technologies, and imaginations. Contemporary architectures of housing are enmeshed in the logics of real estate speculation, many of them connected to territorial processes of massive urbanization and global migration, and increasingly transformed by technological mediations, while continuing to appeal to different traditions and ambitions of stability. In the midst of transcontinental migrations, newly-imagined landscapes, and

**14** Declan Walsh, "Facebook Envy Lures Egyptian Teenagers to Europe and the Migrant Life," *The New York Times*, June 23, 2016, http://www.nytimes.com/2016/06/24/world/middleeast/facebook-envy-and-italian-law-lure-egyptian-teenagers-to-europe.html/.

**15** In the Fall of 2014—when the research for the Triennale was initiated—the realities of migration had not yet attained the wide media coverage they have acquired today. As media theorist and human rights scholar Thomas Keenan has argued, the media coverage of a social crisis is the final site where a public reaction towards the conflict is articulated, and where a possible outcome soothing "impulses for action"—either as a military intervention or as humanitarian assistance—are designed. Primarily

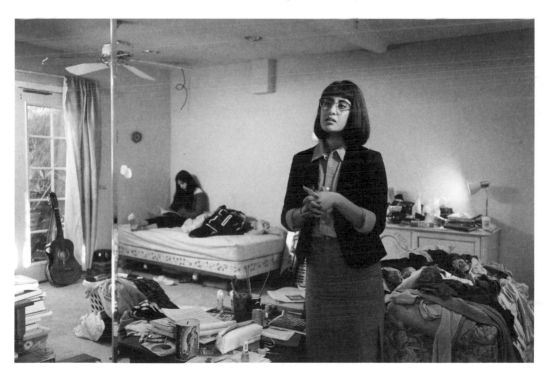

"Boomerang Kids," a series of portraits of young adults who have had to move back home with their parents after college for financial reasons, or who have never been able to leave home. High student loan payments, a competitive, educated job market and graduating into a recovering economy are a large reason why there is a trend to stay home longer. Photograph by Damon Casarez, 2014. Courtesy of the author.

Established as an extension of the Norwegian welfare network located outside the borders of Norway, the hotel Reuma-Sol in the city of Alfaz del Pi, Alicante (Spain), mostly hosts Norwegian pensioners for periods ranging from 6 to 12 weeks where they enjoy the benefits of the Mediterranean sun in the treatment of certain illnesses. Photograph by David Frutos, 2016. Courtesy of the author.

concerned with the role of television in the Sarajevo War, Keenan points to the main place where social conflict representations and its associated discourses are dealt with: the domestic environment. See Thomas Keenan, "Publicity and Indifference (Sarajevo on Television)." *PMLA* Vol. 117, No. 1, Special Topic: Mobile Citizens, Media States (Jan., 2002), pp. 104–116.

16 The expression "imaginary communities" was famously coined by Benedict Anderson in his work on modern nationalism. Benedict Anderson, *Imagined Communities*, rev. ed. (London and New York: Verso, 1991).

17 See, for example, Pierre Bourdieu, "The Berber House or the World Reversed," in Social Science Information 9, no. 2 (1970) and the more general arguments by Amos Rapoport, "Socio-cultural factors and house form," in *House Form and Culture* (Englewood Cliffs, NJ: Prentice Hall, 1969).

financial speculation, traveling constituencies continue to make themselves at home in different conditions: for example, Norwegian retiree resorts along the Spanish Coast, in which architecture mediates the advantage of the chosen location with aesthetic and material links to the community of origin.

*After Belonging* additionally considers the different understandings of residence as they relate to the legal definition of citizenship and as a form of cultural binding to a territory and a nation. Moreover, this Triennale also speculates on architecture's articulation with different kinds of "imagined communities" that have become substitutes for the family and religion as the primary forms of social stabilization in technologically advanced, neoliberal, global contexts.[16] And yet, the nation, family, and religion still continue to take new forms in these contexts, with architecture decidedly participating in their articulation. For example, the contested sovereignty of airport spaces like Oslo Gardermoen—and their complex role in the filtering of individuals and objects— is in some cases countered by a decided effort by nations to present themselves as cohesive units to communities in transit. New techno-spatial articulations are also operating in transnational congregations of religious communities such as those of Charismatic-Pentecostalism in sub-Saharan countries.

*After Belonging*'s approach differs from the structuralist impulse to relate the architectural forms of the house with social practices in different global contexts.[17] The discursive framework of the Triennale goes beyond this exploration of isolated architectural productions and their local contexts (which reinforce traditional forms of belonging), by orienting itself towards the understanding of the cultural, technological, and material links—whose effects have been variously described as "freak displacements," "disjunctures," and "frictions"— configuring the different spatial articulations of contemporary culture.[18] The house, in these contexts, no longer relates to phenomenological ideas of place or community stability, but with "the estranging sense of the relocation of the home and the world in an unhallowed place" that many have explored through the condition of the "unheimleich" (unhomely) and through postcolonial studies.[19] The architectures built with remittance money arriving to different Latin American countries, for example, perfectly illustrate this condition. But this case manifests how the sense of home and the uncanny condition of contemporary forms of residence exceed the aesthetic problem of representation of both individuals and communities, aiming to make themselves at home in different architectures. Indeed, there are specific bodies at stake here, as well as specific resources and material transactions. And while money, in this case, seems to travel swiftly between the nations of emigration and immigration, technical knowledges are modified in their translation between the two for the construction of these characteristic architectures, and individuals are often trapped by borders, or have their defining forms of citizenship change while crossing the border.[20]

The architectures associated with the aforementioned transactions and operations sometimes entail the definition of a homogenous landscape. On other occasions, the architectures respond to the construction of differentiated (or decidedly differentiating) representations of identity for diverse geographical contexts or "imaginative geographies" within this global landscape.[21] In some cases they result in material boundlessness, while in others they are manifested in the definition of material boundaries.[22] Considering these changing forms of identity construction, distributions of property, and constructions of enclosure, the explorations that this Triennale pursues are as far from the advocacy of nomadism, as they are from the celebration of a return to local traditions and rooted communities. Many critical projects exploring nomadism in the last decades have been grounded in the pursuit of a cosmopolitan, secular society, freed from local ties.[23] However, the same mobility that these projects celebrated has been coincidental with neoliberal

18 Homi Bhabha, "The World and the Home," *Social Text* 10, no. 2 (1992); Arjun Appadurai, "Disjuncture and Difference" in *Modernity at Large: Cultural Dimensions of Globalization* (Minneapolis: University of Minnesota Press, 1995); Anna L. Tsing, *Friction: An Ethnography of Global Connection* (Princeton, N.J.: Princeton University Press, 2005).

19 See Bhabha, "The World and the Home," 141–2: "The unhomely is the shock of recognition of the world-in-the-home, the home-in-the-world.… Although the 'unhomely' is a paradigmatic post-colonial experience, it has resonance that can be heard distinctly, if erratically, in fictions that negotiate the powers of cultural difference in a range of historical conditions and social contradictions." The notion of the uncanny, originally a Freudian notion, has additionally been linked by Julia Kristeva to an analysis

House built with remittances in El Salvador. Photograph by Andrés Asturias, 2010. Courtesy of the author.

of otherness that includes both one's own other as well as an understanding of the stranger as part of one's own self. See Julia Kristeva Strangers to Ourselves (New York: Columbia University Press, 1991), 181–2: "One cannot hope to understand Freud's contribution, in the specific field of psychiatry, outside of its humanistic and Romantic filiation. With the Freudian notion of the unconscious the involution of the strange in the psyche loses its pathological aspect and integrates within the assumed unity of human beings the otherness that is both biological and symbolic and becomes integral part of the same. Henceforth the foreigner is neither a race nor a nation. The foreigner is neither glorified as a secret Volksgeist nor banished as disruptive of rationalist urbanite. Uncanny, foreignness is with us: we are our own foreigners, we are divided.… My discontent in living with the other— my strangeness, his strangeness—rests on the perturbed logic that governs this strange bundle of drive and language, of nature and symbol, constituted by the unconscious always already shaped by the other."

20 As Jacques Derrida has problematized, subjects do not carry rights and duties during their physical transit: these are continuously negotiated at each side of the border line. See Jacques Derrida, *Of Hospitality: Anne Dufourmantelle Invites Jacques Derrida to Respond*, trans. Rachel Bowlby (Stanford, Calif.: Stanford University Press, 2000).

21 Edward W. Said, "Imaginative Geographies," in *Orientalism* (London: Penguin, 1978).

regimes that have led to the precarization of labor, massive concentrations of wealth, and dispossessed populations kept in transit.

In order to pursue this goal, *After Belonging* develops different platforms with the aim of rehearsing research strategies, articulating diverse formats and modes for architectural practice, and testing work protocols, which in turn offer new forms of engagement for architects with our contemporary changing realities. The main platforms of the Triennale are articulated in two sections:

— A triennale *On Residence,* in which to collectively analyze the spatial conditions that shape our ways of staying in transit and the definition of our contemporary spaces of residence.

— A triennale *In Residence*, in which architects and professionals concerned with the built environment will engage in local collaborations in Oslo, the Nordic region, and around the globe, to intervene in the transformation of residence.

## On Residence

*On Residence* analyzes the architectures involved in contemporary constructions of belonging, documenting the ways in which these architectures redefine the spaces of residence, and the spatial, aesthetic, technical, and sociopolitical implications of this redefinition. Architecture takes here different forms beyond the building, from arrangements of objects and their logistics, to territorial configurations and digital systems of organization; and both the discipline and the profession, and their effects, also assume changing and diverse forms. These architectures have the capacity to convey new articulations between individuals, societies, and institutions, which this section seeks to analyze.

*On Residence* manifests itself in two forms: an exhibition located at the Norwegian Centre for Design and Architecture, DOGA, and the texts by guest contributors in this volume that expand the conversation, employing different narratives, theoretical arguments, and historical case studies. *On Residence* understands both the space of the gallery and that of the book as parallel sites of architectural production and experimentation that inform each other, while exploiting the possibilities of their own media. Both are organized as an accumulation of evidences and speculations, collectively unveiling the multiple scales and media involved in these architectures, rehearsing research and design tools needed to approach them.

The contributions to *On Residence* gravitate around five areas: *Borders Elsewhere, Furnishing After Belonging, Sheltering Temporariness, Technologies for a Life in Transit,* and *Markets and Territories of the Global Home.* These contributions are both constellated around the five topics (inhabiting the buffer of uncertainty between them), as well as with the other pieces. Their accumulation attests to the coalescence of objects, spaces, and territories (as well as their relations with individuals, societies, and institutions) which constitute the architectures addressed by each of the projects presented. The exhibition refuses any bold categorization of the pieces, which would map an illusory coherence onto the extremely fragmentary and fluid scenarios in which belonging is nowadays redefined. The aim of singling out only some of the layers of their defining parameters is to offer a point of access to analyze their architectural implications.

**Borders Elsewhere** — addresses the diverse material artifacts and technologies defining a liminal space that mediates between polities, social constituencies, legal and economic frames, and aesthetic regimes—reaching beyond the construction of walls alone. The effects of borders are also manifested elsewhere, bringing the frictions they enact to our spaces of residence, in which different forms of belonging are defined and contested. On the one hand, borders filter the transit of bodies, defining particular forms of citizenship and sovereignty, and functioning as "theatrical" backgrounds in the construction of identities.[24] On the other hand, borders regulate the circulation of the belongings of these bodies. In that sense, the border has become a privileged testing ground to interrogate the political implications of design, as well as the ways in which architecture contributes to enclose, or divide, populations.

**Furnishing After Belonging** — inspects the new status of objects (and their relations) in an ever-circulating (both physically and digitally) domestic landscape, assessing the transformation of their modes of production, their networks of commercialization, their scales of appreciation, and their triggering of affections. Furnishing is understood not only as the personalization, decoration, or equipment of architecture, but also as part and parcel of the articulation of spaces of expression, relation, and communication for individuals and communities, serving to untangle ideas of personal and national identity. Additionally, furnishing objects can be considered as a lens to understand how traditional systems of property, ownership, and legacy are being currently recodified by the proliferation of privatization, technologically mediated peer-to-peer exchanges, reuse strategies, and ever-more-efficient logistical networks of commerce.

**Sheltering Temporariness** — explores the different permanence spans affecting the regulation of the spaces of residence, as well as the forms of settlement built for individuals and communities in transience. Shelter is not considered merely as a refuge for a sole person or the group defined by family ties, but also as the architectures hosting collectivities with shared realities and aspirations, where other transactions, connections, and solidarities occur. A different articulation of the infrastructures and networks of resources and spaces supporting these forms of cooperation and cohabitation has the capacity to transform the attachments between individuals and architecture, as well as the relation between communities and the territory. Questioning the universal notions underlying the traditional understanding of shelter and inspecting its temporary condition brings into focus the specific and local regulations (both public and private), the individual and collective practices, and the agendas that shape its architectures.

**Technologies for a Life in Transit** — reflects upon the media and modes of organization shaping contemporary networked geographies and the social-bonding and mutualization systems they make possible. This section

**22** Gilles Deleuze reported from the work of Felix Guattari how we might live in "a city where one would be able to leave one's own apartment, one's street, one's neighborhood, thanks to one's (dividual) electronic card that raises a given barrier; but the card could just as easily be rejected on a given day or between certain hours; what counts is not the barrier but the computer that tracks each person's position—licit or illicit—and effects a universal modulation." Gilles Deleuze, "Postscript on the Societies of Control," *October* 59 (Winter 1992): 7

**23** Edward W. Said, for example, understood the potentials of exile as a form of freedom from local ties and detachment from orthodoxy. "The exile knows that in a secular and contingent world, homes are always provisional. Borders and barriers, which enclose us within the safety of familiar territory, can also become prisons, and are often defended beyond reason or necessity. Exiles cross borders, break barriers of thought and experience." Edward Said, "Reflections on exile," [1984] in *Reflections on Exile and Other Essays* (Cambridge, Mass.: Harvard University Press, 2000), 147.

**24** See Wendy Brown, *Walled States, Waning Sovereignty* (New York: Zone Books, 2010), 82. The genealogies for the relationship between research and practice and a particular understanding of research and practice could be very diverse, but it would be worth mentioning the tradition started by the "Learning from…" studios developed by Denise Scott Brown and Robert Venturi at Yale in the late 1960s (most famously including

Temporary living premises for workers at Statoil Mongstad. Photograph by Helge Skodvin, 2016. Courtesy of the author.

the "Learning from Las Vegas" studio and the resulting publication), and the "Project on the City" studios developed by Rem Koolhaas at the Harvard GSD starting in the 1990s. Felicity D. Scott's piece in this volume appeals to more contemporaneous projects related to this understanding.

**25** According to Keller Easterling, "it would seem appropriate for architecture"—often rendering itself as "innocent of the wide world and its operators"—to perform from "a position of corruption," as the discipline "shares a political disposition with the most successful global development paradigms in the world today—paradigms that insist on the same

considers technologically-enabled forms of socialization, as well as changing relations between data on the one hand, and bodies, objects, and spaces on the other, which generate bounded spaces defining forms of inclusion and exclusion (and constructions of otherness). These forms of belonging result in changing understandings of sovereignty and alternative political constituencies. Additionally, architecture is here concerned with new understandings of territories (both physical and digital), as well as with our forms of navigation and positioning within them, resulting in mediated forms of affiliation to resources and communities, and their associated affections and validations.

**Markets and Territories of the Global Home —** considers the multi-scalar cultural and material transactions articulating the sense of familiarity, as well as the possibility of housing for different constituencies around the world. A particular focus of this area is to consider the home as no longer defined at an architectural scale, but having territorial implications when positioned within global financial transactions, international legal frameworks, and commercial and touristic networks. Additionally, this area addresses the possibility of considering the territory as a home, that is, an environmental entity and a unit of resource management, as well as a system of social organization where conflicts are addressed and negotiated.

## In Residence

*In Residence* focuses on a selection of sites—in Oslo, the Nordic region and around the globe—that encapsulate the contemporary transformation of belonging. This section constructs a speculative platform organized around a series of *reports* and *intervention strategies* for those sites. Sites include: the border spaces, technologies, and transit areas of the Oslo Airport in Gardermoen; the negotiation of resources in Kirkenes, on the Norwegian border with Russia; a transnational neighborhood that forms part of the Million Housing Programme on the outskirts of Stockholm; self-storage facilities in New York City; an asylum seekers' reception center in Oslo; a patient room and the related urbanisms of the Dubai Health Care City; the technological spaces linking religious communities in Lagos; an apartment in Copenhagen rented through digital sharing platforms; the houses resulting from remit-tances sent to the coffee growing region of Colombia; and the Italian textile factories associated with one of the biggest Chinatowns in Europe. *In Residence* challenges ideas of "site" as a unit primarily concerned with geometric boundaries, legal limitations, and contextual references. Sites are instead considered as unstable nodes within wider networks, submitted to ongoing alterations and redefinitions.

*In Residence* will be exhibited at the National Museum—Architecture as a series of reports and intervention strategies which are included in this volume respectively as case studies and as an archive of works in progress. Reports about the ten sites have been commissioned from a group of inter-national architects, artists, journalists, and other professionals. Intervention strategies have been selected for the Nordic sites through an international call in order to rehearse tactical, long-term forms of engagement with them. Through these two formats (reports and intervention strategies), *In Residence* aims to expand architectural forms of practice and seeks to regain relevance

Prefabricated metal homes at the Azraq camp for Syrian refugees in northern Jordan. Photograph by Khalil Mazraawi/AFP, January 30, 2016. © Getty images.

innocence, the same immunity or political quarantine." Keller Easterling, "Believers and Cheaters," *Log* 5 (Spring/Summer 2005), 33–6.

**26** Ultimately, In Residence attempts to lay out alternatives to ideological patronage in architectural practice—that is, a paternalistic attitude by which the architect levels his or her own personal condition to that of the "client," a phenomena which especially surfaces when dealing with post-colonial situations. This notion of ideological patronage, in which notions of architect-as-savior rely, was first expounded by Walter Benjamin in 1934, to be later unfolded by art historian Hal Foster to dissect the appropriation of ethnographic techniques by diverse 1980s artistic manifestations. In advocating for a direct intervention into the means of production of an artwork, Benjamin argues that the author should never position himself "next to the proletariat," as this would suppose to end up acquiring the role "of a benefactor, that of an ideological patron—an impossible place." Walter Benjamin, "The Author As Producer" in *Reflections* (New York: Shocken Books, 2007) and Hal Foster, "The Artist as Ethnographer" in *The Traffic in Culture* (Berkeley: University of California Press, 1995). The application of design operations onto situations of precariousness could result in the aesthetic and programmatic consolidation of the very forms of authority responsible for those conditions. Yet, the withdrawal to intervene due to the consideration of these situations as exceptional, accepts the complicity of design practices with the forms of power causing this very precariousness.

For example, philosopher Slavoj Žižek has urged to overcome the consideration of migration as an exceptional, transitory phenomena. Slavoj Žižek, "The Non-Existence of Norway," London Review of Books: LRB Online, September 9, 2015, http://www.lrb.co.uk/2015/09/09/slavoj-zizek/the-non-existence-of-norway/.

Thanks to Megan Elizabeth Eardley, Marcelo López-Dinardi, Anna-Maria Meister, and Manuel Shvartzberg for their feedback on earlier versions of this text.

for the analysis and transformation of the architectures at stake in this project. Rather than separating research and practice, the research on the selected sites plays a critical role in shedding light on new realities, opening up the possibility of alternative forms of knowledge and modes of practice. Even more, both reports and interventions build on a long standing disciplinary tradition of developing research not just to inform practice, but as a form of practice in itself, which probes not only the limits of the profession but its goals as well.[25]

With the intervention strategies, architecture is conceived very broadly as a practice that includes the establishment of protocols negotiating the relations between objects, spaces, and territories as well as the different agents, institutions, and technologies through which they are managed. Intervention strategies map out attitudes and techniques which coalesce around practices of resistance, contestation, reformulation, infiltration, exposure, or exacerbation, amongst many others. The interventions include: the digital mediation of the property systems of objects, seeking to create everyday intimacies and negotiations throughout the city; the production of a city guide by and for asylum seekers that facilitates new forms of interaction, connection, and integration of the citizens within Oslo's public sphere; a series of cartographies and a public spatial archive aiming to create a forum for imagining a future transnational, eco-political Arctic governance; the exposition and subsequent alteration of the user-homogenizing experiences of airports through the design of new physical and digital apparatuses; and an online exchange platform that offers alternative ways of meeting asylum seekers' needs through new notions of adaptability and hospitality, and which ultimately aims at reimagining housing policies in Norway. The teams selected include practicing architects, educators, and researchers as well as professionals from different disciplines including urban planners, graphic designers, and sociologists, expanding the networks within which architects operate.

In confronting these scenarios associated to current configurations of belonging with the set of agendas undergirding architectural practice, *In Residence* aims to test the capacity of architectural expertise to alter—whether by consolidating, ameliorating, exacerbating, or suppressing—the conditions of these sites.[26] Far from reclaiming architecture as a problem-solving discipline, *In Residence* aims to untangle the agency of spatial interventions as well as the capacity of the architect in transforming the definition of these spaces in relation to legal, political, and economic frameworks.[27]

Together with the *On Residence* and *In Residence* sections, other platforms expand the discussion pursued by the Triennale: *The Embassy, the Academy,* and the *After Belonging Conference*. This publication collects all these platforms and contextualizes their speculations within wider disquisitions, while fostering conversations between them.

In closing, all the formats, media, and contributions contained in this volume aim to collectively address and imagine the architectures of new constructions of belonging, new ways of being together, new collectivities, and new forms of managing our belongings. And this pursuit is characteristically defined by a forward looking project. In fact, the "After" before "Belonging" cannot be reduced to mean "post." The topic of this Triennale does not arise from a nostalgia for a lost understanding of belonging, or from an interest in reviving it. This "After" in "After Belonging" refers to a search, a pursuit.

# Taking Stock of Our Belongings

**Preface to *After Belonging: A Triennale In Residence, On Residence and the Ways We Stay in Transit***

Felicity D. Scott

*After Belonging: A Triennale In Residence, On Residence and the Ways We Stay in Transit* engages with a pressing if complicated contemporary issue: how we might reconceive and reconfigure notions of belonging, or potentially move beyond such a concept today. Closely connected to traditional notions of selfhood, to questions of identity, and to structures of identification (social, cultural, sexual, religious, ethnic, racial, and political), as well as to forms of citizenship proper to the modern nation-state, belonging is a measure at once of inclusion and of exclusion. Notions of belonging have become, however, increasingly complex, if not simply rendered outdated, by the structural ambivalences now at play within conventional demarcations—inside/outside, citizen/foreigner, fixed/transitory, here/there, access/foreclosure, shelter/exposure, us/them—at work within contemporary political, informatic, and geopolitical landscapes. In place of such binaries, new topologies are increasingly visible and many observers speak, instead, of structures and processes of "differential inclusion," "inclusive exclusion," and "exclusive inclusion," convolutions perhaps most evident in the status of migrant workers and refugee communities but also, as *After Belonging* insists, impacting forms of life across a much broader spectrum.[1]

At a current moment characterized by extensive human unsettlement—sometimes voluntary, sometimes not—and by the seemingly ever-more-exacerbated if also increasingly monitored and regulated circulation not only of people but also of goods and information, the semantics and the politics of belonging thus appear today as a heterogeneous and radically unstable field. We might even read this field as a battleground upon which transforming infrastructures and epistemologies both of modernity and of capitalist processes of globalization are struggling to take command. Such fluidity, movement, and communication are often celebrated as markers of increased freedoms under liberalism—and for some this is certainly the case. Circulation within this global milieu is not, however, simply liberatory: the increasingly mobile bodies, signs, objects, aesthetics, and economic and political paradigms are quickly reterritorialized within new forms of stasis, new hierarchies, new institutional frameworks, and new economic, political, and geopolitical formations. The contemporary landscape remains evidently marked by incessant forms of violence, inequity, discrimination, exclusion, securitization, militarism, and exploitation characteristic of neoliberal capital as it touches down unevenly within national contexts and across the planet. These forces too are mobile.

1 On "inclusive exclusion" and its inverse, see Giorgio Agamben, *Homo Sacer: Sovereign Power and Bare Life* (Stanford: Stanford University Press, 1998); and Adi Ophir, Michal Givoni, and Sari Hanafi, eds., *The Power of Inclusive Exclusion: Anatomy of Israeli Rule in the Occupied Palestinian Territories* (New York: Zone Books, 2009). On "differential inclusion" see Etienne Balibar, "Strangers as Enemies: Walls All over the World, and How to Tear Them Down," *Mondi Migranti*, no. 1 (January 2012): 7–25; and Sandro Mezzadra and Brett Neilson, *Border as Method, or, the Multiplication of Labor* (Durham: Duke University Press, 2013).

Moreover, it is a world in which one's differential ability to cross a border or access time-sensitive information is for some a nuisance or inconvenience, while for others a matter of life or death. The ambivalences and instabilities of this contemporary landscape thus come with attendant risks, requiring ongoing scrutiny to render them visible and hence open to critique. But such fluidity can also be read as a precondition for what Michel Foucault has theorized as the structural reversibility of power, and even as opening onto possibilities of politically progressive revalencing, refunctioning, and redirection, at least in the right hands.[2]

It is with this sort of ethos in mind, and cognizant of the distinct and at times incommensurate subject positions that appear within this battleground, that *After Belonging* turns to interrogate the semantic instabilities and the potentialities inherent to tropes of "belonging," "belongings," "residence," "resident," "residency," and "shelter," along with those immanent to contemporary modes of living "in transit." The triennale does so not in order to celebrate the resilience of such terms or their capacity to harbor humanist values in the face of contemporary forms of uprooting, temporariness, and insecurity, let alone to "solve" such "problems" as such or to forge a nostalgic return to earlier, seemingly more stable or clear-cut definitions, valences, and options. Rather, eschewing the often-nationalist and identitarian logics inhering within traditional forms of belonging and residence, *After Belonging* asks, instead, how we might think them differently, recognizing the importance of speculating upon what else they might allow us to do. That is, while recognizing the complexity of the issues at stake, and the ethical minefields to which they give rise, this triennale continues to question how we might navigate within and operate upon this ambivalent terrain and its concomitantly unstable contexts *otherwise*.

*After Belonging* is not, however, just a triennale addressing tensions, aporias, and hierarchies born of capitalist globalization; it is an *architecture* triennale, an event seeking to address what architecture has to do with or say about such concerns, along with the social, subjective, economic, mediatic, and geopolitical regimes informing contemporary reconfigurations of belonging and residence and the artifacts that mediate those reconfigurations. The competition, exhibitions, residencies, objects, buildings, images, research, publications, encounters, exchanges, and events affiliated with the triennale thus come with disciplinary and professional stakes. Not in the normative sense: indeed, although the triennale's foci of investigation often veer away from Architecture (with a capital A) and from strategies seeking an autonomous domain for the discipline, we are also a long way from attempts to normalize architecture's relation to capitalist forces or commercial vernaculars familiar from the generation of *Learning From Las Vegas*.[3] But buildings, spaces, objects, and images—including vernacular ones—remain central to this enterprise, as does the possibility that architects have a certain expertise in decoding and deploying them.

2 On Michel Foucault's figure of the reversibility of power, see Michel Foucault, "Le Discours ne doit pas être pris comme..." (1976), cited by Arnold I. Davidson,"Introduction" in Michel Foucault, "Society Must Be Defended": Lectures at the Collège De France, 1975–76, translated by David Macey (New York·Picador, 2003); Maurizio Lazzarato, "From Biopower to Biopolitics," Tailoring Biotechnologies 2, no. 2 (Summer-Fall 2006): 17. See also Felicity D. Scott, "Taking Time," in 2000+: The Urgencies of Architectural Theory, ed. James Graham (New York: Columbia GSAPP Books on Architecture); 86–197; and Felicity D. Scott, Outlaw Territories: Environments of Insecurity, Architectures of Counterinsurgency (New York: Zone Books, 2016).

3 Robert Venturi, Denise Scott Brown, and Steven Izenour, Learning from Las Vegas (Cambridge: MIT Press, 1972).

Architecture, we might recall, has long enjoyed a privileged relation to historical notions of belonging—establishing material, formal, and organizational
protocols for, as well as visual and representational paradigms of, enclosure,
protection, cultural identity, and place; it has long served to mediate between
what is inside and what is outside. The residence and resident have also
remained privileged figures of settlement and claims to belonging. While architecture remains important to mediating boundaries, identities, and desires, it is
not just a technology to put people in their place or to cement the identity of
places and populations. As I have argued in *Outlaw Territories: Environments
of Insecurity/Architectures of Counterinsurgency*, architecture also serves as
a less stable mechanism of governance and biopolitical regulation in modernity,
as a vehicle of environmental and subjective conditioning, including through
the circulation of bodies, information, and goods.

Such programmatic dimensions of architecture are also not necessarily
fixed, but remain subject to strategic and tactical rethinking. Moreover, as
I have underscored on many occasions, architecture triennales and biennales
have often served as important institutional platforms for technological, aesthetic, and political experimentation, offering occasions or testing grounds for
architecture to address gaps or limits within the field, in order to engage new
questions in a manner not always so easily undertaken in the professional
domain.[4] At once slightly removed or suspended from the realpolitik of professional life, while remaining all too central to architecture's capacity to launch
other possible futures or future imaginaries, triennales—like exhibitions
more generally, along with magazines and research programs—thus provide
occasions both to take stock and to invent. This one is no exception and
the organizers have identified five key thematics to interrogate: Technologies
for a Life in Transit, Borders Elsewhere, Furnishing After Belonging, Markets
and Territories of the Global Home, and Sheltering Temporariness. What, the
triennale asks through each of these lenses, have architecture and design had
to say about the construction of more democratic forms of residence or belonging, *after belonging,* and what else might they have to offer? How might
designers and writers be called upon to reinvent tools, concepts, processes,
practices, and sites in order to participate in such an undertaking?

**4** This is an important
claim at the heart of
the program in Critical,
Curatorial, and
Conceptual Practices
in Architecture (CCCP),
that I founded within
Columbia University's
Graduate School of
Architecture, Planning,
and Preservation in 2008
and now co-direct with
Mark Wasiuta. See Felicity
D. Scott, "Operating
Platforms," *Log 20*
(October 2010): 65–69.

*After Belonging* is not just any architecture triennale but the *Oslo* Architecture
Triennale; it is hosted in a European city that, like many others today, is experiencing the ongoing effects of capitalist globalization, amongst which is an
increased influx of migrants and refugees and with it, unfortunately, a backlash
of rising nationalism and xenophobia often taking the form of anti-Islamic
sentiment. This situation is certainly not unique to Norway, nor does it define
Oslo; but in the face of such pressures, *After Belonging* recognizes that
to ask questions from within and about Europe today, it is important to try to
think from the dual perspective of local and global arenas, paying attention
to distinctions and to interconnections between scales and locales. Hence,
the associated residencies are located not only in Oslo and other border spaces
and transnational neighborhoods in Norway, but also in equally complex

sites in North America, Latin America, the Middle East, Africa, and southern Europe—participants likewise deriving from multiple contexts and straddling multiple borders—all while seeking to understanding how global formations of power and governance touch down in very specific ways.

At a historical moment characterized (once again) by seemingly ever-increasing deracination, on the one hand, and by the anachronistic return of nationalisms, on the other, and with architecture ever-more integrated into the machinations of global capital driving this chiasmatic condition, it seems a particularly important time to revisit the concept of "belonging." Architecture might even contribute to another pressing question, one posed by Judith Butler in a conversation with Gayatri Spivak and one that has haunted my own work: "Are there modes of belonging that can be rigorously non-nationalist?"[5] In addition to having a privileged relation to historical notions of belonging, as suggested above, architecture has often served as a tool of nationalism, helping to cement claims to belonging, whether acting as a means of claiming an authentic relation (or rights) to a place, or as a means of conferring a partic-ular identity. The conception of an architecture proper to a particular place or people—wherein consistency and identity arise from climatic conditions, local materials, cultural patterns, or even racial or ethnic origins—is precisely what, within traditional accounts of the field, facilitated one's ability to identify "German architecture," "French architecture," "Italian architecture," or "Norwegian architecture," along with "American architecture," "Japanese architecture," or the architecture of the Dogon, etc.[6] But in a world so thoroughly reorganized by transit and communication, such claims on behalf of specific populations are not always necessarily so desirable, even potentially acting as a form of exclusion. "[T]he great 'accomplishment,' we might say, of nationalism as a distinctly modern form of political and cultural identity," Aamir Mufti reminds us, "is not that it is a great settling of peoples—'this place for this people.' Rather its distinguishing mark historically has been precisely that it makes large numbers of people eminently unsettled."[7] Like Butler, Mufti is recalling the legacy of the brutal dispossessions of the twentieth century. Indeed, both are avowedly indebted to Hannah Arendt's seminal philosophical reading of the collapse of the "old trinity of state-people-territory, which still formed the basis of European organization and political civilization," as evident in the aftermath of the breakup of Austria-Hungary and the Russian Empire after World War I but even more violently so by the denationalization and mass displacement and murder of minority populations under Nazi rule in wartime Europe.[8] Whether we think of interwar, wartime, or postwar Europe, or "state-people-territory," continues to haunt any conception of belonging and of nationalism in the present, including the unsettling that is the subject of After Belonging.

Architecture has, of course, questioned this nexus and its unsettling of people and boundaries on earlier occasions, not only due to war but also in relation to technological and other geopolitical transformations. For instance, in 1926, Hannes Meyer claimed mobility to be central to the "New World." "Ford and Rolls-Royce burst the confines of the city center, nullify distance, and efface the boundaries between city and countryside," he announced. "Airplanes glide through the air: 'Fokker' and 'Farman' increase our mobility

5 This is the question Judith Butler distills from Arendt's important work on totalitarianism. See Gayatri Chakravorty Spivak and Judith Butler, Who Sings the Nation-State?: Language, Pol-itics, Belonging (London: Seagull Books, 2007), 49. Central here is also the work of Etienne Balibar on questions of territory and citizen-ship. See, for instance, Balibar, We, The People of Europe?:Reflections on Transnational Citizen-ship, trans. James Swenson (Princeton: Princeton University Press, 2004),and Balibar, "Europe as Borderland," Environment and Planning D: Society and Space 27 (2009): 190–215.

6 On such nationalist claims see Meyer Schapiro, "Race, Nationality and Art," Art Front (March 2, 1936): 10–12. See also Eyal Weizman, Hollow Land: Israel's Arch-itecture of Occupation (London: Verso, 2007).

7 Aamir Mufti, Enlighten-ment in the Colony: The Jewish Question and the Crisis of Postcolonial Culture (Princeton: Princeton University Press, 2007), 13.

8 Hannah Arendt, "The Decline of the Nation State and the End of the Rights of Man," in The Origins of Totalitar-ianism (New York: Schocken Books, 2004), 376.

9 Hannes Meyer, "The New World," (1926) trans. Don Reneau, in *The Weimar Republic Sourcebook*, ed. Anton Kaes, et al., (Berkeley: University of California Press, 1994), 446. On Meyer's internationalism see Peter Galison, "Aufbau/Bauhaus: Logical Positivism and Architectural Modernism," *Critical Inquiry* 16 (1990): 709–752.

10 Walter Gropius, "Scope of Total Architecture," in *Scope of Total Architecture: A New Way of Life, World Perspectives* (New York: Harper and Brothers, 1955), 169.

11 Ibid., 172.

12 Ibid., 181.

13 Reprinted from *Uppercase*, in Alison Smithson, ed., *Team 10 Primer* (Cambridge: MIT Press, 1968), 51. The entire section of the *Team 10 Primer* dedicated to "Urban infra-structure" addressed this increase in mobility and its implications for contemporary architecture.

14 See Kenneth Frampton, "Towards a Critical Regionalism: Six Points Towards an Architecture of Resistance," in *The Anti-Aesthetic: Essays on Postmodern Culture*, ed. Hal Foster (Port Townsend: Bay Press, 1983), 16–30; and the essay from which Frampton derived the term, cited in the former as Alex Tzonis and Liliane [sic] Lefaivre, "The Grid and the Pathway: An Introduction to the Work of Dimitris and Susana Antonakakis," *Architecture in Greece* 15 (1981): 178. See also Alexander Tzonis and Liane Lefaivre, "Critical Regionalism," in *The Critical Landscape*, ed. Michael Speaks (Rotterdam: 010 Publishers, 1996), 126–147. For a critique of this notion see Alan Colquhoun, "The Concept of Regionalism," in *Postcolonial Space(s)*, ed. Gülsüm Badyar Nalbantonglu and Wong Chong Thai (New York: Princeton Architectural Press, 1997), 13–24.

and distance us from earth." Beyond automobiles and warplanes, dwellings too, Meyer noted enthusiastically, exhibited liberating possibilities via a mobility that was "disrespectful of national borders." "Our dwellings," he explained, "become more mobile than ever: mass apartment blocks, sleeping cars, residential yachts, and the Transatlantique undermine the local concept of the homeland. The fatherland fades away. We learn Esperanto. *We become citizens of the world.*"[9] In 1955, Walter Gropius, too, acknowledged the "sweeping transformation of human life" brought about by advancements in communication—automobiles, planes, radio, film, gramophones, x-ray technology, and telephones—a transformation of the world, in his assessment, from static, "seemingly unshakable" conceptions to those of "incessant transmutation."[10] To him, however, this condition led to a "perilous atomizing effect on the social coherence of the community," nowhere more apparent than in the US with the "baffling spectacle of a nation whose citizens are, voluntarily or involuntarily, so much on the move."[11] Designers, it seemed to Gropius, were thus faced with the task of re-integrating that atomized world into an organic whole or "true synthesis" he deemed "total architecture."[12] Members of a postwar generation, Alison and Peter Smithson responded instead by embracing that atomization. "Mobility has become the characteristic of *our* period," they announced. "Social and physical mobility, the feeling of a certain sort of freedom, is one of the things that keeps our society together. …Mobility is the key both socially and organizationally to town planning, for mobility is not only concerned with roads, but with the whole concept of a mobile, fragmented community."[13] We could go on….

In addressing technological infrastructures and geographical displacements, *After Belonging* seeks no such universalism, integration, or celebration of mobility as such, even if it hopes to transform architecture's relation to conditions of deracination. The new modes of belonging and residence this triennale interrogates also remain distinct from later twentieth century attempts to restore to architecture the markings of a "particular place" or to idealize "locally inflected culture" in the face of a universalized paradigm of civilization: attempts such as critical regionalism.[14] *After Belonging* does not—it seems to me—seek return to a more authentic or static way of living or of belonging to the land (let alone to a region or nation), but continues to ask how architecture and design objects and images might serve as technologies to dwell while adrift within a condition of territorial insecurity.[15] Here we might recall Bruce Robbins formulation from *Cosmopolitics: Thinking and Feeling Beyond the Nation,* his suggestion that forms of belonging that emerge in the wake of geographical displacements are complex and multiple. Such cosmopolitanism, however, is no longer "understood as a fundamental devotion to the interests of humanity as a whole," as transcending difference or enmity.[16] "To embrace this [complex and multiple] style of residence on earth," he argues moreover, offering us an important lesson, "means repudiating the romantic localism of a certain portion of the left, which feels it must counter capitalist globalization with a strongly rooted and exclusive sort of belonging."[17] Turning to readings of cosmopolitanism as particular rather than universal, and as located (albeit not in a simple sense) and embodied, even at times paradoxically "vernacular," Robbins writes, "instead of an ideal of detachment, actually existing cosmopolitanism is a reality of (re) attachment, multiple attachment, or attachment at a distance."[18] Faced with a "life in transit," a life in which one would never return home, strictly speaking, a life in which architecture and design become the occasion for "sheltering temporariness" and accumulating, at least temporarily, mediating devices for new forms of life, the triennale suggests that architects might participate in forging what I call new cartographies of dwelling, even new cartographies of drift for the twentieth century.[19]

Finally, *After Belonging* is not just the Oslo Architecture Triennale: it is the *2016* Oslo Architecture Triennale, and its reception is necessarily marked by this moment. The theme was conceived prior to the moment when Western media turned their attention to the wave of refugees from Syria, Iraq, Afghanistan, and many countries in Africa, along with other places torn apart by war, conflict, and occupation, as well as by economic and environmental catastrophes, to name only part of a litany of disaster. With the refugee crisis no longer able to be regarded as a Third World "problem," but more evidently a European one, such questions are currently at the forefront of popular and architectural discussions in the West. To be clear, such precarity and the conditions driving this mass migration are hardly new, as has been all too evident to those in other parts of the world; and, as noted above, Europe itself was the site of massive human displacement caused by the two World Wars and, in turn, by the breakup of the former Yugoslavia. But this recent increase in visibility has cast a new spotlight on a long-standing discussion, an important visibility but not necessarily one always accompanied by subjecting architecture's involvement to adequate scrutiny. One is tempted, in this regard, to read *After Belonging* as an implicit critique of the rising professional status and attention paid to designers of "emergency architecture," a response to humanitarian emergencies that is typically assumed to be architecture's most appropriate role. The Pritzker prize committee has effectively institutionalized "the architecture of emergency" as a new norm, granting consecutive prizes to Shigeru Ban and Alejandro Aravena; *Foreign Policy* magazine even anointing Ban as "architecture's first responder." Such a response, however, raises the question of just how the discipline might relate to emergencies born, at least in part, of the military, territorial, and environmental consequences of the expansionist logics of capitalism.

Emergency shelters are often conceived as "solutions" to a design problem, that of providing low-cost, easily-transportable, rapidly-deployable, supposedly-temporary housing for those displaced or rendered homeless due to states of emergency. But such technologies to "shelter temporariness"—to offer shelter without residence—can be read, in turn, as imbricated within a set of economic, political, geopolitical, and policy decisions that are often understudied. Something as apparently simple as a shelter enters into the scene of humanitarian aid in a complex way, whether knowingly or not. Without adequate understanding of the political factors at play, or even sometimes assuming that such factors remain outside the purview of a specific

**15** I am drawing here from my work on émigré architect Bernard Rudofsky. See Felicity D Scott, "Not at Home," in *Émigré Design Cultures*, ed. Elana Shapira (London: Bloomsbury Publishing, 2017). In press.

**16** Bruce Robbins, "Introduction Part I: Actually Existing Cosmopolitanism," in *Cosmopolitics: Thinking and Feeling Beyond the Nation*, ed. Bruce Robbins and Pheng Cheah (Minneapolis: University of Minnesota Press, 1998), 1.

**17** Ibid., 3. As Robbins insisted, "The devastation covered over by complacent talk of globalization is of course very real. But precisely *because* it is real, we cannot be content to set against it only the childish reassurance of belonging to "a" place. The indefinite article is insufficient. Yes, we are connected to the earth— but not to "a" place on it, simple and self-evident as the surroundings we see when we open our eyes. We are connected to all sorts of places."

**18** Ibid. 3.

**19** I am thinking here of my unpublished work on Bernard Rudofsky. See also Felicity D. Scott, *Disorientation: Bernard Rudofsky in the Empire of Signs* (Berlin: Sternberg Press, Critical Spatial Practice series, 2016).

**20** For important scholarship on the politics of humanitarian aid in architecture, see Manuel Herz, ed. *From Camp to City: The Refugee Camps of the Western Sahara* (Zürich: Lars Müller Publishers, 2012); and Eyal Weizman, *The Least of All Possible Evils: Humanitarian Violence from Arendt to Gaza* (London and New York: Verso, 2011).

**21** In addition to Herz and Weizman noted above, see, for instance: David Rieff, *A Bed for the Night: Humanitarianism in Crisis* (New York: Simon & Schuster, 2002); Rony Brauman, "Learning from Dilemmas (Interview with Rony Brauman)," in Michel Feher, ed. *Nongovernmental Politics* (New York: Zone Books, 2007), 131–147; and Didier Fassin and Mariella Pandolfi, eds., *Contemporary States of Emergency: The Politics of Military and Humanitarian Interventions* (New York: Zone Books, 2010).

**22** See, for instance, the work of Eyal Weizman, Sandi Hilal, Alessandro Petit, Laura Kurgan, and Keller Easterling.

field of expertise (such as architecture), such technocratic approaches remain blind to and can even obfuscate the political dimensions of a crisis.[20] Moreover, beyond remaining blind while all too proximate to extant techniques of power, in the worst cases these approaches might even perpetuate violence. I am thinking here of the important scholarship on the "humanitarian paradox," wherein forms of aid potentially serve (whether inadvertently or cynically) to exacerbate, perpetuate, or even institutionalize and normalize process of dispossession. In other words, shelter, too, can have counterproductive effects.[21] This is not to say that those rendered homeless should not be afforded shelter from the elements and a place to reside, nor that improving such technologies cannot at times be beneficial. Rather, the intention is to underscore the importance of paying attention to the larger apparatus within which such shelter operates, and also to interrogate other ways such a shelter might function, for better or worse. Some emergency shelters resonate less as successful design solutions to a crisis than as symptomatic and visible markers of misery and insecurity that, wittingly or unwittingly, inscribe the inhabitants not as citizens or individuals but as a misfortunate lot, a population reduced to being in need of humanitarian aid, mere elements of a humanitarian catastrophe. In other words, the structures can speak also of exposure to a radical insecurity and the ways in which subjects circulate differentially within a larger apparatus of power.

After Belonging actively invokes the language of crisis, precarity, intervention, and asylum, and, in so doing, recognizes the sense of urgency or even the emergencies at hand to which architects should respond, and to which architecture might indeed have something important to contribute. Yet this triennale enters into such a playing field not with a ready prescription for design of shelters but—following in the footsteps of other architectural activists, researchers, and scholars—with a productive uncertainty and a critical mode of questioning just how, when, where, or through what tools and expertise architecture should act.[22] Architecture, that is, can offer something beyond more or better "first responders" and designs for emergency shelters, especially when functional directives are expanded to unsettle political, semiotic, and regulatory domains. Architecture's priorities might even include the construction of platforms through which to think less reactively and more critically or extensively about this nexus of architecture and emergency. The answer, to reiterate, may not always lie in more affordable, efficient, or even pleasing or "humane" forms of minimal shelter. In some situations, the most miserable looking camp is the least permanent one, while in others a more desirable environment is precisely what is needed to bring political questions to the foreground. So we are not offered a simple utopianism, nor a classical reformist attitude or claims to radicalism. Rather, the ambition is to advance a strategic hope, suggesting that architecture might intervene not *only* by offering design "solutions"—although it might, of course, continue to do that, the question being who decides and what effects such decisions might have—but through forging new concepts, tools, and practices for rendering the contours of emergent techniques of power visible and contestable.

Having suggested that conventional notions of belonging might be obsolescent, *After Belonging* does not attend only to those individuals and populations most evidently cast as not-belonging or other—such as migrants and refugees. Rather, it reads these quintessential figures of displacement as contemporaneous with, if distinct from, other mobile or precarious subjects—tourists, transient workers, students, strangers, foreigners, even citizens. More specifically, *After Belonging* takes the knowing risk of asking if and how we might think about these populations together, as all subjected to an interconnected global phenomenon, albeit in different ways. This is not to overlook historical and political specificities or the differential abilities of migrants and refugees to cross borders or find a place to reside and to work. (Residence and labor often go hand in hand).[23] At stake is recognizing how and when particularities and identifications surface to make political claims or how they are created to otherwise interrupt capitalist abstractions or render its machinations visible. The wager, that is, is that the more evidently violent forms of dispossession might be productively thought about alongside other types of insecurity impacting contemporary forms of residence "in transit."

An important objective, then, is to be able to recognize forces informing the new subjectivities emerging, as Paolo Virno suggests, within a condition of "belonging to unstable contexts."[24] In "The Ambivalence of Disenchantment" Virno offers us one of the most forceful readings of the persistence of divergent senses of belonging within a contemporary post-Fordist condition dominated by information technologies and the forms of life it attempts to sponsor. He recognizes a tactical shift at play in the desire for "belonging as such," even in a paradoxical condition of "belonging to uprooting."

> What kind of belonging could I mean, after having unrelentingly insisted upon the unexpected absence of particular and credible "roots"? True, one no longer "belongs" to a particular role, tradition, or political party. Calls for "participation" and for a "project" have faded. And yet alienation, far from eliminating the feeling of belonging, empowers it. The impossibility of securing ourselves within any durable context disproportionately increases our adherence to the most fragile instances of the "here and now." What is dazzlingly clear is finally *belonging as such*, no longer qualified by a determinate belonging "to something." Rather, the feeling of belonging has become directly proportional to the lack of a privileged and protective "to which" to belong.[25]

Virno is not simply lamenting this turn but recognizes in its degree zero, or refusal of nostalgia for a "rooted" identity, a type of dissident potential that insists on forging forms of life *after belonging*.

*After Belonging* asks, from a different perspective, what forms our belongings now take in the social, material, and geopolitical sense, inviting architects and designers to think differently about belonging and belongings while insisting that architectural expertise can be productively brought to bear on examining and designing objects, places, images, trajectories, processes, and protocols, as well as in understanding subjective and territorial formations that pertain to them. To this end, the exhibition and this publication offer an important catalog or contemporary archive of the ways artifacts and environments "shelter" or

23 With this type of mobility we find ourselves at questions of the distribution of labor and shifting geographies and modalities of work, reminding us, as Etienne Balibar and Sandro Mezzadra have argued, that borders are rarely simply open or closed but operate as mechanisms of regulation and of differential distribution. See Balibar, "Strangers as Enemies," 20.

24 Paulo Virno, "The Ambivalence of Disenchantment," in *Radical Thought in Italy: A Potential Politics*, ed. Paulo Virno and Michael Hardt (Minneapolis: University of Minnesota Press, 1996), 21.

25 Ibid. 32.

otherwise mediate conditions of mobility and new forms of belonging "after belonging" within a contemporary "regime of circulation," whether for worse or, potentially, for better.

When *After Belonging* interrogates how architecture might respond to a historical condition *after belonging* (in the conventional sense, for belongings evidently persist), a condition in which we are increasingly called upon, as the curators put it, to "manage our belongings" in the social, material, technical, legal, proprietary, economic, and psychological domains, they point to an important fact. Architecture—as a discourse, a discipline, and a profession—is already and always imbricated within the multifaceted apparatus of capital driving the new patterns of migration, travel, and stasis with which I began. Beyond conceiving of architecture as the provision of buildings, spaces, or shelter as such, that is, the discipline has been and remains proximate to, and at times informs, technologies, markets, laws, policies, information, goods, media, and other forms of regulation and governance. It is from such an expanded conception of the discipline, one that I share, that After Belonging Agency invited participants to collaborate on this project of thinking belonging otherwise, manifesting the desire for identifying and forging practices that remain tactically out of sync with the violence born of neoliberal capital. Inviting collaborators to participate in this venture, *After Belonging* understands that such dissidence is not always spontaneous but has to be continuously sponsored, even at times actively constructed, both in relation to architecture as a discipline and in relation to the world. This catalog, like the exhibition and events it accompanies and the research it documents, is testament to the importance of *After Belonging*'s critical and curatorial project in this regard, providing evidence of the many insights and openings that such invitations and provocations can elicit.

# Bŏŕdęrs Elšęẁhere
## Texts

# Traumatic Exit, Identity Narratives, and the Ethics of Hospitality[1]

**Arjun Appadurai**

**1** This text was first delivered as a lecture at the Berlin Institute for Integration and Migration on November 4, 2015.

Forced exits can be created by traumas of environment, economy, or national civil war. They produce refugees who are invariably traumatized. Their claims on the hospitality of the nations in which they land always lie in a grey zone between hospitality, sanctuary, and incarceration because the refugees are usually in a categorical gray zone which combines features of the stranger, the victim, the criminal, and the undocumented visitor. The trauma of the forced refugee provokes the deepest anxieties of the modern nation-state, which relies on boundaries, censuses, taxes, and documentation. The heart of the new traumas of the forced refugee in the new country is that he/she has a plot (a narrative, a story) but no character, identity, or name. The challenge of evolving a new form of legal and ethical hospitality is one of creating a name to fit the plot, an identity to fit the narrative. The challenge of the modern nation-state is that its key narratives of identity rely on fixed starting points (blood, language, religion, territory), but the forced exit is usually produced precisely by originary traumas of blood, language, religion, or location. The purpose of this lecture is to open the question of how to build a new relationship between plot and character in modern nation-states which exist in a world of forced exits and lack an ethical foundation for seeing traumatic movement as the pivot of a serious identity for some of their citizens.

## Migration and the Crisis of the Nation-State

After the famous treaty of Westphalia in 1648, the principle of territorial sovereignty becomes the foundational principle of the nation-state, though many other ideas affect its cultural self-imaging and self-narrativizing: these include ideas about language, common origin, blood, soil, and various other conceptions of ethnos. Still, the fundamental political and juridical rationale and basis of the system of nation-states is territorial sovereignty—however complexly understood and delicately managed in particular post-empire settings.

Throughout the world, immigrants, cultural rights, and state protection of refugees are growing problems, especially since very few states have careful ways of defining the relationship of citizenship, birth, ethnic affiliation, and national identity. The crisis is nowhere clearer than in Europe today, where the struggle to control and manage the intensified wave of migrants from the Middle East and North Africa is threatening to unravel the very foundation of European ideas of full citizenship, asylum, and refuge, and to expose the exclusionary foundation of European thinking about cultural markers of national belonging. But in many countries, problems with immigrants, race, birth, and residence are becoming problems of one or another kind. Think, for example, of Mexicans in the United States, Rohingya Muslims from Bangladesh and Myanmar in other countries in South East Asia, and migrants from the rest of Africa in South Africa. One source of this problem is that modern conceptions of citizenship, tied up with various forms of democratic universalism, tend to demand a homogeneous people with standardized packages of rights. Yet the realities of ethno-territorial thinking in the cultural ideologies of the nation-state demand discrimination between different categories of citizens even when they all occupy the same territory. Resolving these conflicting principles is inevitably a violent and uncivil process.

Territory thus can be seen as the crucial problem in the contemporary crisis of the nation-state or, more precisely, of the crisis of the relationship between nation and state. Insofar as nation-state ideologies rest on some sort of implicit idea of ethnic coherence as the basis of state sovereignty, they are bound to minoritize, degrade, penalize, or expel those seen to be ethnically minor. Insofar as these minorities (either as guestworkers, refugees, or illegal aliens) enter into new polities, they require reterritorialization within a new civic order whose ideology of ethnic coherence and citizenship rights they are bound to disturb, since all modern ideologies of rights depend, ultimately, on the closed group of appropriate recipients of state protection and patronage. Thus second-classness and third-classness are conditions of citizenship which are inevitable entailments, however plural the ethnic ideology of the state and however flexible its accommodation of refugees and other weakly documented visitors.

Now, none of these realities would be a problem except that the conditions of global economic, labor, and technological organization create both dramatic new pushes and pulls in favor of uprooting individuals and groups and moving them into new national settings. Since these individuals and groups have to be cognized within some sort of vocabulary of rights and entitlements, however limited and harsh, they pose a threat to the ethnic and moral coherence of all host nation-states, a coherence that is, at bottom, predicated on both a singular and an immobile ethnos. In these conditions, the state as a push factor in ethnic diasporas is constantly obliged to push out the sources of ethnic noise which threaten or violate its integrity as an ethnically singular territory. But, at the same time, virtually every modern nation-state is either forced or persuaded to accept into its territory a whole variety of non-nationals, who demand and create a wide variety of territorially ambiguous claims on civic and national rights and resources.

Here we are at the heart of the crisis of the nation-state. It looks at first glance as if the crisis of the nation-state is the fact of ethnic plurality that is the inevitable result of the flow of populations in the contemporary world. But on closer inspection, the problem is not ethnic or cultural pluralism as such, but the tension between diasporic pluralism and territorial stability in the project of the modern nation-state. What ethnic plurality does (especially when it is the product of sudden population movements) is to violate the sense of isomorphism between territory and national identity on which the modern nation-state relies. More exactly, what these diasporic pluralisms expose and intensify is the gap between the powers of the state to regulate borders, monitor dissent, and distribute entitlements within a finite territory and the fiction of ethnic singularity on which all nations ultimately rely. In other words, the territorial integrity that justifies states and the ethnic singularity which validates nations are increasingly hard to see as seamless aspects of one another.

## Migration, Memory, and Media

2 Arjun Appadurai, *Modernity at Large: Cultural Dimensions of Globalization* (Minneapolis: University of Minnesota Press, 1996).

3 Arjun Appadurai "The Capacity to Aspire: Culture and the Terms of Recognition," in Rao, Vijayendra and Michael Walton (ed). *Culture and Public Action* (Redwood City: Stanford University Press, 2004).

In my book, *Modernity at Large*,[2] I suggested that in the era of globalization, the circulation of media images and the movement of migrants created new disjunctures between location, imagination, and identity. More specifically, I suggested that in many social locations throughout the world, especially those characterized by media saturation and migrant populations, "moving images meet mobile audiences," thus disturbing the stability of many sender-receiver models of mass communication. This has many implications for what I then called "the work of the imagination," and I particularly stressed the new potentials that this situation created for the proliferation of imagined worlds and imagined selves.

Migrants, especially the poorer migrants of this world, are not thriving in a world of free markets, consumer paradises, or social liberation. They are struggling to make the best of the possibilities that are opened to them in the new relationships between migration and mass mediation. There is no doubt that migrants today, as migrants throughout human history, move either to escape horrible lives, to seek better ones, or both. The only new fact in the world of electronic mediation is that the archive of possible lives is now richer and more available to ordinary people than ever before. Thus, there is a greater stock of material from which ordinary people can craft the scripts of possible worlds and imagined selves. This change does not mean that the social projects that emerge from these scripts are always liberating or even pleasant. But they are exercises in what I have called "the capacity to aspire."[3]

Muslim migrants from North Africa, Syria, Turkey, and Iraq sometimes drown in the Mediterranean as they seek to swim to the shores of Italy, Greece, or Spain from illegal boats, as do their Haitian counterparts in the waters of Florida and others in the containers that cross the English Channel. It is also true that young women from the ex-socialist republics often end up brutalized as sex workers in the border zones between the old and new Europe, as do Philippine domestic workers in Milan and Kuwait, and South Asian laborers (both male and female) in Dubai, Saudi Arabia, and Bahrain. Such examples of the brutalizing of migrants can be multiplied: poorer migrants today frequently end up as undocumented citizens, objects of racist laws and sentiments, and sometimes as targets of ethnocidal violence in locations from Rwanda to Indonesia.

But is this suffering the whole story? Does it tell us everything we need to know about how these projects for movement were formed; about what efforts it took to summon the resources to move; of what was made possible by meager remittances; of how the relationship of men and women is often recalibrated under the conditions of migration; of the doors that are opened for migrant children; and, finally, of the value of negotiating for new opportunities, even in harsh circumstances? The work of the imagination, especially for poorer migrants, is critical for exercising the capacity to aspire. Without developing this capacity, which may also lead to rape, exploitation, and death (for migration is a world of risk), poor migrants will always remain captive to the wishes of the vanguard, to the prison of their own domestic tyrannies, and to the self-fulfilling prophecies of those business-class revolutionaries who always know, in advance, how poor people should best exercise their agency and which level of risk is most appropriate to them.

So I insist that the work of the imagination is not a privilege of elites, intellectuals, and cosmopolitans but is also being performed by poor people, notably in the worldwide pursuit of their possibilities to migrate, whether to near or far locations. Denuding these proletarian projects of the dimension of fantasy, imagination, and aspiration, reducing them to mere reflexes of the labor market or of some other institutional logic, does nothing for the poor other than to deny them the privilege of risk-taking. This is the opposite of what Charles Taylor calls "the politics of recognition."[4]

In this perspective, what can we say about the place of archives, narratives, and memory in the building of migrant identity? Here the idea of the living archive becomes especially useful. Migrants have a complex relationship to the practices of memory and, thus, to the making of archives, for several reasons. First, because memory becomes hyper-valued for many migrants, the practices through which collective memory is constructed are especially subject to cultural contestation and to simplification. Memory, for migrants, is almost always a memory of loss. But, since most migrants have been pushed out of the sites of official/national memory in their original homes, there is some anxiety surrounding the status of what is lost, since the memory of the journey to a new place, the memory of one's own life and family world in the old place, and official memory about the nation one has left have to be recombined in a new location. Migration tends to be accompanied by a confusion about what exactly has been lost, and thus of what needs to be recovered or remembered. This confusion leads to an often deliberate effort to construct a variety of archives, ranging from the most intimate and personal (such as the memory of one's earlier bodily self) to the most public and collective, which usually take the form of shared narratives and practices.

Media plays a critical role in the construction of the migrant archive since circulation, instability, and the disjunctures of movement always cast doubt on the "accidental" trace through which archives are sometimes assumed to emerge. In the effort to seek resources for the building of archives, migrants thus often turn to the media for images, narratives, models, and scripts of their own story, partly because the diasporic story is always understood to be one of breaks and gaps. Nor is this only a consumer relationship, for in the age of the internet, literate migrants have begun to explore social media, chat rooms, and other interactive spaces in which to find, debate, and consolidate their own memory traces and stories into a more widely plausible narrative. This task, never free of contest and debate, sometimes does take the form of what Benedict Anderson disparagingly called "long-distance

4 Charles Taylor, *Multiculturalism and The Politics of Recognition* (Princeton: Princeton University Press, 1992).

5 Benedict R. O'G.
Anderson, *Long-
Distance Nationalism.
World Capitalism and
the Rise of Identity
Politics, The
Wertheim Lecture 1992*
(Amsterdam: Centre for
Asian Studies, 1992).

nationalism."[5] But long-distance nationalism is a complex matter, which usually produces many sorts of politics and many sorts of interest. In the age in which electronic mediation has begun to supplement and sometimes even supplant print mediation and older forms of communication, imagined communities are sometimes much more deeply real to migrants than natural ones.

Interactive media thus play a special role in the construction of what we may call the diasporic public sphere (an idea I proposed in *Modernity at Large* to extend the insights of Habermas, Anderson, and others about national public spheres), for they allow new forms of agency in the building of imagined communities. The act of reading together (which Anderson brilliantly identified in regard to newspapers and novels in the new national-isms of the colonial world) are now enriched by the technologies of the web, Facebook, Twitter, and Google, creating a world in which the simultaneity of reading is complemented by the interactivity of messaging, searching, and posting. Thus, what we may call the diasporic archive, or the migrant archive, is increasingly characterized by the presence of voice, agency, and debate, rather than of mere reading, reception, and interpellation.

But the migrant archive operates under another constraint, for it has to relate to the presence of one or more narratives of public memory in the new home of the migrant, where the migrant is frequently seen as a person with only one story to tell: a story of abject loss and need. In his or her new society, the migrant has to contend with the marginalization of the migrant archive, of the embarrassment of its remote references, and of the poverty of its claims on the official "places of memory" in the new site. Thus, the electronic archive becomes a doubly valuable space for migrants, for, in this space, some of the indignity of being minor or contemptible in the new soci-ety can be compensated for, and the vulnerability of the migrant narrative can be protected in the relative safety of cyberspace.

What is more, both new electronic media as well as traditional print media among migrant communities allow complex new debates to occur between the memory of the old home and the demands of public narrative in the new setting. Migrant newspapers in many communities become explicit sites for debate between micro-communities, between generations, and between different forms of nationalism. In this sense, the migrant archive is highly active and interactive, as it is the main site of negotiation between col-lective memory and desire. As the principal resource in which migrants can define the terms of their own identities and identity-building—outside the strictures of their new homes—the diasporic archive is an intensified form of what characterizes all popular archives: it is a place to sort out the meaning of memory in relationship to the demands of cultural reproduction. Operating outside the official spheres of both the home society and the new society, the migrant archive cannot afford the illusion that traces are accidents, that documents arrive on their own, and that archives are repositories of the luck of material survival. Rather, the migrant archive is a continuous and conscious work of the imagination, seeking in collective memory an ethical basis for the sustainable reproduction of cultural identities in the new society. For migrants, more than for others, the archive is a map. It is a guide to the uncertainties of identity-building under adverse conditions. The archive is a search for the memories that count and not a home for memories with a pre-ordained significance. This living, aspirational archive could become a vital source for the challenge of narrativity and identity in contemporary times.

## Narratives Without Identities

Citizenship in modern nation-states — such as Germany — is built on a tight fit between plot and character (or story and actor, or narrative and identity). The legal and bureaucratic origins of the modern nation-state seek to provide a territorial ground for stabilizing and connecting plot and character in verifying legitimate citizens. The story of birth to parents who are citizens is the strongest example of this convergence, for it implies territorial, personal, and sanguinary stability. Legal naturalization procedures — on the basis of marriage, work, or investment — also produce this stability and convergence between plot and character by allowing changes in the present status of an immigrant from refugee or illegal to full citizenship or quasi-citizenship by "naturalizing" their ties to the national territory. For refugees, asylum-seekers, and almost all other undocumented migrants, the problem is that their stories (however painful and dramatic) come with names (personal names) but no characters — that is, no identities which fit the legal narrative requirements of legitimate migration. This disjuncture exists not simply because they arrive suddenly, traumatically, and violently within the new national space or to a transitional national space on their way to their preferred final destination. It is because, in the eyes of their new hosts, they are truly "nobodies"— that is, they have no identities that fit their new circumstances.

Here, the main problem is that the modern nation-state has room only for narratives which are based in the past (blood, birth, parenthood, language, etc.) or in the present (work, marriage, student status, etc.) and not for those based primarily on the future: on the aspiration for a better home, a safer life, a more secure horizon. There are no aspirational narratives for refugees, in the way that there are aspirational narratives for work or skill-based applicants for immigration. The fact is that refugees are today *supplicants* who wish to become *applicants* for citizenship in countries like Germany. Their stories of suffering, oppression, and violence in their home countries or in the camps which they have elected to leave on their tortuous journeys to their aspirational destinations, are stories of abjection and supplication; and these stories are not easy to convert into the narratives of application and aspiration.

Here then are the narrative challenges that goes beyond the policing, administrative, and legal challenges that face migrants in today's Europe and their hosts. How do we create stories based on imagined future citizenship in a context where the past (birth, parenthood, and blood) is still the currency of most citizenship laws? How can longing be turned into belonging? How can hospitality to the stranger be made a legitimate basis for the narrative of citizenship?

To provide deep and sustainable answers to these questions, we can consider two approaches. The first is to help the strengthening and deepening of migrant archives, seeing them not only as storehouses of memory but also as aspirational maps. This effort might allow us to see the common ground between the aspirations of the refugees and our own and thus to find a richer cultural road to the legal and bureaucratic solutions currently being debated. The second approach — finding ways to make migrant narratives and identities a basis for secure citizenship — will require re-thinking the very architecture of sovereignty in the contemporary world. That daunting task cannot be addressed today, but I hope I have described the conditions that make it an unavoidable challenge.

# Liquid Traces: Contesting the Lethal Architecture of the Mediterranean Sea

**Charles Heller and Lorenzo Pezzani**

"When you have a land border: here is country A, and therefore the subject of law is country A, and here is country B. There is no limbo in-between. At sea it's different. Here you have country A, here you have the high seas, and here begins the jurisdiction of country B. But in-between, on the high seas, things are a little bit delicate...."[1]
—Commander Borg, Armed Forces of Malta

If geography expresses in its very etymology the possibility to write and therefore read the surface of the earth, the liquid territory of the sea seems to stand as the absolute challenge to spatial analysis. Constantly stirred by currents and waves that seem to erase any trace of the past, the sea appears to be, in Roland Barthes's words, a "non-signifying field" that "bears no message." Furthermore, the lack of stable habitation on its surface leads events at sea to occur mostly outside the public gaze and thus remain unaccounted for. The deaths of illegalized migrants at sea and the violation of their rights are no exception.[2] Between 1988 and February 2016, the press and NGOs reported more than 22,000 deaths at the maritime frontier of the EU, including more than 13,000 in the Sicily Channel alone. But the conditions in which these deaths have occurred have rarely been established with precision, and the responsibility for them has seldom been determined. Many more lives have been lost without being recorded, other than in the haunting absence experienced by their families.

In an attempt to document the deaths of migrants at sea and the violations of their rights, despite the challenges posed by this liquid frontier, we started the Forensic Oceanography project in summer 2011. This endeavor was spurred by the new demands for accountability that emerged in the aftermath of the Arab uprisings. The fall of the Ben Ali regime in Tunisia and the Qaddafi regime in Libya allowed migrants to at least temporarily re-open maritime routes which had been sealed off through collaboration between the EU and the North African states. Shortly afterwards, the civil war that has engulfed Syria since 2012 in turn led to the largest exodus since the Second World War. While the majority of population movements unleashed by conflicts in the region have occurred on the southern shore of the Mediterranean, record numbers of people have also sought to reach the EU by boat. This situation, on the one hand, has lead to momentous transformations in (non-)assistance and bordering practices that have transformed the Mediterranean into a veritable laboratory where novel legal arrangements, surveillance

[1] Quoted in Silja Klepp, "A Contested Asylum System: The European Union between Refugee Protection and Border Control in the Mediterranean Sea," *European Journal of Migration and Law* 12 (2010): 1–21.

[2] We use the term "illegalized" migrants, instead of the more common "illegal," to highlight that illegality is a product of state law rather than an intrinsic feature of migration.

technologies, and institutional assemblages have emerged at dazzling speed; on the other, this situation has exacerbated the issue of migrant deaths at sea, turning the Mediterranean into what the United Nations' High Commissioner for Refugees (UNHCR) has defined as the "deadliest route" for migrants in the world, the epicenter of those "landscapes of deaths" that characterize global borders.[3]

As we will show, however, migrants do not only die at sea but through a strategic use of the sea. Even when they drown following a shipwreck or starve while drifting in the water's currents, there is nothing "natural" about their deaths. To understand how the sea has been made to kill, we have had to attend to the way the liquid expanse has been mobilized to alternatively connect and make movement flow smoothly or to separate and add friction to this movement. This dual character of the sea has been a recurring trope in much geographical thinking, often inflected with deterministic undertones. Ellen Churchill Semple, in her "Influences of Geographic Environment," famously argued that amongst many different types of "natural boundaries" that "set more or less effective limits to the movement of peoples and the territorial growth of states,… the sea is the only absolute boundary, because it alone blocks the continuous, unbroken expansion of a people." Yet, in another passage, she also remarks that the sea can be "domesticated" to bring people into contact: "Man, by appropriating the mobile forces in the air and water to increase his own powers of locomotion, has become a cosmopolitan being."[4] Formulated in more contemporary and less deterministic terms following Elisabeth Grosz, we can argue that the sea, like any geographic environment, can be considered to be endowed with a "geopower," a term by which Grosz refers to "forces that precede, enable, facilitate, provoke and restrict 'life'."[5] Conversely political practices shape the way this geopower operates, and affect the ways some are empowered and others restricted by that power. Recognizing the crucial agency of the sea and its geopower, our project could not limit itself to reading the sea in order to document specific incidents, but demanded that we attempt as well to understand the broader conditions that have led the sea to become a liquid grave for so many at a time when 90% of global trade and thousands of passengers move across the oceans without apparent effort or danger. In this short article, we will retrace some of the ways in which we have attempted to pursue these simultaneous aims—looking at the policies, practices, and discourses that have turned the Mediterranean into a lethal border zone—and discuss the methodologies we have developed to document some of the incidents that are its manifestations. In the process, we will both chart and mobilize the legal and political geographies of this liquid territory, or what we might call the "architecture of the sea."

## Reading liquid traces, mapping fluid geographies: the "left-to-die boat" case

Evoking architecture, arguably one of the most "terrestrial" of disciplines, as an analytical category to understand the spatiality of the sea might appear at first counterintuitive, as it goes against the already-recalled popular image of

3 Joseph. Nevins, *Operation Gatekeeper: The Rise of the "Illegal Alien" and the Making of the U.S.-Mexico Boundary* (New York [u.a.]: Routledge, 2002), 144

4 Ellen Churchill Semple, *Influences of Geographic Environment on the Basis of Ratzel's System of Anthropo-Geography* (New York: Henry Holt and Company, 1911), 214 and 292.

5 Kathryn Yusoff et al., "Geopower: A Panel on Elizabeth Grosz's Chaos, Territory, Art: Deleuze and the Framing of the Earth," *Environment and Planning D: Society and Space* 30, no. 6 (2012): 973–975.

the sea as an empty and lawless space without history and beyond the reach of society. Carl Schmitt famously described the sea as an anarchic space in which the impossibility of drawing long-standing and identifiable boundaries made it impossible for European states to establish durable legal order or found claims of sovereignty. "The sea," he wrote, "has no character, in the original sense of the word, which comes from the Greek charassein, meaning to engrave, to scratch, to imprint."[6] And yet, nothing appears more far from reality once we start to look at the sea a bit more closely. The sea, we demonstrate, does bear traces, and power is exercised across its space by combining a form of mobile policing and a complex political geography.

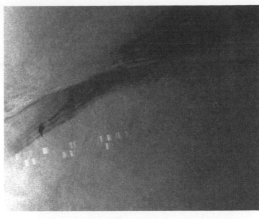

Figure 1: Synthetic Aperture Radar (SAR) image taken on March 28, 2011 by the European Space Agency's Envisat satellite.

The image reproduced as *Figure 1* is a good illustration of our claim. Taken on the 28th of March 2011 by the European Space Agency's Envisat satellite, the image depicts a portion of the Strait of Sicily between the coast of Libya, in the lower left corner, and Malta, towards the top. As a "Synthetic Aperture Radar (SAR)" image, it was not created by an optical sensor, but rather by the reflection of the satellite's beamed microwaves on the sea's surface. If we look carefully at this image, we begin to distinguish different textures that clearly disprove the popular conception of the sea mentioned above. A remote sensing specialist would be able to determine, for instance, that the darker area that crosses the whole image diagonally, at times bordered by wave patterns, represents an area of calmer sea. The sharply defined dark feature in the mid-left portion of the image, instead, probably represents an oil slick caused by illegal tank-washing. When released on the surface of the sea, oil decreases the amount of microwaves reflected back to the satellite, hence appearing as a black hole, a veritable information gap. Just below that feature, a striping pattern was most likely caused by an error in the sensor response. Finally, the brighter dots scattered across the image represent large ships. Emerging at the intersection of electromagnetic and physical waves, what we see here is not simply a new representation of the ocean, but a new ocean altogether, one simultaneously composed of matter and media.

Images such as this one are routinely used for the policing of illegalized migration, but we repurposed it as evidence of the crime of non-assistance in the frame of our investigation into the "left-to-die boat" case.[7] This incident concerns how seventy-two migrants fleeing Libya in March 2011, at the height of the NATO-led military intervention against Libya, were left to drift in the Central Mediterranean for fifteen days, despite distress signals sent out to all vessels navigating through this area, and several encounters with military aircrafts and a warship. The reluctance of all actors to rescue the drifting passengers led to the slow deaths of sixty-three people. By combining the already-mentioned satellite image with a drift model that maps the trajectory of the boat after it ran out of fuel *(Figure 2),* we were able to establish that

6 Carl Schmitt, *The Nomos of the Earth in the International Law of the Jus Publicum Europaeum,* trans. G. L Ulmen (New York: Telos Press, 2003), 42–43.

7 See: http://www.forensic-architecture.org/case/left-die-boat/

| Id | Length | Confidence |
|---|---|---|
| 29_0 | 75m | 80% |
| 29_1 | 75m | 70% |
| 29_2 | 75m | 95% |
| 29_3 | 75m | 80% |
| 29_4 | 75m | 70% |
| 29_5 | 75m | 90% |
| 29_6 | 225m | 95% |
| 29_7 | 75m | 80% |
| 29_8 | 75m | 70% |
| 29_9 | 75m | 80% |
| 29_10 | 75m | 80% |
| 29_11 | 150m | 95% |
| 29_12 | 150m | 95% |
| 29_13 | 75m | 80% |
| 29_14 | 300m | 95% |
| 29_15 | 150m | 95% |
| 29_16 | 75m | 80% |
| 29_17 | 75m | 95% |
| 29_18 | 300m | 95% |
| 29_19 | 75m | 80% |
| 29_20 | 75m | 80% |
| 29_21 | 75m | 70% |
| 29_22 | 150m | 95% |
| 29_23 | 225m | 95% |

*Figure 2:* Analysis of the March 29, 2011 Envisat satellite image showing the modeled position of the "left-to-die boat" (yellow diagonal hatch) and the nearby presence of several military vessels which did not intervene to rescue the migrants.

the bright pixels scattered across the image represent large ships that were located in the vicinity of the migrants' boat just as it ran out of fuel and began to drift. All vessels in the area had been informed of the distress of the passengers on board the migrants' boat, as well as its position, and could have easily rescued them but chose not to intervene.

Satellite imagery is one of the many techniques that we have used to offer an alternative reading of the ocean and reconstruct with precision this dramatic event. In the absence of external witnesses, we corroborated the survivors' testimonies by mobilizing, against the grain, the vast apparatus of remote sensing devices (optical and thermal cameras, radars, tracking and satellite imaging technologies) which have transformed the contemporary ocean into a vast and technologically mediated sensorium. Instead of replicating the technological eye of policing and its untenable promise of full-spectrum visibility, we chose to exercise what we have called a "disobedient gaze," redirecting the light shed by the surveillance apparatus away from illegalized migration and back towards the act of policing itself.

However, in addition to reading the traces left by the events, the spatialization of these traces across the EU's maritime frontier has been equally crucial *(Figure 3)* in order to determine the degree of involvement of each of

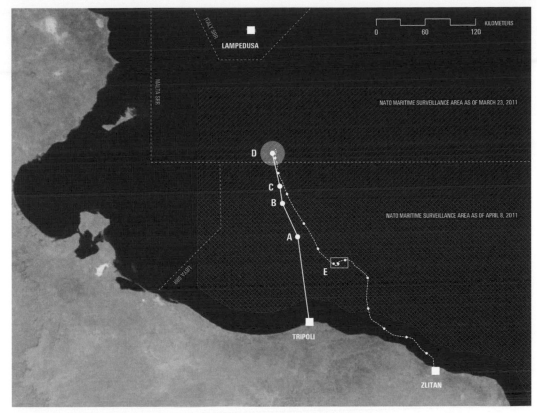

*Figure 3:* Chain of events in the "left-to-die boat" case as reconstructed by Forensic Oceanography. For a detailed key to this map, see: http://www.forensic-architecture.org/case/left-die-boat/.

the parties involved and to allocate responsibility to them. In the process, we have had to understand the complex legal structure of the Mediterranean— which, we argue, is intrinsic to the violence perpetrated in the "left-to-die boat" case and many others—and mobilize the political geography of the sea to allocate responsibility where states sought to evade it.

At sea, the moment of border crossing is expanded into a process that can last several days and extends across an uneven and heterogeneous territory that sits outside the exclusive reach of any single polity. The spatial imaginary of the border as a line without thickness dividing isomorphic territorial states is here stretched into a deep zone "in which the gaps and discrepancies between legal borders become uncertain and contested."[8] While, as a vast literature on the subject has already demonstrated, this uncertainty is true of every border—even those situated on firm land—this condition is pushed in the Mediterranean to its limits and acquires the clarity of a paradigm. As soon as a migrants' boat starts navigating, it passes through the various jurisdictional regimes that crisscross the Mediterranean: from the various areas defined in the UN Convention on the Laws of the Sea to Search and Rescue regions, from ecological and archaeological protection zones to areas of maritime surveillance *(Figure 4).* At the same time, the migrants' boat is

**8** Brett Neilson, "Between Governance and Sovereignty: Remaking the Borderscape to Australia's North," *Local-Global Journal* 8 (2010): 126.

JURISDICITONAL AREAS DEFINED BY UNCLOS
- Internal waters
- Territorial waters
- Exclusive Economic Zone

ENVIRONMENTAL PROTECTION ZONES
- Ecological Protection Zone
- Ecological and Fisheries Protection Zone
- Fisheries Protection Zone

SEARCH AND RESCUE ZONES
- SAR Zones

OVERLAPPING CLAIMS
- Overlapping SAR zones
- Other overlapping claims

*Figure 4:* Map of maritime jurisdictions in the Mediterranean, based on data compiled by www.marineplan.es and the International Maritime Organization. Design: Forensic Oceanography.

caught between a multiplicity of legal regimes that depend on the juridical status applied to those onboard (refugees, economic migrants, illegals, etc.), on the rationale of the operations that involve them (rescue, interception, etc.), and on many other factors. These overlaps, conflicts of delimitation, and differing interpretations are not malfunctions but rather a structural character-istic of the maritime frontier that has allowed states to simultaneously extend their sovereign privileges through forms of mobile government and elude the responsibilities that come with them. For instance, the strategic mobilization of the notion of "rescue" has in several occasions allowed coastal states to justify police operations on the high seas or even within foreign territorial waters for which they would otherwise have little legal ground, thus de facto extending their sovereign capabilities through their patrols. Conversely, for sev-eral years, the Mediterranean coastal states have been involved in diplomatic scuffles over their respective obligations to assist migrants distressed at sea. One of the most notorious and longstanding conflicts has, until recently, been between Italy and Malta, which have repeatedly attempted to pass onto each other the burden of rescue, basing their claims on the different versions of the International Convention on Maritime Search and Rescue (SAR) to which they each are signatories. Here, it is not the absence of law, but rather the prolifer-ation and spatial entanglement of different legal regimes across the maritime border—what we might call with Keller Easterling its "disposition"—that has created an "unfolding potential," an "inherent agency" that "makes certain

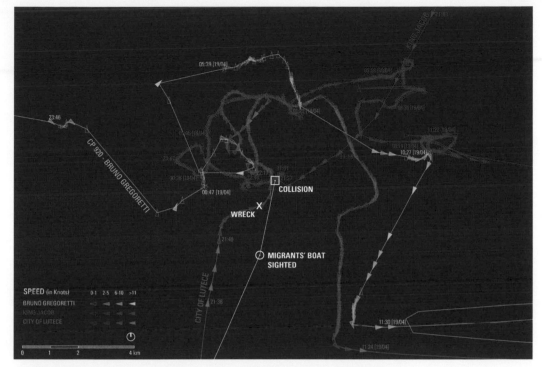

*Figure 5:* The frantic tangle of Automatic Identification System (AIS) vessel tracks in the Mediterranean following the April 18, 2016 shipwreck reconstructed in the "Death by Rescue" report. Credit: Forensic Oceanography. GIS analysis: Rossana Padeletti. Design: Samaneh Moafi.

things possible and other things impossible," ultimately producing violence on a large scale.[9]

It is because of this distinctly spatial dimension of violence at sea that mapping has represented such an important aspect of our investigations: if violence is exercised through space, mapping can help locate the indices where this "infrastructure that evades representation"—the violence of the maritime border—"nevertheless leaves its imprint and creates its own specific forms."[10] In the specific case of the "left-to-die boat," mapping has been useful to re-inscribe responsibility across the complex legal geography of the sea. Plotting the trajectory covered by the boat onto the various juris-dictional areas of the Mediterranean was crucial in pointing to the multiplicity of agencies that, at different times, had specific responsibility for the rescue operations but did not intervene.

## Against the sea's mobilization towards deterrence: the "Death by Rescue" report

More recently, in our report titled "Death by Rescue," our work has focused on another disturbing form of killing at sea that we saw emerging in early 2015.[11] The week commencing April 12, 2015 saw what is believed to be the largest loss of life at sea in the recent history of the Mediterranean. On April 12, four hundred people died when an overcrowded boat capsized due to its

**9** Keller Easterling, *Extrastatecraft: The Power of Infrastructure Space* (London; New York: Verso Books, 2014), 14.

**10** Julieta Aranda, Brian Kuan Wood, and Anton Vidokle, "Editorial 'Structural Violence,'" e-flux, no. 38 (October 2012), http://www.e-flux.com/journal/editorial-29/.

**11** See: https://deathbyrescue.org/

passengers' excitement at the sight of platform-supply vessels approaching to rescue them. Less than a week later, on April 18, a similar incident took an even greater toll in human lives, leading to the deadliest single shipwreck recorded by the UNHCR in the Mediterranean. Over eight hundred people are believed to have died when the migrants' vessel sank after a mis-maneuver led it to collide with a cargo ship that had approached to rescue its passengers. More than twelve hundred lives were thus lost in a single week. As Médecins Sans Frontiers (MSF) commented at the time, these figures eerily resemble those of a war zone.

Beyond the huge death toll, what was most striking about these events is that they were not the result of the reluctance to carry out rescue operations, which we had previously identified as a structural cause of migrants' deaths. In these two cases, and other similar ones that had taken place in previous weeks, the actual loss of life had occurred during and partly through the rescue operation itself. Based on Automated Identification System (AIS) vessel tracking data *(Figure 5)*, the detailed reconstruction of these two successive tragedies provided in our report shows, however, that in all likelihood the merchant vessels involved complied with their legal obligations and did everything they possibly could to rescue the passengers in distress. While it could appear that only the ruthless smugglers who overcrowded the unseaworthy boats to the point of collapse are to blame, the report focuses on the deeper responsibilities of EU agencies and policy makers, showing how their policies created the conditions that made the April shipwrecks inevitable. The report reconstructs the institutional process that unfolded after the announcement of the Italian government's intention to discontinue the military-humanitarian operation Mare Nostrum (MN). The latter, which began in October 2013, had deployed unprecedented means to rescue migrants in distress close to the Libyan shore but had also attracted increasing criticism for allegedly constituting a "pull factor" for migrants and hence causing more deaths at sea. On November 1, 2014, EU institutions responded to the imminent end of Mare Nostrum by starting the Triton operation led by Frontex, the European border agency, which deployed fewer vessels in an area further away from the Libyan coast, and which did not consider rescue operations as their main priority. In early 2015, as a result of this retreat of state-led assets, the burden of extremely dangerous search and rescue operations was ceded to large merchant ships, which, as has been repeatedly emphasized by the shipping industry, are ill-fitted to conduct them. The EU's decision not to dispatch assets near the Libyan coast to provide SAR assistance to migrants in distress at sea thus created the conditions in which the twin April shipwrecks were bound to happen, ultimately leading to assistance becoming deadly.

What is perhaps most relevant in this context, however, is that not only were EU agencies aware that cutting back rescue operations would lead to an increase in the number of fatalities; these agencies were also explicitly seeking to use the increased risk for migrants as a means of deterrence. Through an in-depth analysis of newly-acquired technical documents produced by Frontex, official statements by policy makers and EU officials, and minutes of operational meetings (what we have referred to as a form of "policy forensics") *(Figure 6)*, our report demonstrates that the rationale for this

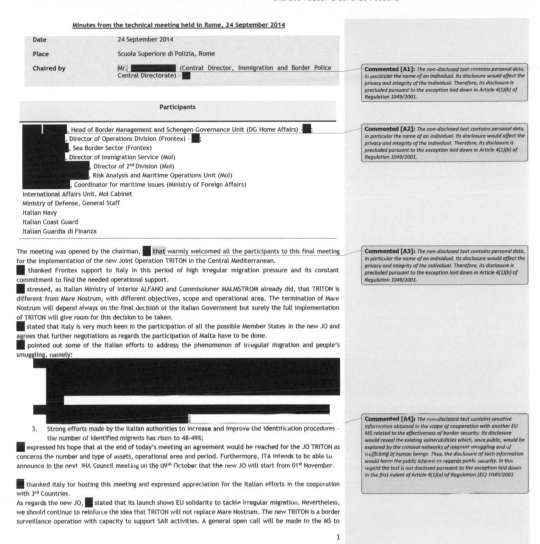

Figure 6, part 1: Minutes of a technical meeting held in Rome on September 24, 2014 between representatives of the European Commission; Frontex; and the Italian Ministries of Interior, Defense and Foreign Affairs; as well as the Italian Coast Guard Border Police and the Navy. In the meeting, an increase in search and rescue operations foreseen as a result of the end of Mare Nostrum is discussed.

retreat from state-operated rescue was to create a deterrent for migrants and smugglers with the aim of stemming crossings. As explicitly stated in a Frontex Tactical Focused Assessment for operation Triton, "the fact that most interceptions and rescue missions will only take place inside [Triton's] operational area could become a deterrence for facilitation networks and migrants that can only depart from the Libyan or Egyptian coast with favorable weather conditions and taking into account that the boat must now navigate for several days before being rescued or intercepted."[12]

The notion of deterrence is here of particular interest because it reveals how the sea as an environment has been factored into the logic of border

12 Frontex, *JO Triton 2015 Tactical Focused Assessment*, 14 January 2015, p. 2. The document can be accessed in full at: https://deathbyrescue.org/assets/annexes/7.Frontex_Triton%202015%20Tactical%20Focused%20Assessment_14.01.2015.pdf

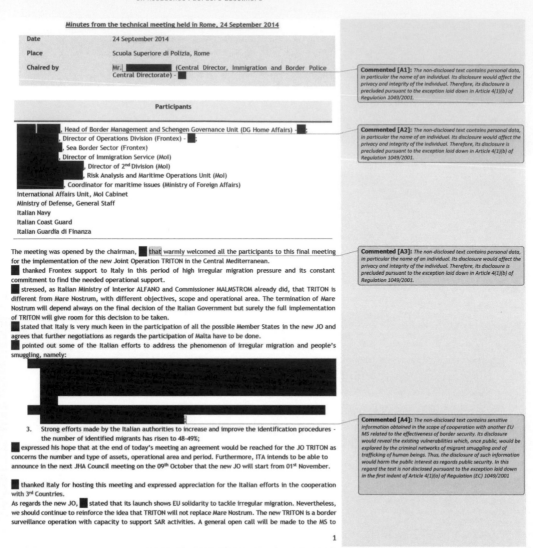

Figure 6, part 2: Minutes of a technical meeting held in Rome on September 24, 2014 between representatives of the European Commission; Frontex; and the Italian Ministries of Interior, Defense and Foreign Affairs; as well as the Italian Coast Guard Border Police and the Navy. In the meeting, an increase in search and rescue operations foreseen as a result of the end of Mare Nostrum is discussed.

control. While the notion of deterrence has of course a long history in military thinking and criminology, it appears to have first been explicitly mobilized in the context of the "war on migration" along the Mexico-US border. Here the notion of "prevention through deterrence" was adopted by US border guards as early as 1993. This enforcement strategy calls for the deployment of massive numbers of agents along the sections of the border that are easiest to cross, usually around urban areas. These concentrations, in turn, lead migrants to attempt to cross in areas that are much more hostile and, therefore, more difficult to traverse and much easier to control.

A logic of deterrence has long been at play as well across the maritime borders of the EU. In an important report submitted in 2003 to the EU

Commission by CIVIPOL—a semi-public consulting company to the French Ministry of the Interior—the authors explain that in order to "hold a maritime border which exists by accident of geography," it is necessary to go well beyond an understanding of the maritime border as delimited by the territorial waters of the EU states.[13] To exploit the geopower of the sea and use its physical characteristics to reinforce the border, surveillance has to cover "not just an entry point, as in an airport, nor a line, such as a land border, but a variable-depth surface." The unbundled sovereignty at work in the high seas enabled European and non-European coastal states—assisted since 2001 by NATO as part of its "Operation Active Endeavour" and since 2006 by Frontex— to deploy maritime border patrols using boats, helicopters, airplanes, and the aforementioned surveillance technologies to intercept incoming migrants.

Moreover, these means of control should be primarily deployed along what the CIVIPOL report calls "focal routes [...] which account for more than 70%–80% of detected cases of illegal immigration by sea" and whose locations are dictated by geography—"straits or narrow passages where Schengen countries lie close to countries of transit or migration: the Straits of Gibraltar, the Sicilian Channel, Adriatic Sea, the Dodecanese island channels, the Canary Islands Channel and the Gulf of Finland." These places are ones where "the surveillance required is highly intensive, detailed and semi-permanent in virtually constant areas." However, the result, as the CIVIPOL report notes, is ambivalent, since "the increasing deterrent effective [sic] of improving the surveillance and control mechanisms of the Spanish and Italian authorities on the Straits of Gibraltar and the Sicilian Channel is shifting the focus towards riskier passages, the Canary Islands Channel and the Gulf of Sirte," which in turn leads to greater numbers of deaths. As such, rather than stopping the inflow of illegalized migrants, the increasing militarization of the maritime frontier of the EU has instead resulted in the splintering and funneling of migration routes towards longer and more perilous areas of crossing. This mechanism has been a constant one, which we can also expect to continue operating in the aftermath of the March 2016 deal between the EU and Turkey. The latter has managed to almost bring to a halt crossings using the relatively safe route via the Aegean. While it is still too early to precisely assess the effects of this last closure, many have argued that it will again lead to an increase in crossings from Libya or Egypt, which are substantially longer and more dangerous routes.

As this discussion demonstrates, the strategic use of the maritime environment as a frontier zone turned the sea into an unwilling killer, while at the same time distancing the deaths of migrants further from the eyes of the European public and shifting the blame for them onto the sea itself. Seen from this perspective, the sea and its very materiality stop being a mute background on which tactics of border enforcement unfold, becoming instead a constitutive element of boundary making in the same ways that border guards, institutions, and surveillance systems are.

## Liquid Lands

What emerges from our investigations into particular cases of deaths at sea and our attempt to understand the conditions that led to them is an

13 This and successive quotes from: CIVIPOL, "Feasibility Study on the Control of the European Union's Maritime Borders" (European Commission (JHA), April 7, 2003), 8, http://www.ifmer. org/assets/documents/ files/documents_ifm/ st11490-re01en03.pdf.

impression of the EU's maritime frontier as a highly complex space, in which conflicting and overlapping jurisdictions, mobile militarized patrols, and the assemblage of a surveillance system enabled by a pulsating "sea" of electromagnetic waves converge to create a space of deeply hierarchized and a-rhythmic mobility. Here the geopower of the sea can, in the words of Vyjayanthi Rao "oscillate between states of fluidity, enabling the passage of people, forms and ideas and states of solidity, blocking passage under given political and historical circumstances."[14] This complexity should not make us lose sight, however, of the profound divisions of the Mediterranean space marked by enduring colonial asymmetries and socio-legal inequalities that are crucial in determining who can travel freely and who cannot. The sea has become a crucial device for sorting global populations through the migration policies and bordering practices of the EU, relegating the majority of the populations of the global South to spaces of banishment, and transforming those who seek to contest their spatial assignment by crossing this liquid frontier into illegalized and precaritized subjects. The form of violence that is exercised at and through the sea, is the necropolitical supplement of this selective mobility regime. This maritime deathscape echoes with many others, scattered across time and space, in which a harsh environment—be it the sea, the desert, or the mountains—has been made to kill without touching.

Inasmuch as the sea does not constitute an anarchical space that lies outside the reach of state power, it should also not be seen as a space that is absolutely separate and different from firm land. Although, as we have argued above, it certainly offers particular conditions that both enable and constrain actors operating across its liquid plain, the particular form of government characteristic of the maritime space—in which the line of the border has become elastic, expanding and retracting with the movement of patrols and migrants' boats, ebbing and flowing to the rhythm of shifting operations—does not stop at the coastline but rather spills over onto firm land. Echoing the government of routes at sea, border functions on the land have increasingly been decoupled from the limits of territorial borders, becoming increasingly dispersed and mobile, and following certain bodies as they move across space. From the notion of "Routes Management," which revolves around the charting of clandestine migrant routes, to that of "Integrated Border Management," which seeks to control migration "before, at, and after the border," practices of border control seem to have increasingly done away with fixed territorial thinking. As such, rather than the "solidification of the sea"—a term that was suggested a few years ago by the artist collective Multiplicity to describe the progressive invasion of the terrestrial logics of bordering into the sea—what we observe here might be qualified as the "liquefaction of the land," with the coastline simply turning into a point of "logistical tension" along which the different practices and rationalities that operate at sea and on land meet and sometimes clash.[15] A new spatial imagination is needed to understand this topography of borders. Contrary to the predicament that has often sidelined the sea as an exceptional aberration from the standard of contemporary territoriality, the spatiality of the sea might prove instead a crucial starting point to think through the challenges posed by this novel situation.

**14** Vyjayanthi Rao, "Speculative Seas," in Güven İncirlioğlu and Hakan Topal, eds., *The Sea-Image: Visual Manifestations of Port Cities and Global Waters,*(New York: Newgray, 2011), 124.

**15** Craig Martin, "Shipping Container Mobilities, Seamless Compatibility, and the Global Surface of Logistical Integration." *Environment and Planning A* 45, no. 5 (2013): 1021–36.

# Deconstructing the Threshold: Waste Lands / Trauma / Hospitality

Merve Bedir

Until the revolution in Syria, Turkey had been a territory of transit for refugees moving towards Europe. As a consequence of migration during the last five years, and especially after its recent agreement with the European Union, the country is transforming into a threshold, a border, and a fortress. In this context, the philosophical, political, and cultural implications of politico-geographic borders and hospitality; the relations between hosts and guests and between institutions and their constituencies; and the violence and coloniza-tion of language are being rendered visible in urban space. An etymological analysis of hospitality, and a spatial analysis of migration and (non)belonging in and around Turkey could help to develop an understanding of the phenom-enon called the "refugee crisis" today, as well as the problematic of security, the decay of the nation-state, and social welfare.

## A Critique of Hospitality

> "[T]he foreigner is first of all foreign to the legal language in which the duty of hospitality is formulated, the right to asylum, its limits, norms, policing, etc. He has to ask for hospitality in a language which, by definition is not his own, the one imposed on him by the master of the house, the host, the king, the lord, the authorities, the nation, the State, the father.... This personage imposes on him translation into their own language, and that's the first act of violence."[1]

1 Jacques Derrida, *Of Hospitality* (Stanford: Stanford University Press, 2000).

Turkey passed a law concerning foreigners and international protection in 2013, for the first time in its history. This law imposes different titles for foreigners and their statuses, such as asylum seeker, conditional refugee, subsidiary refugee, temporary protection, humanitarian residence permit, and victim of human trafficking residence permit. Concerning refugees, the hierarchy underlined by these words in the national law is reinforced by an extant hierarchy within the international protection system that privileges those who qualify for official UN refugee status over those who do not.

The current "refugee crisis" needs to be confronted through the perspective of the heightened borders created by these highly hierarchical national and international definitions, and the inherent hostility embedded in them. Language is used to denigrate asylum seekers by assigning them to certain categories, enacting further legislation to tighten borders, and forming regional agreements to hinder the free movement of people seeking asylum.

In addition, common political discourse asserts the language of guest, host, and hospitality, instrumentalizing these notions to suspend the universal agreements on human rights (for instance the freedom of movement, mentioned in the UN's Universal Declaration of Human Rights (1948)).

### The Host and the Guest

The words host, guest, hospitality, ghost, hospice, hostile, and hostage, all derive from the same linguistic origin, and describe the complexity of social and legal obligations and tensions that are embedded in the relationship between the host and the guest. Why is the guest at the door? Where did he come from? What is his name? Does he have a name? How important is it for us to know his name? What does he want? Do I have to open the door? What happens when I open the door? The responses to these questions determine the rules of hospitality.

**2** Ibid.

**3** Immanuel Kant, *Perpetual Peace: A Philosophical Text,* 1795.

As Derrida[2] has conceptualized in detail, the words "host" and "guest" both stem from the Proto-Indo-European root "ghostis," which embeds three meanings. The first denotes the guest as a stranger, with an emphasis on enmity. For instance, "hostis humani generis" is a legal term for enemy of humanity. The second denotes a host, a guest, or a stranger, with an emphasis on hospitability and "hospitality;" and the third inverts the hostility of the first, and refers to the "victim," the one who is besieged. The host is sometimes the "hostage."

Related to these terms is the word xenos (guest-friend),[3] defined as a foreigner or stranger who is unknown, not a member of the community, and who either receives another's hospitality or, conversely, is a host. Xenos comes from a word of Greek origin, xenia, which is the necessary respect, generosity, and courtesy shown among the hosts and the guests. This definition is far from a legal one, neither created nor instrumentalized by the state.

### Istanbul's Spaces of Hospitality

Istanbul is a city of guests, and the city is the ultimate host given its history of internal and international migration. A series of cases in the city illustrate how urban space displays the various meanings of hospitality: a detention center appropriated from a former court building by the Ministry of Interior; a summer camp of the State Railway Works, which was designed for use by its employees, but is being used as a refugee camp for an indefinite period; social housing built by the State; and a stadium built by one of the local municipalities.

The first example, *Kumkapı yabancılar misafirhanesi* (Kumkapı Foreigners Guesthouse) is a second-degree monument building, which belonged to the Armenian community. The building was confiscated by the

Still from the film "Are there any palm trees in Grozny?" Palm trees decorating the beach/night club next to the camp. Banu Cennetoğlu, 1995.

State and used as a court building until 2007, when it was transformed into a detention center and renamed. While the name Kumkapı Foreigners Guesthouse contains the meanings of enemy versus hostage and parasite versus guest, the name also signifies the complete opposite. The detainees are kept hostage. They are perceived, by both the state and the citizens, as parasites who are looked after with the taxes of citizens, who are dangerous and should not be released into the city or society. They thus become invisible.

Still from the film "Stadium." Mimar Sinan Stadium, Fatih, Istanbul. Artıkişler Collective, 2015.

In 2004, the State Railway Works *summer education camp* was turned into a temporary refugee camp on the Anatolian side of Istanbul, located between a beach/night club, an army barracks, and a former shopping mall. Here, 160 Chechen "refugee-like persons," who had escaped to Turkey during the Russia-Chechnya War, became *ghosts*, an apparition on the news as well as a new legal category (refugee-like-persons), but their presence was not manifested in reality, or visible in the city. Their arrival in Istanbul was briefly mentioned in the news. The president at the time had facilitated their transfer to Turkey from Georgia. Thereafter, barely a trace of them was perceptible for a long time. The users of the nearby beach club did not know of the presence of the refugees due to fencing and landscaping. Those in the army barracks avoided them.[4] The Chechen guests stayed there until 2014. Nobody knows where they went afterwards.

In 1989–90, the Mass Housing Administration of Turkey (TOKİ) built affordable housing for migrants with Turkish ancestry, who fled after the fall of the communist regime in Bulgaria. Residential districts were developed at the periphery of Istanbul as part of TOKİ's housing scheme, not much different from other social housing typologies in Turkey. The infrastructure built for these districts caused more informal settlements at the periphery, thus becoming part of the history of Istanbul's urban sprawl. The migrants from Bulgaria were never named as refugees, but they were actually the subjects of refuge. Later on, they were given Turkish citizenship.

In the final case, African immigrants have been running their own football league using a stadium managed by the local municipality in the Fatih neighborhood of Istanbul. They have established an NGO to organize the games, but also to manage possible transfers to the national Turkish football league. Managers of big teams in Istanbul go to watch the games there. The *football stadium*, in a way, has been transformed into a space of solidarity and resistance for and by the immigrants, whose role has changed from "guest" to "host." The NGO is the representation of this transformation.

Hannah Arendt[5] claimed that the modern history of minorities goes together with the history of those without a state, those who have been displaced by created emergencies. Since this situation means the repatriation or naturalization of the displaced, it shows the limited hospitality granted either by the sovereign from whom the refugee is escaping, or by the sovereign

4 Banu Cennetoğlu, *Are there any palm trees in Grozny?*, 2005.

5 Giovanna Borradori, *Philosophy in A Time of Terror: Dialogues with Jurgen Habermas and Jacques Derrida* (Chicago and London: University Of Chicago Press, 2003).

extending the refuge. Tarlabaşı and Aksaray, two neighborhoods of Istanbul that function as arrival neighborhoods, exemplify the two cases of Arendt's argument.

Internally displaced Kurdish people and refugees from different countries live in Tarlabaşı. The situation there suggests that the condition of solidarity should be added to Arendt's statement. Often, the residents of Tarlabaşı unite, as when they mobilize against the police, who want to evacuate them from their houses.

In Aksaray, refugees from Syria have already opened bookshops, restaurants, hair salons, etc. Shop windows display at least two languages. Another vocabulary has emerged for various streets, squares, parks, and parts of the city. For instance Istiklal Street is called "Mille Mindele" (a thousand white faces), whereas Sıra Selviler Street has been renamed Sylvester Stallone Street for the convenience of pronunciation.[6]

## Camp As The Space of Trauma

Turkey had very few temporary/short-term refugee camps within its territories before the refugees from Syria arrived. More than twenty state camps along the border with Syria are equipped with the most recent digital technology and excellent containers, tents, and common facilities with solar panels. The "residents" of the camps are given chip-cards, which are valid as ID, but can also be used to shop at the supermarket, for instance. On the other hand, the municipal camps are much less "luxurious," but more permeable for the host community to enter and leave and spend time together with the guests.

The state refugee camp in Nizip, Gaziantep has three layers of fences, with two layers of buffer zones in-between, ten watch towers, established rules for getting permission to go in and out, bolted-down containers, and extra layers of fences within and between the school, the supermarket, the hospital, etc. It is a space of hostage for people.

Considering that the Syrian refugees are categorized under "temporary protection" status in Turkey, which is the most ambiguous legal condition of all, holding no prospect of a future as a legal refugee, this camp promises to be the living environment for them for an indefinite time. The refugee camps in Turkey have been around for five years now, but the average time a person spends in a refugee camp, globally, is seventeen years. This condition makes the camp into the space of trauma, the trauma of a future yet to come, a future that is not decided by themselves, a future that might include any enemy coming from any direction, a timeless space.

Derrida[7] writes that a traumatic event is not only marked as an event by the memory, even if unconscious, of what took place. Yet, the schema of trauma must be complicated, questioned in its "chrono-logy"—that is, the thought and order of temporalization the term seems to imply. For the wound remains open because of terror of the future and not only the past. The ordeal of the event has as its tragic correlate not what is presently happening or what has happened in the past but the trauma to be produced by the future, by the to come, by the threat of the worst to come, rather than by an aggression that is "over and done with." But, here is another

**6** Abd Nova, Basem Nabhan, Auguy Lufuluabo, Metehan Özcan, *take place*, 2015.

**7** Giovanna Borradori, *Philosophy in A Time of Terror*.

Gaziantep Nizip formal camp for Syrian asylum seekers. Photograph by Merve Bedir, 2013.

paradox, which is the anonymous invisibility of the enemy because of the undetermined origin of the terror, because we cannot put a face on such terror, because we do not know what an event of the unconscious or for the unconscious is.

Robin Mackay[8] opposes the wound as for the reason for trauma. He talks about a geotrauma, a trauma that is not a hole punched into the organic by exteriority, nor even a founding event synonymous with the constitution of the organic individual per se, which constricts his or her path to death. Trauma is a perennial boring or a vernacular inhabiting of the organic by the inorganic. Trauma is not personal; it is a physical reality, where the time of earth is recorded, accreted, and knotted up inside us. All human experience is an encrypted message from Cthelll (the memory of the terrestrial crust of the earth) to Cosmos; geotrauma is a planetary neurosis. McKenzie Wark looks at the camp, the urban space, the site of ruin as the site of geotrauma and suggests pushing beyond the atomized images to imagine not what passes but what is created at the end of human time. The permanent legacy of humans will be chemical, he emphasizes, not architectural:

> "After the concrete monoliths crumble into the lone and level sands, modernity will leave behind a chemical signature, in everything from radioactive waste to atmospheric carbon. This work will be abstract, not figurative. The chemical signature of modernity, the end of human time."[9]

The refugees living in the informal camps around Amman have a perception of trauma, time, and space that brings them back to their being before modernity. They prefer not to be settled in a formal camp, or in the city. They refer to Bedouins, who can move freely and quickly, according to their needs. In the last decades, this condition happened to Palestinians, to Iraqis, and now to Syrians, spreading further in the region.

> "I don't need to build another house that will be destroyed by an enemy, that I don't know who, when, and from where might be coming. The sky is my home."[10]

8 Robin Mackay, "A Brief History of Geotrauma," in *Leper Creativity: Cyclonopedia Symposium.* Ed Keller, et al, eds. (Brooklyn: Punctum Books, 2012).

9 McKenzie Wark, "An Inhuman Fiction of Forces," in *Leper Creativity: Cyclonopedia Symposium.* Ed Keller, et al, eds. (Brooklyn: Punctum Books, 2012).

10 Quote from conversation with an immigrant in Gaziantep, 2014.

Left over life jackets in Lesvos. Photograph by Merve Bedir, 2016.

## Extraterritorial Black Holes

11 Henry Giroux, *Zombie Politics and Culture in the Age of Casino Capitalism* (New York: Peter Lang Publishing, 2011).

In his book, *Zombie Politics and Culture in the Age of Casino Capitalism*,[11] Henry Giroux examines the emergence of the culture of sadism, cruelty, disposability, and death. His metaphor, the Zombie, is a pertinent one: dead but not quite dead, the Zombie does not make autonomous decisions but is driven by higher powers of security, religion, and finance. The Zombie nevertheless wreaks considerable havoc, kills, terrorizes, traumatizes, and disposes of bodies with ease. The Zombie derives its power from the anxieties of the common man and woman.

The agreement on the exchange of Syrian refugees between the European Union (EU) and Turkey, signed on March 20, 2016 has, in fact, effectively altered the physical borders of Greece, by excising some of the Greek islands in the Aegean Sea from Greece, making them into waste lands. All "aliens" arriving on these Greek islands, or intercepted in the waters around them, are denied mainland access for the asylum application process, treated with mandatory detention, and, in time, returned to Turkey. This agreement breaches constitutions and the human-rights and asylum conventions of the United Nations (UN). Refugees are a threat to the security of nations, hence they should be imprisoned, but they are still part of humanitarian discourse.

Robben Island in South Africa, Manus and Christmas Islands in Australia, and Alcatraz in the US are all extraterritorial spaces that have long been used to detain outsiders, dissenters, and individuals who challenge mainland authorities; and, in this case, the Greek islands of Lesvos, Chios, Samos, Rhodos became such places for the EU. Carceral systems are designed to isolate the asylum seekers completely from the outside world, criminalizing

Calais Jungle (left) and formal camp for asylum seekers (right). Photograph by Merve Bedir, 2016.

them, by denying them access to the environment of social contacts and legal rights. With security and efficiency as a priority, detention centers are im-
permeable, impenetrable, and isolating, surrounded by concrete stanchions
supporting electrified barbed wire fences, and monitored by guards—built to
restrict movement.

Through this agreement, Lesvos is becoming an offshore island for the
EU to keep the unwanted migrants away. But, onshore "islands" are also
emerging, for instance in Idomeni, or Grande Synthe and Calais, where the
law does not protect the asylum seeker. People in these camps today are not
even registered, so there is no exact reckoning of numbers and names. These
spaces have been transformed into extraterritorial waste lands, black holes,
managed by private international companies profiting from national governments or the EU, which outsource their responsibilities. This corruption leads
towards the decay of the nation-state and social welfare.

McKenzie Wark[12] asks about the connection between molecular trauma
and the planetary limit: "How can the revolutionary subject, through deepening
and widening its traumas, attain topological and categorical equivalence with
the universal absolute?" As Greece and Turkey are becoming the waste land
of the EU, and at the same time Turkey is transforming into Fortress Europe,
we need to look, through the traumas, for the possibility to imagine new
existences. For example, transnational citizenship, which has been visible
in the great effort of volunteers from several countries working with the
refugees between Turkey's shores and the Greek islands, is a case of xenia
(guest-friendship), and proposes a new understanding of an open border
society, embracing otherness, self-determination, solidarity, and collectivity.

12 McKenzie Wark,
"An Inhuman Fiction
of Forces."

# The Destabilized Boundary

**Thomas Hylland Eriksen**

You are bound to have noticed: something has happened to the way we speak and think about boundaries, borders, and the distinction between the self and the other. It is as if a world of borders has been replaced with one of fuzzy frontiers; it is as if a social universe where boundaries were once crisp and clear has been superseded by one difficult to decipher, where every social relationship seems to be under negotiation. I am not the first person to make this observation, and, naturally, the nature of boundaries has been interrogated before. Two centuries ago, William Blake was reputedly asked why he drew outlines around creatures and objects, since nothing has an out-line in reality. According to Gregory Bateson, Blake once answered that wise men see outlines, and therefore they draw them. But on another occasion, he allegedly said that *mad* men see boundaries, and they therefore draw them.[1]

A century later, Nietzsche mused, in the aphoristic *The Wanderer and his Shadow* (§67), which forms the final part of *Human, All Too Human*:

> The general imprecise way of observing sees everywhere in nature
> opposites (as, e.g., "warm and cold") where there are, not opposites,
> but differences in degree. This bad habit has led us into wanting to
> comprehend and analyse the inner world, too, the spiritual-moral world,
> in terms of such opposites. An unspeakable amount of painfulness,
> arrogance, harshness, estrangement, frigidity has entered into human
> feelings because we think we see opposites instead of transitions.[2]

In other words, life is process, difference is a continuum rather than some-thing marked by rupture and sharpness, and transitions are everywhere if you just care to look for them. This floating world may seem attractive, but it is never fully realized. Communities draw boundaries around themselves and have always done so, even if criteria for membership vary: sometimes, you have to prove common descent, and sometimes it is sufficient to settle and follow local custom. When we classify the world, we also think in terms of bounded, contrasting entities. A male is not a female. A sun is not a moon. Broken skin leaks bodily fluid and is problematic because it reveals a fissure in the body's boundary that may have detrimental long-term effects.

Bounded entities give a feeling of order, security, and empowerment, and we soldier on, bravely facing the Sisyphean task of tidying up the chaos of the world. This is why controversy erupts, and uneasiness results, when boundaries are being challenged.

**1** Gregory Bateson, *Steps to an Ecology of Mind* (New York: Ballantine Books, 1972).

**2** Friedrich Nietzsche, *Human, All Too Human: A Book for Free Spirits.* Trans. R. J. Hollingdale. (Cambridge: Cambridge University Press, 1996 [1880]).

In our time, more boundaries are being questioned, interrogated, and destabilized than has been the case for a very long time. There is a nervousness about Europe these days, an insecure anxiety which drives the constituent parts of the continent towards withdrawal and increasingly desperate attempts to reinstate unambiguous internal boundaries, while simultaneously solidifying the external borders through militarization of the Mediterranean and strict policies on refugees from non-Europe.

Norway is no exception. The gender boundary is being destabilized, e.g. through the rise of the LGBT movement and discourses about gender equality (or equity). The nature/culture boundary is also being challenged through the growing awareness that the very success of cultural projects is also a recipe for their ultimate failure through the destruction of the very conditions for their long-term survival. Last but not least, the boundary of the national community is continuously being questioned: Who should have the right to call themselves Norwegians? How should the flows through the osmotic membrane enclosing the national community be regulated? What kinds of variation are acceptable? Is it possible for the country to leave the ethnic and racial ideas about nationhood behind once and for all? Or, in an even more radical bid, does nationhood matter at all, or should a broader cosmopolitanism or universal humanism serve as a moral compass when we encounter global crises, inequalities, injustices, and catastrophes? There is no easily discernable hegemonic discourse, but rather multiple polarizations and opposing views made visible at every crossroads. No available map fits the territory perfectly. The anxiety is not so much a result of boundaries being crossed, but rather their tendency to dissolve, or move, or change, before our very eyes.

The destabilization of boundaries has also been observed in the academic world. For a hundred years, anthropologists studied the Other, and, although there was considerable disagreement over the nature of the Other and his or her origins, the boundary between the civilised, academic self and the remote, exotic other was rarely put into question. For a brief period in the late twentieth century, the study of the self-as-other became fashionable, and metropolitan anthropologists wrote about their own group, relying on a suspension of disbelief (sometimes contrived, sometimes credible) in their readers, as if their subjects of study were Trobriand islanders or Zulu tribesmen. At this time, the boundary was already destabilized, never again to return intact. It has become increasingly clear that the craft of anthropology—the study of human variation and diversity—has now transmuted into the study of the boundary as such, seen as a wriggling, shapeshifting, foggy, and slippery thing, a "now you see it, now you don't" kind of phenomenon which we cannot, however, afford to discard.

Two major statements about boundaries were published in the 1960s: Fredrik Barth's *Ethnic Groups and Boundaries*[3] and Mary Douglas' *Purity and Danger*.[4] Barth showed how persons, ideas, and things could flow across the ethnic boundary separating groups. Under certain circumstances, one could even change ethnic membership, as has happened in the recent past when Travellers have become Norwegians, eradicating every visible trace of their background (more on this subject below). However, Barth did not question

**3** Fredrik Barth, ed., *Ethnic Groups and Boundaries: The Social Organization of Culture Difference* (Oslo: Scandinavian University Press, 1969).

**4** Mary Douglas, *Purity and Danger: An Analysis of Concept of Pollution and Taboo.* (London: Routledge, 1966).

*[handwritten margin note: border reviews will could be crossed]*

the boundary as such. One could cross it and penetrate the osmotic membrane of the social cell, but one could not destroy it.

Coming from another theoretical background, and representing a very different genre of anthropological writing, Douglas was concerned with the relationship between the boundaries of the body and the social order, exploring how the latter reflected the former. Like Barth, she studied border work, but had a more acute understanding of the amount of effort that goes into the maintenance of boundaries, which continuously need to be defended against the forces of chaos and disruption. Notably, she spoke of anomalies in classificatory systems as to what does not fit in, and to that which is neither/nor or both/and: the abhorrent pig in Hebrew culture; the strange pangolin among the Lele of Kasai; and, we may safely add, the inscrutable, secretive and potentially threatening Travellers of contemporary Norway.

*[handwritten margin note: border itself under threat]*

Building on, but also departing from complementary insights in Barth and Douglas, social theorists have later critically investigated, subverted, and destabilized the boundary itself, through concepts such as hybridity,[5] cultural creolization,[6] the frontier as an alternative to the boundary,[7] and so on. Neither the gender boundary, the cultural boundary, nor the ethnic boundary has any reason to feel safe from unexpected assaults for now. A question asked by many during the last couple decades is how long the national border and the governmental politics of identity will be able to withstand the pressure from dissolving boundaries. The answer is that these institutions are likely to go down fighting. For the time being, the winds are blowing in a direction strengthening both national borders and social boundaries, but this trend will change again, as it has in the past. It is nevertheless likely that a major controversy across the continent in the coming years or decades will concern the meaning and implications of the word "we," that sticky ticket to the realm of belonging.

In a city museum somewhere in Germany, I once saw an old engraving depicting the city and its border, clearly delineated by a city wall patrolled by armed guards. Beyond the city were wild beasts, bandits, and barbarians; inside it was an orderly hierarchy based on a set of rules enabling everyone to find their rightful place. On the wall itself sat, spread-eagled, a grinning witch. Neither wild nor domesticated, neither civilized nor barbarian, she threatened the very boundary separating nature from culture. Therein lay the main threat of the witch in traditional European society: she transgressed boundaries and questioned their validity, making fun of squeamish conformism and making light of constraining rules.

Against this background, the attempt on the part of many European governments to control, eradicate, or expel the Roma may rightfully be called a witch-hunt. They threaten to rip open the fabric of society by consistently breaking rules of conformity holding society together as a moral community: they reject wage work, ignore national borders, disrespect the laws of the state, and they have neither permanent addresses nor exam papers. In Norway, as elsewhere on the continent, the salient categories of the local culture are made visible through responses to Roma transgressions.

In recent years, the number of itinerant Roma visiting Norway for a few weeks or months at a time has grown, and Roma beggars have become a

**5** Homi Bhabha, *The Location of Culture* (London: Routledge, 1994).

**6** Ulf Hannerz, "The World in Creolization," *Africa* 57 (1987): 546–559.

**7** Anthony P. Cohen, *Self Consciousness: An Alternative Anthropology of Identity* (London: Routledge, 1994).

common sight in Norwegian towns. On occasion, the Roma have established makeshift camps in parks and forest areas near Oslo, moving elsewhere when evicted, and invariably leaving a trail of rubbish behind. As my colleague Cathrine Moe Thorleifsson has shown, Norwegian outrage at the misbehavior of the Roma is not so much motivated by economic anxieties—unlike in other European countries—but by their transgression of the nature/culture boundary.[8] Being Norwegian entails respecting the purity and intrinsic value of Norwegian nature. The Roma are the abject Other, human waste as Bauman would put it, superfluous and disposable.[9] While Syrian refugees are feared by many Norwegians for their sheer numbers and assumed religious fanaticism, itinerant Roma are feared for their ability to subvert core values and break down established boundaries, in spite of their being few and politically weak.

The Roma can unequivocally be defined as being the opposite of good Norwegians, and their subversions consistently confirm the boundaries of the moral community and the invisible but real norms reproducing it. They seem to make every mistake in the book, and of course, they do not want to be part of the greater family of Norwegians any more than Norwegians will accept Roma into that family. With another Gypsy group, the situation is different, and this circumstance sheds light on the politics of boundary work and belonging in another way. While Roma are "matter out of place" and "human waste," the Travellers, or *tatere*, are an anomaly, like the mediaeval witch. Neither fully inside nor fully outside, they are physically indistinguishable from ethnic Norwegians; they speak the language without an accent and are usually economically self-sustaining; and yet, they insist on maintaining cultural practices and values which the Norwegian state has tried to eradicate for generations, with limited success.

First described in the sixteenth century, there has been disagreement as to whether Travellers should be considered Gypsies at all. Their origins have been variously attributed to Gypsy immigration and the domestic underclass. The truth must lie somewhere in between. Many Travellers describe themselves as "a mixed people." Their language, known in Norway as *Romani* (as opposed to the *Romanés* spoken by Roma), is classified as a Gypsy language, but it contains many Scandinavian words. Today, around five thousand persons identify as Travellers, but only a few hundred, at the most, speak the language well. There are also Swedish and Finnish Travellers who consider themselves members of the same group as the Norwegian ones.

Travellers have historically engaged in many of the same economic activities as the Roma, but have also taken on seasonal work at farms, and have been known for having a good hand with horses. Following decades of persecution and brutal assimilation on the part of the state, Travellers are today mostly settled, but many do travel extensively in the summer months. They are sometimes turned down at campsites, discriminated against in the labor market, and treated with suspicion in welfare offices, but also praised for their handicrafts and their musical traditions, and envied for their ethos of freedom and independence.

We might say that the Roma fit into the overall scheme of classification and boundary work engaged in by ethnic Norwegians. They can easily be

8 Thomas Hylland Eriksen and Cathrine Moe Thorleifsson, "Human waste in the land of abundance: Two kinds of Gypsy indeterminacy in Norway." Forthcoming.

9 Zygmunt Bauman, *Wasted Lives: Modernity and its Outcasts* (Oxford: Polity Press, 2004).

depicted as the opposite of us; everything that "we" are not. With Travellers, the situation is trickier. They can become us, and they cannot. They are already us, but then again, they are not. They straddle the city wall. Their cultural influence seeps through the openings of the osmotic membrane of the cell. Indeed, they themselves flow in and out. Like transgender people, adopted children, and halfies with one Norwegian and one foreign parent, they are indeterminate and anomalous.

It is not the abject Other that threatens the integrity of the boundary. They can be excluded easily enough. The danger lies in the indeterminate: those who cannot be classified because they are neither inside nor outside, those who are both at the same time. This paradox is why the image of the drowned child on a Greek island made such an impression on so many Europeans. They realized that this child could have been their child, or their sibling's child. In social boundary making, the difficult part does not consist in dehumanizing or excluding people who appear to be profoundly different from ourselves, but in finding the proper place, or niche, or opening, for those who resemble us without quite being "us." This dilemma brings us full circle back to the most complex of all questions asked in social science or social theory, namely what the word "we" should be taken to mean. Probably one of the first ontological questions asked by humans, it has lost none of its potency or difficulty. And we are nowhere near a final answer.

# Bŏŕdęr Dēfĵnitiŏn
## in Oslo Airport Gardermoen

Located about fifty kilometers from the city center, the Oslo Airport in Gardermoen has experienced a continual increase in the number of passengers in recent years. In 2015, it received a total of 24,678,165, of which approximately a third were tourists.

The architecture of airports materializes the divisions and boundaries of the differing sociopolitical, economic, and aesthetic conditions of nation states. As such, the airport acts as a two-fold regulator. On the one hand, its spaces filter the transit of bodies into and out of the country, defining the subjects' belonging to a specific political, social, and legal status. On the other hand, through luggage control and taxes, it administers the circulation of these bodies and their belongings.

The Oslo Airport Gardermoen is characterized by an insistence on the tropes of the Nordic, embodied in the dialogue between the wooden interior textures of the airport and a landscape project which merges the facility with the surrounding forests. On entering these spaces, individuals cross one of the biggest areas of duty-free shops in Europe. On leaving, their bodies pass through "state-of-the-art" airport security.

Amongst those departing are a record number of undocumented migrants waiting to be extradited at the neighboring Trandum Detention Center. Despite the Nordic architectural veil, Gardermoen is the scene for wider conflicting sovereignties, such as the US Customs and Border Protection preclearance system for inspection before boarding a direct flight to the United States.

Within the Oslo Airport, we can examine the contemporary use of aesthetics and technologies in the spaces that some can call home, that some can access while in transit, and that some are not allowed to enter.

Duty-Free Shop at Oslo Airport Gardermoen. Photograph by Ryszard Parys, 2014. Courtesy of the author.

Wayfinding

James Bridle

The Stille Rom at Oslo Airport Gardermoen is a square, wood-panelled chamber on the busy domestic concourse, conveniently located just past security, between gates A4 and A6. A small table serves as an altar, with a Norwegian bible and a Koran available for visitors. A dusty pot plant takes up one corner; one day I found it hid an Albanian prayer book and a sheaf of Marian pamphlets. Metal chairs line three of its walls, while the fourth is dominated by a wide tapestry by the Norwegian artists Jan and Benedikte Groth. The tapestry is a black field, divided by a white stripe which shoots up the centre of the cloth: a trail of paint; a flash from heaven; a plane or soul ascending. In one corner of the Stille Rom, next to a pile of Islamic prayer mats, scratched into the wooden floor and repeated again above the skirting board, is a ballpoint arrow, which aligns the supplicant with the 'qibla:' the direction of Mecca, 4,800 kilometres to the southeast.

The airport is a place of trajectories, of tracking, guiding, and orienting flows of people, machines, and information. In the airport's Operations Centre, separate desks, banked with monitors, watch over the hundreds of security cameras, fire alarms, and interlocking technical systems. Each screen is divided into rows and columns of maps, figures, flow charts, and video feeds. Any discrepancy, slow-down, logjam, or alert is instantly displayed to the operators, who can see into any part of the building and act upon it. One central screen depicts the airport's twin runways, 01L/19R and 01R/19L, which are oriented at 10 and 190 degrees. Overlaying them are compass roses displaying the current temperature and wind direction. After the Operations Centre, only the Control Tower has more authority over the airport, because, as the OC's manager puts it, the people working there are "closer to God."

The distinctive blue and yellow signage systems and the visual profile of Gardermoen were created by the Danish designer Per Mollerup, whose studio Designlab also worked on identities for the Copenhagen and Stockholm airports. The design and practice of environmental signage is commonly known as "wayfinding," a term coined by the urbanist Kevin Lynch in his seminal text, *The Image of the City,* published in 1960. Lynch proposed that our direct awareness of our surroundings was in constant communication with an ever-shifting mental map, our perception "not sustained, but rather partial, fragmentary, mixed with other concerns. Nearly every sense is in operation, and the image is the composite of them all." With the title of his 2007 book *Wayshowing,* Per Mollerup updated Lynch's term to better emphasise the role of the designer in assisting the often unconscious wayfinding processes of the individual. In that book, he wrote: "the directional traffic arrow is as much a regulatory sign as a directional sign."

1 The Stille Rom (interfaith chapel) at Oslo Airport Gardermoen, featuring a tapestry by
  Jan and Benedikte Groth. Photograph by James Bridle. Courtesy of the author.

2 The arabic word *qibla* with direction arrow, drawn above the skirting board in the Stille Rom
  (interfaith chapel) at Oslo Airport Gardermoen. Photograph by James Bridle. Courtesy of the author.

*Wayfinding* is additionally supported by the Office for Contemporary Art Norway: OCA.

1

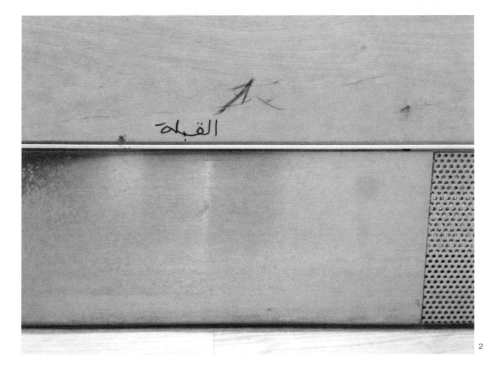

2

1

The maps released every month by FRONTEX, the European Border Agency, record the migratory routes taken by those seeking to enter the European landmass illegally. While noting that "one of the biggest entry routes for migrants into the EU is via international airports," the maps depict the main overland routes as a series of wide, coloured arrows, helplessly reminiscent of military maps and the iconography of invasion. Between January and March of 2016, the agency's figures admit 18,694 illegal border crossings across the Central Mediterranean (from North Africa to Italy), and 153,082 through the Eastern Mediterranean (from Turkey to Greece). For 2015, the total figure was estimated at over a million, 97% of which were made by sea. Over 1,200 are thought to have died. Planners have a name for paths which are worn into the landscape by travellers regardless of the intention of authorities: they are called "desire paths."

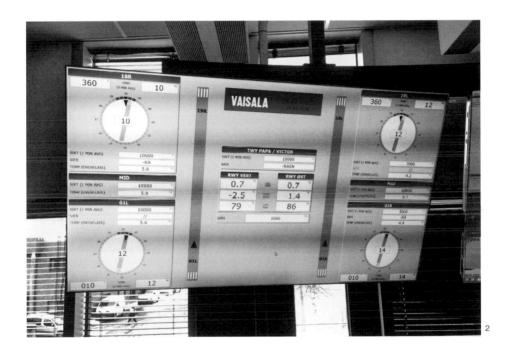

2

1 Per Mollerup Designlab, "Wayshowing design at Oslo Airport Gardermoen (OSL)," arrows and placement, March 2009. Copyright © Per Mollerup Designlab, Copenhagen, courtesy of the author.

2 Flickr user riouj, "Oslo Airport Gardermoen signage system, designed by Per Mollerup Designlab," photograph licensed under Creative Commons.

One of the biggest entry routes for migrants into the EU is via international airports: most of those who currently reside in the EU illegally, originally entered in possession of valid travel documents and a visa whose validity period they have since overstayed.

**Main migratory routes into the EU / land & sea**

▶ Western African route
▶ Western Mediterranean route
▷ Central Mediterranean route
▷ Apulia and Calabria route
▶ Circular route from Albania to Greece
▶ Western Balkan route
▷ Eastern Mediterranean route
▷ Eastern Borders route

■ Schengen area
■ Schengen associate countries

Canary Islands

"FRONTEX Migratory Routes Map, April 2016." Image courtesy of frontex.europa.eu.

# Bŏŕdęrs Elšęẁhere
## Works

## Longing for Belonging

### Frida Escobedo and Guillermo Ruiz de Teresa

During the 1980s and 1990s, Mexico experienced a dramatic neoliberal restructuring that triggered northbound migration. Driven by the decline of rural economies throughout the country, migration rates from Mexico to the United States have grown exponentially since then. Labor migration, however, offers a promise of progress that is rarely fulfilled. This journey entails numerous costs not only for the ones who leave but also for those who stay behind. In many cases, the resulting shrinking rural population faces a burden of newfound responsibilities, undermining the local economy and providing even fewer opportunities for the least privileged members of the family that remain.

According to Svetlana Boym, nostalgia (from *nostos* — return home, and *algia* — longing) is a longing for a home that no longer exists or has never existed. As Boym states, nostalgia is, at first glance, a longing for a place, but actually it is a yearning for a different time. Immigrants — whether living in voluntary or involuntary exile — embody and attest the disjunctions of Nostalgia. The sentiment of loss that suffuses the immigrant's daily life is Janus-faced: simultaneously perpetuating and contesting a cycle of dislocation.

Among the key manifestations of a successful enterprise of migration are remittances. Sending money home to the family goes beyond responding to financial need, for remittances are also one of the markers of continued belonging to the community. The opportunity for better income comes with the capacity to transform these resources into opportunities. Paradoxically, the result of these processes is often the provision of material resources for the migration of the next generation. It is through financial ties that the sense of belonging and community gets tested.

The financial investment materialized through the remittance is nothing other than the investment of nostalgia, a longing for a past that is no longer there and a future that may never come. The promise of progress is never fulfilled: the regular conveyance of the money order actually delays the homecoming indefinitely.

The remittances are often invested in land, as it is known to be the most "stable" form of patrimony. Paradoxically, as the migration rates keep growing, land increasingly loses its value. The act of investing a remittance in securing a piece of land back home is an *Odyssey*-like task: it weaves and unweaves the possibility of a possible return home.

The mechanisms of exchange that occur in transnational families as a product of migration, redefine the very concept of *home and territory*. From family structure to aesthetic choices, all the factors that define *the place where we belong* are disrupted.

The migrant families, therefore, become builders of a new world order, spearheading an extractive process in their new destination, while redefining the terms of exchange back home. The remittance, and the piece of land derived from it, become the spatial manifestation of nostalgia, a material testament of longing for a place and time, while becoming the instrument of this place and time's own extinction. It is the nostalgic — by being simultaneously sick of home and home-sick — that challenges the physicality and potential of a territory, forcing us to challenge the notions of border and belonging.

1  Frida Escobedo and Guillermo Ruiz de Teresa, "Roadside Ruin." Google Earth screen shot, 2016.
2  Frida Escobedo and Guillermo Ruiz de Teresa, "Remittance Equation," 2016.

Formula:

---

Initial area: IA = I
Area at the end of the exhibition:

EA = {I - TC - IE - Dx - [(CL+CL)-CL] - X}

---

Speed would be equal to the differential between both areas

I = XX year investment (Capital spent throughout the XX years in sending remittances)

TC = Transaction costs of the remittance throughout the XX years

(Commission from: local remittance receiver + International transmission entity + Paying agents (banks or savings entities) or exchange houses as well as the varying exchange rates when the money is deposited and then received)

IE = Investment expenses of said migrant on migrating

(Trip(s) from Mexico to the US + Coyote or broker in charge of the crossing + Mordida or fees paid to officials and facilitators throughout the trip)

Dx = Depreciation of the land of origin due to the shrinking of that community

CL = Cost of living for the migrant in both new homes (Mex/US) in relationship to the cost of living back home

X = Intangible costs the migrant incurs on due to the fact that he is away from his family for XX years

## Air Drifts

Kadambari Baxi, Janette Kim, Meg McLagan,
David Schiminovich, Mark Wasiuta

*Air Drifts* reinterprets scientific visualizations of air pollution and depicts the aftereffects of toxic aerosols as they flow from emission sources across boundaries and into high-altitude atmospheres. This project tracks how anthropogenic air pollutants drift into new territories and challenge existing regulatory norms and forms of global responsibility.

The action of minute airborne particulate matter at massive spatial and temporal scales is almost impossible to perceive. *Air Drifts* collaborates with NASA to explore its "GEOS-5 Nature Run" high-resolution supercomputer model that "mirrors" earth systems. This model accumulates five million data points every six hours, combining ground observations and satellite monitoring, and rendering atmospheric aerosols in space and time as spectral smog, creating renditions of the "invisible" environment permeating our habitats. Here, plumes of particulate matter become computational data clouds. By rendering these high-resolution visualizations of the pollutants circulating freely across borders, *Air Drifts* analyzes these parallel real-virtual worlds as surreal objects haunted with earthly territories that also foreshadow the effects of climate change yet to come.

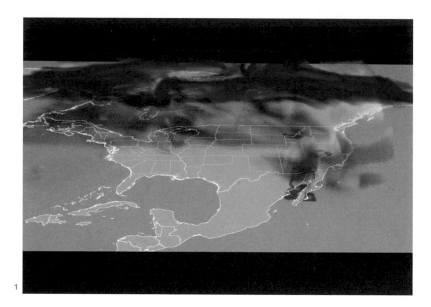

1

1 Stratospheric ozone intrusions shown as "data clouds" (computer simulation by NASA Scientific Visualization Studio).

2 Sulfur dioxide (SO2) pollutants in global atmospheres (computer simulation animation by NASA) + Polar mesospheric "night-shining" clouds (increased observations of these clouds are attributed to global warming [image acquired by the NASA crew of the International Space Station]).

All images: Computer model simulations, NASA-GMAO. Courtesy of NASA.

Project Team: Kadambari Baxi, Janette Kim, Meg McLagan, David Schiminovich, Mark Wasiuta in collaboration with NASA-GMAO (Global Modeling and Assimilation Office), Maryland, USA.

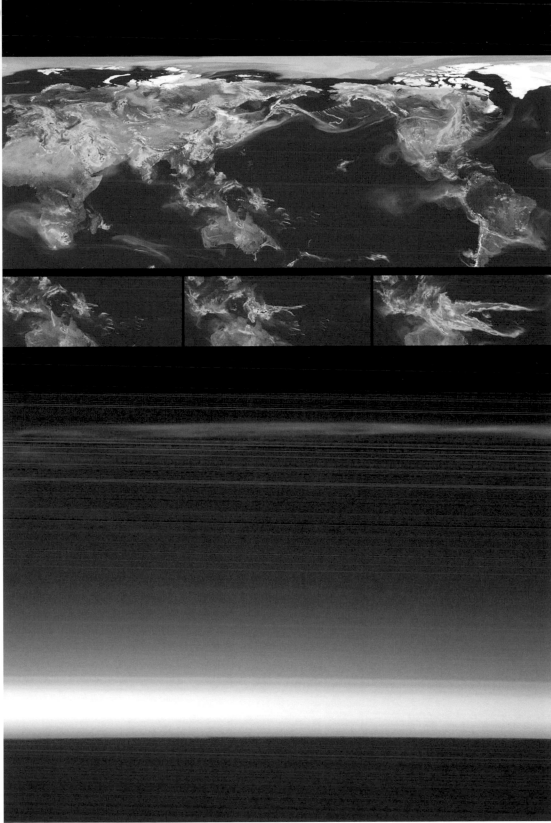

### An Old World in a Former New World

**Cooking Sections (Daniel Fernández Pascual and Alon Schwabe)**

1

Over three million United States citizens are currently planning to retire overseas for better weather and less expensive health care. Some 550,000 retired Britons are already living abroad. As a byproduct of the recent crisis in temperate "developed" countries, affordable retirement in the US and Europe is becoming financially uncertain. Pensioners are venturing into resettling in Anglophone, Francophone, Lusophone, and Hispanophone former colonies in order to seek a better quality of life. Nations that were utilized in the past to provide fertile land to harvest "exotic" produce for their former parent states, are today providing the ground to host a frenetic wave of sun-oriented migration. According to the Annual Global Retirement Index, Belize, Panama, and Ecuador are competing to build bespoke fully-catered retirement towns to meet the demands of a growing speculative market. These real estate operations for the housing of pensioners from overseas rely on farmland acquisitions. In Brazil, US investment giant TIAA-CREF started a global fund in 2012 to buy farmland, drawing investment from Swedish and Canadian pension funds. Retirement is becoming a machine of global capital that not only constructs space anew, but is also actively shaping deforestation, land dispossession, and displacement of civilians behind the multi-million euro land grabs in "forever summer" parts of the world.

A "planter's chair" is a piece of colonial furniture around which domestic architecture used to be organized. It epitomizes the connection between comfortable living and the yielding of secure revenue. Developed for Dutch and English colonists in the Caribbean and Indo-Pacific, the planter's chair used to provide comfort for the white man supervising the revenue of a plantation under weather he was not accustomed to. The chair furnished the climatic comfort of the outdoor shaded verandah, while body comfort was addressed through the arms' retractable extensions that allowed the user to rest his legs on top. The planter's chair was also known as the "lazy chair:" it helped the planter wait for the lands to yield vast profits while lying comfortably. Today, in a world of post-plantation economies, the extraction of value from land has shifted from foodstuffs to financial products. An *Old World In a Former New World* reacts to the holdings of pension funds and their level of transparency. The analysis of these funds exposes the body to changing positions of comfort or discomfort through a new chair typology that ranges from zero gravity to the forced expulsion of the body.

1 The real ocean view from the upper deck of your future development. 2015, Barbados.

2 Sun loungers on the non-turquoise beachfront of an island that turned tropical mangroves into offshore banking. 2015, Grand Cayman.

3 Fortified resort along the public coast. 2015, Barbados.

All photographs © Cooking Sections, Courtesy of the author.

## In the Frontiers of Climate Change

### Paulo Tavares

Along the southern and eastern edges of the continental Amazon basin, vast tracts of tropical forests and savannahs are being rapidly converted into scorched fields to open space for industrial soy plantations. A large part of the production of these plantations is exported to Norway to be used as fish feed in the high-tech aquaculture farms that supply most of the salmon consumed in the Global North. Monoculture capitalism operates across a global conveyor belt tying deforestation in Amazonia with the depletion of fish stocks in the Nordic Seas.

Enabled by heavy doses of fertilizers and pesticides produced by the multinational corporations Monsanto and Syngenta, this endless, toxic desert landscape is not only lifeless, harboring much less biodiversity than neighboring forests and savannahs; it is also lethal. Consider the life worlds of some of the traditional inhabitants of these lands: for example, peccaries, a mammal that plays a fundamental role in the diet and the cosmology of various indigenous groups. As trees are destroyed, lands are fenced off, and soy plantations expand, peccaries are evicted by the transformation and shrinking of their natural habitats. Like indigenous people, they become refugees in their own lands.

In the frontiers of Amazonia, the displacement and cleansing of vegetal and animal life to clear land for the expansion of the plantation ecology is historically and structurally associated with the displacement of native peoples and the extermination of their culture, a process which in turn leads to the advancement of deforestation and consequently enhances global climate change.

1 "Changing the climate." The making of the plantation ecology operates according to an expansive and destructive logic that typically starts with the selective logging of the most commercially valuable trees, followed by the clear-cutting of the thinner vegetation and recurrent burnings. The interactions between logging and fire create a highly fractured and debilitated ecosystem much more vulnerable to future burnings and further release of carbon stocks into the atmosphere. Forests are transformed into pastures, which are later re-engineered into high-tech plantations connected to the geometries of the global market.

Project by Paulo Tavares. Photographs by Armin Linke and Giulia Bruno. Satellite imagery analysis designed by Erin Yook and Paulo Tavares based on collaborative research with Forensic Architecture, Wederã Media Lab – Xavante Land of Pimentel Barbosa (Leandro Parini'a and Francisco Caminati), and Conflict Shorelines Studio – Princeton University (Rennie Jones, Igor Bragado Fernandez and Eduardo Cadava).

2 "Frontier Landscape." A geometric matrix of recently opened roads and vast deforested fields dominates the southern region of the Amazon basin, Mato Grosso state, Brasil.

3 "Refugees." A flock of Rheas feed in a field set to be converted into soy agriculture. The large-scale transformation of the tropical savannahs of southern Amazonia into pastures and plantations is leading to the dramatic shrinking and fragmentation of wildlife habitat. Displaced from their natural environments, animals such as the *Rhea americana*, globally considered a species under "near threat" of extinction, must find food in the toxic soils of soya farms.

All photographs by Armin Linke and Giulia Bruno.

## Sonic Sketches for Rroma Utopias
### FFB

At least 10% of Romania's population is Rroma. Facing discrimination and oppression in many countries, Rroma communities in Bucharest have been able to consolidate centers for cultural life, where artists and activists gather amid crowds and beats.

FFB's past research on the Rroma communities in Norway has now shifted to the architectures of these Eastern European Rroma cultural hotspots. The project consists of a compilation of interviews, field-sound excerpts, music clips, and other on-site recordings in an attempt to produce a portrait of the Rroma culture and the role of architecture in the construction of their identity. A limited-edition of sound records featuring a series of Rroma-utopias will present speculative futures for the Rroma communities of Europe.

All photographs: FFB, "Sonic sketches for Rroma utopias." May 2016, Bucharest.

### The City of Islams

**L.E.FT (Makram el Kadi and Ziad Jamaleddine)
in collaboration with Lawrence Abu Hamdan**

In July 2014, the so-called Islamic State of Iraq
and Syria announced itself as a new Islamic
Caliphate. The day after, its ruthless members
proceeded to demolish religious shrines and
mosques of other Islamic sects. Their brutal
propaganda videos are usually set either against
a bare desert (recalling the Arabian landscape
of Prophet Muhammad's era), or a religious
structure, like the neo-classical Grand Mosque
of Mosul. The architecture of the Mosque became
a critical part of this extremist visual construct.

*The City of Islams* is an exhaustive historical
research re-situating 1,400 years of the architectural typology of the Mosque, unveiling the
evolution of the mosque plan across civilizations and geographies. At every historical turn,
the mosque proved itself to be one the most
hybrid (and impure), ever evolving, religious
archetypes that still stand as a living witness
to the historical multiplicity of Islam. Architecture and urbanism act here as resistance to the
autonomous and reactionary discourse that
wants us believe in the pre-determinism of
our cultural landscape.

L.E.FT (Makram el Kadi and Ziad Jamaleddine) in collaboration with
Lawrence Abu Hamdan, "The City of Islams." Collage, 2016.

# Movement as Civil Disobedience:
## Mapping Migration and Solidarity on Lesvos Island

Nora Akawi, Nina V. Kolowratnik, Johannes Pointl, Eduardo Rega

1

In Lesvos, Greece, in the summer of 2015, most refugees traveling through Turkey arrived on the northeast coast of the island, around seventy to ninety kilometers from the first registration point in the port of Mytilene: a white container in the parking lot of what used to be the city's public swimming pool. Refugees arriving on Lesvos were denied access to public transportation, taxi cabs, and hotels. The few buses chartered by the municipality, the Port Authority, MSF, and UNHCR left the majority of people along the route, having to make their way by foot. Islanders and tourists were arrested for taking refugees to Mytilene in their private vehicles. It took around two days to cross the island on foot to reach the registration point. The grassroots organization Agkalia was set up by the priest and community activist Papa Stratis in the town of Kalloni in the center of the island. Networking with local volunteers, doctors, taxi drivers, police officers, and others, this organization provided the refugees who were left out of the government's aid operation with transportation, a resting place, food, and some basic

1 Swimming pool and first registration point near the port of Mytilene, Lesvos.
  Photograph by Eduardo Rega Calvo, August 1, 2015.

2

medical attention when necessary. Agkalia was part of a rapidly growing network of small-scale activist and volunteer organizations working in solidarity to protect refugees' right to movement.

*Movement as Civil Disobedience* focuses on the emerging networks and spatial organizations of independent human rights activism facilitating the movement of refugees, both regular and irregular, along their journey from the Turkish coast to Lesvos, Greece, as they flee towards northern Europe. This project considers the tension between the intensifying fortification and militarization of nation states on the one hand, and the way their borders are continuously transformed by the movement of refugees and its facilitation by migration activists on the other. Moving beyond the static representation and understanding of identities, borders, and territories, this project depicts their unstable and fluctuating reality. The resulting mappings are an attempt at visualizing movement across borders as the central element that defines contemporary territories and geopolitical terrains.

2 Resting space provided by the Agkalia grassroots organization at Kalloni, Lesvos.
  Photograph by Nina V. Kolowratnik, August 2, 2015.

## The Dead are Coming

### Center for Political Beauty

Every day, hundreds of migrants die trying to cross Europe's aggressively sealed-off borders. These borders are the world's deadliest. The victims of this cordon sanitaire are buried en masse in the hinterland of Southern European states. They have no names. No one looks for their relatives. No one brings them flowers.

The Center for Political Beauty carried the bodies of these dead immigrants from the European Union's external borders right to the heart of Europe's mechanism of defense: Berlin, the German capital. Those who died of thirst or hunger at the EU's borders on their way to a new life, were thus able to reach the destination of their dreams beyond their death. Together with the victims' relatives, the Center for Political Beauty opened the graves, identified and exhumed the bodies, and brought them to Germany.

1 The Center for Political Beauty exhumed a mother who had drowned on her way to Europe and was buried as "unknown" by the authorities in Sicily. The Center for Politial Beauty took her to her loved ones in Germany. They were not allowed to bury her two-year-old child with her. Center for Political Beauty, June 16, 2015, Berlin-Gatow. © Nick Jaussi.

2 The Center for Political Beauty managed to free a sixteen-year-old from the shackles of bureaucracy. He had collapsed on the trip of horror across the Mediterranean, and his body was held by the authorities for ten weeks in order to get his relatives to testify against their smuggler. Center for Political Beauty, June 19, 2015, Berlin-Schöneberg. © Nick Jaussi.

# Rēsoūrće Negotiąţjòns
## in Kirkenes

Located on the border with Russia in the furthest northeastern area of Norway, Kirkenes now constitutes a limit of the Schengen region. Following the end of the Cold War, stronger ties and peaceful contacts across borders were fostered throughout the northernmost parts of Finland, Sweden, Norway, and Russia, formalized in 1993 by the signing of the Barents Euro-Arctic Region Cooperation Agreement in Kirkenes. The maritime border between Norway and Russia was recently delimited after a forty-year-long dispute over the control of an area rich in oil and gas, yielding a series of legal treaties for the mutual benefit of the two countries. With the Pomor Visa (2010), exchanges between Barents Russia and Northern Norway are facilitated even further, giving rise to a transnational industrial and economic zone, known as the Pomor Zone.

Once a fishing town in the far northern region of the planet, Kirkenes has a built environment that has been transformed into a strategic point for the industrial, scientific, and touristic sector. The interest of global energy companies in new sites of extraction in the region has intensified speculation on future constructions of land-based infrastructure for oil and gas, possible plans for a rail link with Finland, and hypothetical new shipping routes. With the melting of the Arctic, new cargo ships are expected to stop in Kirkenes en route from China and South Korea to the West.

The specific case of Kirkenes, with its contentious landscape and its heterogenous floating population, allows an inquiry into the way architecture contributes to territorial creation and collective forms of residence in this territory embodying geopolitical and environmental frictions.

Photograph by Mathis Herbert, 2009. Courtesy of the author.

Boris Gleb Bar
Transborder Studio

The Cold War represented a period of hostility in relations between the East
and the West. Consequently, local ties across the Norwegian-Soviet border
were effectively cut off. But one historic event during this period stands out
as a contrast to the general situation of separation. For better or worse, this
incident is a symbol of borderland potential and the unique program that can
evolve from this condition.

The event happened in Boris Gleb, a small area five kilometers south of
Kirkenes, just across the border from Norway. Following the completion
of the Norwegian-Soviet hydroelectric power plants on the Pasvik River in
1965, the Communist travel agency *Intourist* put up a tourist compound there
with a bar, a cinema, an exhibition space, and a liquor shop in the barracks
built for the visiting Norwegian construction workers. Visa-free access to the
area was given to all Nordic citizens, a sensation considering the political
climate at the time.

The Russian government wished to continue the arrangement, but Norway
refused, suspecting that Soviet agents used the place to recruit Norwegian
informants. But for fifty-nine lively days during the peak of the Cold War, local
Norwegians flocked to the Soviet Union to enjoy cheap vodka, propaganda
cinema, and live music.

The Boris Gleb Bar represents a significant landmark in the history of the borderland, a point where a symbiotic existence between both sides of the line
of demarcation came into being in spite of externally imposed limitations.
As with all borderland events, the Boris Gleb Bar contained a strange brew
of geopolitics, hidden and open agendas, and a basic local need for finding
ways of everyday living.

The report on Kirkenes and the Norwegian-Russian borderland is in the form
of a spatial, performative recreation of the Boris Gleb Bar. In the framework
of this unique historical event, the idiosyncrasies of the borderland are investigated, and a platform for speculations on its future is created.

Project Team: Øystein Rø, Espen Røyseland, Håvard Skarstein, Fredrikke Frølich, Emilie Bergrem, Søren Olav Saanum Bessesen.

All images: Boris Gleb Bar, date unknown. Courtesy Varanger Museum.

# Fũŕņĭşhing Áf̧tėr Bełonġing
## Texts

# Alternative Belongings: Instituting and Inhabiting the Iranian Underground

**Pamela Karimi**

"Who is it?"

"Hi, I noticed someone is ill in this house, and I have come to help."

"Yes, please come in."

"I am wearing red shoes."[1]

**1** *"Justijuhay-e shabaneh dar khanehay-e mardom* [Investigating People's Homes in the Middle of the Night]," *Khandaniha*, 14, no. 13 (1333/1954): 11–13. Translation by the author.

**2** Ibid.

Conversations using coded language, like this one, were essential to internal communications among activist groups of leftists in Tehran in the years preceding and following the 1953 coup which—sponsored by the CIA and MI6—overthrew the democratically-elected Iranian Prime Minister, Mohammed Mosaddeq. More specifically, these obscure bits of dialogue were used by the members of the Marxist-Leninist Tudeh party, who held their meetings in rented modern houses and apartments in Tehran. These homes served as storage depots for firearms, and operated as production venues for propaganda posters and pamphlets. At times, other communist artifacts such as statues of Lenin and Stalin could be also found in these dwellings.

In the late 1950s, the expressions used in conversations like the one cited above were finally decoded by members of the Shah's secret police, enabling them to access this network of homes, arrest their occupants, and force them to collaborate in locating other Tudeh members.[2] Yet, these arrests did not put an end to the use of homes as loci for anti-establishment activities in Iranian cities, which were then undergoing processes of modernization. Covert underground Tudeh cells and members of other anti-Shah groups continued the use of housing as a place of retreat during the 1960s and 1970s. These homes were often occupied by members of the Tudeh party that acted like families. As time went by, the utilization of these homes became increasingly sophisticated. Although simple and apparently family-friendly, they became the hub of some of the most radical activities of the party. Many were located on corner lots, providing broad vistas onto the street. The residents could thereby observe the activities of passersby, as well as keep an eye out for the cell's members as they came and left. Over time, some of these homes became double-shell buildings. A simple family unit, for instance, could accommodate a "threshold" in the kitchen cupboard from which one could leave the "outer" house and enter an "inner" home, where the most sensitive materials and documents were kept, and the most important meetings were held. Later on, these homes became known as "team houses" (khaneh-haye teemi) or "group homes" (khaneh-haye dasteh jamii).[3]

To actually understand the significance of this network of alternative spaces, one should consider their proliferation in parallel to the modernist architecture fostered before and during the reign of Mohammad Reza Shah Pahlavi, between 1941 and 1979. In fact, overcoming their association with a specific political movement, the production of such alternative and covert spaces outgrew communist or anti-capitalist ideology. Ultimately, these forms of dwelling manifested larger social reactions to the rapid modernization of Iran—and, of special interest here, to the rushed proliferation of modern architecture and highly controllable modern public space—which ultimately led to the Islamic Revolution in 1979.

"Investigating People's Homes in the Middle of the Night," Khandaniha 14, no. 13 (1333/1954): 11–13. Image in public domain.

In 1953, facing a lack of revenue following the nationalization of the oil industry, the Shah sought economic assistance from other countries—first and foremost, the Truman and Eisenhower administrations in the United States. Subsequently, financial and technical aid emerged from a variety of American institutional sources, including those initiated through the Point IV program, the Ford Foundation, and the Smith-Mundt and Fulbright Acts.[4] In the 1950s, a plethora of foreign specialists ranging from lesser-known construction companies to world-renowned architectural firms erected housing complexes in major Iranian cities.[5] In the years that followed, most residential and public buildings designed by Iranian architects began to adopt imported "rationalist" and functionalist models. While many of these builders followed instructions given by on-site foreign advisors, others followed the guidelines of translated texts such as the lengthy United Nations Modular Co-ordination in Housing pamphlet of 1966, endorsed by many professional designers and educators, as well as contractors. The modular and carefully coordinated spaces of modernity became imbricated within a global market which fueled the gradual disappearance of the traditional Iranian architecture.

The global urban-planning projects of the post-WWII era offered not only "standardized" and "rational" ways of life in lieu of existing traditional and regional ones, but also new modern spaces that seemed "alienating" to those who occupied them. As Karl Marx had envisioned, while the pervasion of machinery lessened the burden on workers, technology also became an "alien power," setting labor more frantically into motion, and transforming people into mere appendages.[6] Patrick Geddes, for instance, produced a series of abstract diagrams to show the process of urban evolution; and, inspired by Buckminster Fuller's geodesic dome plans, the urban planner Jaqueline

3 This information was extracted through personal interviews with former members of the Tudeh Party who wish to remain anonymous. Spring and summer 2015.

4 Kristen Blake, The Soviet Confrontation in Iran (1945–1962): A Case in the Annals of the Cold War (New York: University Press of America, 2009), 53.

5 Among others, the English studio Fry, Drew & Partners and the Greek planner Constantinos Doxiadis. For more information on these developments, see, for example, Neta Feniger and Rachel Kallus, "Israeli planning in the Shah's Iran: a forgotten episode," Planning Perspectives 30, no. 2 (2015): 2–21; Ali Madanipour, "The limits of scientific planning: Doxiadis and the Tehran Action Plan," Planning Perspectives 25, no. 4 (2010): 485–504.

6 Karl Marx, The Grundrisse, trans. Martin Nicolaus (London: Penguin Books in association with New Left Review, 1973), 690–712.

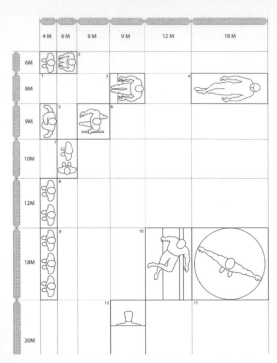

**Figure showing "modulated measurements in relation to the human body" from the translated edition of the United Nations pamphlet *Modular Co-ordination in Housing* (1966). Reproduced from the original by Pedram Karimi.**

Tyrwhitt developed a generic model of hexagonal grids for deindustrialized metropolises.[7] Not only did these new spaces seem abstract on paper—having emerged from an amalgam of datasets, codes, and diagrams—but they gave the same impression in their built forms. Above all, they were abstract in terms of their processes of production: processes that rendered utterly out-of-date the aspects of social life which were formerly marked by distinctions between center and periphery, or between industry and agriculture. Nonetheless, when studying the new industrial city of Mourenx, built in the 1960s in western France, the Marxist philosopher and sociologist Henri Lefebvre asserted how, in the name of efficiency and profitability, modern architecture led to a *separation* between people and activity, triggering the passage from *the production of things in space* to the *production of space itself*.[8] In 1974, in his widely-cited book *The Production of Space*, Lefebvre characterized the modernist built-environment as *abstract space*, evaluating it in a negative light.[9] The terms "absolute" and "abstract" were both drawn from Karl Marx's deliberations on the Hegelian concepts of absolute and abstract knowledge, as well as on Marx's own critique of abstract labor.[10] Marx interpreted industrial capitalism as a process of abstraction in which useful products were converted into the abstract value of the commodity form. As such, *use value* became synonymous with *exchange value*, and concrete kinds of work were transformed into *abstract labor*, which nonetheless structured real social existence. Similarly, "if one were to try and enumerate the 'properties' of abstract space," wrote Lefebvre, "one would first have to consider it as a medium of *exchange*... tending to absorb *use*."[11] Hence, according to Lefebvre, *abstract space* manages to propose itself as neutral in buildings, places, and modes of human interaction with space. And this interaction is conditioned, in Lefebvre's thoughts, by no *real* concern for qualitative differences. "The space that homogenizes," Lefebvre wrote, "thus has nothing homogeneous about it."[12]

Ultimately, Lefebvre understood "abstract space" as leading to dispersion and division.[13] With the expansion of exchange value into the "totality of daily life"—either in the private or the public realm—commodities and money reigned supreme, and builders in association with bankers and realtors, promised security as long as they could stealthily control the freedom of the populace. Hereafter, lived experience in both the public and the private domain was, in keeping with Lefebvre, seized both economically and ideologically. Several scholars have alluded to the ways in which Lefebvre's ideas

**7** See Ellen Shoshkes, *Jaqueline Tyrwhitt: A Transnational Life in Urban Planning and Design* (Farnham, UK: Ashgate, 2013), 103–117.

**8** Henri Lefebvre, "Les nouveaux ensembles urbains (un cas concret: Lacq-Mourenx et les problèmes urbains de la nouvelle classe ouvrière)," *Revue française de sociologie* 1, no. 2 (1960): 186–201. For an in-depth analysis of Lefebvre ideas concerning space and architecture, see Lukasz Stanek, *Henri Lefebvre on Space: Architecture, Urban Research and the Production of a Theory* (Minneapolis: University of Minnesota Press, 2011).

**(right) Modernist housing in Arya Shah with modified balconies and windows the residents. Photograph by the auth**

**9** Henri Lefebvre, "From Absolute Space to Abstract Space," in *The Production of Space*, trans. Donald Nicholson-Smith (Oxford, UK and Cambridge, USA: Blackwell, 1991), 229–291.

**10** See Robert C. Tucker, ed., *The Marx-Engels Reader* (Princeton: Princeton University Press, 1978), 109–125.

**11** Henri Lefebvre, "Contradictory Space," in *The Production of Space*, op. cit., 307.

**12** Ibid., 308.

**13** Ibid., 304.

**14** Wing-Shing Tang, "Where Lefebvre Meets the East: Urbanization in Hong Kong," in *Urban Revolution Now: Henri Lefebvre in Social Research and Architecture*, ed. Lukasz Stanek, Christian Schmid, and Akos Moravanszky (Burlington, VT: Ashgate, 2014).

**15** Similar assertions are made in Andy Merrifield, *Henri Lefebvre: A Critical Introduction* (New York and London: Routledge, 2006), 112.

**16** Ibid., 111.

cannot always be applied worldwide. For instance, dissecting the case of Hong Kong, Wing-Shing Tang points to how urbanization in that city did not fit into Lefebvre's modernization model of the forced separation of the rural—periphery—and the urban—center. Rather, against all odds, Hong Kong's modernization simultaneously experienced, as Tang remarks, a ruralization of the city, and an urbanization of the countryside.[14] Nonetheless, as the Iranian case reveals, Lefebvre's observations partially resonate with global narratives of modernization including the Global South.

During the mid-1960s, in Iran—as in much of the rest of the developing world—newly modern spaces of living became the model for hundreds of row houses, apartments, and large-scale housing complexes that crowded the margins of the old city centers. Space began to look not only more methodical, but also, in a Lefebvrian sense, more abstract, more indifferent, and more peripheralized. In the 1970s, upper- and middle-class luxury apartment complexes mushroomed in and around the prosperous suburban areas in the form of gated communities, complete with Western-style shopping centers that abetted the avoidance of a commute to the marketplaces of the old city center. The broadened streets and parking lots stirred the desire for more car possession.

Although spearheaded by foreign experts, the new modern housing concepts imported from the West swept everybody along. Their forms and their fragmentation of function recast the lifestyles of their new residents, producing a myriad of peripheries, as in turn they peripheralized centers.[15] Furthermore, most new residential developments suffered from poor commercial services, obliging the residents to purchase their daily food in the markets of the old city centers. To borrow from Lefebvre, these new spaces falsified a superficial unity out of real social disintegration.[16]

The modernist structures in Iran also contributed to the isolation of different class groups by separating the built environments where they lived. For instance, in lower-income neighborhoods, new constructions peripheralized the core of the house and its purpose. All two-story homes followed the same floor plan: they were constructed in rows, and each individual property was divided by low walls between the courtyards. All the windows were the same size, regardless of whether they faced north or south. Large glass windows and second-floor balconies allowed direct visual access to courtyards—and even parts of the interior—of neighboring homes. Many single-story units lacking a courtyard introduced the addition of a small enclosed glass box known as the *passiu*— a variant of the patio—which

*Figure 4:* Perspectival view of row houses in Shiraz with direct visual access to neighbors' courtyards: view from the upper level of the row houses. Drawing by the author.

housed plants, presumably to replicate the aura of the garden in the traditional courtyard house. With its glass ceiling, the *passiu* was the only means for allowing natural light and air into the living room. But rain would also often accumulate on the glass, causing mold to grow—so much for the efficiencies of modernist "abstraction."

The proliferation of modern dwelling spaces in Iran resulted in two main consequences. On the one hand, as new modern typologies flouted traditional Muslim taboos against mixing public and private areas, many families began to conform to the dictates of public life in the "private" spaces of their houses. For example, women in more traditional households would wear the veil all day, even at home. On the other hand, inhabitants altered these modern regimes of transparency to allow for more privacy—for example, blocking balconies and dividing shared entrance thresholds.[17]

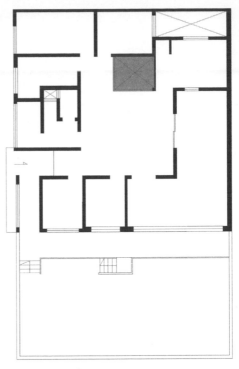

A one-story family-type house from the Mehran housing complex in central Tehran. The area highlighted above on the plan is the *passiu*. From *A Study of Nine Residential Districts in Tehran* (study conducted under the supervision of Building Research and Codes Division, Ministry of Housing and Development, Tehran). Manuscript 2.62 (1351/1972), n.p. Reproduced from the original by Parham Karimi. The patio under discussion corresponds to the grey area on the plan.

Beginning in 1978, the revolutionary supporters of the establishment of an Islamic Republic challenged the order of the carefully choreographed and surveilled spaces of the Shah's administration by occupying public squares and streets in Tehran. But once in power, the revolutionary administration had firsthand evidence of the chaos and disorder to which the orderly modernist public spaces fostered during the Shah's regime— and partly planned to allow authorities to control the activities of the citizenry could succumb, as proved by events such as Black Friday in Jaleh Square. In the absence of widespread closed-circuit television technology, the new Islamic authorities instituted public monitoring through the regulation, appropriation, and modification of public spaces so that they could *architecturally* impose moral codes, subject both to the "eyes of God," and especially, to the watchful gaze of the Revolutionary Guard. But political activists were not the only group targeted by the new authorities. As Iranian society became more gender-segregated, physical spaces were more carefully monitored. Segregation

*Figure 6:* Demonstration of September 8, 1978, the sentence on placard: "We want an Islamic government, led by Imam Khomeini." Image in the Public Domain.

was extended to even the most implausible places, including the Caspian Sea. Only a few months after the revolution, most of the accessible beaches banned mixed-gender swimming, subsequently separating portions of beach and sea from each other by long, tall curtains. What might have appeared like a Christo and Jeanne-Claude installation to contemporary Western eyes was, in fact, nothing short of an ideological intervention in nature.

A curtain used to separate men's and women's swimming areas. Photograph by Stephen Alvarez. Courtesy of Getty Images.

17 These modification strategies of modernist housing projects even emerged in the most delicate interventions by prominent Iranian architects. Consider, for example, the 1977 Shushtar New Town by the Iranian DAZ architectural group led by Kamran Diba. The complex was carefully composed of intricate brickwork, courtyards, and rooftop entertaining spaces resembling the features of vernacular architectural culture. Yet, it also emulated modern design in its attempt to push residents to coexist in similar spaces, even forcing them to share parts of their domestic realms with their neighbors. Although highly photogenic, the mere fact that inhabitants of these units altered them to allow for more privacy in their homes—blocking balconies and dividing shared entrance thresholds—attests to the failure of the idealistic revival of traditional Iranian architecture. Pamela Karimi, *Domesticity and Consumer Culture in Iran: Interior Revolutions of the Modern Era* (New York and London: Routledge, 2013), 140.

Yet, as mentioned above, long before the Iranian public space became a stage for revolutionary acts, the house had already served as a platform for countercultural activism of all sorts. To follow Hannah Arendt's account of the intimate correlation between public-political and private space in an ideal society, private space for the "idealist" activists in Iran was important only as long as it legitimated their participation in public-political affairs.[18] So, despite the even greater repression of leftist and anti-government groups after the Islamic Revolution of 1979, team houses or *khaneh-haye teemi* lingered. In the first few years in the aftermath of the revolution, the Tudeh party and other communist groups, as well as members of other anti-Shah groups, continued to use private family homes as places of retreat as they had been doing since the Islamic Revolution of 1979. A former member of a branch of the Iranian communist Left in the southeastern city of Shiraz, describes the *khaneh-haye teemi* as follows:

> Everything had to be sacrificed for our ideology. My husband and I were just married. But we often had little privacy in our own home, which was converted into a major venue for the active members of a provincial branch of the Iranian Left, *Chirik-e Fadaie*. Our "team house," left little room for privacy; we slept by the printing facilities and worked day and night, assuring the publication of our magazine and other propaganda posters, pamphlets, and brochures. When we were not home, we were busy at our own jobs followed by long teaching sessions for young people about our group's ideology. But most of the activities were conducted in our house. Although we tried our best to secure the house, we were reported by some external elements that came to know our whereabouts. My husband and I were arrested on an afternoon in the fall of 1983 as we were entering our house or what we called the team house. Several of our other members were arrested on the same day at other locations. This led to a couple of years of imprisonment and torture followed by half a decade of home arrest.[19]

After the mid-1980s, fearful of being arrested and executed, leftists and anti-revolutionaries soon abandoned the team houses as an anonymous entity and sought refuge in the homes of their relatives, especially the elderly, who drew less attention from the authorities. Sometimes a whole neighborhood collaborated to ensure that these individuals remained hidden. But it was not just the leftist groups and the anti-revolutionaries who were subject to policing, control, and interrogation: in order to suppress any possible anti-revolutionary uprising, the government subjected the entire nation to monitoring.

AV performs its play *Melpomene* in an old underground thermal bath in central Tehran. The AV theatre method is based on music, movement, dialogue, and a close relationship with the audience, reminiscent of *Gardzienice* or Polish experimental theatre. Courtesy of the photographer Jeremy Suyker.

In the Islamic Republic, disguise became a common characteristic of spatial design. While the pro-revolutionaries utilized it to show their disapproval of the mixed-gender spaces permitted by the Shah's administration, the anti-revolutionaries and the general public embraced the secretive and the hidden to lead their lives in any way they wanted, rather than following the ideals of the revolutionaries. Thus two kinds of "concealed spaces" emerged around the time of the Iranian Revolution in 1979: the conservative Islamic one, opposing the Shah's administration; and the dissident one, countering Islamic revolutionary precepts. Scholars, journalists, and cultural critics have a term for Iran's heterotopias or sites where "unlawful" activities take place. They call these places *zirzamini* or the "underground." Indeed, the term "under-ground" has become a cliché, referring to certain sites in Iran where "unlawful," "alternative," and "anomalous" practices occur.

As early as 1986, the artist Farah Osuli, in conjunction with filmmaker Khosrow Sinaie, curated the first mixed gender, Westernstyle art exhibitions inside the home of the attaché of the West German embassy. In 1994, with the help of the Christian community in central Tehran, the Iranian underground music band Kiosk began to rehearse inside a Greek Orthodox Church at the heart of the capital, and an out of sight greenhouse on the outskirts of Tehran became the rehearsal venue for 124, a fusion music band. Later on,

18 Hanna Arendt, *The Human Condition* (Chicago: University of Chicago Press, 1958), 63–67.

19 Personal interview, May 2016. The interviewee wishes to remain anonymous.

The work of publically anonymous underground mural artist, Qalamdaar (pseudonym), who appropriates abandoned homes to exhibit his art. Courtesy of Parham Salimi.

anonymous graffiti artists, such as Black Hand and Qalamdaar, appropriated abandoned homes to exhibit their art and the avant-garde theater group AV opted for an old underground thermal bath in central Tehran.

The creative agents hosting underground manifestations in Iran did not just modify spaces, but also gave rise to a new ethos of design. By appropriating principles such as the mechanisms of the physical segregation of the sexes, or the palpable separation of the public and the private, many architects gradually incorporated these strategies into singular design processes. In this regard, their actions resonate with the thinking of the French philosopher, Jacques Rancière: "[I]n order to enter into political exchange, it becomes necessary to invent the scene upon which… objects may be visible."[20] Rancière invites us to think about the ways in which non-human agents can enter the political field. He bears witness to how humans slough off and relegate practical and moral responsibilities, assigning them to objects that act on their behalf. Although sounding simplistic at first, Rancière nonetheless allows us to make a case for material objects, at those moments when they "act" independent of humans. This way of thinking about objects is helpful for decoding how subtle and indirect forms of resistance function in a society like Iran. In particular, this mode of thinking allows us to consider the ways in which buildings become active agents, even if not without human consequences.

Consider the Sharifiha House, located in an affluent neighborhood in northern Tehran, which was completed in 2013 by the Tehran-based firm. This building was completed in 2013 by the Tehran-based firm, Next Office. While carefully separated from the public, the private life of the inhabitants can be

**20** Jacques Rancière and Davide Panagia, "Dissenting Words: A Conversation with Jacques Rancière," *Diacritics* 30, no. 2 (2000): 113–126. Also see Ines Weizman, "Introduction" in *Architecture and the Paradox of Dissidence*, ed., idem (New York and London: Routledge, 2014), 3–5.

made visible to passersby if the house's mutable façade is altered. For example, the guest room can literally rotate with a push of a button, depending on whether there is a guest or not, utilizing an imported small-scale German anchor and mooring winch originally intended for maritime use.[21] The lead architect, Alireza Taghaboni, seems to suggest an alternative lifestyle using the system's own dictates, by alternately concealing the interiors from the outsider's gaze and then revealing them. In this way, the inhabitants become active agents taking control of their private lives and also, though perhaps unintentionally, defying the obligatory spatial regulations of the regime. Unlike habits that are blind repetitions of traditional ways of life, the Sharifiha House creates, in Pierre Bourdieu's sense of the term, an *habitus*: a mechanism that resists, as much as it adapts and improvises.[22]

Upholding that architecture has nowadays become a mere tool of the capital, rather than sustaining its intended social mission, the architect Reinier de Graaf writes that "[Today] the logic of a building no longer primarily reflects its intended use but instead serves mostly to promote a 'generic' desirability in economic terms. Judgment of architecture is deferred to the market. The 'architectural style' of buildings no longer conveys an ideological choice but a commercial one: architecture is worth whatever others are willing to pay for it."[23] While such an assertion could be applicable to many countries that have been affected by the mainstream global economy, it has yet to be scrutinized in the few situations where anomalies and alternative patterns—economic

**21** Personal interview, March 2015.

**22** Pierre Bourdieu, *The Logic of Practice*, trans. Richard Nice (Stanford: Stanford University Press, 1990), 68.

**23** Reinier de Graaf, "Architecture is now a tool of capital, complicit in a purpose antithetical to its social mission." *The Architectural Review* (April 2015): 1–21. Quotation from page 13.

Sharifiha House by the lead architect of the Next Office, Alireza Taghaboni. Photographs by Parham Taghioff.
Courtesy of the Next Office.

or otherwise—still prevail and where neoliberalism and capitalism have emerged but not in the conventional form. The irregular Iranian post-revolutionary economy, followed by years of sanctions, has created cultural manifestations perhaps even more dramatic than the arcane financial symptoms which emerged with industrialization and spurred Karl Marx's theories. An irregular economic system that bans the importation of standard building technology, but is ambivalent toward individual entrepreneurs who pay—allegedly, through their Central Asian bank accounts—for minor gadgets such as the aforementioned small-scale German marine technology, can be said to have had an impact on the commodity form itself: instead of homes serving as abstract, economically-equivalent units of production, economic sanctions, coupled with ideological constraints, have provided opportunities for young architects and their nouveau-riche clienteles alike, to deviate from the "norm." As such architecture's *use-value* has become sanctioned by the social currency of *defiance*. The more unconventional, the higher the worth of a house in a desirable neighborhood in northern Tehran. "Peripheries" have thus become "central," infused with an endless web of connotations. Iranian architecture today—even with its tendency to function in secretive ways and despite its seemingly indeterminate appearance—has combatted and overcome the modernist "abstraction" that troubled Lefebvre.

# Home Page

**Jeffrey Schnapp**

In the course of a long career dedicated to poking fun at social conventions, Bruno Munari designed a number of objects that point beyond the notions of domesticity, functionality, and well-being championed by the modern movement in architecture and design. Among these contentious objects, there are useless machines, folding sculptures for travelers, and alterable environments like the *Abitacolo* children's play space. My personal favorite, however, is the *Chair for Very Brief Visits*. Sketched in 1945 as Allied bombs were raining down on Milan and produced in an edition of nine by Zanotta in 1991, the chair bridges two cultures of sitting in place while pointing beyond. It is a belonging that gestures towards the present era's ambivalence towards homecomings: dreams of emancipatory forms of workplace or domestic nomadism, nostalgias for a secure sense of home or place, and fears regarding the fragility of both belonging and belongings with the demise of social protections and the dislocations prompted by poverty, natural disasters, and war.

The first culture of sitting is what I would call the *classical* (or pre-industrial) in which hospitality is demonstrated by providing the visitor with a throne-like seat whose robust construction and soft padding convey a sense of confidence that the visit is something of a homecoming, an enactment of the expression, "My home is *your* home." Here, the chair marks the point of departure and completion of the epic *nostos*.

The second is the *industrial*. Its spirit of sped-up, circumscribed hospitality is captured by the more calculated, ambivalent greeting: "Welcome to *my* home." Here, sedentariness is no longer understood as given or, for that matter, as an inherent good. Sitting in place has been recast in functionalist terms: as a time-bound transaction in which the competing demands of hospitality, relative comfort, productivity (however defined), and the host or visitor's freedom to move on must be managed. No longer a cathedra, the chair operates instead as a kind of friendly slow-motion turnstile, pacing flows in and out of the home in keeping with industrial-age concepts of recreation, value, property, and propriety. Whether for work or for play, this chair is an office chair.

Munari summons up memories of classical seating by endowing the *Chair for Very Brief Visits* with a stout wax-finished walnut frame ornamented with inlay ornamentation. He summons up memories of industrial seating by pairing the chair's hardwood back with a smooth anodized aluminum seat. But here the memories end and the troubles begin. Thanks to the seat's forty-five-degree slope, the iconic place of welcoming, the visitor's temporary throne, the seat of hospitality, homecoming, and social belonging is exposed as little more than a comforting illusion. Every chair is a *chair for very brief visits*; only, in this case, transience is wired into the ergonomics. One can *lean* against the *Chair for Very Brief Visits*, but one surely cannot *sit* on it. The metallic seat is not just sloped but so slippery that it tenders a not-so-subtle invitation to hit the road. Munari's chair is a springboard more than a seat, the icon of an era in which a gleeful homelessness is flanked by the

Bruno Munari, *"Chair for Very Brief Visits."* 1945. Edition of nine by Zanotta in 1991. Courtesy of Zanotta SpA-Italy.

abiding reality of mass dislocation. Even the intarsia decorations have come unmoored in the course of Munari's breach of ergonomic codes, sliding asymmetrically up and down the legs and crossbars as if threatening to run away from home.

I have opened this brief rumination on contemporary ambivalence towards sitting in place and the passion for mobile devices with the *Chair for Very Brief Visits* because it anticipates features of the dromological world that have taken shape in the transition from the era of industry to that of information. In a deep sense, nothing has changed during this (or, for that matter, any preceding) historical transition. Today, each and every human existence remains little more than a *brief visit* and, in the course of this fleeting sojourn, humans establish fictions of homefulness (and collections of belongings such as chairs) as bulwarks against the cosmic certitude of death and loss, even as much of humanity remains deprived both of belongings and of any sense of belonging due to poverty, disease, and natural disasters. Instead of declining in the ways once imagined by the social housing movement, literal homelessness appears on the rise in the world's most advanced economies, walking hand-in-hand, as it were, with the new adventure of digital nomadism.

As regards beliefs and expectations, however, much has changed. Thanks to a complex of factors—the near ubiquity of communications networks, the ascendancy of the knowledge economy, the relative ease and speed of travel, the extension of life spans, the demands of 24/7 global markets—we live in an era with a popup ethos. Lifetimes have become much longer sojourns, homes are imagined as indices of consumer choice, and mobility has been consecrated as the aspirational norm for a sovereign existence in which workplace and play space are everywhere and nowhere.

The nomadisms of the present are built upon the nomadisms of the recent historical past. They piggyback on the history of mobile, migratory, and momentary industrial homes, from the Sears kit houses of the early decades of the twentieth century to Airstreams and Winnebagos to various tides of enthusiasm for prefabrication, both past and present. These nomadisms remain powerfully present in the world of furnishings: in the abundance, for instance, of flat-pack, portable, foldable, and disposable furniture. Heirs to a half-century of experimentation—countercultural as well as industrial—with alternatives to conventional furnishings, these products extend the lineage of the many plastic, steel, and aluminum descendants of such agents of sedentary disruption as Gerrit Rietveld's 1934 Zigzag chair, flaunting their devotion to novel construction, modes of assembly, design, or looks over the values of comfort or durability.

But the ultimate portable/folding/popup habitats that are informing contemporary dreams and anxieties regarding our sense of identity, presence, and place are the networked devices that you and I are transporting in our pockets and pocketbooks at this very moment. (Is yours fully charged? A discharged battery=death.) As ubiquitous as they are transformative, these devices are the belongings that anchor, support, and sustain the key facets of contemporary social life.

The process of migration from home base to home screen began, long before the popup era, on the nineteenth century battlefield. This transformation was prototyped by modernizing commanders such as Napoleon Bonaparte. Wherever Napoleon bivouacked, he established the mobile double of his imperial study complete with a field chair, a folding campaign desk, and a purpose-built portable library of one thousand carefully curated and indexed small format (duodecimo) volumes, each with an average thickness of five hundred to six hundred pages. Napoleon's books were printed to precise specifications so as to fit into his custom-built portable bookcases. To maximize data compression, typefaces were simplified, and margins were reduced to a bare minimum. To guarantee rapid access, flexible covers and sprung bindings were adopted. In constituting his traveling library (modeled upon eighteenth century voyagers' libraries), Napoleon sought a precise balance between the memoirs of great men across the centuries, and works of history, religion, poetry, and drama. In short, Napoleonic encampments wove

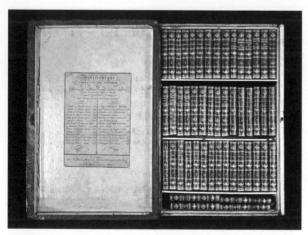

"Bibliothèque portative du voyageur." 1802–1815, Paris. Leslie Weil Memorial Fund, University of North Carolina, Chapel Hill Library.

together fixtures of domesticity with ready-at-hand information resources, the instruments and measuring tools of war, and architectures of rapid access in order to forge a unified nomadic node. The aim was both to create a sense of home away from home while sustaining on-the-fly acts of calculation, strategic decision making, and record keeping, as well as gestures of self-memorialization.

Napoleonic ideals of efficiency shaped the then-emerging/expanding domain of white-collar labor, fueled by the needs of the industrial revolution and by the rise of nation-state bureaucracies. Whereas, in factories, work had implied manuality, physical mobility, and fatigue, the clerk's arena of activity was circumscribed by the contours of the desktop, consisting in tasks such as reading, writing, filing, scheduling, computing, recording, and communicating. At the desktop's hub sat an industrial chair-machine, the modern office chair, designed not for coziness but instead for efficient rolling and rotation, forward and backward bending, and vertical adjustability in keeping with the variegated character of clerical labor. Since the labor in question was information-centric, desks were designed as freestanding islands combining the functionalities of a filing cabinet, a library, and a work station. (Similar notions would gradually invade the design of domestic spaces and transform the home into a laboratory of home economics, the home office into a mirror of the clerical office.)

By the turn of the twentieth century, typewriting was well on its way to supplanting handwriting in commercial communications. Personal communications would follow soon thereafter. Dials and keyboards were also becoming the interface between individuals, the workplace, and the world, as devices like telegraphs and telephones became essential fixtures in modern offices. Office chairs had metamorphosed into typing chairs. Fed by reproductive technologies like carbon copying, mimeography, and xerography, the scale and volume of paper records became bloated to such a degree that, though a theater of accelerating clerical operations, the workplace seemed ever more distant from the battlefront. Files had earned themselves dedicated domiciles of their own: the wall-like cabinets that became the mid-century office's signature furnishings. Their immediate successors were the room-sized computers, flanked by libraries brimming over with reels of magnetic tape, of the first cybernetic age.

The second cybernetic age dramatically downsized the office; the third miniaturized it down to the scale of shoulder bags and pockets. The entire universe of calculating, recording, filing, and writing tools that once populated physical desktops was absorbed into a single appliance. As telephony, telegraphy, and facsimile transmissions (or their digital descendants) joined the suite of capabilities only two tethers to fixed physical locations still stood in the way of workplace nomadism: the need for a power supply and an ethernet connection. Extended-life batteries and wireless connectivity completed the move back under Napoleon's tent. They finalized the transformation of what started life as an integrated workspace into the defining social prosthesis of the present era.

The consequences of this transformation are evident not only among pioneering tribes of digital nomads but in cities everywhere. *Homo digitalis* now drifts about, zombie-like, under the spell of pixel dust. The species vociferates and gestures into the thin air like the madmen of a century ago, only marginally aware of their immediate surroundings. All eyes are riveted to screens, the secondary task of navigating the world's physical perils having been apportioned to peripheral vision. The ears too are wired shut, though ghostly voices or throbbing beats leak out now and then, betraying the nature of the data flows. The selfie is the daily sacrament that affirms the power of the device to anchor selfhood *somewhere*.

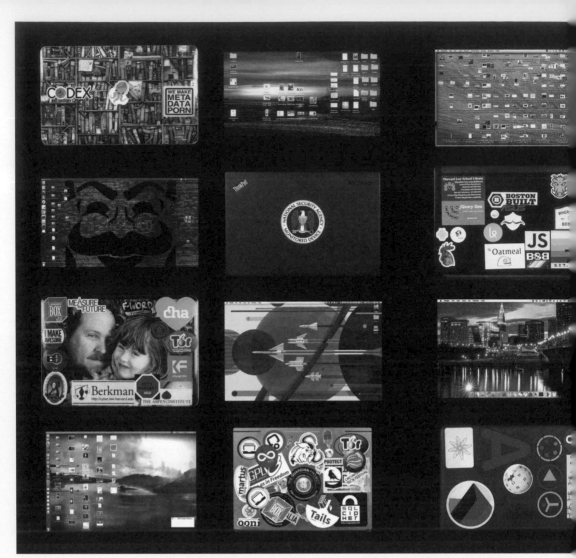

Sarah W. Newman and Jeffrey Schnapp, "Laptop homescreens and cases from the metaLAB (at) Harvard community." Twenty-four photographs, dimensions variable, 2016. Courtesy of the artists.

The communion between individual, network, and device knows few limits of place or time; it proves both mutable and scaleable. The device operates indifferently as a civic space, a factory, an office, an entertainment center, a shopping center, a living room, a café, or an intimate boudoir. The device carries in its train access to a library exponentially greater than the Library of Alexandria, to a gallery of images more extensive than those held by all of the world's museums, to a marketplace as big or small as the entire globe…. Yet the device is strangely intimate. The object of whispers, touching, fumbling, and stroking, we press it to our face and plant it on our lap. It has to be personalized, customized, protected, and re-encased.

Practices of interior and exterior decoration consecrate the role of the networked device as a focal point of contemporary identity formation. The home screen (even if vulnerable to home invasion) is a private place

to which only the invited are privy. The screen is wallpapered, arrayed with photographs like a private mantelpiece. The arrays of files—messy, ordered according to ideal geometries, constellated, tightly packed or stacked—open up a window onto the soul, something like casting a furtive peek in through a half-closed closet or bedroom door.

　　Like the steamer trunk of yore festooned with luggage labels at every station or port of call, the external surface of the portable device is cumulatively reskinned with the marks of people, places, causes, and products of either personal or tribal significance. If, by contrast, the home screen functions as a private retreat or study, here one stands face to face with the façade. The external surface is a place of self-staging, for projecting an image of self out into the world, to hint at the riches contained within before disembarking at the next port of call.

# Stuff During Logistics

Jesse LeCavalier

That's all you need in life: a little place for your stuff. That's all your
house is—a place to keep your stuff. If you didn't have so much stuff,
you wouldn't need a house. You could just walk around all the time.

A house is just a pile of stuff with a cover on it.
—George Carlin[1]

1 George Carlin, *A Place for My Stuff*, Atlantic Records, 1981, audio recording.

2 Ibid., emphasis added.

3 Ibid., emphasis added.

By suggesting that architecture is in service of the accumulation of belongings,
American comedian and social critic George Carlin pointed to the trappings of
US consumer culture that he spent much of his career lampooning. Recorded
on the 1981 album, *A Place for My Stuff*, Carlin elaborated that a house is
"a place to keep your stuff while you go out and get... *more stuff!*" He suggested that the volume of one's possessions drives domestic habits and that
the feeling of being out-of-place at another location is because "there's no
room for *your* stuff."[2] Describing a vacation scenario of traveling to an island
with suitcases and then, on short notice, to a friend's house on another island, Carlin invoked the language of a military operation, "You're really getting
extended now when you think about it. You got stuff all the way back on the
mainland; you got stuff on another island; you got stuff on this island. I mean,
supply lines are getting longer and harder to maintain."[3] While the routine
was recorded in 1981, it still serves as a helpful entry point into a discussion
of furniture "after belonging" partly because of its refrain of "stuff" but also
because of the themes of replication ("a suitcase is a smaller version of your
house") and logistics. Carlin neatly crystalized the tensions between stability
and mobility, between originality and reproducibility, and the role that logistics
plays within both. This article uses the furniture company IKEA—one of
the most significant actors within networks of domestic consumerism—
to better understand the relationship between logistics and stuff, especially
as impulses to accumulate "more stuff" get replaced by the same impulses
to secure more experiences (as a form of status and social capital, among
other things). While IKEA's line of "flat pack" and "knockdown" furniture
serves as a symptom of a culture defined by disposable consumerism, it
is possible that the reliable availability of domestic infrastructure that IKEA
provides also enables inquisitive modes of living that challenge acquisitive
modes. In other words, the similarity and universality of some of IKEA's
products take them out of circuits of status and accumulation and allow them
to act in the background to support the daily lives of their owners. The BILLY

bookshelf for example, though embedded in global networks of extraction
and exploitation, exists for many not so
much as a durable domestic object but
more as a durable domestic concept, a
reliable household utility whose specifications remain consistent because of
a globally-coordinated set of production
standards. These same standards govern
the methods by which the combination of
woodchips, glue, and sawdust are transformed into IKEA's ubiquitous fiberboard,
an example of logistical "stuff" capable
of being shaped into a wide range of
furniture elements and equally capable of
being loaded onto trailers or into shipping
containers. Like William Cronon's observation in *Nature's Metropolis* that the
pig, along with whiskey, was the most effective way of getting corn to market,
IKEA's flat pack furniture is a way of turning trees, a natural resource, into
revenue."[4] However, as IKEA has become a global brand, its frontiers of competition have also expanded. While the company has a stable of products that
remain the same, year after year, it also continues to develop new products.
By looking at some of these cases and by comparing them to IKEA's more
familiar products, this article looks for ways to understand the role of stuff in
the time of logistics.

Starting in 1995, IKEA launched a small boutique line of domestic
objects which it called "PS," for "Post Scriptum." Under the catchphrase
"Democratic Design," IKEA debuted its PS line at the 1995 Milan Furniture
Fair, the largest furniture trade fair in the world. In the company's language,
IKEA PS is "the design statement of IKEA... which puts focus on cutting
edge modern Scandinavian furniture design without losing sight of what
makes IKEA unique—affordable, quality design for the many people [sic]."[5]
During the 1995 premier of IKEA's PS line, the *New York Times* reported that
the Swedish company upstaged the more established lines and designers,
even though those same houses were also unveiling more affordable "bridge
lines." The review called the IKEA show "dazzling" and admired the way the
collection was "flaunting its price tags like war medals." It suggested that the
effect of the exhibition was to "put Milan's design intelligentsia on notice."[6]
The article went on to quote an American furniture buyer who, disappointed
in not being able to sell more expensive pieces to his customers, quipped,
"Everyone is talking about the third millennium... but why does it have to
be made out of particleboard?"[7] Rather than IKEA clamoring for design
credibility, one might read the company's debut in Milan as a confirmation
of something many already knew: that its ability to design, manufacture,
distribute, and sell modern furniture for dramatically less money had already
polarized the furniture market. With 1.9 billion visits in Finanvial Year 15, the
volume of the company's sales has changed and continues to change the
way a great number of people think about and inhabit the places where they

**IKEA° PS 2014
Collection**

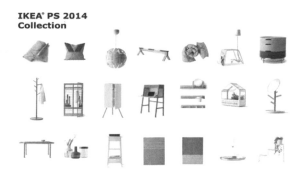

Overview of the IKEA PS 2014 collection, accessed June 15, 2016, http://
www.ikea.com/ms/en_US/pressroom/press_materials/IKEA_PS_2014_
press_kit_fin.pdf.

**4** William Cronon,
*Nature's Metropolis:
Chicago and the Great
West* (New York: W. W.
Norton, 1992), 226.

**5** IKEA PS Collection
2012, May 2012, 3.

**6** Suzanne Slesin,
"Little People, Milan
Loves You," *New York
Times*, April 13, 1995,
http://www.nytimes.
com/1995/04/13/garden/
little-people-milan-
loves-you.html.

**7** Ibid.

**8** IKEA.com,"Welcome inside our company," accessed June 26, 2016; http://www.ikea.com/ms/en_US/this-is-ikea/company-information/.

**9** In an early example of a patent for "knockdown furniture," the patent describes the invention as "an improvement of sitting furniture of the knock-down type, such as easy-chairs and sofas, and a special object of the invention is to provide means enabling the parts of the sitting furniture to be mounted and interlocked in mounted position in a particularly simple way *without any tools whatever* and using a minimum of furniture fittings." Folke Ohlsson, "Sitting Furniture of the Knockdown Type," US Patent 2,650,657, September 1, 1953.

**10** Saabira Chaudhuri, "IKEA Can't Stop Obsessing About Its Packaging: Retailer increasingly designs furniture with shipping costs in mind from the start," *Wall Street Journal*, June 17, 2015, http://www.wsj.com/articles/ikea-cant-stop-obsessing-about-its-packaging-1434533401.

**11** IKEA PS 2014 Press Kit, April 2014, 4.

**12** Adam Davidson, "Its Official: The Boomerang Kids Won't Leave," *The New York Times Magazine*, June 20, 2014. http://www.nytimes.com/2014/06/22/magazine/its-official-the-boomerang-kids-wont-leave.html.

**13** IKEA PS 2014 press kit, 16.

**14** *IKEA Autumn 2014 Trend Report*, 44, emphasis added, accessed June 15, 2016. http:// www.ikea.com/ms/ en_US/pressroom/press_ materials/IKEA_Trend_ FALL_2014.pdf.

live.[8] IKEA develops its products through an intersection of design ingenuity and logistical relentlessness, a combination evident in the company's reliance on designs that optimize packing density while minimizing excess space (flat pack), shifting the work of delivery and assembly to its customers (knock-down), and through its line of wood-based fiberboard manufactured by its subsidiary, Swedwood (particle board).[9] Indeed, for IKEA, design and logistics are intertwined because designing a piece of furniture includes designing its manufacture (cheap), delivery (fast), packaging (flat), and assembly (easy). This process is also one of constant improvement, as evident, for example, in the company streamlining the packaging of its EKTORP sofa to make the packaging 50% smaller, lowering the price by 14%.[10]

Although technical innovations such as flat pack, knock-down, and wood fiberboard are fundamental to the company's success, they are not evident in its most recent PS Line from 2014, called "On the Move." As IKEA's promotional copy describes, the PS 2014 collection "targets creative young urbanites. Therefore, it was important that it was designed by the very same creative young urbanites."[11] The pieces shown in the press kit appear surrounded by the implied habitat of this elusive demographic: natural light, unfinished floors, or evidence of interrupted projects. These images are appealing and, of course, aspirational fantasies just as much as the lifestyles suggested by the attendant promotional material. While the "target" for the PS 2014 collection is young and creative and urban, a recent report found that one in five college graduates in the United States is now back living at their parental home.[12] In copy that acknowledges transient situations while also valorizing them, the promotional material indulges in a number of clichés about this class of young creative urbanites. It describes the "mobile and multi-functional" furniture line as being about "living here-and-now" and that "it's here to help you make the most of life at home. No matter if that home is somewhere you're just crashing for a while or somewhere you'll stay put."[13] The pieces themselves tend to focus on supporting work or making more space for storage (e.g. Keiji Ashizawa's "wall shelf with 11 knobs" or Matali Crasset's wire mesh wardrobe cage). That these objects are thoughtfully designed and, seemingly, made with care is secondary to the images of urban life that the campaign promotes. The line caters to and seeks to justify the unsettled conditions that its target audience is experiencing and uses the PS 2014 objects to turn a condition many are forced to adopt into something aspirational instead. According to the company's Autumn 2014 trend report: "For Millennials, *stuff isn't enough anymore*. Instead, they crave brands and products that have meaning, stories and experiences embedded in them. They are less focused on financial success, and more interested in making a difference and living lives defined by meaning. Furniture and products for life at home need to have a greater value beyond form or function."[14] As part of the PS2014 line, IKEA also commissioned a report from the market research company YouGov about the changing demographics that the line is attempting to address.[15]

IKEA's emphasis on the transience of its target audience is condensed in a promotional video for the PS 2014 line, striking as much for what it included as for what it leaves out.[16] In a series of vignettes of urban fantasies, groups of joyful young people (all either white or Asian) make their way through their respective cities—San Francisco, Warsaw, Tel Aviv, Shanghai, Manchester, Marseille, Malmö, and Tokyo—with furniture in hand. In almost every city, the characters spend time walking toward the camera with their featured items, or are shown in a variety of transport configurations. The ad, in its short two-and-half minute duration, goes to great lengths to demonstrate a commitment to public transportation in what amounts to a kind of giddy mobility checklist as the protagonists make their way through the city in an elevator, cable car, city bus, subway, outdoor escalator, a folding bicycle, commuter train, a minibus, a street car, a rickshaw, and even some kind of amusement park ride. By including this catalog of transit modes, the ad signals a dependence on the public sector for transport mobility. People are filmed in groups, walking Abbey-Road style past a building façade or landscape, often sharing the weight of one of the furniture pieces. No one is shown driving a car, nor are there any shots of interiors. Likewise, though all the products require putting together, they are all shown fully assembled, suggesting that viewers are witnessing some kind of relocation process. The only protagonists who seem to reach their destination are two of the characters in Shanghai, both holding one handle of the "Kick Bench" as they navigate, laughingly, through crowded streets. The scene ends with a view through traffic of them placing the bench and talking animatedly.

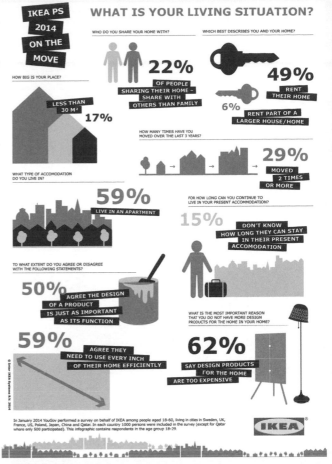

Figure 2: An infographic summarizing the results of a report commissioned from YouGov by IKEA for its PS 2014 collection.

With its subtitle, "For people and homes in constant motion," the ad suggests that unsettlement is something new for IKEA, when in fact it has been enabling such mobility since the company's founding. The difference in the PS 2014 line is the suggestion that these objects are durable goods rather than transient ones. Instead of leaving them behind when moving, as IKEA's externalized costs and design stability allow, these objects, the ad suggests, are important enough to take with you.[17] Viewers are actively placed in the scenes through hand-held and eye-level camera work as if walking alongside the characters, all to the tune of a buoyant and nostalgic Swedish pop song, "Find Your Way." The implication, reinforced by the song's chorus, is that viewers are on this journey as well and are also searching for some elusive home.

15 "The collection was inspired by homes—and homeowners—that are in constant motion. According to a global survey commissioned by IKEA, nearly 60 percent of American city dwellers, aged 18–29, desire to move within the next two years." IKEA PS 2014, accessed June 15, 2016. http://www.ikea.com/us/en/about_ikea/newsitem/031314_product_IKEAPS2014.

16 "The IKEA PS 2014
collection focuses on
the young urban residents
that have ever-fluctuating
living situations, whether
it's where they live or
with whom they share a
space," said Janice
Simonsen, Design Spokes-
person, IKEA U.S. "This
line brings flex-ibility
to everyone by combining
form, function,quality,
sustainability and an
accessible price point."
Accessed June 15, 2016.
http://www.ikea.com/us/
en/about_ikea/newsitem/
031314_product_IKEAPS2014.

17 In what could be read
as a tone-deaf response
to the contemporary mig-
ration crisis, IKEA's
images of happy young
people wandering through
the streets with their
sole possession lands
flatly amongst the streams
of images of forced mig-
ration where mobility
is a matter of survival.
Emma Sulkowicz's 2014–
15 piece, *Mattress
Performance (Carry That
Weight)*, an endurance
art piece in protest of
Columbia University's
handling of her sexual
assault case invokes an
additional set of asso-
ciations that render
IKEA's urban fantasies
less whimsical.

Simultaneously evoking a sense of nostalgia and anxiety, the ad creates a condition of displacement for viewers and offers IKEA products as its solution.

In a similar way, the IKEA showroom functions as a kind of ersatz home for its shoppers. Publicists for IKEA Australia launched a contest whose winners got to spend the night in an IKEA showroom. In scenes that seem taken from Albert Brooks's *Real Life* or David Byrne's *True Stories,* lucky couples and families were filmed waking up to a live string quartet, breakfast in bed, and groups of puppies.[18] The display of intimacy and the turning out of private life into the shared and controlled space of the IKEA showroom is something already familiar to anyone who has ever visited one. As is perhaps well known, one of IKEA's key marketing innovations was to stage fully-formed domestic tableaux into which visitors could insert themselves, often in full view of other customers, trying on different lifestyles the way one might try on different clothes. This condition has become ubiquitous enough that people visit IKEA stores not to shop but to simply use the furniture.

For example, in a recent photo series published by *The Telegraph*, customers in IKEA locations in China are shown in repose on the company's beds and sofas.[19] At once humorous and uncomfortably intimate, the series takes IKEA's display approach to a logical conclusion. It also connects to some of the country's pressing urban migration issues as large numbers of rural residents are making their way to urban areas, even though the government contests their status. These migrants are referred to as a "floating" population. Similar images of family moments within the semi-public spaces of IKEA's showrooms are on display in Guy Ben-Nur's film "Stealing Beauty" (2007), in which the artist staged a series of dramatic scenes about banal domestic issues within the company's stores. Since Ben-Nur filmed without IKEA's permission, a sense of nervous assertion characterizes the scenes. Working with his family as the other members of the cast, Ben-Nur kept the

Still from video. Promotional cross-over between IKEA and Air BnB. IKEA Australia, "Sleeping in the IKEA store on Airbnb," (YouTube Video), 2014.

camera rolling until someone at IKEA compelled them to stop, forcing the crew to pick up the scene where they left off but in a different setting. The result is a continuous stream of dialog against a shifting background. One bedroom scene, for example, unfolds in five different spaces. In addition to the surprising aesthetic and formal effects these disjunctions produce, Ben-Nur's critiques of property emerge as another layer of content of the piece. While explaining ownership to his son, the artist says, "We evolved. We rose up on our two feet so we can free our hands to point at objects and say, 'This is mine.'"[20]

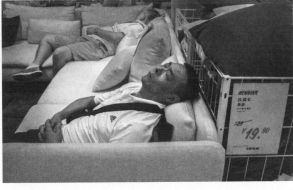

Kevin Frayer, "Chinese Shoppers Make The Most Of IKEA's Open Bed Policy." © Getty Images.

In the context of IKEA's larger furniture cosmology (bracketing momentarily the suggestions of their PS 2014 line), questions of ownership and personal attachment remain present. In Ben-Nur's project—like people actually sleeping in IKEA showrooms—the artist treats the company's interiors as a kind of commons to be appropriated, even if only temporarily and tenuously.

Consider two polarities: one that ranges between the transient and the durable; and another that spans between an actual, original object, and the idea–image of that object. Crossing these two axes generates four categories: the transient original; the durable original; the transient image; and the durable image. The *transient original* could be understood as an archival experience—something that does not last, but that is recorded and celebrated. The *transient image* might correspond to something more evanescent or disposable, an experience that is not archived or even archiveable. On the durable side, an *enduring original* might correspond more closely to something like an heirloom, while the *durable image* could be used to describe a sustained category of an idea of an object. In many cases, IKEA's line of its best-selling furniture fits into this last category in the sense that while a single instance, say of a BILLY bookshelf, might be abandoned upon relocation, the category of the object is stable enough that its replacement can be easily established in the new place.

The BILLY bookcase is, in many ways, less like a piece of furniture and more like an index of an industrial engineering process. Through the optimization of hardware and wood fiberboard, the bookshelf can be broken down into a dense brick of material capable of being shipped and delivered in a minimum amount of space. In *Bookshelf*, Lydia Pyne writes, "Every IKEA bookshelf is born out of its box, lives in a room until it is no longer needed, and then goes away."[21] Citing Bourdieu and his idea of using objects within the "travelling space" of culture to establish social stability, Pyne argues that IKEA bookshelves like BILLY tap into a mythos and can "navigate cultural expectations."[22] In the context of a discussion about stuff, mobility, and ownership, the predictability and affordability of BILLY, for example, suggest that the furniture system exists as both as an actual object and as an idea of an object, a kind of object-image that is more of a platform. If one is moving

18 According to IKEA, these are based on the top answers to a survey about waking up.

19 "Ikea shoppers in China fall asleep in furniture room displays," *The Telegraph UK*, accessed June 26, 2018, www.telegraph.co.uk/ news/picturegalleries/ worldnews/10950697/ Ikea-shoppers-in-China-fall-asleep-in-furniture-room-displays-in-pictures.html.

20 Guy Den-Nur, *Stealing Beauty*, 2007, http://www.ubu.com/ film/ben-ner_beauty.html.

21 Lydia Pyne, *Bookshelf* (New York: Bloomsbury, 2016), 95.

22 Ibid. Pyne writes, "The predictably and affordability—indeed, the rather ubiquitous presence—of IKFA bookshelves offer straightforward bookshelves, but they also offer possibility. Just as a *bauplan* gives a basic body plan for an organism, IKEA bookshelves offer building blocks for other bookshelf-based objects. Few bookshelves outside of the cheap veneer of TKFA offer such anticipation and expectation in their respective life cycles," 98.

# 30 Years of Creating a Better Life at Home.

IKEA has been helping consumers live a better life at home in the US for the past 30 years. Through the principles of democratic design, IKEA has been creating well designed home furnishings

with the right combination of form, function, quality, sustainability, and at a low price. Let's take a look back at some iconic products to see how they have changed since entering the US in 1985.

1985 price: $82

1985 price: $25

1985 price: $395

1985 price: $148

BILLY bookcase
$59.99
PE391149

KLIPPAN loveseat
$299
PE249666

LACK side table
$9.99
PE551406

POÄNG chair
$69
PE170826

**Need more information?**
For additional product suggestions, images or product loans, please contact:
Christine.Soner@IKEA.com or Noreen.Lennon@IKEA.com.
To schedule an interview with the IKEA Design Spokesperson, please contact:
Janice.Simonsen@IKEA.com

**IKEA**®

A comparison of prices of some of IKEA's bestselling products between 1985 and 2015 on the company's 30th year anniversary in the United States.

to a new location in which there is an IKEA store and if one has purchased a bookcase in the past, it might be more convenient and economically feasible to abandon the shelf given that its structural integrity rapidly decreases with transit. Rather than disassembling it, moving it, and then recreating it in a compromised condition, many choose to simply get a new one upon arrival, as they probably have to go to IKEA to get some other stuff anyway.

This bookshelf operating as a platform is just one moment within a longer material-intensive logistical process. As Erich Fromm notes "the words indicate that we are speaking of fixed substances, although things are nothing but a process of energy that causes certain sensations in our bodily system."[23] Moreover, the material possesses a kind of uni-directional utility in that it is easy to assemble but dismantling something like the BILLY bookcase makes it hard to subsequently reassemble. The combination of glue, woodchips, sawdust, and plastic laminate that constitute the

23 Erich Fromm, *To Have or to Be?* (New York: Bloomsbury, 2010), 67.

24 Deborah Cowen, "Containing Insecurity: Logistic Space, U.S. Port Cities, and the 'War on Terror,'" in *Disrupted Cities: When Infrastructure Fails*, ed. Stephen Graham (London: Routledge, 2009), 69-84. Emphasis added.

plank of an IKEA shelf seems to embody idealized logistical "stuff." This stuff has no innate form but is capable of being molded to the consumer's desire, while obscuring the mechanism that propagates it. As Deborah Cowen writes, "Without the rapid and reliable movement of *stuff* through space—from factories in China to U.S. big box stores, for instance—cheap labor in the global South cannot be 'efficiently' exploited, and globalized production systems become as inefficient economically as they are environmentally."[24] At the same time, the social role that the BILLY bookcase can play, for example, perhaps differentiates its crystallization of this particular amount of stuff.

IKEA's recently commissioned report found that 50% of respondents thought design was just as important as function, a surprise given the company's past emphasis on frugality and utility. Sara Kristoffersson's *Design by IKEA: A Cultural History* demonstrates how IKEA and Swedish identity are both mutually constitutive and linked to ideas of modern "Scandinavian" design. The 1930 Stockholm Exhibition and the later travelling exhibit "Scandinavian Design" of 1954 (a decade after IKEA's founding) are largely credited with defining and spreading an idea of Scandinavian functionalist design and the social democratic ideals that it embodies. In many ways, the PS 2014 line seems to go against some of the foundational design ideas of IKEA in its efforts to respond to changing lifestyles. In Emilio Ambasz's 1972 exhibition, "Italy: The New Domestic Landscape, Achievements and Problems of Italian Design," the curator laid out three categories as a way to assess the state of design in Italy: objects selected for their formal and technical means (conformist); objects selected for their sociocultural implications (reformist); and objects selected for their implications of more flexible patterns of use and arrangement (contesting).[25] Through this classification, Ambasz attempted to make a case for the dearth of the last, of those designs that challenge preexisting normalized forms of living: "The objects in this section are flexible in function, permit multiple modes of arrangement and use, and propose more informal patterns of behavior in the home than those currently prevailing." In a closing essay about the work of Archizoom and Superstudio, Filiberto Menna wrote that the designers "have made a decisive contribution to the protests against design regarded as purely the execution of objects for consumption, and to the invention of a new typology for the equipment needed for daily life."[26] He went on to write, "If these designers really have to build something, they prefer to make structures and environments that will enlist the active participation of the user, in the first person, in the shaping and enjoyment of his own surroundings."[27] This mode of design engagement echoes what Erich Fromm describes as a being mode rather than a having mode. Fromm argues that the difference between being and having is not just about consuming and possessing things but is also about ideas and experiences. He uses knowledge as an example: "Optimum knowledge in the being mode is to know more deeply. In the having mode it is to have more knowledge."[28] In other words, a desire to possess and accumulate characterizes the acquisitive mode, even if the objects of that desire are immaterial. Within the emerging experience economy that IKEA alludes to in its PS 2014 campaign, the objects in the collection are offered as infrastructure in support of lifestyle.

In the context of furniture in the contemporary experience economy, Ambasz's critique from 1972 might still hold. With the PS 2014 collection, the problem might be that IKEA is asking *things* to become "equipment for daily life" instead of looking to those objects of domestic infrastructure that become backgrounds and platforms. Moreover, these could engage logistical systems *outside* of logistics—i.e. in inquisitive not acquisitive modes. The BILLY bookshelf, as a platform and as a medium, as something whose logistical transience is foregrounded, becomes a kind of conceptual infrastructure, or an infrastructural armature to allow the collection and storing of books, a repository of memories to support being. If experiences are the new things, logistical furniture can help resist their commodification.

25 Emilio Ambasz, *Italy: The New Domestic Landscape, Achievements and Problems of Italian Design* (New York: MoMA, 1972), Table of Contents.

26 Filiberto Menna, "A Design for New Behaviors," in *Italy: The New Domestic Landscape* (New York: MoMA, 1972), 405-418.

27 Ibid., 413.

28 Fromm, 26.

Special thanks to Brendan Comfort, Chau Tran, and Yuliya Veligurskaya.

# A Prisoner of Air

**Hu Fang, translated from Chinese by Daniel Nieh**

A window is just like a screen. Looking out my window, I can see that the sky is overcast, the low-hanging clouds divided into discrete shapes that pile together and stretch into the distance. The trees, mostly bare of leaves, form peculiar shapes that seem to stab upward into the gray sky, a strand of vitality amid the cluster of identical buildings. The snow banks on the rooftop of the opposite building have not yet melted. An elderly man, tightly bundled, walks alone in the middle of the street. The frozen lake in the distance sparkles with the reflection of dim blue light.

A person wakes up every morning and paces back and forth in a tiny room, imagining the possibility of being let out for some air.

"No, there was no way out, and no one can imagine what the evenings are like in prison." These words by Camus in *The Stranger* moved me deeply. As I see it, the azure Mediterranean waters and dazzling sunlight captured in the book foretell a prison cell with a window, a prison cell from which the stars could be seen, a prison cell with time cycles and air circulation: one in which time and place are no longer implements of punishment.

However, Camus made me realize that even nights spent in prison can be happy ones. For a long time, I did not tell anyone my complicated feelings on the subject. But in my buildings, one can sense that we are always ready to go over everything once more, and, even in the most desperate of circumstances, it is still possible for us to choose to better ourselves.

This sort of epiphany can occur in schools, hospitals, factories, and art museums, but also in prisons: "Right now, I am facing a night filled with stars and silence, and opening my heart to this cold world for the first time."

There are many spatial techniques associated with the design of prisons that serve to facilitate the disruption and collapse of human perceptive systems: a room without natural light and no way to tell time; a deathly still space with no indications of life; or, quite the opposite, a space bisected by a one-way mirror that allows you to see the grieved and despairing face of someone you love. Perhaps, early one morning, you are sent to familiar streets or a familiar park. Someone lights a cigarette for you and tells you: "You can have your freedom this instant, as long as you're willing to…." The warden quietly calls your name, so that you know that as soon as you enter prison, you are nothing more than a serial number, and you will never be seen as a person.

Tomorrow, interrogations will be conducted as usual, and the day after tomorrow, they will continue, until you realize that you no longer recognize yourself. You cease to care who you are; you cease to care about the dignity you once cherished.

Then, when I see the photograph, it abruptly brings me back to awareness, and I fully realize the significance of prison design.[1]

1 A documentation photo presented at Hohenschönhausen, Berlin. Photo retaken by Hu Fang.

In the Hohenschönhausen prison of East Berlin, a prisoner used meditation as a method of refusing to answer questions. This photograph comes from that prison, it was used to document and analyze the prisoner's unorthodox method of resistance. The prisoner's name was Günter Schau.

Meditation, practiced at the highest level, becomes the art of survival, relating to both self-preservation and self-sacrifice—or perhaps the two have always gone hand-in-hand. The humiliated man is beautiful because he uses a strong will to endure an insult that an ordinary person could not endure. He lives on, and could it be that he finds survival in humiliation? A world without humiliation is like an earth without gravity.

I begin to imagine a prison space in which separation from the outside world leads to spiritual tranquility. By limiting perceptions, this space could provide the soul with the refinement of enlightenment. An emphasis on introspection and spiritual transformation would not necessarily mean that the place would be comfortable, but it must be a space that lends people a certain spiritual intensity. All of the movements of modern history have undoubtedly been movements to reform people. They add up to a continuously evolving New Life movement which has over time produced countless and diverse spatial transformation movements.

Looking back to when I first started out in prison design, I recall that I was truly inspired by Fučík's description of a movie theater. That might be because I have always been a film buff, but it is also related to how we have obliviously entered an age of images.

Again and again, I flip through the yellowed pages of my copy of *Notes from the Gallows* to the mesmerizing Preface:

> Sitting at "attention," your body rigidly erect, your hands gripping your knees, eyes riveted on the yellowing wall of a room in the former Petchek bank building—this is certainly not a position conducive to meditation. But who can force your thoughts to sit at attention?
>
> We shall never know who or when, but someone once called this hall in Petchek building "the Cinema." The Germans called it "domestic imprisonment," but "Cinema" was a stroke of genius. The spacious hall contained six long rows of benches, occupied by the rigid bodies of those under investigation. The bare wall before their staring eyes became a screen on which they projected more scenes than have ever been filmed, as they waited to be called to another hearing, to torture, to death.

Fučík continues:

> I have seen the film of my life a hundred times, thousands of details. Now I shall attempt to set it down. If the hangman's noose strangles before I finish, millions remain to write its "happy ending."

Today, the price of becoming an image-addict is to sell one's whereabouts to countless data companies and receive in compensation nothing more than an endless sea of time-killing films, shows, and videos. Thus, the whereabouts of an image-addict are superlatively easy to obtain. His curiosity about the world and his bored, comfort-seeking heart are ceaselessly stimulated by immersion in image. His heart anxiously palpitates and contracts, but he never realizes how images are already steering him to his prison. Perhaps this does not count as irony. If I put video equipment in every prison cell and played clips of the best moments from each of our lives, then those pure images might allow us to repent and start anew.

The "Cinema" metaphor implies that the question of what put us in this prison space—whether an oppressive system of authority or a consciously committed crime—is irrelevant. These two possibilities are two sides of the same coin, because we are talking about a prisoner with a consciousness and how the prison space allows this consciousness to be expressed. All the prisoners are given a chance to face themselves. After the "movie" is over, they will all ultimately leave the "cinema" and return to society.

This is how people disappear from the spaces of their own everyday lives: they flow toward different places, and I am uncertain whether prison spaces can contain all people of this type. In the final analysis, other than those people who hate humankind, we have no true enemies.

After I finish the design of this prison space, I am willing to shrink, to unreluctantly draw back into my body and withdraw from questions of right and wrong. When I touch my face, and the wrinkles on my forehead, I can vividly perceive that I am still lodged within this body, this prison cell, built by man for the soul.

# Trãṇsńātıòńaĺ Ñeiĝhbòrhoòd
## in Tensta, Stockholm

Located northwest of central Stockholm, Tensta is one of the neighborhoods resulting from the Million Dwelling Program—one million residences built by the Social Democratic government of Sweden between 1965 and 1974. Similar to other European initiatives, this program aimed to alleviate the housing shortage in the growing urban areas of the country. Considering that approximately 90% of the neighborhood's population now has diverse migrant backgrounds, Tensta provides a framework where the realms of domesticity and identity are constantly negotiated.

The homogenous landscape of blocks and the standardized designs of two and three bedroom apartments—originally conceived for Swedish working class families—have been enriched and transformed by a diversity of domestic occupations, with a large number of inhabitants from the Middle East and North Africa. The abstract sequence of late modernist facades is now punctuated by a plantation of satellite antennas, which bring remote sounds and images to the local scene from distant countries that build the new global domestic landscape.

Amidst the changing European political context and the current migration and refugee crises, Tensta allows us to question how architecture and urbanism have contributed to the integration of migrants in the last decades. Moreover, Tensta can be considered an arena to discuss the original ambitions of the welfare state project and the lasting effects of housing policies. It raises questions about homeownership, integration, and cohabitation, both regarding the adaptation of the existing stock of housing for new inhabitants and the future development of the city.

"Restructuring Swedish Modernist Housing," Million Housing Apartment in Tensta. Photograph by Matti Östling, 2012. Courtesy of the author.

## Same Time Next Day
Ahmet Öğüt and Emily Fahlén

The reigning narrative on Tensta is dominated by a focus on dramatic *events*, on crime and uprisings. Actual everyday life, however, is characterized by the un-dramatic and the un-eventful. By exploring the notion of a chronic temporality, this research investigates continuities and repetitions, ongoing processes that lack defined beginnings and ends, by considering the daily routines of the founder of a news network for the Eritrean diaspora, the industrious enthusiast behind a local women's association, and the most famous poet of Kurdistan who smokes every waking hour. They all move in the same centre squares, linked together by bridges separating traffic.

This is how the repetition starts: He wakes up in the morning, and like every other day, it is exactly 8:00. He turns on the TV. For two hours, he watches the TV. Then, he takes a shower, gets dressed and goes out, passing Glömmingegränd, Kämpingebacken, a bridge, the car park, the subway station, the fountain.

He meets acquaintances, stops and chats, stops and gets stuck in a conversation about the news, stops and talks to a young person who has grown older. Then, into Tensta gången, all the way to the café where he sits down by the people he knows. Looking at the poet who sits in the same corner every day. He lights one cigarette after another, smoking in competition with the clock, writes until 12:00. He only drinks one cup of coffee but he pays for more. He writes with a yellow lead pencil with an eraser at the top, and he writes small and erases a lot, as he will the next day. At 12:00, he gets up and packs his stuff, walks through Tensta gången and out, again passing the fountain, the subway station, the car park, a bridge, Kämpingebacken and into Glömmingegränd. He does not greet anyone on the way because he does not see them, deeply embedded as he is in his thoughts.

The next day, he wakes up at 8:00. He turns on the TV, and watches it for two hours. Then, he takes a shower, gets dressed and goes out, passing Glömmingegränd, Kämpingebacken, a bridge, the car park, the subway station, the fountain. At the café, he sits in the far corner, orders a coffee, and writes in tiny letters with a yellow lead pencil:

*Beneath the surface of this exhausted*
*And wounded soul*
*The hours of exile*
*Are like wagons of a train*
*connected to each other.*
*Every day they travel back and forth.*
*At the station of waiting,*
*At the station of farewell*
*Their restless doors*

*continuously*
*open and close me.*
*Every pain that gets off*
*is replaced by a hundred new ones.*
*Such a long tunnel of exile!*
*where is it leading me?*
*Tears well up behind my eyes,*
*but it is leading me…*
*leading me.. leading me.*

—Sherko Bekas (1940–2013)

Then, he erases what he just wrote and begins anew.

Project team: Ahmet Öğüt and Emily Fahlén with Hatice Akalınlı, Halo Bekas, and Nuraden Mohammed Ali (voices in the film); Josua Enblom (photographer); Alexander Widerberg (producer).

1

2

1 Graphics for radio Arkokabay. Network for
  Eritrean media. Photograph by Nuraden
  Mohammed-Ali. Courtesy of the author.

2 Sherko Bekas monument in Azadi park, "the
  park of liberty" in Sulaymaniyah. Photograph
  by Shwan Kamal. Courtesy of the author.

1 Ahmet Öğüt and Emily Fahlén. Still from the film *A Report on Tensta*.
Photograph by Josua Enblom, 2015. Courtesy of the author.

| | Måndag | Tisdag | Onsdag | Torsdag | Fredag |
|---|---|---|---|---|---|
| 9³⁰-12³⁰ | SVENSKA 1 Nesma | SVENSKA 3 Fatih | SVENSKA 1 Nesma | SVENSKA 3 Maria | SVENSKA A Fariborz |
| 9³⁰-12³⁰ | Svenska 2 Gülgün | ARABISKA Hanan | VENSKA 2 Gülgün | MATTE Hanan | MATTE Hanan |
| 9³⁰-12³⁰ | SVenska Nesma | | Joga Kicki | Systuga Muna | |
| 13⁰⁰-16⁰⁰ | Turkiska Gulgün | Systugan Muna | Svenska A Fariborz | DATA Nesma | |

1 Ahmet Öğüt and Emily Fahlén. Still from the film A Report on Tensta. A café in Tensta centre. Photograph by Josua Enblom, 2015. Courtesy of the author.

2 Schedule at the Women's centre in Tensta Hjulsta.

# Fũŕņĩşhiñg Áf̧tėr Bełongjnğ
## Works

## The First Whole Moon Catalog
Unfold

*It is easier to see the forest when we distance ourselves from the trees.*

In December 1972, three astronauts left the Earth for what would be the last human visit to the Moon. At a distance of approximately 45,000 kilometers, the astronauts took a picture of the Earth through the spacecraft's rear-view window, forever changing the way we look at the "Blue Marble" we call *home*. This photograph spurred the environmental movement and graced the cover of *The Whole Earth Catalog,* the bible of American countercultural movements in the 1970s and the precursor of user-generated knowledge sharing.

By 2050, mankind intends to return to the Moon. If humanity aims to settle on the satellite permanently this time, the question is not only how human beings can survive in a context with a complete lack of atmosphere and reduced gravity, but also in a scenario characterized by a paucity of raw materials. Uniformly covered in a thick layer of regolith, a glass-like dust resulting from the impact of millions of micrometeorites, the surface of the Moon lacks the organic materials — such as wood, cotton, and oil — traditionally used for object production.

So: What if high-tech tools are available for production, but the only material available in abundance is a fine dust containing a mixture of metals and glass? How can we produce the objects necessary for daily life in this new context? What objects would be essential for our daily needs and our emotional well-being? How could we make these objects sustainable? Settling on the Moon, humanity would start with a blank slate, as the troglodytes did. Is it then possible to outlive material scarcity by developing a new material culture (and ultimately, new forms of culture) using Earth-conceived technology?

*The First Whole Moon Catalog* explores the issues surrounding the production and the meaning of our belongings by transposing them into the exceptionality of an extra-terrestrial context.

Unfold, "The First Whole Moon Catalog," 2016. Based on the cover of *The Whole Earth Catalog.* Menlo Park, California: Portola Institute, 1968.

# The First Whole Moon Catalog

*access to tools*

**$5**

Sept 2016

## Home Back Home

### Enorme Studio and PKMN Architectures

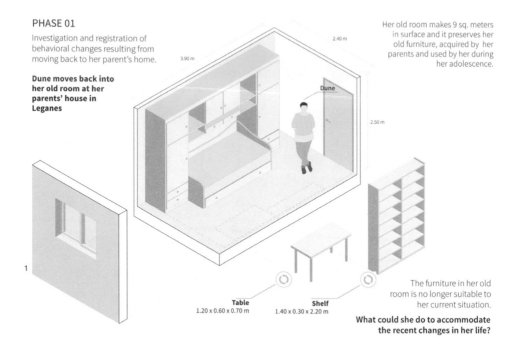

**PHASE 01**

Investigation and registration of behavioral changes resulting from moving back to her parent's home.

**Dune moves back into her old room at her parents' house in Leganes**

3.90 m

2.40 m

Dune

2.50 m

Her old room makes 9 sq. meters in surface and it preserves her old furniture, acquired by her parents and used by her during her adolescence.

1

**Table**
1.20 x 0.60 x 0.70 m

**Shelf**
1.40 x 0.30 x 2.20 m

The furniture in her old room is no longer suitable to her current situation.

**What could she do to accommodate the recent changes in her life?**

*Home Back Home* is a prototyping initiative for the analysis, monitoring, and treatment of new domestic models emerging from contexts of economic collapse. This project specifically interrogates the return to the childhood family residence of young professionals aged from 25 to 40 in a process including the re-habitation of childhood rooms filled with obsolete belongings and mementos.

Emancipation has been conventionally constructed as a linear sequence, unambiguously aligning with the strengthening of personal autonomy, in a progression which includes: training, working, abandoning the family home, and, lastly, creating a new family. Yet, in contexts of economic resource deprivation, the abandonment of the family home has ceased to be irreversible and, quite frequently, has become impossible in the first instance. Furthermore, the rupture

of socially-accepted biographical options has displaced success in the traditional progression as a marker of the transition to adulthood, no longer validating these personal choices as necessary in the constitution of one's own personal biography.

In *Home Back Home,* the return to the family house is not considered an anomaly in the conventional sequence, but a chance to *de-standardize* pre-established emancipation narratives. Through collaborative design methodologies, this initiative provides a series of tools to encourage pro-active strategies within contexts of economic instability and crisis. Ultimately, *Home Back Home* develops processes of accompaniment, negotiation, and intervention involving all home co-habitants— as well as agents from academic, cultural, and activism milieus—to conceive more efficient and friendly living prototypes.

Home Back Home is a project that was initiated by PKMN Architectures. Enorme Studio is the new office created by three of the four members of the disbanded PKMN Architectures office and is the developer of this contribution to *After Belonging.*

## PHASE 02
Spatial Distribution. Enhanced furniture.

### EXPLODED AXONOMETRIC
### SEWING STATION PROTOTYPE

From co-design sessions conducted with Dune and workshop participants, a piece of furniture is designed and built. It is a transformed element built from two reused pieces of Dune's old furniture.

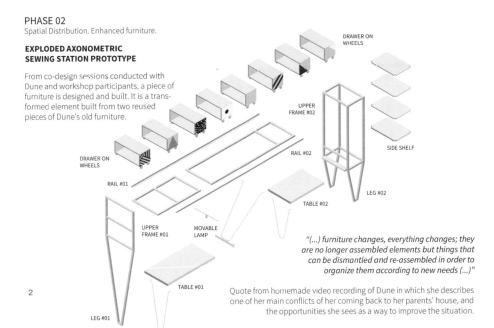

DRAWER ON WHEELS

UPPER FRAME #02

RAIL #02

SIDE SHELF

LEG #02

TABLE #02

DRAWER ON WHEELS

RAIL #01

UPPER FRAME #01

MOVABLE LAMP

TABLE #01

LEG #01

2

*"(...) furniture changes, everything changes; they are no longer assembled elements but things that can be dismantled and re-assembled in order to organize them according to new needs (...)"*

Quote from homemade video recording of Dune in which she describes one of her main conflicts of her coming back to her parents' house, and the opportunities she sees as a way to improve the situation.

### HOW DOES THE PROTOTYPE ADDRESS STORAGE NEEDS AND THE USE OF SPACE IN DUNE'S BEDROOM INTERIOR?

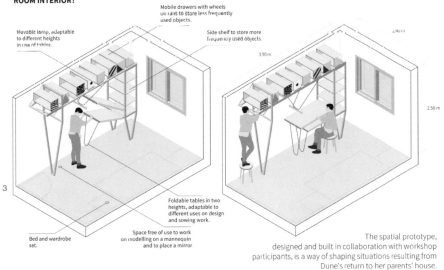

Movable lamp, adaptable to different heights in use of tables.

Mobile drawers with wheels on rails to store less frequently used objects.

Side shelf to store more frequently used objects.

3.90 m

2.40 m

2.50 m

3

Bed and wardrobe set.

Space free of use to work on modelling on a mannequin and to place a mirror

Foldable tables in two heights, adaptable to different uses on design and sowing work.

The spatial prototype, designed and built in collaboration with workshop participants, is a way of shaping situations resulting from Dune's return to her parents' house.

1  Research and registration of behavior changes involved in moving back to parents' house.
2  Spatial Distribution. Enhanced furniture. Optimized furniture.
3  Prototype implementation.
   All drawings courtesy of PKMN Architectures.

1

Home Back Home proposes to deal with this new temporary housing situation, working from the architecture's field.

To drive a positive change in young people and strengthen the confidence in their own abilities

Home Back Home transforms unuseful furniture from the former room promoting the second life of objects.

1  Dune in her teen room. Courtesy of PKMN Architectures.

2  The prototype implemented in Dune's room.

3  The collaborative design process developed at the Do-It-Yourself Institute.

All Drawings: Home Back Home Platform.

2

Home Back Home is a platform for making visible, discussing and cooperating, taking decissions about new alternatives to this change of housing model.

To connect people by building social cohesion and emotional participation around this collective problem.

3

Home Back Home is developed through open workshops of co-design and co-production

## 2014 Deconstruction Montagne du Parc: Large Scale Salvage Operation Concerning Interiors by Christophe Gevers & Jules Wabbes

### ROTOR / ROTOR Deconstruction

In 2014, Brussels-based design collective Rotor founded a spin-off project specifically concerned with demolition practices. Dubbed "Rotor Deconstruction," the project develops tools and strategies to *undo* buildings in such a way that at least some of the materials involved can be repurposed as building components elsewhere.

The salvage of building components has been quite common throughout history — for instance, Stonehenge is believed to be a secondhand structure that was moved at least once. But this ambition, which a priori seemed such a simple idea, was gradually confronted with the complexity of the industrial building complex as it exists today. Although demolition is a highly codified and regulated trade, the main challenge for this practice lies in inverting one of the logics governing design today: the need to produce materials according to specifications when more standardized components would be more amenable for reuse. Specificity, therefore, constitutes the ultimate flaw for the reutilization of secondhand building components.

Following the decision to demolish the former headquarters of the "Générale de Banque" opened to the public in 1973, BNP-Paribas / Fortis contacted Rotor to coordinate a salvage operation to save the iconic corporate interiors by the well-known designers Jules Wabbes and Christophe Gevers. Rotor's mission comprised the identification and inventory of all significant and salvageable materials, the organization and supervision of their removal, as well as the placement of the salvaged materials in new locations and projects. In total, around two hundred tons of materials—the entire cafeteria, thousands of square meters of ceilings and floors, and a myriad of architectural decorations— were diverted from landfills with this operation.

1

Commissioned by BNP-Paribas / Fortis & Rotor.

1 Rotor, "Vade-mecum for Off-SiteReuse."

All other images: Deconstruction of the interiors of Générale de Banque (currently BNP-Paribas-Fortis) designed by Jules Wabbes.
© Rotor Deconstruction.

# The Proposal: The Barragán Archives

## Jill Magid

### The Proposal

Agreement between the Barragán Family and Jill Magid

This agreement is made and entered into this __23__ date of __Sept. 2015__ by and between the Barragán family (hereinafter the "Family") and Jill Magid (hereinafter the "Artist").

The Family is the heir, descendant, and owner of the remains of Luis Barragán Morfín (hereinafter the "Architect"), which are currently located at La Rotonda de los Jaliciences Ilustres in Guadalajara.

This agreement follows from a discussion with the Family, whose members, for the purposes of this agreement, include: Hugo Barragán Hermosillo, Alfredo Vásquez Barragán, Juan José Barragán Hermosillo, Martha Barragán Hermosillo, Oscar Barragán Gortázar, Alfonso Barragán Gortázar, Liana Barragán Gortázar, Luisa Barragán Gortázar, Miguel Barragán Gortázar, and Rayo Barragán Morfín. In this discussion, all expressed their strong desire that the professional archive (hereinafter the "Archive") of the Architect return to Mexico. They also expressed their ardent support of The Proposal (hereinafter the "Artwork"), made by the Artist, as a unique, open, and independent gesture.

This discussion occurred on July 19, 2014, at the Museo de Arte de Zapopan. There, the Family visited the exhibition Woman with Sombrero and the Artist presented to the Family her plans for the Artwork.

In order to ensure clear and direct communications between the Family and the Artist, the Family has collectively nominated Hugo Barragán Hermosillo as the Family's agent in all matters related to this agreement and to the Family's relationship with the Artist. Furthermore, the Family has agreed that Alfredo Vásquez Barragán shall act as the Family's successor agent, in all matters related to this agreement and to the Family's relationship with the Artist, if Hugo Barragán Hermosillo is unable to do so.

The following document describes the Artwork, generally, and then the specific agreements made between the Family and the Artist.

### The Artwork

Contents

The Artwork will include a diamond made from the cremated remains of the Architect, set into a ring mounting (hereinafter the "Ring"); a ring box; a letter, written by the Artist, to Federica Zanco, Director of the Barragan Foundation (hereinafter the "Archivist"); and a series of relevant documents, including a Certificate of Authenticity for the diamond, provided by its Swiss based fabricator, Algordanza AG (hereinafter "Algordanza").

Realization

The Artist will hire a mortuary agent to collect twenty-five percent of the Architect's cremated remains at La Rotonda de los Jaliciences Ilustres in Guadalajara, at the soonest possible date after the signing of this agreement. The mortuary agent will place the rest of the remains back into La Rotunda. A notary public will certify this process.

The Artist will personally transport and deliver the Architect's remains from Guadalajara to Algordanza, in Switzerland, for creation of the diamond. Upon the diamond's completion, the Artist will return to Algordanza to recover the diamond, which Algordanza will release to her for immediate setting.

The diamond will be made from the remains of the Architect. According to the sales contract entered into by the Artist and Algordanza, the diamond shall weigh two carats, polished but not augmented from its natural octagonal shape. It will carry the micro laser inscription I am wholeheartedly yours.

The diamond will be set into a ring mounting provided by the Artist. The Ring will be fitted to the Archivist's finger once her size has been determined.

Periods

The Artwork will exist in two periods: the proposal period and the engagement period. The Artwork will be displayed during both periods, as described in The Agreement.

The Artist will offer the Ring to the Archivist, in Switzerland, at the first exhibition of the Artwork. This offer will initiate the proposal period. In order for the Archivist to receive the Ring, she must agree to relocate the Archive from the Barragan Foundation, in Birsfelden, Switzerland, to a publicly accessible site or institution in Mexico. The Archivist may accept the Ring and the terms of the offer at any moment.

If the Archivist accepts the offer, the Family, the Archivist, and other relevant parties will negotiate the terms of the Archive's relocation. Once negotiations have concluded, the Artist will give the Archivist the Ring and a copy of the Certificate of Authenticity from Algordanza. At this moment, the engagement period will begin. The remaining materials, less the Ring, will constitute the Artwork. Once the Archivist is in possession of the Ring, the Artist and the Family will relinquish all claims to it.

1

The Barragán Archives is an extended, multimedia project examining the legacy of Mexican architect and Pritzker Prize winner Luis Barragán (1902–1988). The Barragán Archives considers both Barragán's professional and personal archives, and how the intersections of his official and private selves reveal divergent and aligned interests, even within the institutions that have become the archives' guardians.

Along with the vast majority of his architecture, Barragán's personal archive remains in Mexico while his professional archive, including the rights to the architect's name and work, was acquired in 1995 by the Swiss furniture company Vitra, under the auspices of the newly founded Barragán Foundation. By developing long-term relationships with various personal, governmental, and corporate entities, The Barragán Archives explores the intersections of the psychological and the judicial, national identity and repatriation, international property rights and copyright law, authorship and ownership, the human body and the body of work.

Courtesy of Until Then, Paris; RaebervonStenglin, Zurich; LABOR, Mexico City.

## he Agreement

### The Family and the Artist Agree to the Following

he Family shall generously give the Artist twenty-five percent of the Architect's remated remains, understanding that four hundred and fifty grams is the minimum amount necessary to manufacture a diamond solely of those remains.

In exchange for the remains, the Artist shall transform them into a diamond, ointly owned by the Family and the Artist, according to the above specifications, and subject to the risks outlined in her contract with Algordanza, as part f the Artist's original Artwork. As the diamond grows, the Artist shall regularly form the Family of the diamond's progress by sharing Audit Protocol notices om Algordanza.

The Family may designate two of its members to accompany the Artist to ecover the diamond and also to attend the first exhibition of the Artwork. The rtist shall bear responsibility for the travel costs of said family members.

During the proposal period, the Artist shall ensure that the Ring is always on ublic display. For three years after the Artist offers the Ring to the Archivist, e Artwork may be loaned for exhibition throughout the year. After three years, e Artwork shall be displayed within its permanent location in Mexico for a inimum of six months per year.

The Artist shall decide where the Artwork is loaned for exhibition. The Family hall have the right to approve a publicly accessible institution in Mexico within vhich the Artwork is permanently exhibited.

The Family shall have the right to approve the terms of the Ring's release o the Archivist. Accordingly, the Family will enjoy the ability to approve the rrangements by which the Archive is made accessible, including a permanent ocation in Mexico. The Artist shall have no ownership of the Archive.

The Family shall not bear financial responsibility for any aspect of the production of the diamond, nor for any aspect of the Artwork, including its production, exhibition, insurance, etc.

### Official Version

his agreement has been prepared in English and Spanish, and the Spanish ersion thereof shall prevail nnd be binding upon the parties. The English ersion, which the parties shall also sign, shall serve as the Artist's version, for urposes of exhibition.

### Conformity to Law

he interpretation and enforcement of this agreement shall be governed by the ederal laws of the United States of America and by the laws of the State of Vew York not inconsistent therewith

N WITNESS WHEREOF, the parties hereto have executed this agreement as f the day and year first written above.

_____
he Barragán Family

_____
ill Magid

3

1  Agreement between Jill Magid and the Barragán family regarding The Proposal, signed by Jill Magid and Hugo Barragán Hermosillo on September 23, 2015. Jill Magid, "The Family Agreement," 2015. Designed by Philipp Hubert.

2  Certificate confirming that Algordanza, Switzerland, received Barragán's ashes and has transformed them into a rough-cut blue diamond. Diamond Certificate by Algordanza, 2016.

3  Jill Magid, "Rough Diamond in Cell," 2016. Chur, Switzerland. Photograph provided by Algordanza AG. © Jill Magid. Courtesy LABOR, Mexico City; Until Then, Paris; RaebervonStenglin, Zurich.

4  Gemmological Report. Laboratory-grown diamond report from GGTL Laboratories, dated March 30, 2016.

## Electronic Cartographies: Paper Electronic Modules, Circuit to Link, Anatomical Board of a Speaker

Coralie Gourguechon

The purpose of *Electronic Cartographies* is to reveal information which cannot be experienced, either because of a scaling relationship or due to the immateriality of a concept. Despite the pervasiveness of technology in the mediation of everyday life, the miniaturization of electronic devices has rendered them as increasingly inaccessible, both leaving users without the possibility of understanding their operational logics and obscuring the conflicts emerging from the production of electronic waste. *Electronic Cartographies* relies on mapping as a means to democratize electronics by simplifying their codes of representation. These maps do not merely *represent* the circuits: the use of materials such as conductive ink or the addition of components allow these representations to become working paper electronic devices.

*Paper Electronic Modules* is a freely available design interface, containing a library of modules, patterns, and electronic circuits to print out, allowing for the creation of electronic devices in Open Source.

The form and techniques are built up simultaneously, creating a "white box" out of the blank page: the object no longer covers the circuit; the circuit becomes the object.

The aim of the project *Circuit to Link* is to demystify electronics by simplifying the execution of simple circuits. Their assembly requires the use of conductive glue, and tracks are made with a special conductive-ink pen. The user connects the various elements of the circuit with the help of instructions, in an operation that conceptually reconciliates the conventional electronic diagram with a simplified version of a circuit.

*Anatomical Board of a Speaker* is an educational anatomical chart which graphically unveils the operation of hidden electronic systems. When detached from the sheet, the speaker forms a cone, allowing for the mechanical amplification of sound. Returning the speaker to a flat condition by unfolding the cone opens the circuit and the speaker is turned off, mechanically creating a switch system.

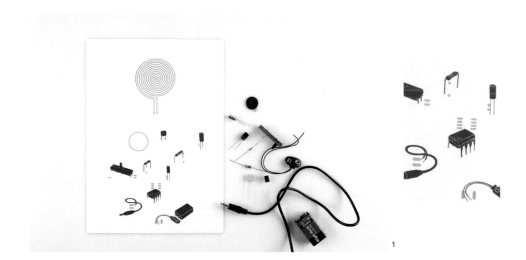

1

These projects are part of a Master Thesis in Design, completed at Institut Supérieur des Arts de Toulouse, ISDAT. The name of the general research is "Electronic Cartographies." The thesis title is "Rebuild the Electronic and Digital Tools."

1 "Circuit to Link," 2013.
2 "Anatomical Board of a Speaker," 2013.
3 "Paper Electronic Modules," 2013.
All images: Coralie Gourguechon, co-production ISDAT.

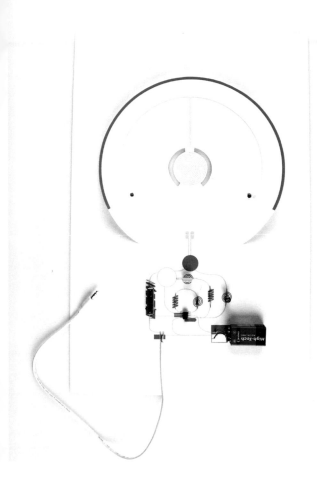

2

3

# Found

**Superunion Architects (Johanne Borthne, Vilhelm Christensen, Haakon Walderhaug, Jonathan Værnes, Magnus Garvoll)**

*Found*—understood as an adjective, the past participle form of the verb *find*, and the English translation of *finn*—is a collection acquired and composed by sorting through the more than 10,000 giveaway objects advertised at *finn.no,* the local Norwegian version of the worldwide object and services exchange platform Craigslist.

The *Found* collection, acquired during the specific time frame of a 24-hour span by contacting offers posted, in its majority, during that same period,

investigates the relation of objects to temporary living. With the acceleration of household relocation resulting from new economies and lifestyles, and the spread of new modes of production, object giveaway and the purchase of new furnishing products is often considered more convenient than moving household goods, debasing notions of historical value and quality systems relying on ideas of craftsmanship and materials.

Superunion Architects, "Found," 2016. Collage using photographs uploaded by users from www.finn.no (accessed June 30, 2016).

The *Found* collection interrogates the relation between the lack of economic or exchange value of these objects, and the accumulation and construction of historical or affective value. At *finn.no,* user-assembled low-cost furniture is juxtaposed and blends together with antique furniture, in a compilation which establishes new systems of appreciation. Losing the context through which meaning was constructed by former owners, belongings are transformed into simple matter,

circulating through new generations of owners with different interests and backgrounds.

What are the individual stories hidden within these vast numbers of objects, and what could be the continuity of these narratives in contexts different from the ones through which they were constructed? Does the repurposing of these objects grant them new meanings? What is the value of craftsmanship techniques and notions of quality in temporary living?

## Jerry Can: Construction of Computers Through Recycling

**Kër Thiossane and Fablab Defko Ak Niëp**

A jerry is a self-assembled computer using recovered hardware (motherboards, CPUs, disks, etc.) and some sewing equipment (closures, sewing threads...) as well as any other elements that can be utilized for decoration. All these pieces are mounted in a 20-liter container, on which open source, freeware applications are installed. The name "jerry" comes from the English noun "jerry can."

The jerry was born from the initiative of individuals sensitive to the conflicts of our time. In the era of over-consumption and planned obsolescence, this recycled computer invites to the sharing of knowledge, to creativity, and to greater individual autonomy in the use of digital tools. Where some see a new market to monopolize, others see it as the symbol of a renewal of the values of sharing and "common good."

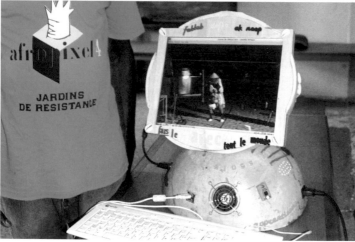

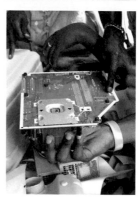

**Jerrys workshop. Fourth Afropixel Festival, May 19–21, 2014. All images by Kër Thiossane.**

In collaboration with Woelab–Togo, and Defko Ak Niep. A Jerry workshop was first organized as the inauguration of the École des Communs of Ker Thiossane, during the Afropixel Festival, running from May 19–21, 2014.

# Sēlf Ştoragę Façĭlĩtĩeš
## in New York

With more than thirty facilities within Manhattan, the self-storage industry has an increasing presence in the urban fabric of the financial capital of the United States. The accelerated life cycling of housing associated with an ever more dynamic job market has transformed the profile of the personal storage industry, which was originally targeted to affluent suburban households and has increasingly come to support young professionals moving frequently within global metropolitan networks.

These infrastructures, with their regular distribution of stacked corridors and homogenous colored metal doors, are no longer limited to the unused leftovers of affluent suburban life, but also include materials associated with daily dynamics. With storage spaces ranging from the size of a locker to that of a garage, many storage facilities are open 24/7. They complement the domestic space both in response to current peaking consumption and accumulation of goods, as well as to precarious housing conditions. The formerly popular suburban facilities have been superseded by big, fat volumes located in strategic urban locations. These buildings are also submitted to the logics of real estate, functioning as capital repositories. New storing trends are intertwined with these transformed architectures, the changing location of the facilities, and are supported by aggressive media campaigns.

The proliferation and typological changes of these storage facilities render visible shifts in the ways in which we relate to objects: many times, belongings remain fixed despite constant changes of residence; other times, objects keep circulating regardless of the length of a stay in a specific residence, as long as they can be stored.

Manhattan Mini-Storage building in New York City,
Photograph by Brett Beyer, 2015. Courtesy of the author.

Blocks of Blabla

First Office (Anna Neimark and Andrew Atwood)


Despite the traditional image of Manhattan as a city of monuments, some
beautiful buildings in New York are not monumental. They do not stand
out or stand on pedestals; they do not speak of a company's power or an
architect's will; they do not proclaim autonomy. They are perhaps unique
precisely because they do not exhibit any unique character. There are no
specific qualities that distinguish these buildings from their contexts; and
so they tend to blend, quite literally, into the background. It is because they
are so common that they so deeply impress themselves upon our minds.
We use the word "impress," because they produce something of a relief.
Relief in both of its senses: mental and material. We feel relief when we
encounter these blocks, when we find ourselves in front of their ordinary
façades. They exhibit a weak attitude; they are like architecture in size only,
or so it seems at first glance. They have windows, once in a while a door,
and sometimes a fire escape. But these architectural parts rarely perform
any function. Windows are hardly ever glazed; entrances are often filled-in
with block or brick. The details that do remain appear now as extravagances.
Meaning—if we can still use that term to refer to architectural syntax—
has been stretched over the elevation: the purpose of each component now
seems to be absorbed into the thin surface of paint. What was once an
articulate foreground becomes a mute backdrop. So we come to the second
sense of relief. The building is a relief: a continuous surface of paint that
does not distinguish among the materials it coats. The addition of paint
subtracts delineations between one part and another, between one detail
and another. It fuses all possible meanings into one—but it is a meaning
that no longer speaks to us. These buildings might be our Towers of Babel,
except that they defeat language without a monument: they are not towers,
they are multiple, and they are indistinguishable. There are so many of these
blocks that they become mere presence; they just fill space. Rather than
Towers of Babel, perhaps we can call them blocks of blabla. We thought we
should make a map, or at least jot down some addresses for you; make a
list, so to say. But someone beat us to it, on Google maps, under "self
storage." Go ahead, take a look; everything is there.

Project Team: First Office team includes Aubrey Bauer, Brooke Hair, and Jon Gregurick in collaboration with SCI-Arc
students who participated in the workshop: Deborah Garcia, Connor Gravelle, Daniel Hapton, Alissa Lopez (Princeton
University), Kyla Schaefer, and Tidus Ta. With the additional support of University of California Berkeley and Southern
California Institute of Architecture.

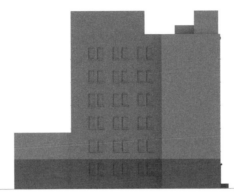

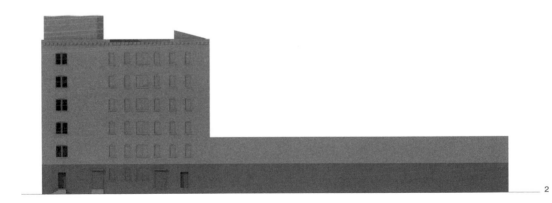

1  261 Walton Avenue, Bronx: South Elevation.
2  261 Walton Avenue, Bronx: East Elevation.
   All images by First Office, 2015.

1  261 Walton Avenue, Bronx: East, South, West, and North Elevations.
2  29 Review Avenue, Long Island City: East, South, West, and North Elevations.
3  30 Starr Avenue, Long Island City: East, South, West, and North Elevations.
4  541 West 29th Street, New York City: South, West, North, and East Elevations.

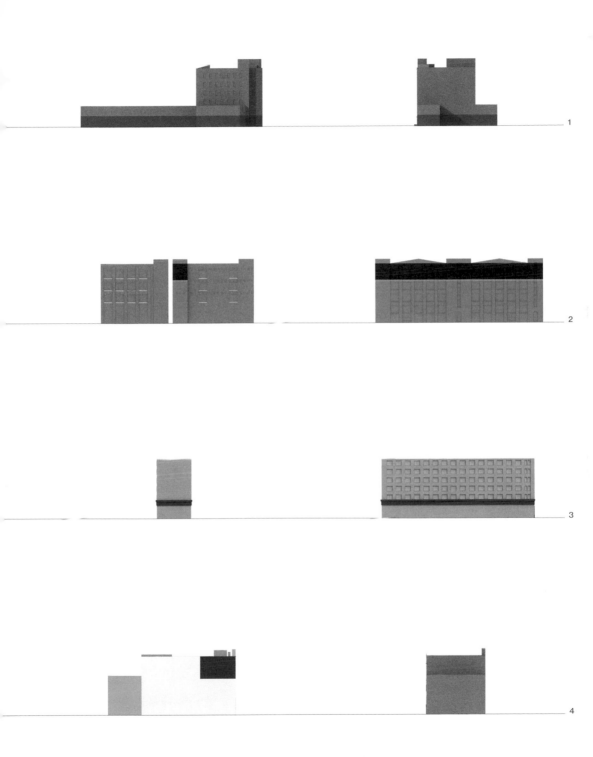

1

2

3

4

541 West 29th Street, New York City: West Elevation, by First Office, 2015.

# Sheltering Ṭėmpòrariñęšs
## Texts

# Architectures of Inhospitality

Didier Fassin

In the beginning, they hailed from South Asia and Southeast Asia: Pakistanis, boat people from Vietnam, and Tamils from Sri Lanka fleeing conflict and repression. Then, the Berlin Wall fell, and Yugoslavia broke up: they were Poles in search of employment, Croatians and Kosovars escaping civil war. With the destabilization of the Middle East after Western military interventions, Kurds from Iraq and Afghans followed. Many were also from Africa, having crossed the Sahara and the Mediterranean: Somalis, Sudanese, and Eritreans who had endured persecution, violence, misery, and the dreadful perils of the uncertain journey. Finally, the Syrians arrived, the most numerous and the most desperate to reach England.

Didier Fassin, "The grocery store Welcome to the City," January 8, 2016, Calais. Courtesy of the author.

Didier Fassin, "The legal center before it was burnt down by arson," January 8, 2016, Calais. Courtesy of the author.

In the beginning, one hardly noticed their presence in the city: they were few and just spent a handful of days there before crossing the Channel. Then Great Britain passed the 1993 and 1996 Asylum and Immigration Acts, making it much harder to obtain refugee status or residency documents, but much easier to detain those who tried to enter the country. In Calais, they became more numerous, slept in the parks or on the streets, received tents and food from local organizations, started to face the hostility of the inhabitants. In 1999, as the situation grew worse, the French left-wing government opened a warehouse in Sangatte under the auspices the Red Cross: the two hundred people were soon more than fifteen hundred. In three years, 65,000 refugees and migrants passed through the center, which the activists called a camp. When the conservative party returned to power in 2002, the government closed the warehouse, affirming that the closure was for security and humanity reasons, and signed an agreement with Britain, authorizing the presence of its police in the port and the tunnel. Having nowhere to go, they now camped on the beaches or hid in bunkers abandoned by the Germans at the end of the Second World War. Constantly harassed by law enforcement officers,

Didier Fassin, "Shacks, tents, cart and swamp on a dry day," January 8, 2016, Calais.
Courtesy of the author.

their shelters systematically destroyed and their belongings ruined, they
wandered along the coast in quest of a way to get to England.

In 2014, after more than a decade of a repression as inhumane as
it was ineffective, the socialist government, back in power, resolved to let
them occupy a former dump site devoid of basic sanitary equipment and
situated next to chemical plants. Yet, with the assistance of British and French
non-governmental organizations, the migrants and the refugees managed to
make this wasteland a place to live; in the strongest sense of the word, they
inhabited the undignified location they had been given by contempt more
than benevolence. Indeed, in the "jungle," as it came to be known, there
were tents and shacks, bars and restaurants, barber shops and grocery
stores, a mosque and a church, a primary school and a legal center. Although
there was mud everywhere and although, when it rained, the ground was
transformed into a swamp, people moved around, solidarity networks operated,
a form of dignity was restored. This was at least the case in the "jungle" during
the day, because every night hundreds of migrants and refugees left the camp
to try to cross the Channel by road, train, or boat. Several died every month,
being run over by a truck, electrocuted on the rails, or drowned (in 2015, twenty-
four lost their life as a consequence). The others were chased and teargased by
the police, assaulted by their dogs, sometimes beaten, occasionally arrested (in
a survey, 80 percent declared they had been victims of such violence). In the
morning, most returned to the camp, aggrieved and injured.

Didier Fassin, "Syrian refugees in front of their makeshift shelter," January 8, 2016, Calais. Courtesy of the author.

Didier Fassin, "Installation of the shipping containers surrounded with wire fencing," January 8, 2016, Calais. Courtesy of the author.

Eventually, the same government that had let them settle in this squalid environment decided to take it away from them, installing large white shipping containers and surrounding them with wire fencing. The new housing, which had neither bathrooms nor kitchens, could only shelter one third of the estimated number of people living in the "jungle." Residents were to be registered, the control of their entry being monitored by handprint technology and a prolonged absence being penalized by the loss of their place. Many regarded this housing as a prison meant to prevent them from crossing the Channel and anticipated their relocation to reception centers elsewhere in France. One morning, despite a decision of the administrative tribunal contrary to the eviction, bulldozers protected by the police destroyed a large part of the camp—shanties, stores, restaurants, places of worship—hardly leaving time for the occupants to evacuate their belongings. Those who resisted were chased with tear gas and hit with batons. Soon, the "jungle" turned into a desolate landscape of torn canvas, broken boards, and crushed objects. And most of the evictees—men, women, and children—became forced nomads once more, having lost their last refuge. It was still winter.

Philologists tell us that hospitality and hostility have the same Latin root. Ironically the linguist who explored this conspicuous connection, Émile Benveniste, was born in Aleppo, the martyr city in Syria from which many refugees have fled over the past four years. He showed that *hostis* initially meant the stranger with whom relations of equality and reciprocity were established. With time, as the sentiment of the Roman nation developed, the distinction between citizen and stranger hardened and the term took on a negative connotation. The stranger became the enemy. Another word was therefore created to retain the original sense and *hospes* signified the guest. Hostility derives from the first root; hospitality from the second. Contemporary politics towards refugees and migrants are heirs of this etymological lineage. The international laws of hospitality inscribed in the 1951 Geneva Convention on Refugees, which guarantee protection for those who fear persecution on political, religious or ethnic reasons in their home country, have turned into policies and practices of hostility.

Architectures of inhospitality reflect this ambivalence. They are made of tents, shacks, military blockhouses, industrial warehouses, benches in parks, or hollows in the sand. The environment of these architectures is comprised of waste grounds and dump sites, sometimes surrounded by wire fencing and barbed wire, sometimes simply in the middle of no man's land. In fact, these architectures can fit any environment where the indignity of the condition of the migrant or refugee can be recalled, exhibited, and experienced. Insecurity must also be permanent, fear must be present, a sense of humiliation and hopelessness must be felt. Only under these conditions can the true goal of the politics of inhospitality be attained: deterrence.

At the entrance to the "jungle," on the pier of the bridge from which the police watched over the comings and goings of migrants and refugees, the street artist Banksy stenciled a picture that represents Steve Jobs carrying a computer with a bundle on his shoulder, in the attitude of a clandestine alien—a reminder that the biological father of the founder of Apple was Syrian. At his feet, near a small blue tent, someone had put together the remains of grenades used to teargas the residents of the camp. The small cluster formed a derisory altar which seemed to ironically celebrate the violence of the French state. A little further, on the same concrete pile, awkwardly written graffiti reads: "Nobody deserves to live this way!"

Didier Fassin, "Steve Jobs by Banksy on the bridge pier at the entrance of the jungle," January 8, 2016, Calais. Courtesy of the author.

Didier Fassin, "Nobody deserves to live this way — on the bridge pier," January 8, 2016, Calais. Courtesy of the author.

# Prisoners of the Present: Transient Populations, Sovereign Thoughts, and Depoliticization of Housing in the Postwar Era

Ijlal Muzaffar

transience, *n.*
1 The action or fact of soon passing away; also, the condition or state of being transient, transiency.
*Oxford English Dictionary*

Transience by definition is contradictory. What is transient must change, is changing, yet it needs to be fixed in space and time to be defined *as* changing. Transience presents a problem of attributing a phenomenological state to something that cannot have a state. This state-crossing is thus frequently a State problem. Transient states of populations and politics threaten the State as they continuously cross boundaries of space and time, claiming new territories and articulating new futures.

The UN was founded in 1947 to guard against the possibilities of another nuclear war. But the first deadly threat the organization identified in its reports was of a different order: it was the "world housing crisis" that was seen as threatening the new geo-economic order being forged for the postwar era. How could a global order be managed if the transient population flowing into the cities of the decolonizing world—overflowing onto their surrounding hills, filling their ravines, and clogging their streets—turned them into spaces of political and economic uncertainty?[1]

Housing the world's transient population, thus, was a project of taking unpredictability out of change and turning it into a calculus of choice. It is important to remember that when housing starts to figure as a "world crisis," the idea of housing as it had figured in the expertise-driven discourse of "blight removal" in the Anglo-American context has already been turned upside down. If, in the Anglo-American context, unpredictability was reckoned as a series of choices for the expert, as variables to be determined in the plan; then, in the development arena, the presence of unpredictability was presented as moments of choice for the inhabitant herself. To accept housing is to accept an invitation or a demand to make the contradictory pulls of history on your life yield to the singular expectations of progress. Housing is a figuration of making the transient appear to be a manageable phenomenon, for there are no populations and no migrants who move from the "village" to the "city" simply in search of a better life. The concerns of the transient are polymorphous, and their politics many. Their spaces are overlapping and interwoven, cutting across administrative and cartographic categories. Housing as a "world crisis" is a figuration that makes this collection of concerns and experiences appear as steps in a sequence.

1 See Charles Abrams, *Man's Struggle for Shelter in an Urbanizing World* (Cambridge, Ma.: MIT Press, 1964), 23. We see this sentiment expressed from the very first UN reports to the later World Bank Urbanization Sector Working Papers. See *Urbanization Sector Working Paper*, June, 1972; *Housing Sector Policy Paper*, May, 1972.

*This* curious figuration of housing was certainly on the minds of UN housing experts in the 1950s. In a series of advisory "missions" to West Africa, South Asia, and Southeast Asia between 1956 and 1959, Charles Abrams, the famous American housing advocate, and Otto Koenigsberger, the head of the Development Planning Unit at the Architectural Association in London, would situate this sequencing under the umbrella of self-help architecture, an earlier version of the current discourse on "public engagement architecture," where the future inhabitants are asked to build their own houses over

Nadeem F. Paracha, "Visual Karachi: From Paris of Asia, to City of Lights, to Hell on Earth," 2014.

time.[2] On their joint missions, Abrams and Koenigsberger wrote reports and proposed housing schemes for "refugees," "migrants," and "squatters," from Ghana to Pakistan to the Philippines. These proposals present a snapshot of a major institutional approach—self-help architecture—which formed the medium and mode through which the majority of the world's population encountered the immense Third World development discourse. The proposals also provide a window into a major epistemological transformation in the figuration of architecture from a vehicle of patronage to an instrument of finance in the global arena.

To chart this transformation, let us begin with an instance of self-help proposed by Abrams and Koenigsberger in which housing is presented literally as an invitation to enter the world of investing:

> In the long run… a sign on land made available which reads "Settlers Welcome" will produce more acceptable, more durable and more morally-structured neighborhoods than the timid "no trespass" sign that is respected more in the breach than in the observance[3]

This declaration is indeed a strange one. Instead of barbed wire around vacant lots in Karachi, Accra, and Manila, one can imagine Abrams and Koenigsberger's "settlers welcome" signs attached to lone poles, issuing a squeaking invitation as they wave in the coastal winds to all passersby. Architecture had been held up to make morality durable in the past. What is new in Abrams and Koenigsberger's coupling of architecture and morality, however, is the unique figuration in which the architecture is summoned not as an object, but as an absence, a potential. Order is invoked not by presence, but by promise, not by form, but by the sequence in which architecture is made to appear.

The experts called this approach the "roof loan" scheme: the inhabitants were given money to buy the roof and start living under it, as they built up the walls and the rest of the house. This arrangement, the experts argued, would unleash a dormant potential lying fallow on the streets:

> [E]verywhere in the cities we saw people of small and moderate means saving building blocks and storing them in the areaways and in backyards…. Block-savings has more implications than appear on the surface. Savings which normally might be channeled into long-term investments lie

2 Abrams and Koenigsberger went on joint missions to the Gold Coast (Ghana), Pakistan, the Philippines, Singapore, and Nigeria. The reports for these missions were published by the UN as follows: *Report on Housing in the Gold Coast*, prepared for the government of the Gold Coast by Charles Abrams, Vladimir Bodiansky, Otto H.G. Koenigsberger (New York: United Nations Technical Assistance Administration, 1956); *A Housing Program for Pakistan with Special Reference to Refugee Rehabilitation*, prepared for the Government of Pakistan by Charles Abrams and Otto Koenigsberger, September 14, 1957 (New York: United Nations Technical Assistance Administration, 1957); *A Housing Program for the Philippine Islands*, by Charles Abrams and Otto Koenigsberger (New York: United Nations Technical Assistance Administration, 1959).

3 *A Housing Program for Pakistan with Special Reference to Refugee Rehabilitation*, 19.

4 *Report on Housing in the Gold Coast*, 21.

5 Ibid., 77.

6 Ibid.

*sterilized* in blocks that will probably never see the mason's trowel or shelter an occupant. The cement used in the blocks is paid for with money that goes out of the country but produces no wealth within it. In that sense it is even less constructive than the purchase of local gems as a form of savings. The family foregoes purchase of other necessities in favour of the futile block and despite the need, the product rarely contributes to the production of the housing for which it was intended. Often the blocks are actually set up, but the house remains unfinished because of inability to finance the purchase of a roof or the other final elements of the structure.[4]

*Manual on Self-help Housing*, United Nations, 1964. "Roof-loan variant of 'core' housing in Ghana."

The roof-loan schemes would not only "ease the perplexing problem of the 'unfinished house,'" the authors asserted, "[but it would] even bring into being the 'unstarted house,' represented by the vast stocks of sterilized building blocks punctuating city streets."[5]

How does a house turn sterile material into a fertile investment, and what or whom does the scheme impregnate? By putting the roof before the house, the scheme makes the present pregnant with potential. Everything the inhabitants do while living under the roof counts as investment, including the money they will save on rent elsewhere, but also the improvements they will make on the site, and the savings they would be incentivized to make to finish the house sooner.

This reproductive logic, however, is not as straightforward as it might seem. The line between fertility and sterilization is also a demarcation of risk. Since the "[l]oans on the roof would be represented by the last section of the building," argued the authors, "[it] enable[d] the lending agency to be selective in its loans and reduce the danger of defaults in completion. The loans would be made only when, after inspection, the roofless building was found to have a good foundation and a solid wall structure."[6] Whom does this strategy, this inversion, benefit: the lender or the inhabitant?

It appears that the inhabitant/worker takes on greater risk by accepting the roof over her head. If she defaults now, she doesn't just lose the roof, but the house itself. Those concrete blocks that previously sat idle in the street, were now assembled under the roof owned by someone else. The roof loan inscribed the inhabitants' savings into the calculus of finance at the least risk to the financial institutions and the greatest risk to the inhabitants.

Two time frames collide in this risk management strategy: the time of labor and the time of finance. A roof-loan house thus is simultaneously a spatial structure and a temporal infrastructure. By situating the roof as a pregnant system, Koenigsberger and Abrams situate housing as a containable risk. The risk is contained not in space, but in time. This time, the time of living under the roof, however, is a perpetual present, a pregnancy without birth, a risk forever contained, as long as the inhabitants keep investing in the house. This figuration of housing as a potent *system*, a temporal infrastructure, something that connects things in time, spreads risk by expanding the time of the present to infinity. We will return to this systemization of housing later. For now, let us stay a bit longer with the dimension of time this systemization emphasizes: the present.

## Perpetual Present

French philosopher and historian of labor, Jacques Rancière, has described a similar perpetuation of the present in post-1968 France in his book, *Chronicles of Consensual Time*.[7] Rancière argues that the twentieth century has experienced a new arrangement of time in Europe and America: "flexible time." With the increasing mobility of capital, the clear division between work and leisure is muddled. In contemporary industrial societies, the worker is now asked to be available all the time. If he resists, he is simply seen as not being of the times, of not understanding the demand of time, the spread of globalization, the flux of open markets, and the speed of capital. If he resists, he does not understand his place in the fast, global, interconnected, interdependent world. He must be ready to show up for work at night, just because it is daytime in China then. Even though it is the weekend here, it is high time for business somewhere else.

7 Jacques Rancière, *Chronicles of Consensual Time* (London: Continuum, 2010).

This demand for flexibility, Rancière argues, degrades all visions of the future as well as deflating those of the past. When the worker is asked to be present all the time, forced to yield to the demands of flexible time, he is forced to forgo any demands for the future or appraisals of the past.

The present takes on the form of a forced consensus. We cannot speak of futures or past anymore. If we do, we are called rigid and inflexible to the demands of the present. The present demands full flexibility. The present is itself nothing but flux: of capital, of markets, of trends, of cities, of social networks. To fully answer to the demands of the present, we as workers cannot be rigid, ask for regular workdays and predictable hours. We are to make ourselves available for work at all times. That absolute flexibility is the highest work value in the world of the present. It is the sign of entrepreneurship, an understanding of globalization, a commitment to democracy and capitalism. It is the measure of creativity in a rapidly changing world. To demand anything else would be to show signs of ignorance, to be outdated, to be irrelevant.

The worker is asked to be flexible because that is all that remains as the goal. Flexibility does not lead to any recognizable goal outside itself. Flexibility is its own promise, its own result. In return for flexibility, workers are not promised greater wages, or more secure rights. Those demands, those visions of the future, are themselves seen as outdated hindrances to flexibility. What is offered instead is relativism.

The effects of this historical turn towards flexibility, however, are not limited to Europe. It is supported by a figuration of undifferentiated labor and time elsewhere. Before the process of undoing the welfare state took hold in the center in Western democracies, it spread out to the Third World as a strategy of preventing the welfare state from emerging in the first place. It is the long shadow of this strategy that is cast by Abrams and Koenigsberger's "settlers welcome" sign.

With these two simple words Abrams and Koenigsberger not only sought to spell the end of politics, but also kill history. The "settlers welcome" sign is not only an invitation but also a demand. The words stipulate the terms on which occupation is offered. They insist that squatters redefine themselves as settlers and, in settling once and for all, give up the resistive edge of the encroachments that had been filling up the empty spaces at Karachi's seams, building congestion, piling up refuse, threatening to make the threads of "law and order" come loose. The sign asserts that the members of its audience must give up the political demands they have come to shape from living in those conditions. The sign asks them to forget the past and enter the present and remain there, only in the present. The sign assures them that they will always be welcome in this *now* as long as they do not disturb the ghosts of the past that might call on the specters of other possible futures.

The roof-loan scheme, also called the "core" house in some instances by Abrams and Koenigsberger, is indeed the perfect instrument for making this demand. The roof-loan scheme had no predetermined plan or form that could be seen as a goal to be delivered, an end to be achieved, or a recognition of a struggle. The scheme was a step ahead of concurrent discussions of determining some semblance of "minimum standards" of space and construction that still concerned questions of housing in international agencies. The scheme made no promises for the future, and heeded no murmurs from the past. Sometimes the projects provided just a plinth and the roof, at others, they just provided a land title tied to a loan. Abrams and Koenigsberger made the house—the architectural object—disappear from the architectural project. And with the house, the recognition of what housing stood for disappeared as well: "shelter" as a historical and political demand.

This claim might appear outright untenable in light of the title of Abrams' renowned book, *Man's Struggle for Shelter in an Urbanizing World*. This book indeed presents shelter as the central theme of the reports written by Abrams for various governments on his international missions. Yet, as the title betrays, the term shelter is strung together with other specific terms: struggle and urbanizing. And it is in the stringing of these particular words together that the particular demands for shelter from specific contexts discussed in the book are excluded in favor of a general one that does not, and cannot, speak to any of them. We see this push toward generalization in the Abrams and Koenigsberger's description of the situation in Karachi:

> The housing problem as such is therefore no longer purely a "refugee problem…." If there had been no refugees from India, the problem would have confronted Pakistan, as indeed it confronts other developing countries to-day. Our first underlying recommendation is therefore that while certain aspects of the housing problem are emergency in nature, the problem as a whole must be viewed as *long term*, requiring *long term* programming and *long term* treatment [emphasis added].[8]

**8** *A Housing Program for Pakistan*, 2.

It is this "long term" that becomes a perpetual present. Yet this perpetual present does not appear to be the same for all. Its unending expanse is marked by a silent division, a flip side. There are those who can see this underside and understand the blueprint of the present etched on it. And there are those who wander its desert without a map.

## Flexible Labor

We are here reminded once again of Jacques Rancière's work, but this time of his seminal first book, *Nights of Labor*, that describes the incredible intellectual activity of workers in nineteenth century France.[9] What Rancière found astonishing was that despite the extreme variety and depth of thinking carried out by workers in their precious after-work time—Rancière documents the activity of individuals in debate societies, poetry readings, writing groups, and political and painting groups, among other forms of intellectual social engagement—the worker was not recognized as a thinking being. Both those who despised and feared workers' political ambitions and those who valorized workers' labor and proclaimed utopian futures for them, defined the worker primarily as a being who does bodily work. This opposition between those who think and those who work could only frame the thinking activities of workers as amateur meanderings, even when these activities were seen with highly sympathetic eyes.

For Rancière, this distinction between two qualities of thought stemmed from the distinction between those who got to define the standard notion of time and those who didn't. Those who owned the means of production could set the standard of time, or define time as a standard. The workers were meant only to follow this standard. They did not own their time, even after work. That time was defined as time for rest, for leisure, for sleep, for food, and for rejuvenation of the body so it could return to work the next morning. Those who defined the order of time, however, could step behind its curtain. They understood how time worked and why it worked. After setting the clock in motion for others, they could stop it for themselves. Stepping off the stage, they could fritter away the hours as they wished. The nights consumed in contemplation, mornings spent in tired slumber, were not wasted. They were of value, as they were seen to write the script on which value was determined.

Workers' thought could not lay claim to stepping out of the confines of time. The Luddites could not stop the clock even when, protesting against the shackles of time on their lives, they set out to break every measuring clock. Their hours of thinking wrested from the inexorable demands of sleep and exhaustion, could only be seen as a waste of that precious time. Even Karl Marx, Rancière would assert, could only recognize workers as workers, not as thinkers.

This historical insight is instructive for us in understanding proposals like those by Abrams and Koenigsberger. The roof-loan house's thin roof arrives before the rest of the house. It does not just provide a shelter to work under, it defines the time and space that the worker works in. The roof sets the foundation of time as flexible, and the living spaces tied to that time as malleable and overlapping. With this shaping, this figuring of time and space, the worker standing under the roof's shade becomes malleable too. She must make her time available, at all hours. She must render all the spaces to which her life is connected as interconnected, summoning resources from the village to the city. If she does not make her life, its space and time, fully available to the project that she is to complete—if she thinks other-wise—her resistance can only be seen as a sign of being behind the times.

9 *Jacques Rancière, Nights of Labor: The Workers' Dream in Nineteenth-Century France*, trans. John Drury (Philadelphia: Temple University Press, 1989). Originally published in French as *La Nuit des Prolétaires* (Paris: Fayard, 1981) and re-released as *Proletariat Nights: The Workers' Dream in Nineteenth-Century France* (London: Verso, 2012).

*Manual on Self-help Housing*, United Nations, 1964.
"Roof-loan variant of 'core' housing in Ghana."

It can only be seen as the resistance of outmoded thought, immature and amateurish thought, thought that cheats her of what her body needs: shelter.

It is not a coincidence, nor a contradiction, that the roof-loan house begins with the claim of providing the most basic "shelter." This definition of shelter determines how the worker's time and space, thought and body, came to be figured in the development discourse. Under this claim of shelter, the worker can only be a worker, not a thinker.

She must listen to her body, and enter the structure of ownership, both literal and figural, through her labor—and flexible labor at that. For that is the mode of labor deemed proper for her. Under the shade of the loaned roof, the variations of her thought, their resistance to the demand for infinite availability and flexibility placed on her body, is blackened out. All the world's air can enter the roof-loan house's open walls, but it has no room for the worker's thought.

## Sovereign Thoughts

But the refugees in Karachi *were* thinking, and thinking through a discourse of displacement and transience. I have described in some detail the political demands of the refugee settlers in Karachi elsewhere.[10] It is sufficient to repeat here that the refugees, though economically and socially marginalized, were actually citizens of Pakistan who had migrated from India during the partition of the Indian subcontinent in 1947. These groups had variously adopted the *mohajir* (refugee) appellation as a political slogan to give their plight the religious symbolism of *hijrat*, the journey taken by the prophet Muhammad and his followers from Mecca to Medina in 678 AD, the year later marked as the beginning of the Islamic calendar.

This thinking of, and through, time and space is obliterated in Abrams and Koenigsberger's figuration of architecture. The invitation to settlement in a forever unfolding long present only recognizes the immediate bodily experience of the settler, and can never recognize her as a thinking, political being. As a site of settlement, the roof-loan house thus inscribes a distinction between flexible thinking and flexible labor. The inhabitant can only provide the latter, the planner/expert the former.

The realm of thinking proper, one which is not reducible to labor, however, cannot be proclaimed without a certain Catholicism which treats engagement with substance as merely transitory, and thinking as a purely spiritual realm. And here, Catholicism figures not just as an analogy, but rather as the very medium of making sense. Why is thinking in and through labor so threatening to development and its national clientele? We find this question answered not in terms of the hardships of the displaced or the shelterless, but the threat their transience poses to the idea of sovereignty. Writing on their mission to the Philippines two years later in 1959, the two experts identified this threat as common throughout the developing world:

10 See Ijlal Muzaffar, "For the Love of (Shared) Politics," in *Grey Room*, no. 61, Fall 2015 (MIT Press).

[Squatting] symbolize[s], the general breakdown of civic responsibility and of respect for public law and private rights. People who get away with appropriating what is not their own, take a cynical view about paying rent and taxes, or about respecting contract or authority. Worse still, others are encouraged by their example, disrespect for law and government becomes epidemic and lawlessness leans upon lawlessness as the structure of the state sags under the challenge. When a program for re-settlement is under way, it suggests that the government is still sovereign; when none is in sight, it puts *sovereignty* in issue [emphasis added].[11]

**11** *A Housing Program for the Philippine Islands*, 29.

**12** Pheng Cheah, *Spectral Nationality: Passages of Freedom from Kant to Postcolonial Literatures of Liberation* (New York: Columbia University Press, 2003).

**13** Bertrand de Jouvenel, *Sovereignty: An Inquiry into the Political Good* (Indianapolis: Liberty Fund, 1998).

The conflation of nationalist and religious ideas is not new. As Pheng Cheah has elaborated, national sovereignty has historically been conceived through ideas drawn from religious sovereignty, a collective belief in an independent entity larger than any of its physical manifestations.[12] It is, however, the *manner* in which questions of national sovereignty, civic "responsibility," and "respect" for law and property relate to a particular aspect of Catholic thought that are of concern to us here.

As we see in the statement above, national sovereignty is not just a question of asserting authority, but also of the claims of legitimacy in the development arena. Abrams and Koenigsberger's statement marks a partic-ular turn in claiming legitimacy for national sovereignty. And the fact that this legitimacy is claimed through an architectural figuration is not insignificant.

As a medium of establishing legitimacy, the roof-loan house ties national sovereignty to a particular spiritual affect: entrepreneurship. To respect national sovereignty through the spatial logic of property and the organization and sequencing of material is not to respect the law out of fear of authority, but to respect the law as a basis of mutual creativity. The flexibility of the roof-loan house is the promise to make material manifestation coincide with economic logic, to bring desire in line with value.

This is the promise, but then there is the rub. Despite presenting itself as the site of creative freedom, the house—and the legal, material, and discursive structures of policy and policing built around it—will only recognize that creativity as flexible labor, not as flexible thinking. To understanding this duality, we have to take another detour through the contradiction inherent in the idea of modern sovereignty itself.

This problem of legitimatizing sovereignty in modern political systems was most influentially discussed by Bertrand de Jouvenel, in his famous book, *Sovereignty: An Inquiry into the Political Good*.[13] For de Jouvenel, modern political systems are continuous with premodern ones, despite many claims to the contrary, inasmuch as they all require securing the legitimacy of the sovereign, be it the nation-state, the monarch, or God. This legitimacy is secured by defining the sovereign as the seat (or the site) of the promotion of the "common good."

Yet de Jouvenel finds it hard to define how the common good could be identified. Every scenario either leads to authoritarianism or relativism. Either someone, or everyone, ends up defining what the common good is, thus mak-ing that good not common at all. The only instances when the common good can be claimed are, strangely, when the rules articulating its premise are not followed but instead sublated by claiming to attend to something deliberately vague. In the chapter titled, "The Problem of the Common Good," de Jouvenel asserts, "[T]here is one phrase in the statement ["act for the common good"] which is almost entirely free of subjectivity: the capacity to act simultaneously or in combination is a concrete fact, which takes us into the domain of the object."[14] But "[t]his agreement is obtained," de Jouvenel acknowledges, "only because of the *vagueness* of the statement...."[15] Thus, ironically, vagueness is precisely what makes concrete and objective action possible.

From acting in accordance with a *vaguely* defined good, to *trusting* in the good action of others, to *believing* in a social *friendship*, society appears to be undergirded for de Jouvenel not by specific rules and laws for each action but by a generalized commitment to *every* possible situation: "Friendships... are seen to be antecedent to political organization properly so-called."[16]

But, we might ask, how can friendship be instituted if it is the basis of all institutions themselves? How can material wellbeing be promoted if what is needed is transcending all material concerns? De Jouvenel resolves this apparent metalepsis by making—relevant to our concerns—a distinction between flexible labor and flexible thinking. It is not the material and the political that can guarantee promotion of friendship, but the presence of sovereign thought, of thought as sovereign.

This distinction is revealed, not without significance, in a section titled "The Problem of Obligations in a Mobile Society." "Naturally," de Jouvenel asserts, "Christian societies have been very progressive ones, in which deeper and swifter transformations have occurred than in any other." This association results, he continues, because the "obligations of the Christian [sic] is no longer limited to the observation of rules." "The Christian [sic] is free from the law [and] his behavior is no longer ordered in detail by a code of precepts appropriate to different circumstances, but it is inspired by a new *spirit*. The specified obligations no longer act as a corset to his conduct; the sense of obligation must now become its very principle [emphasis added]."[17] This claim leads Jouvenel to draw a distinction between Christianity, the religion of the spirit, and Judaism and Islam, the religions of the letter: "Still confining ourselves to the social standpoint, we can see there a major revolution; a precise and detailed code of behaviors to others, such as is found in the Old Testament and the Koran..., is contrary to the genius of Christianity."[18]

The genius of Christianity resides in formulating a spirit, not rules, for the common good. All other postulates for the latter, de Jouvenel asserts, have been lodged in immobility: "It is here that a mobile society confronts the authorities with their major problem, which has never been properly clarified, for all the leading discussions of the common good are based on the postulate of a stationary society. Even revolutionary thought has always been directed to an immobile society which has been renovated once and for all."[19]

## Spirits and Ghosts

We might be able to take free thought out of religion but not religion out of free thought. If we return to Abrams and Keonigsberger's figurations with insights from de Jouvenel's argument, they reveal the same dichotomy between the spiritual and the material at work. Koenigsberger and Abrams

14 Ibid., 130.

15 Ibid.

16 Ibid., 140.

17 Ibid., 144–145.

18 Ibid., 145.

19 Ibid., 146.

found sovereignty threatened in South Asia because squatting undermined the idea of the common good. It promoted individualist gain at the cost of the shared:

> [S]quatting has often come to be an enterprise in itself, and poverty, guile and opportunism compete for the prizes that lawlessness offers. When squatters have begun to feel greater security in their possession, optimism vies with despair and odd evidences of affluence manifest themselves amid the squalor; speculation and turnover increase and as the vested illusion of right begins to ripen, it commands a cash price.[20]

*This* speculation is not entrepreneurial, for it is not founded on the idea of the common good. Even at the poorest level of the society, individualistic interests benefit at the expense of others.

For the other, desired type of speculation and turnover in property to take hold, one that can be properly called investment, the two vectors of the common good and individual interest must be aligned in a society. Inattention to the squatter's "motivation" was, the two experts asserted, one of the fundamental causes of the irresolution of the squatting problem in Pakistan: "The past policy of blindness to the motivating causes of population movements has provided an open invitation to squatting."[21]

Yet, the search for this "motivation" is interrupted before it is inaugurated. The heterogeneity of the causes, their thick boundary, cannot be accommodated in the calculus of development built on indexical choices. Rather, squatter motivation is buried in time, by declaring all its manifestations as *transitory*. This verdict was announced from the Gold Coast. This country, stressed Abrams and Koenigsberger,

> is undergoing a period of social and economic transition which makes it extremely difficult, if not impossible, to set standards of minimum housing requirements that would be uniformly applicable or which would survive the impacts of migration and other economic developments now unforeseen but inevitable [emphasis added].[22]

De Jouvenel had deployed the idea of the Christian spirit to identify and resolve the problem of the union of the individual and the collective. In the development context, that problem is circumvented and resolved by a *deus ex machina*: systems. In his report on land reform for the Ford Foundation titled, *Infrastructure Problems of the Cities of Developing Countries*, Koenigsberger would define systems as the most critical, as well as the most precarious, element of Third World urbanization:

> There is a need to design urban *systems* which respond both to the resources available in various countries and to the different time scales of potential change in these resources. That is: Urban infrastructure systems need to be designed to fit the income levels of different countries, taking account of the ways in which incomes are likely to change *over time* [emphasis mine].[23]

Systems do indeed appear to be akin to the spirit. But their function is different and that difference must be noted: in de Jouvenel's account, the individualized collective spirit figures as the *cause* of a unifying agency. There might

20 *A Housing Program for the Philippine Islands*, 30–31.

21 *A Housing Program for Pakistan with Special Reference to Refugee Rehabilitation*, 18.

22 *Report on Housing in the Gold Coast*, 44.

23 Otto Koenigsberger et al., *Infrastructure Problems of the Cities of Developing Countries*, 1. Koenigsberger here is citing David E. Bell, "Establishing Centers for Research, Development, and Application in Developing Countries," *Ekistics* 30, no. 179 (October 1970): 321–322.

as well also be systems that stem from that spirit. These systems figure as effects of this cause whose origin is transcendental. In the development arena—and at this point we are talking about the generalized framework of an argument that was made by Abrams and Koenigsberger from the Gold Coast to Pakistan to the Philippines over a decade—the inhabitant cannot lay claim to that agency. Her intentions are displaced by system as spirit. Here the system, instead of being an effect, figures as the cause, performing the same function as the spirit in time, anticipating the possibilities of all variations, all changes, ahead of time.

The question of housing then appears in the development arena both as a site of recognizing agency and a foreclosure of that invitation. This duality is necessary to posit the inhabitant as both the agent and the subject of development. As an agent of the development, the inhabitant encounters the house as the site of creativity, initiative, incentive, investment, and productivity. This agency relieves the expert of the burden of identifying the origin, the standard, or the capital needed for planning. This invitation, however, cannot be carried out. The inhabitant who appears at the door cannot be recognized as the guest. Her creativity is polemical and polyvalent. It resists being incorporated into the indexical divisions of the city, the village, the rural, the urban, or even housing and family. This complexity must be displaced or replaced, in time, by invoking transitions and systems. The variants of housing we have discussed in this paper allow the experts to both be relieved of the responsibility of planning and yet be able to plan. The plan, instead of being an instrument of organizing space, becomes one of organizing time.

With the Soviet invasion of Afghanistan in the 1979, the militarized politics of South Asia expanded onto a new scale. The US supported the military government of General Zia-ul-Haq to pass arms to the anti-Soviet factions, the *mujahidins*, in Afghanistan. The military regime, however, armed the *mohajir* movement too to gain a stronghold in Karachi. This policy backfired and the two militarized fronts, the national and the regional, the *mohajir*s and the *mujahidins*, twin echoes of a collision between religious temporality and political space, came to face each other on a hilltop at the outskirts of Karachi.

As the Soviet forces retreated, many of the *mujahidin* joined the stream of Afghan refugees who were migrating to Karachi in search of work, rather than returning to their war-torn country. All of a sudden, Karachi's *mohajir*s had other major groups vying for power. These groups, identifying as ethnically Pushtun, organized under the banner of the ANP (Awami National Party) and formed a closely-linked settlement on a hill called *Manjhopir Pahari* (mountain) overlooking the strongholds of the major *mohajir* political party, the MQM, the Muttahida Qaumi Movement (United National Movement).

The ANP foot soldiers, hardened by a decade of war, had brought back munitions that matched those of the MQM forces. With shifting political alliances and a precarious relationship to governance and power, small skirmishes turned into full-fledged armed conflict, the scale of which had not been witnessed in the city before. In 1986, several Pushtun families were found murdered in their homes on *Manjhopir Pahari*. The ANP retaliated, firing rocket-propelled grenades and sniper bullets from the heights into the neighborhood below. What unfolded over the next decade was a precise yet

Laurent Gayer, "Overlooking the MQM stronghold of Qasba Colony, one of the final destinations of the 'refugees' Abrams and Koenigsberger proposed to settle, as seen in 2011 from the heights of the Kati Paharl (split mountain)," 2011. Courtesy of the author.

elusive calculus of political alliances and criminal enterprise which escaped both logics of governance and geopolitics.

As the 1990s drew to a close, the MQM found itself in the favor of yet another military government, this time under General Pervaiz Musharraf, that would stay in power, and in US favor, for a long decade after the September 11, 2001, attacks in New York. Enjoying a period of power over the ANP in 2005, the young newly-elected MQM-supported mayor of Karachi, Mustafa Kamal, sought to undercut the ANP hold on the infamous hill by repeating a high modernist planning strategy: during the 1960's, another military government (under General Ayub Khan), with USAID's help, had cut through the few stubborn hills that cropped up from the desert surrounding Karachi to construct Pakistan's first high-speed road. Called the "Superhighway," the road ran some one hundred celebrated miles between Karachi and its distant sister city, Hyderabad. Large stretches of highway appeared as if a gigantic hand of modernity had drawn a straight line between the two cities, leveling the hills. The Superhighway became symbolic of the promises of modernity, development, and cosmopolitanism that often led to proclamations of Karachi as the "Paris of Asia" in the 1960s. Kamal invoked this modernist vision from Karachi's

**Front-page news reports on the deadly 1986 Mohajir-Pakhtun riots in Karachi, Urdu daily newspaper, *Jang*, June 1st, 1986.**

24 See Laurent Gayer, "The Battle for Karachi: Changing Patterns of a Permanent Civil War," in Ravi Kalia ed., *Pakistan's Political Labyrinths: Military, Society and Terror* (London: Routledge, 2016), 106–124. Also see Laurent Gayer, *Karachi: Ordered Disorder and the Struggle for the City* (New York: Oxford University Press, 2014).

storied past to control the present. Proposing a highway that cut through the ANP-controlled hill, the MQM government sought to both connect its low-lying neighborhoods with the industrial areas beyond as well as disrupt the movement of ANP forces on the heights overlooking its headquarters. The project was bulldozed through at a lightning pace compared to other infrastructural schemes in the city.[24]

The now bisected *Manjhopir Pahari*, which from then on acquired the name, *Kati-piharhi* (split mountain), did, at first, undercut the ANP strongholds, interrupting the easy movement of munitions around the area. The project also allowed the *mohajir* population to encroach on the heights. Yet, very soon, as the MQM once again lost its hold on power with the fall of Musharraf's military government, the cleaved hill turned into an the abyss that expelled all the ghosts of the past. One side of the hill came to be occupied by the Pashtuns and the other by the *mohajir*s, with bullets now exchanged across the gap. Instead of a gateway to the future, the gap in the hill became a political traffic jam of the present, exposing the residue that decades of national and geopolitical calculations had tried to cover up with their different blueprints.

If one were to risk climbing up the *split mountain* and look below, one would not see Abrams and Koenigsberger's loan-built roofs that once, like shards of broken glass, reflected the sun throughout the *mohajir* neighborhood. Today, those tin structures, which were to align intention and modernity under their shadows, have been replaced everywhere by makeshift concrete frame multistory buildings and concrete block houses. But these new building typologies are a sum of more than the bricks that lay fallow in the streets. They embody a flexibility of politics that could not be captured by flexible financing thought up by flexible minds through narratives of pliable labor and participatory development. Architectural figurations are instruments of claiming sense, summoning muteness of materiality to attest to the expanse of planned thought. Yet thought never flows uninterrupted, and when its echoes return, they might be holding a gun.

# Provisional Demos:
# The Spatial Agency of Tent Cities

Mabel O. Wilson

In the colonies, the economic substructure is also the superstructure.
The cause is the consequence: you are rich because you are white;
you are white because you are rich.[1]
—Frantz Fanon, *The Wretched of the Earth*

Over the past few years, the domes of hundreds of bright red, yellow, blue, and green camping tents have been seen clustered along train tracks, on the edges of highways, below underpasses, and on the land adjacent to border fences. These tent cities form temporary domiciles erected by thousands of political and economic refugees in all the corners of the world. These improvised settlements are the residue of failed global economic development policies from the mid-twentieth century onward. The thin membranes of fabric that offer marginal protection against cold, wind, and rain have arisen along the paths followed by legions of refugees fleeing civil strife in the Middle East and Africa, as bottlenecks at border control stations have produced states of limbo, conditions of having neither arrived nor departed. Tent cities not only house those fleeing political turmoil, but have also become the semi-permanent homesteads for homeless individuals and families, economic refugees who have borne the brunt of the waves of foreclosures and layoffs across the United States in recent years. Tent cities often form outside the oversight of international humanitarian refugee camps or official state detention centers, and against the legal designation of land-use defined by local zoning laws. When non-citizens and poor residents are placed under the supervision of NGOs such as the United Nations High Commission for Refugees (UNCHR) or various religious organizations, their status is nonetheless determined by racial and class differences that disempower them within the various nation-states in which they dwell or through which they pass.[2]

These communities of tents—enclosures fabricated from lightweight nylon designed to be portable for activities of leisure and sport—convey the precariousness of domesticity lived out of backpacks and duffle-bags. But does itinerancy necessarily foreclose political claims to secure more permanent housing, employment, and other rights associated with belonging to a state, whether short-term or long-term? Could a provisional demos, a temporary commons of the people formed within tent cities, assign agency and leverage collective action for economic and political refugees; or is it precisely the tent's lightness, its negligible footprint, that in part contributes to the refusal on the part of the state and cities to commit to long-term settlement?

[1] Frantz Fanon, *The Wretched of the Earth* (New York: Grove Press, 1963), 40.

[2] Michel Agier, "Humanity as an Identity and Its Political Effects (A Note on Camps and Humanitarian Government)," *Humanity: An International Journal of Human Rights, Humanitarianism, and Development* 1, no. 1 (Fall 2010): 29–45.

"Aerial view of migrant tent city in Idomeni, Greece." March 2016. Sceenshot courtesy of Drone Media Studio.

What can tent cities in the past tell us about how these temporary formations might function as sites of political action?

## Resurrecting Rights for the Poor

Tent cities have a long history as sites of political protest. The recent Occupy movement, begun when protestors took over Zuccotti Park in lower Manhattan, represents the politically motivated temporary settlement of an urban space.

"Occupy protester camp in Frankfurt, just hours before its removal." August 7, 2012. Courtesy of Author.

Inspired by the Arab Spring movement, this occupation of a privately-owned public space in 2011, raised collective objections to the hegemony of global financial markets and the invasive spread of economic inequality aided by government complicity. Occupy Wall Street spawned similar protest encampments in many parts of the world—including San Francisco, London, Frankfurt, Tel Aviv, Hong Kong, and Porte Alegre, Brazil. Earlier formations of tent cities that, like the Occupy Movement, promoted specific political agendas can offer important lessons to the most recent waves of temporary settlements about the challenges to rights posed by racial and class differences and how tent city denizens might engage forms of political agency.

In May of 1968, civil rights activists erected a monumental tent city on the National Mall in Washington, D.C. Although major victories had been won in the mid-1960s to secure voting rights for African Americans and fight racial segregation, the problems of poor housing, inadequate medical care, hunger, and joblessness did not disappear. This particular protest, launched by African-American groups but joined by a multi-racial coalition, cast public scrutiny on how racial discrimination produced economic precariousness and sustained inequality.

The widely circulated call for participation in the mass multi-phased protest focused on the fundamental inequities in America's economic and political processes:

> Many nations that are poorer than rich America provide decent incomes and services for all poor people. America spends 10 times as much money on military power as it does on welfare. The government subsidizes big companies and farms, and gives tax favors to rich people, but punishes the poor. American spends more money in one month to kill in Vietnam than it spends in a year for the so-called "war on poverty."[3]

3 Southern Christian Leadership Conference, *The Poor People's Campaign* (Georgia: Atlanta, 1967). See http://www.crmvet.org/docs/68_sclc_ppc_brochure.pdf. Accessed June 17, 2016.

4 Ibid.

This statement was a withering assessment about how war profiteering and income disparity—also an accurate description of the U.S.'s current political and economic state—had misdirected priorities away from the underserved. This document framed the issues at the core of what was called the "Poor People's Campaign." The campaign was organized by the Southern Christian Leadership Conference (SCLC), a key civil rights organization, and Dr. Martin Luther King Jr., who envisioned the campaign as a continuation of his unprecedented March for Jobs and Freedom in 1963 which led to the passage of the Voting Rights and Civil Rights acts of the mid-1960s.

For King, the SCLC, and other activist groups—including the more radical Student Nonviolent Coordinating Committee (SNCC)—the first goal was to build a tent city, which became known as "Resurrection City," on the National Mall between the Washington Monument and the Lincoln Memorial. The presence of these tents would make visible the plight of the nation's poor and raise from the dead the rights of American's living in poverty. While clearly invested in overturning the devastating economic marginalization of black Americans, the Poor People's Campaign recruited "young and old, jobless fathers, welfare mothers, farmers and laborers. We are Negroes, American Indians, Puerto Ricans, Mexican-Americans, poor white people." The campaign aimed to recruit men and women from around the country to convene in Washington, D.C. where

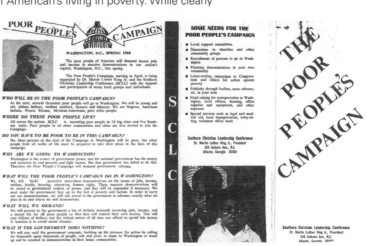

"Poor People's Campaign brochure." Civil Rights Movement Veterans.

Oliver Atkins, "Aerial view of Resurrection City."
Courtesy of Special Collections Research Center,
George Mason University Libraries.

Paul Sequeira, "Activists constructing plywood
A-frame tents of Resurrection City." May 1968.
© Getty Images.

**5** See Jordan Weissman,
"Remembering Marting
Luther King, Jr.'s
Solution to Poverty,"
*Atlantic Monthly*
20 (January 2014).
Accessed online http://
www.theatlantic.
com/business/
archive/2014/01/
remembering-
martin-luther-king-
jrs-solution-to-
poverty/283193/ on June
17, 2016.

**6** For a detailed
account of the Poor
People's Campaign
see Gordon K. Mantler,
*Power to the Poor:
Black-Brown Coalition
and the Fight for
Economic Justice,
1960–1974* (Chapel Hill:
University of North
Carolina Press, 2013).
Accessed June 16, 2016.

they would lobby various agencies and politicians to end
the poverty that crippled, as the brochure had declared,
"35 million persons who do not have enough money for a
decent life."[4]

Dr. King was assassinated in April 1968 before the
Poor People's Campaign could commence. The protest
would have certainly been his most radical attack on the
structural racism that sustained the capitalist exploitation
of black men and women. He vociferously fought against
the ruthless usurpation of black labor and life that had built
the wealth of the United States from slavery through the
Jim Crow era of segregation. The campaign also launched
a counterattack on the underfunded and insufficient
policies of President Lyndon Johnson's War on Poverty, a
package of programs that took on as separate, rather than
interrelated, the problems of housing, work, education,
and health. King wanted to use the campaign to lobby
the government to provide income and work that would
guarantee the poor a middle-class existence. King boldly
demanded that "we must create full employment, we
must create incomes."[5] King and the campaign issued a
clarion call for government to be accountable to all of its
citizens and for those living in poverty to be counted as
political subjects rather than the abject poor.

In the wake of King's murder, the Poor People's
Campaign was led by the SCLC's Rev. Ralph Abernathy. People trekked from inner
city ghettos and back country farms to the nation's capital, with some arriving
by mule train to raise the visibility of their plight and encourage other people to
join the effort. In May 1968, some three thousand men, women, and children
of all ages descended on Resurrection City's temporary encampment. In a short
period of time, the tent city would sprout twenty-eight hundred A-frame structures constructed of wood, canvas, and plastic, designed by a team led by
Washington, D.C. architect John Wiebenson. Builders moored each tent to a
plywood platform so that it could be assembled and dismantled quickly, given
that the occupation of the National Mall was intended to last several weeks.[6]

By demanding "the right to a decent house and the free choice of
neighborhood," the symbolic expression of impoverishment by the placement
of tents on the National Mall drove home the structural inequalities of the housing market, a major hurdle to overcoming poverty. The predominantly black
residents of Resurrection City, as they settled into their temporary ad hoc
camp, set up a vibrant community by renaming the streets Poor Avenue and
other similar symbolic monikers. In big letters across the tent walls people
christened their sections "Soul City," "Funk City," and "Soulsville U.S.A." On the
abundant plywood surfaces, residents painted slogans of militancy, like "Black
Power," and solidarity, such as "Sisters of Watts for human dignity." Volunteers
set up kitchens, a commissary, and clinics to provide healthcare, food, sanita-
tion, and other services. A City Hall built out of plywood served as an important public forum and meeting place. Arriving from Oakland, the Black Panthers,
a militant group committed to black nationalist causes, claimed a presence

amid the many tents, which reveals the many different
conflicting positions within the campaign. The rhythms
of everyday life continued between the protests and
rallies as people shot pool and watched television,
and children played among the wood structures. There
were musical performances and educational classes,
along with intermittent acts of crime, which drew the
attention of the authorities and the ire of those who had
volunteered to maintain order in the tent city of three
thousand. Torrential rains in the first weeks turned the
ground into reddish brown muck but did not dampen
the protesters determination to call for an end to poverty and for recognition of the rights of poor people.

Henry Zbyszynski, "View of U.S. Capitol amid the tents of
Resurrection City." May 1968. Courtesy of Wikimedia Commons.

Organizers planned the Poor People's campaign to culminate in Solidarity
Day on June 19th, a day-long series of militant speeches calling for non-violent
actions around the country. More than fifty thousand people joined the residents of Resurrection City to rally for an "Economic Bill of Rights." The SCLC
had initiated the tent city as the first of three phases of demonstrations. The
second phase was intended to consist of nationwide mass protests and civil
disobedience. The third phase would involve a boycott of industry and commerce to force congressional action to alleviate the nation's crippling poverty.
However, before the latter two phases could commence, the first phase ended
in the violent displacement of the residents of Resurrection City. After forty-two
days and the expiration of the permit of occupation, over one thousand police
officers descended on the encampment on June 24th to remove the residents
by force. In response to a few people throwing rocks, along with other acts of
protest against intimidation, the police, already fearful of recent urban unrest
following King's assassination, resorted to tear gas and force to clear protestors
away from the site. Those who chose to remain in the camp were arrested.

The concentration of poor black bodies on the National Mall—members
of the families and communities that had been trapped in the inner city
and the rural hinterlands in order to keep the suburbs white and prosperous—proved to be a powerful disruption in the orderly symbolic space of
the National Mall, as intended by King and the SCLC. It should be noted that
Washington, D.C with a 70% African American population had its own problems of urban poverty and black political disenfranchisement with deep roots
in the city's history of slavery. Resurrection City—its tents, streets, and civic
sphere—formed a temporary *demos*: a commons for the disenfranchised
and the dispossessed. This commons—constructed within the National Mall,
the symbolic monumental public sphere of the United States whose museums and monuments celebrated the founding principles of liberty and equality—emphasized how the state and corporate interests had failed to sustain
the lives and well-being of poor Americans, especially those members of the
black and brown underclass.

## Subhumanity's Non-Place

In the era of mass civil-rights protests in the 1960s, many black and brown
peoples—those whom the Poor People's Campaign represented—lived in

decrepit apartments and ramshackle houses with no heat, peeling lead paint, pest infestation, and faulty plumbing. Amid these untenable living conditions of the inner city, many people did manage to build strong social bonds, including forming organizations that fought legal battles for better housing. These communities, however, were under constant of threat of removal and displacement by the scorched earth policies of urban renewal.

Given the American condition and the pervasiveness of racially-segregated poor neighborhoods throughout the world, one is confronted with the question: Why has modern poverty always been racialized?

In Europe, during the early modern period, the idea of race was predicated on the invention of "Man." "The Renaissance humanist's epochal redescription of the human," writes Sylvia Wynter, moved away from ecclesiastical conceptions that had allowed the Church and its clergy to rule the "lay world of Latin Christian Europe," and toward the "invention of Man as a political subject of the state."[7] It was the rise of the racial paradigm of human difference, made possible through Europe's colonial quest for commercial gain and territorial expansion, that produced the "empirical effects of which would be the 'rise of Europe' and its construction of 'world civilization' on one hand, and, on the other, African enslavement, Latin American conquest, and Asian subjugation."[8] The nation-state succeeded divine rule as the socio-political formation for the emergent rational self-determined "Man," who as the subject of modern society was also the creator of culture: shared but geographically-distinct values and practices.

Those who did not fit this paradigm were no longer just the cursed descendants of the Bible's Ham, but were placed under a "secular biological variant of Man." Native Americans, Africans, Indians, and Asians were labeled, according to Wynter's cogent analysis, as "sub-human," "sub-rational," "colonized non-white peoples." Based upon the scientific processes of evolution's natural selection, those living or descended from so-called primitive civilizations in Haiti, Brazil, India, and elsewhere were exploitable for their land and for their bio-power, their labor.[9] With the emergence of the modern scientific episteme that rationalized racial difference and the emergence of cultural formations that popularized racism and racial cast, those who possessed the phenotypical mark of black or brown skin continued to be designated as "subhuman." Their racialization made them unrepresentable in the nation-state formations that gave citizens their institutions, rights, and privileges such as decent housing, fair wages, and suffrage.[10]

These marginalized concentrations of poverty lived by black and brown peoples have continued to flourish in contemporary banlieues and favelas, in squats and bad buildings around the world. The proximity of these racial enclaves to valuable urban centers has made them ripe for what geographer Neil Smith has referred to as "uneven development."[11] With the rise of the neoliberal city fueled by surplus capital investment in real estate and facilitated by the liberalization of the land market, waves of gentrifying whites have moved back to cities where the once threatening black and brown bodies have been displaced (by urban renewal), contained (through incarceration), or eliminated (by murder or social neglect). The devastation wrought in New Orleans by Hurricane Katrina offers one example of negligence by the state in ensuring viable living conditions for black communities. The local, state, and federal government's failure to adequately protect New Orleans' low-lying

**7** Sylvia Wynter, "Unsettling the Coloniality of Being/Power/Truth/Freedom: Towards the Human, After Man, Its Overrepresentation—An Argument," *The New Centennial Review* 3, no. 3 (Fall 2003): 263.

**8** Ibid.

**9** Wynter, p 307.

**10** For an excellent historical example of how black slaves and freed people could not be represented as citizens but only as property, see Jefferson's analysis of natural conditions and the human transformation of Virginia in *Notes on the State of Virginia*. See http://avalon.law.yale.edu/18th_century/jeffvir.asp. Accessed June 24, 2016.

**11** See Neil Smith, *New Urban Frontiers: Gentrification and the Revanchist City* (New York and London: Routledge, 1996) and David Harvey, *Rebel Cities: From the Right to the City to the Urban Revolution* (New York: Verson, 2013).

poor neighborhoods—where families had lived in substandard housing stock for decades—from the threat of catastrophic floods posed the first danger. The deluge of waters caused by the breeching of the levees during the storm, followed by the government's abject failure to rescue stranded black residents, proved to be the second great danger. Rather than save lives, local police forces murdered people trying to flee the floods or simply trying to survive the catastrophe.[12] This elimination of black life by neglect and murder, but also by displacement, as witnessed in the forced migration of many black families to other cities, created new swathes of available land for either market-rate development or aesthetic reclamation as parkland.

Warren K. Leffler, "Protestors marching for Poor People's Campaign in Washington, D.C." June 18, 1963. U.S. News and World Report Magazine Photograph Collection, Library of Congress, LC U9-19271-33A.

## Precarity Normalized

In today's tent cities, the personal tent reduces the architecture of the tent city to an architecture of privately-owned structures. This condition is what Andrew Herscher has identified as "voucher humanitarianism," in which "the refugee camp is privatized, its functions distributed across city-as-such, no matter its condition," with the effect of "normalizing precarity."[13] Efforts by private corporations such as IKEA to solve, for example, the need for refugee housing blurs the distinctions between humanitarianism and consumerism. The lightweight construction of the nylon tent leaves a very different kind of footprint on the land in comparison to the heavy wooden structures of canvas and plastic that were built for the Poor People's campaign.

Living in today's "archipelago of Human Otherness," as Wynter has written, "the jobless, the homeless, the poor, the systemically made jobless and criminalized" have been exiled by racialized economic and political forces that keep these populations constantly on the move.[14] In the case of Europe, the build-up of encampments at the borders maintains the conditions of displacement where settlements form away from the central public spheres. Those fleeing conflict—disputes fueled in part by European and American military interventions in the Middle East and Africa—are not citizens in the nations where their tent cities arise. They have become the stateless, wards of the vast NGO and humanitarian economy that oversees 65.3 million displaced people worldwide.[15]

The precarious relationship of the tent to land is the outcome of centuries of implementing a racialized world order that began with Europe's colonial expeditions for territory and resources. What the Resurrection City does offer is a lesson for how a temporary demos, a commons for all, including non-citizens, can be a place where shared causes can be articulated, demands can be formulated, and action can be taken.

12 For an investigative report on police misconduct during Hurricane Katrina and its aftermath, see the extensive report by Propublica, "Law and Disorder: After Katrina, New Orleans Police Shot Frequently and Asked Few Questions." See https://www.propublica.org/nola

13 Andrew Herscher, "Humanitarianism's Housing Question: From Slum Reform to Digital Shelter," E-flux Journal 66 (October 2015): 9. Accessed September 15, 2015.

14 Wynter, p. 321.

15 See the UNHCR report at http://www.unhcr.org/en-us/figures-at-a-glance.html, accessed June 25, 2016.

# Peace in the Valley

Thomas Keenan

> In 1956, when I was only ten, Hungarian relief was very big. Our school had a jar for you to donate what money we could. Usually the change after you bought your lunch. The jar was sitting next to the cash register so when you paid for your lunch, you would drop the change into the jar. I remember it well, when Ed [Sullivan] said Elvis was supporting the Hungarian relief, well, my lunch became a little lighter so I would have more change to put in the jar.
> —Unnamed commenter on "Elvis Insiders" forum[1]

1 Cited in an article on the website of the First Hungarian Elvis Presley Fanclub: "Elvis és az 1956-os magyar segítségnyújtás" [Elvis and 1956 Hungarian relief], posted 06/10/2013 –11:22, http://elvisklub.hu/?q=content/elvis-%C3%A9s-az-1956-os-magyar-seg%C3%ADts%C3%A9gny%C3%BAjt%C3%A1s. I'm grateful to Ariella Azoulay and Bonnie Honig for the invitation to think about the question "what is a refugee crisis?" in terms of a "media object," and for the rich day they organized at Brown University in March 2016 on that question.

2 Michel Foucault, "Pouvoir et savoir," interview with S. Hasumi, October 1977, in Dits et Écrits (1954–1988): III. 1976–1979 (Paris: Gallimard, 1994), 401.

It was in 1956, Michel Foucault once told an interviewer, that the problem of power as such ("dans sa nudité") became apparent to him and those of his generation. Fascism had been defeated, and Stalinism was dying. But in 1956, "something fundamental happened," he said. "The Hungarians revolted in Budapest, the Russians intervened and Soviet power, although it was no longer driven by economic necessity, reacted as we saw. "Like the French war in Algeria, "it was a matter of mechanisms of power that somehow ran by themselves."[2]

We are still living in the shadow of the events of 1956. Perhaps this condition is more obvious in the case of France and Algeria, which seems like an unfinished story with the *Charlie Hebdo* and Bataclan massacres as only the latest chapters. But Hungary is also part of our present, even if in a less obvious way. The mechanisms of power in question there were not simply the military, bureaucratic, or imperial ones of the Communist regime and its Soviet backers, but also the ones arrayed on the other side of the Cold War curtain. And those were likewise not simply governmental: in the aftermath of that military reaction in Budapest, an unlikely and often fractious network of allies—public and private, governmental and non-governmental, local and global, media and pop-cultural—emerged to respond. We need to consider all of these together as a matter of power.

There was no counter-intervention in Budapest—the NATO armies did not flood across the Austrian border to support the uprising. In fact, the flood came in the opposite direction: refugees took advantage of the open border and fled the crackdown. And another response to political repression emerged on the global stage—another form of power to be sure, but one whose unfolding was not entirely commanded by the state and whose dimension of civic solidarity should not be neglected. The "humanitarian" response to what was even then described as a "refugee crisis" can tell us something today, especially about the possibilities of intervening in situations that are, indeed, saturated with politics and with mechanisms of power that somehow run by themselves. They still offer, though, openings, sometimes very significant ones, for initiatives that negotiate with governments and authorities in the name of something else: rights, justice, aid, refuge, and so on. At the height of the Cold War, in one of its hottest moments, an array of actors worked together, sometimes well and sometimes in tension, to shelter hundreds of thousands of people in flight. These actors—powerful states and their militaries, churches and non-governmental organizations, the ICRC and the UN agencies, the media, foundations, universities, and even the icons of popular culture—all found themselves on the side of "Hungarian relief."

Refugees from the Failed Hungarian Revolution on an Airplane to the United States, 1957. US Information Agency.

In June 1956, the *New York Times* finally broke the story of the events of the 20th Congress of the Soviet Communist Party in February. First Secretary Nikita Khrushchev's speech marked an epochal break with, and denunciation of, the repression of the Stalinist period. Four months after the story appeared, in late October, Hungarian students took to the streets of Budapest, and their protests spread quickly across the county. In little more than a week, they succeeded in bringing about the fall of the regime and began negotiations with the USSR for the withdrawal of its forces. Within another week, however, the Soviet leaders rethought their decision and launched a major military intervention. The uprising was crushed by the third week.

But the borders stayed open for much longer, and, in the period between October 1956 and February 1957, roughly 200,000 Hungarians fled the country, most of them to Austria. Some were fighters and others political dissenters, but most, it seems, simply wanted to escape to a better life. As Gil Loescher and John Scanlan note, in their superb study of postwar responses by the United States to refugees, *Calculated Kindness*, "most of the Hungarians who fled their homeland in 1956 and 1957 possessed no well-founded fear of persecution and were not technically refugees when they left Hungary…. Yet the reaction to [them] did not turn on the distinction between the merely dissatisfied and the patently fearful."[3] Nations around the world welcomed them, including their Western European neighbors, led by the UK, West Germany, Switzerland, and France, but also including a number of Latin American countries and, in particular, two North American countries. Canada ultimately resettled some 37,000 Hungarians, and more than 38,000 eventually came to the United States, more than any other country. Loescher and Scanlan suggest that "the reasons for such generosity were largely similar" around the world: "One study of their reception in the United States concluded that 'the Hungarians were viewed as heroes, easily the most popular group of refugees in American history, because of their battle with Communism.'"[4]

Of course, for much of the second half of the 20th century, refugees in the United States were virtually synonymous with fighting Communism. This too started in 1956. Bill Frelick has noted "the pervasive bias in US refugee and asylum policy" during the Cold War, namely that it was effectively "limited to people fleeing communist-dominated regimes or the Middle East….

3 Gil Loescher and John A. Scanlan, *Calculated Kindness: Refugees and America's Half-Open Door, 1945 to the Present* (NY: The Free Press, 1986), 52.

4 Ibid.

An ICEM resettlement officer briefs a family of escapees about their resettlement to the United States, Austria, 1957. International Organization for Migration.

Secretary with telegrams pledging over $100,000 to International Rescue Committee. *New York World-Telegram & Sun* photo by Ed Ford, Nov. 8, 1956.

5 Bill Frelick, "No Place To Go: Controlling Who Gets In," in Carole Kismaric, *Refugees: The Agony of the Refugee in Our Time* (New York: Random House, 1989), 165.

6 Stephen Ross Porter, "Defining Public Responsibility In A Global Age: Refugees, NGOs, And The American State," (Ph.D. diss., Dept. of History, University of Chicago, June 2009), vol. 1, p. 247.

Of the 1,027,497 refugees paroled into the United States between the time of the 1956 Hungarian Revolt and 1979, only 2,000—less than 0.3 percent—were from noncommunist countries." [5]

As historian Stephen Ross Porter argues, "the US response to the Hungarian crisis of 1956 was the country's defining international humanitarian aid initiative during the height of the Cold War."[6] And not simply because of its politics, size, complexity, or the relative efficiency of the response. Aaron Levenstein, in his insider account of the history of the International Rescue Committee, which played a leading role in the events of 1956–57, goes as far as to claim that, "in a very important way, the character of refugee aid had been changed by the Hungarian Revolution. Once the preoccupation of a handful, it had now become the concern of many. Something new had been brought into the awareness of the average American."[7]

The story of this remarkable welcome involves a mixture of elements that will seem familiar today. Drawing from the handful of scholars who have studied this underappreciated moment, we can summarize them quickly under five major headings:

**1 — Conflict media.** Near real-time television coverage of the Hungarian revolt, the Soviet response, and the ensuing flight, helped construct a strong frame for public opinion. "During the height of the uprising, the American television audience had been provided with same-day coverage of students hurling paving stones and Molotov cocktails at Soviet tanks," write Loescher and Scanlan.[8] Or, as historian Carl Bon Tempo puts it: "For two weeks, the story of the revolution and the bravery and fate of the resistance fighters led the news. Reporting in the *New York Times* and the *Washington Post* easily mingled facts, half-truths, and rumors, but a compelling picture emerged," one that centered around the story of "the Hungarian revolutionaries [who] valiantly fought for their freedom against a mighty Soviet military."[9]

**2 — Humanitarianism.** US propaganda and a small covert action program had encouraged the uprising, but President Eisenhower chose not to follow through with more substantial support after the rebellion began. Thus the US government found itself "providing refugee relief in lieu of the military aid that had been withheld."[10] And not only the government: within just a few days of the uprising's beginning, and in the knowledge that the US would not

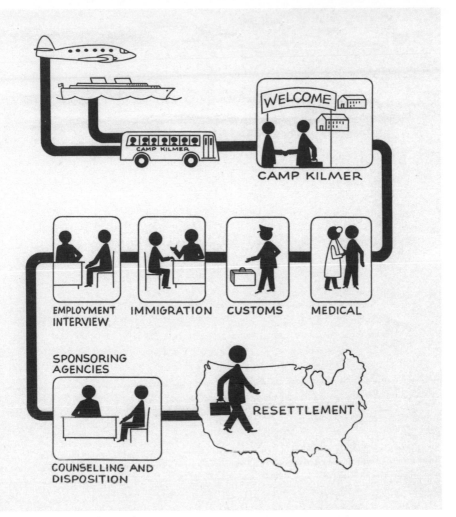

**"Kilmer Reception and Resettlement Procedure. The President's Committee for Hungarian Refugee Relief, "Prospectus for Kilmer Operation," 1956.**

intervene, private organizations began relief efforts. These too made use of the media. Already on October 29th and 30th, *New York Times* headlines read "American Medical and Food Help Starts Via the Red Cross to Rebels of Hungary" and "Austrian Relief Goes to Hungary," reporting "tremendous interest abroad in the humanitarian effort undertaken here" and noting in particular the initiatives of Leo Cherne and Angier Duke Biddle of the International Rescue Committee (IRC), among the most prominent and certainly the most media-savvy of the humanitarian organizations involved, to carry hastily-gathered antibiotics and themselves to Budapest.[11]

**3 — Governmental and non-governmental politics.** The "refugee crisis" sparked an unprecedented, coordinated, governmental and non-governmental partnership in providing relief aid. This effort involved, first, the opening of a

**7** Aaron Levenstein, *Escape to Freedom: The Story of the International Rescue Committee* (Westport and London: Greenwood Press, 1983), 63.

**8** Loescher and Scanlan, *Calculated Kindness*, 52.

**9** Carl J. Bon Tempo, *Americans at the Gate: The United States and Refugees during the Cold War* (Princeton: Princeton University Press, 2008), 65.

**10** Loescher and Scanlan, *Calculated Kindness*, 54.

**11** "American Medical and Food Help Starts Via the Red Cross to Rebels of Hungary," *New York Times*, October 29, 1956, 9; Henry Giniger, "Austrian Relief Goes to Hungary," *New York Times*, October 30, 1956, 17; Andrew F. Smith, *Rescuing the World: The Life and Times of Leo Cherne* (Albany: SUNY Press, 2002), 58–59; see also Leo Cherne, "Thirty Days that Shook the World," *The Saturday Review*, 22 December 1956, 22–23, 31

**12** Bon Tempo, *Americans at the Gate*, 70.

**13** Ibid., 68.

**14** Smith, *Rescuing the World*, 73.

**15** Loescher and Scanlan, *Calculated Kindness*, 59. Arthur A. Markowitz, "Human-itarianism versus Restrictionism: The United States and the Hungarian Refugees," *The International Migration Review* 7, no. 1 (Spring, 1973): 49.

**16** Porter, "Defining Public Responsibility," vol. 1, p. 285.

**17** Ibid., 298.

major loophole in the otherwise strict and restrictive US immigration regulations, with Eisenhower allowing "the attorney general to admit (or 'parole') an alien into the United States on an emergency basis if the admission served the public interest,"[12] and a spectacular fast-track clearance program, which meant that, as Bon Tempo writes, "getting a Hungarian from the queue [in Austria] to an airplane bound for the United States took about four days."[13] "These refugees," Cherne's biographer Andrew Smith writes, "were flown to the United States in Operation Safe Haven, the largest airlift since the Berlin blockade."[14] Second, there was a concerted private and NGO-led effort to resettle refugees. Much of the massive reception center at Camp Kilmer in New Jersey was, according to Loescher and Scanlan, "staffed by volunteers, and they had virtually no difficulty finding sponsors or job opportunities for the migrants entrusted to their care. The entire program was almost completed in 90 days."[15] Porter notes that "the private agencies licensed by the federal Advisory Committee on Voluntary Foreign Aid raised approximately $20 million from their fundraising appeals," an astonishing amount even today.[16]

**4 — Neutrality.** The Hungarian experience led to the emergence of a self-understanding among NGOs that, regardless of this spirit of cooperation and their obvious instrumentalization in the Cold War struggle, their efforts had a different character from those of the government. As Porter writes, in spite of the US government's investment in and growing competence at providing refugee relief, "what [US officials were] discovering, however, was that ma-turing right alongside the state had been the private agencies' organizational sophistication and the accompanying confidence that, while they might need to acquiesce to certain government oversight, the field of humanitarian aid should ultimately be the domain of ethically-based nongovernmental entities, not states."[17] A sense of the seriousness of the pushback can be gleaned from the fierce language of a *New York Times* editorial on November 28th en-titled "The Blunder of Camp Kilmer," which concludes: "Why was this turned into a show for the Army and bureaucracy, instead of its being the great, voluntary, civic operation it should have been—and can still become?"[18]

**5 — Publicity.** Concerned about the predictable isolationist backlash against the sudden influx of large numbers of refugees, Eisenhower's Hungarian relief czar Tracy Vorhees quietly (and privately) secured the services of both the Advertising Council and a leading public relations firm, Communications Counselors, to convert sympathy for the rebellion and antipathy towards Communism into a positive image for the Hungarian migrants. Martin Bursten, in his rich eyewitness account of the uprising and the relief efforts, *Escape From Fear*, notes this "radical departure from the usual government 'standard operating procedure,'" and commends the "spectacular publicity job. There was hardly a magazine, newspaper, radio program, or TV show that was not blanketed with effective and compelling material on the Hungarian project."[19] As Bon Tempo writes, "the Eisenhower administration and the voluntary agencies charged with refugee resettlement understood the need to blunt this criticism. In response, they undertook a concerted effort to 'sell' the Hungarian refugees to the general public as prospective citizens with

Hungarian refugees arriving at McGuire AFB, New Jersey. Still from "The Big Picture: Operation Mercy." US Army Signal Corps, Army Pictorial Service, 1956.

all of the qualities that 'good Americans' supposedly possessed in the late 1950s."[20] Communication Counselors' goal was, as they put it, to create "a great national desire to welcome and care for these refugees."[21]

The amazing story of this PR campaign deserves a much longer retelling—it included everything from a CARE-sponsored visit by American disk jockeys to refugees in Austria, to a *Life Magazine* article titled "They Pour in… And Family Shows Refugees Can Fit In," to the successful project of having the "Hungarian Freedom Fighter" named as *Time Magazine*'s 1956 Man of the Year—but to conclude I will select perhaps the strangest but most exemplary moment. I learned about it first in an almost offhand comment offered by Michael Ignatieff in a December 2015 piece on ISIS and the "refugee crisis." He wrote: "To bar refugees from US borders would allow the enemy to dictate the terms of the battle. The US has every reason—moral, humanitarian, and strategic—to refuse to give in to fear and to continue to provide refuge for those escaping barbarism." And to underline that this project is eminently achievable, he reminded us of Hungary: "Fear makes for bad strategy. A better policy starts by remembering a better America. In January 1957, none other than Elvis Presley sang a gospel tune called 'There Will Be Peace in the Valley' on 'The Ed Sullivan Show' to encourage Americans to welcome and donate to Hungarian refugees."[22]

Elvis Presley? The fall and winter of 1956–57 were not only notable for the Hungarian rebellion and its aftermath, but also for the explosion in American media of the extraordinary phenomenon that was Elvis Presley, and his celebrated appearances on the most popular live television program of the time, "The Ed Sullivan Show." Presley performed three times—in September, October, and January—and those appearances catapulted him into superstardom.[23]

At the end of Presley's second appearance, on October 28, five days after the uprising began in Budapest and as the UN Security Council debated the issue, Sullivan had, himself, closed the show with Hungary. "I've been asked by the Hungarian groups of our city to call your attention to the plight of the Hungarian people, who have been putting up this magnificent fight against the Commies over there. If you contact Mrs. Thomas B. Watson, she'll tell you how to help them out."[24] A week later, on November 4, Sullivan had allowed an emergency appeal from his live audience by the IRC's Cherne, who had just returned from his spectacular flying visit to Hungary. For a full four minutes, Cherne stood up "to tell the story of Hungary's glory and need," showing "a shredded and soiled flag with the hastily improvised red cross," and "Sullivan closed with an appeal for financial support for the IRC, asking viewers to send in at least a dollar apiece. The appeal generated $455,000 in donations, which was unprecedented in television history."[25]

Two months later, on January 6, 1957, with the Communications Counselors public relations campaign well underway, refugees pouring into New Jersey, and the guardians of moral purity up in arms about Presley's capacity to drive the teenage girls in his audience into a frenzy, Elvis made his third and final appearance on Sullivan's show, this time famously filmed only from the waist up. Presley historian Susan Doll sees the show as a decisive moment in the production of what she calls "the other Elvis," centered around support for charities and humanitarian engagements. She writes:

**Stills from Elvis Presley's performance of "Peace in the Valley," "The Ed Sullivan Show," CBS Television, Jan. 6, 1957.**

18 "The Blunder of Camp Kilmer" (editorial), *New York Times*, 20 November 1956, 34

19 Martin A. Bursten, *Escape From Fear* (Syracuse: Syracuse University Press, 1958), 163.

20 Bon Tempo, *Americans at the Gate*, 73.

21 Ibid., 77.

22 Michael Ignatieff, "The Refugees and the New War," *The New York Review of Books*, December 17, 2015.

23 The three shows are collected in *Elvis: The Ed Sullivan Shows*, three-DVD set (Image Entertainment, 2006), which is the source for all my quotations from the performances.

**24** For a summary of the entire show, see Sheila O'Malley, "Elvis Presley's 2nd Ed Sullivan Appearance: October 28, 1956," *The Sheila Variations* [blog], October 28, 2014, http://www.sheilaomalley.com/?p=45585.

**25** Smith, *Rescuing the World*, 68; see also Bursten, *Escape From Fear*, 43.

**26** Susan M. Doll, *Understanding Elvis: Southern Roots vs. Star Image* (New York and London: Garland Publishing, 1998), 91.

**27** Sean Michaels, "Elvis Presley to be named honorary citizen of Budapest," *The Guardian*, March 3, 2011.

**28** Lindsay Terry, "Story behind the song: 'Peace in the Valley,'" *The St. Augustine (Fl.) Record*, May 1, 2015 http://staugustine.com/living/religion/2015-05-01/story-behind-song-peace-valley#

"The final appearance on the Sullivan program was perhaps [Presley manager Colonel Tom] Parker's attempt to showcase this burgeoning side to Presley's image on a national scale."[26] The final song he sang that night was the gospel hit "Peace in the Valley," and in introducing it Sullivan noted that Presley would soon fly to California for, among other things, "a big Hungarian relief show" (which did not in fact occur). "But," said Sullivan, "because he feels so keenly, this young man feels so keenly about Hungarian relief, he urges all of us throughout the country to remember that immediate aid is needed. So long before his benefit show is put on, he wants to remind you to send in your checks to your various churches, Red Cross, etc. And now he's gonna sing a song. He feels that this is sort of in the mood that he'd like to create: 'Peace In the Valley.'"

Written in 1937 by one of America's most celebrated black gospel songwriters, Thomas Dorsey, originally for Mahalia Jackson, the song had been a country-and-western hit in 1951. Presley, backed by the four-man Jordanaires, performed it without any introduction of his own, and without visible instruments, but with a restrained, tightly-wound, intensity, his eyes often looking up and sometimes closed. He sang only the first stanza and the refrain, and the performance was finished in a minute and a half. The song conveys a passionate plea for deliverance—for relief, in fact—from weariness and trouble, and a prayer for a place free from "sadness and sorrow." The performance communicates feeling, but of a cool and controlled rather than a painful sort. It looks forward, with confidence, to the promise of peace.

Presley's appearance was rewarded in a number of ways. The appeal for "immediate aid" was met handsomely: one account suggests that it raised some $25 million Swiss francs for the ICRC.[27] Presley himself earned something valuable too. In closing the show, Sullivan offered Presley a handshake and his personal seal of approval: "I wanted to say to Elvis Presley and the country that this is a real decent, fine boy."

Years later, Dorsey told a journalist that the song, for all its Biblical spirituality, had decidedly political origins. They were not the obvious ones, either, however clear and deep the metaphors of slavery, suffering, and a longed-for emancipation are. Dorsey said: "It was just before Hitler sent his war chariots into Western Europe in the late 1930s. I was on a train going through southern Indiana and saw horses, cows and sheep all grazing together in this little valley. Everything seemed so peaceful. It made me question, 'What's the matter with mankind? Why can't men live in peace?' Out of those thoughts came 'Peace in the Valley.'"[28]

Relief is not the same as peace, of course, and whatever its political and ethical complexities, the Hungarian refugee program was a tactical move in the Cold War. But it was not simply that. The story of the welcome those refugees received reminds us that the field of power relations is always rich and differentiated, and that opportunities—for hospitality and solidarity, among other things—can arise at unexpected moments, and be seized by unlikely agents.

# Ašylūm and Șheļter Prŏyjsiōn
## in Torshov, Oslo

The *Torshov Transittmottak,* located in the borough of Sagene in Oslo, is a transit center run by Norwegian People's Aid. The facility has the capacity for two hundred asylum seekers, who are each assigned a bed and a locker in rooms that can accommodate from four to eight people. Defined by the legislation as a "basic/sparse but safe" space, shelter is provided through all the phases of the asylum granting process in receiving, transit, and ordinary centers. The asylum seekers are meant to stay in Torshov only during the resolution of their applications by the Norwegian Directorate of Immigration, which can last for several years. While staying in these centers is voluntary, the expansion of the resolution procedures eventually provides this transitory condition certain state of permanence.

The architectures that host asylum seekers render visible the entanglements between social concerns, policies, and legislation. In 2015, more than 31,000 individuals sought asylum in Norway. Coming from different locations, the shifting population at Torshov is an index of current international con-flicts, which are often replicated in the frictions provoked by the tight spatial standards; these are manifested in attempts to take control over televisions, radios, and the internet, as audiovisual content subverts the condition of the center as neutral soil. These facilities are now mostly operated by private commercial agents through short term contracts. Consequently, the concept of shelter is defined through spatial economies tied to the market.

From the design of their distributions and common spaces, to their participa-tion in the logics of the city, asylum seeker centers allows us to question the ways in which architecture provides what is conceived of as temporary shelter.

"Moments of Freedom," Asylum Seeker's Center in Oslo. Photograph by Javad Parsa, 2013. Courtesy of the author.

## The Orchard
Eriksen Skajaa Arkitekter

> *These counter-spaces [...] are well recognised by children. Certainly, it's the bottom*
> *of the garden; it's the Indian tent erected in the middle of the attic; or still, it's...*
> *on their parent's bed where they discover the ocean, as they can swim between*
> *the covers, and the bed is also the sky, or they can bounce on the springs; it's the*
> *forest as they can hide there; or still, it's night as they can become ghosts between*
> *the sheets and, finally, it's the fear and delight of their parents coming home [...]*
>
> — Michel Foucault, "Les hétérotopies," Radio Conference on France Culture
> (December 7, 1966).

The garden is both the whole world and outside the world.

The asylum centre at Torshov inhabits several buildings on former farmland
bought by a local teacher in 1877 in order to establish a school for mentally
disabled children. Today, the site and buildings are owned by a Norwegian
real-estate company that in the long term seeks to develop a large-scale
housing project on the plot. Some of the buildings, formerly used as student
dormitories, were leased by the asylum centre in 2004. The other buildings
are used as schools and pre-schools, as well as studios for artists and meeting spaces for local organisations. There is also a temporary housing barrack
at the north end of the area, mainly used by Portuguese guest workers. The
surrounding housing development is popular with the middle class, although
originally built as worker housing in the first quarter of the twentieth century.

On the eastern edge of the site, on a slope facing the Torshov Valley park,
there is an abandoned fruit orchard, uncared for and overgrown for reasons
unknown. The orchard is used by the residents at the centre as a free source
of fresh fruit, as an area for collective action, and as a retreat from daily life.
The orchard as a heterotopic space, using Michel Foucault's terminology,
is a space of otherness. This site can also be seen as a space where new
collectives become possible through the harvest.

In asylum seeker centres there is a dualism between the need for intimacy
and the need to take part in the complex's collective life. The orchard works
both as a collective space and a possible escape from the dense living
quarters in the facility, something that is both an outside and an inside, place
and non-place. The paradise, as in the perfect gardens of Eden, the Jewish
Pardes, and the Islamic Jannah, are places of perfection and harmony.
Could the orchard also be a single real place that juxtaposes several spaces,
a microcosm of different environments?

Project Team: Arild Eriksen, Joakim Skajaa, Cathrine Finnema, Joachim Haug, and Mattias Josefsson with Sullivan
Lloyd Nerdrum who had the idea for the apple press and Jorid Bertelsen from Norwegian People's Aid.

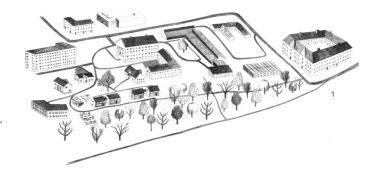

1  Eriksen Skajaa Arkitekter, *The apple orchard at Torshov reception centre,* a view of the centre and the apple orchard. © Eriksen Skajaa Arkitekter.

All other images are stills from the film "Eplepressen," 2015, Torshov. Photography by Christer Fasmer / Flimmer Film, © Eriksen Skajaa Arkitekter.

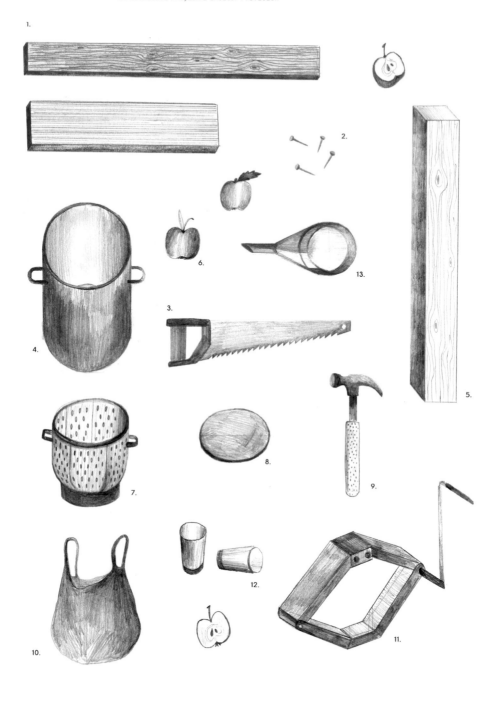

1. 2 X 2 PIECES OF WOOD APROX 100 CM   2. NAILS   3. SAW   4. BIG PAN   5. HEAVY POLE FOR MASHING APPLES
6. APPLES   7. SIEVE   8. LID THAT FITS THE SIEVE'S DIAMETER   9. HAMMER   10. PLASTIC BAG TO COLLECT JUICE
11. CAR JACK   12. GLASSES   13. FUNNEL

Eriksen Skajaa Arkitekter, *Tools for apple press*, Drawing showing the tools
and materials needed to build the apple press. © Eriksen Skajaa Arkitekter.

# Sheltering Tėmpörárıňěšs
## Works

## Monuments of the Everyday

**Sigil (Khaled Malas, Salim al-Kadi, Alfred Tarazi, Jana Traboulsi)**

The common conception of alchemy is that it is the art of transforming base substances into more valuable ones, such as the transmutation of waste into gold. Alchemy is a powerful art which is primarily articulated visually, much like architecture and its infrastructures. "Knowledge is power," we are told repeatedly, yet what specifically could this mean for an architect and citizen today? What powerful knowledge could one imagine being performed in these capacities? We seek a knowledge that is eloquent, critical, fearless, and dutifully applied. Such performances are sincere attempts to move away from the conceived and perceived spaces of mere imagery, illusion, and representation into the experienced spaces of action and performance. It is only then that knowledge attains its poetic, and thus truly revolutionary, potential. Charged with its newfoundpower, such knowledge transforms all landscapes and beings that come into direct or indirect contact with it. Acquiring multiple forms, and scattered within the contemporary catastrophe—detached and unknown to most from afar—such knowledge is present in Syria today.

The conditions, as one can easily imagine, are dire. Yet people have not lost hope. It is at this moment that one can recognize creative resistances in the face of tyranny and catastrophe. This empowering resistance originates within the everyday experiences of those who dare to diligently think and act differently. It is amongst these brave men and women that we have located our collaborators. Amongst other forms, this resistance is given material expression in a series of humble, sometimes invisible, rural and semi-rural architectures.

In Syria, where opposing forces turn land into the site of multiple cycles of excessive violence, the comprehension of past struggles in and for space and its meanings also becomes most essential. These projects stem from a firm conviction that architecture can perform a transmutational role and that it is capable of transcending the oft-unquestioned distinctions between building and monument. As such, these political projects attempt to forge new ways of building in accordance with the circumstances of the Syrian context today.

Project team: Sigil (Khaled Malas, Salim al-Kadi, Alfred Tarazi, and Jana Traboulsi) in collaboration with Yaseen al-Bushy (Architect and Photo Journalist, Istanbul); Abu Ali al-Kalamouni (Blacksmith, Eastern Ghouta); The Higher Commission for Civic Defence (Deraa, Syria).

Sigil, "Building the windmill." Photograph by Yaseen al-Bushy, July 2015.
Courtesy of the author.

203

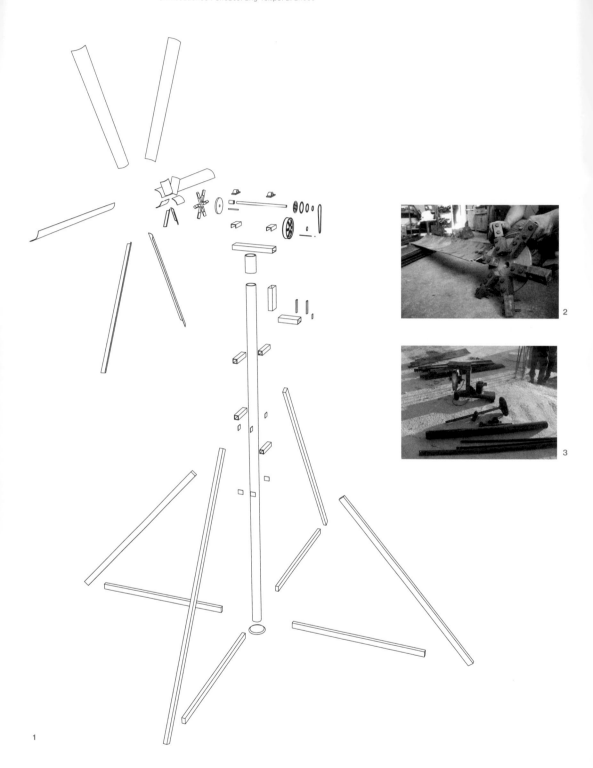

1

2

3

1  Sigil, "Exploded Windmill." Drawing by Eva Goula, February 2016. Courtesy of the author.
2–3  Sigil, "Building the windmill." Photograph by Yaseen al-Bushy, July 2015. Courtesy of the author.

## Welcome Hotel

estudio SIC | Vivero de Iniciativas Ciudadanas VIC
(Esaú Acosta, Mauro Gil-Fournier, Miguel Jaenicke)

The *Welcome Hotel* is a paradoxical place for the urban and social concentration of Madrid's evictions. A temporary accommodation not only for tourists, but also for political refugees, undocumented migrants and families that have been evicted from their homes. Even though there are more than 260,000 empty homes in Madrid, around 300,000 mortgages have been foreclosed on since 2009 in the city.

The socio-material process of evictions has composed an urban assemblage where different co-isolated entities mediate: banks, financial and vulture funds, legal and economic initiatives, government agencies, public institutions, and security forces. This process separates citizens from their material and affective homes, communities, and families. *Welcome Hotel* aims to describe how those co-isolated and connected entities form this urban assemblage.

In this context, the Platform of People Affected by Mortgage (Plataforma de Afectados por la Hipoteca, PAH)—a citizen initiative of resistance and action—defends the interests of residents from the banks that have been rescued with public money. The PAH is a self-organized platform and network that provides collective assistance and mutual support for the needs and lives of the members or any citizen.

There are also alternative networks that operate in Madrid after the evictions take place. New models of informal urbanism have emerged for evicted people—forward and back migrations, informal economic markets for squatting, circulation of objects from houses to storage spaces and digital selling platforms—unfolding affections that recapitalize the bodies and objects of the citizens.

The aim of this research is not only to render visible the evictions process and its complexities, but also to propose possible urban assemblages that respond to this new condition.

Spain's housing crisis. Photograph by Andres Kudacki, 2013 © The photographer.

Project team: Esaú Acosta, Mauro Gil-Fournier and Miguel Jaenicke with Poli del Canto, Jorge Pizarro, Miguel Cantoral, Domingo Arancibia, Donovan Theodore Gracias, Amelyn Ng, Juan Luis Pereyra, Raúl Alejandro Pérez, Thiago Pereira, Wala Saoul. Project in collaboration with PAH Madrid (Plataforma de Afectados por la Hipoteca). Special thanks to Carolina Pulido and Rafael Iván. The experiences of Marceline Rosero, Lamine Nunmke and Irene González are crucial to the "Welcome Hotel" research project.

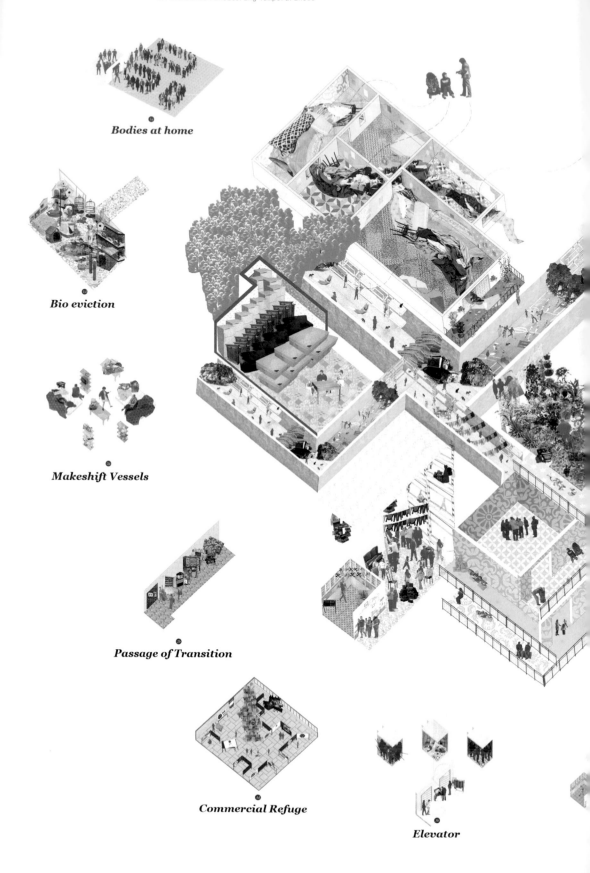

*Bodies at home*

*Bio eviction*

*Makeshift Vessels*

*Passage of Transition*

*Commercial Refuge*

*Elevator*

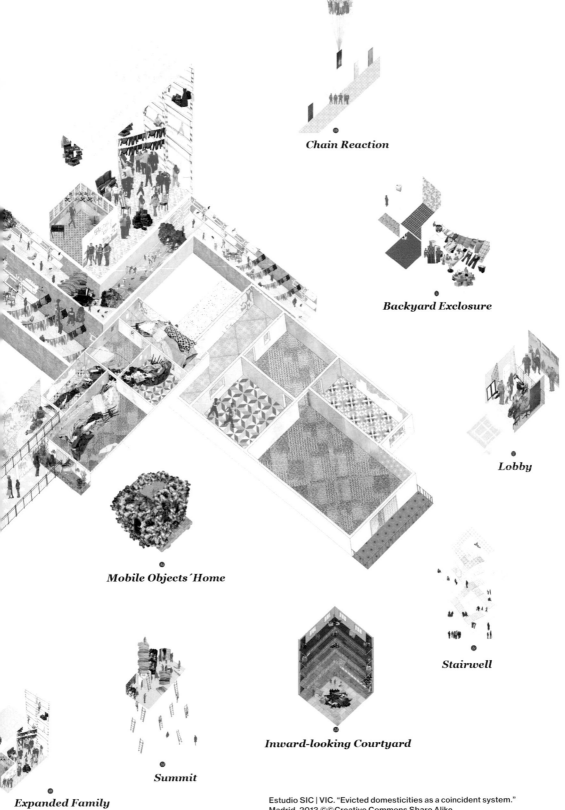

**Chain Reaction**

**Backyard Exclosure**

**Lobby**

**Mobile Objects´Home**

**Stairwell**

**Inward-looking Courtyard**

**Summit**

**Expanded Family**

Estudio SIC | VIC. "Evicted domesticities as a coincident system."
Madrid, 2013 ©© Creative Commons Share Alike.

## Autonomous Infrastructure: Forms of Decay

### Martha Rosler and Pelin Tan

Discussions of "infrastructure" have recently intensified and have become urgent when considering towns under curfew; cities experiencing urban warfare, siege, or natural disaster; and urbanized refugee camps. Creating a temporary infrastructure—in dwelling and survival—advances a discursive realm about autonomy and collective imagination. Just as "infrastructure" denotes a tool (as well an outcome) of hegemony and colonization in most urban spaces and conflict zones, infrastructure can also be a tool of decolonization and a structure of autonomy. Infrastructure has also recently been described as an active network linking economy, administration, and politics.

Thus, autonomy and collective self-management constitute the other side of the coin of infrastructure.

Is it possible to define autonomy as a collective action, as a practice of commoning?

*Autonomous Infrastructure: Forms of Decay* is an open seminar that brings together practitioners from different fields to present their projects. This online course will focus on questions of autonomous infrastructure and examples posed by temporary dwellings and non-belonging. The aim of this platform is to discuss the concept of infrastructure from different perspectives, territorial contexts, and scales.

### Seminar List

1. Autonomous Infrastructure
2. Camps as Commons
3. Neoliberalism and Urban Infrastructure
4. Border Infrastructure and Action Research
5. Extrastatecraft—Colonization of Infrastructure
6. Solidarity as Autonomous Infrastructure
7. Solidarity and Archive as Infrastructure

### Participants

Sandi Hilal
Ayat Al Thursan
David Harvey
MAP Office [Gutierrez + Portefaix]
Teddy Cruz
Fonna Forman
Cruz & Forman

Miguel Robles Duran
Keller Easterling
Zeynep Sıla Akıncı
Mezra Öner
Kamal Musawwak
Tangör Tan
The Silent University Athens

1

autonomousinfrastructure.tumblr.com/Seminar4

Autonomous Infrastructure:
# Forms of Decay

A piece by Martha Rosler and Pelin Tan for the Oslo
Architecture Triennale 2016: After Belonging.

About    Participants    Reader    Calendar    Content    Links    Ask Questions

Seminar 1. *Autonomous Infrastructure* Seminar 2. *Camps as Commons*
Seminar 3. *Neoliberalism and Urban Infrastructure* Seminar 4. *Border
Infrastructure and Action Research* Seminar 5. *Extrastatecraft -
Colonization of Infrastructure* Seminar 6. *Solidarity as Autonomous
Infrastructure* Seminar 7. *Solidarity and Archive as Infrastructure*

Seminar 4
## Border Infrastructure and Action Research

**Date:** 06/17/2016 | 7pm-9pm

**Time zones:** (EST) Eastern Standard Time

**How do borderlines simulate and establish infrastructures?
What are the form and function of these infrastructures? How does
border infrastructure affect the everyday life, neighborhood
settlements, and socio-economic conditions of the residents? What
does "civic infrastructure" mean nowadays?**

This seminar will consist of a conversation between Teddy
Cruz, Fonna Forman, and Miguel Robles-Durán about their
experiences and their use of action research methodologies.

Cruz and Forman, and Robles-Durán have been actively
engaged in discussing the urbanism and social conditions of the
border zone encompassing Tijuana, Mexico, and San Diego, in the U.S.
For both of them, the border is both a space to be researched, and a
space for action.

**Participants:** Teddy Cruz, Fonna Forman, Miguel Robles
Duran, Martha Rosler, Pelin Tan

Designed and developed by Eli Cayuela & Eugenio Garcia.

2

1  MAP Office, still image from the first online session: Neoliberalism and Urban Infrastructure, June 2016,
   Hong Kong. Conversation between David Harvey, MAP Office [Guttierrez + Portefaix], and Pelin Tan.
   Courtesy of the authors.

2  Autonomous Infrastructure: Forms of Decay blog page screenshot [afterbe.tumblr.com/seminar4], 2016.

# The Seaman, The Wet Feet Series, and The Constellations Series

## Bouchra Khalili

1

The combination of *The Seaman* (digital film, 2012), *The Wet Feet Series* (photography, 2012), and *The Constellations Series* (2011)—three distinct bodies of work—questions ideas of emancipation and resistance as shaped and developed by members of political minorities.

The Seaman offers an exploration of Hamburg harbor, the second biggest container terminal in Europe and the first to be automated. While showing the ghostly choreography of gigantic automated cranes, a young Filipino seafarer delivers a sharp reflection on global capitalism and the condition of the working class at sea. *The Wet Feet Series* offers a metaphorical documentation of forced illegal immigration between South America, the Caribbean, and the United States. *The Constellations* re-maps the Mediterranean region from the perspective of forced illegal journeys.

Connecting the North Sea, the Atlantic Ocean, and the Mediterranean Sea, these three projects invite viewers to reflect on issues of globalization, migration, and mobility, and—eventually—the struggle for emancipation.

1  Broken Container, Fig. 1. From "The Wet Feet Series." 2012. C-Print. 100×120cm. Courtesy of the artist and Galerie Polaris, Paris.

2 The Constellations, Fig. 7. From "The Constellations Series." 2011. 8 silkscreen prints on paper. Mounted on aluminium and framed. 42×62cm. View at "The Opposite of Voice-Over," solo exhibition, Färgfabriken Konsthall, 2016. Photo by Jean-Baptiste Béranger. Courtesy of the artist and Galerie Polaris, Paris.

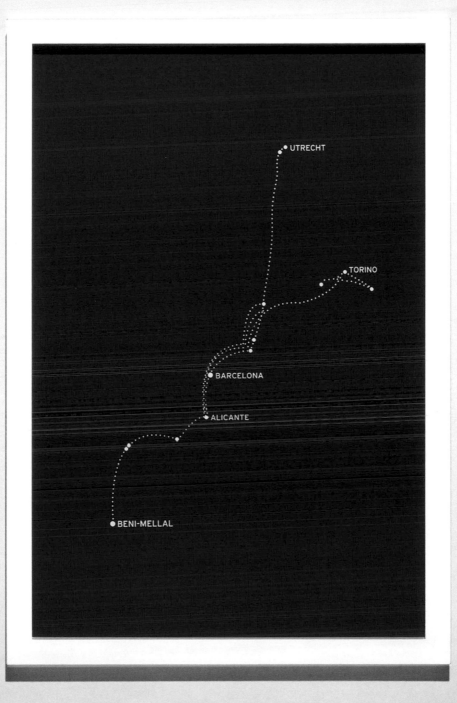

## Lo que el barco se llevó

### Supersudaca

While much of the discussion about migrants concerns how they can be integrated in the more affluent parts of the world, little thought is given to the influence of affluent travelers on developing countries. About 1.2 billion international tourists travel every year worldwide to multiple destinations, and their impact on the local social and physical fabric of underdeveloped regions remains a marginal note. Supersudaca has surveyed how mass tourism operates in the Caribbean through its two most poignant manifestations: the all-inclusive resort and the cruise ship industry, since this region is the leader in both types of tourism, home to the largest number of all-inclusive resorts in the world and almost 50% of world cruise tourism.

*Lo que el barco se llevó* shows not only how cruise ships are becoming large enough to resemble a city, but also reflects on how this new condition severely impacts the future role of the destination in the tourist game. The improbability of the cruise ship's sublime and growing scale goes hand-in-hand with the perfectionist scheme that ensures that everything one could dream about is embedded in the ship: multiple neighborhoods, cinemas, nightlife, running tracks, surfing waves, various restaurants, gambling, shopping areas, and an endless list of activities. Although this

new form of cruise ship encapsulates the dream of a floating city and is surely a remarkable technological achievement, the impact of the new ships on the ports of call is becoming alarmingly tricky. If the ship is turning into the ultimate destination, why should cruise ships negotiate with the ports about the location of piers, the impact of their waste disposal, or even the paying of taxes for docking? Furthermore, the latest trend in the new generation of cruise tourism in the Caribbean also questions the actual need for an existing destination since cruise ships operators can instead either fabricate an artificial island fantasy far from the coast or lease an island for their own management as they do in Labadee, Haiti.

An intriguing question then is: If all money and time spent by the tourists is consumed on the boat and in controlled ports of call, why should the developing world welcome these giant machines in the future? *Lo que el barco se llevó* is a visualization of the scale and diversity of the current generation of cruise ships that now go hand-in-hand with their controlled ports of call, shopping malls, and private beaches. It hints that, in fact, the upcoming generation of cruise tourism in the Caribbean has emptied any possibility of benefit for the local cultures and economies which are still welcoming these mega-boats with awe and naiveté.

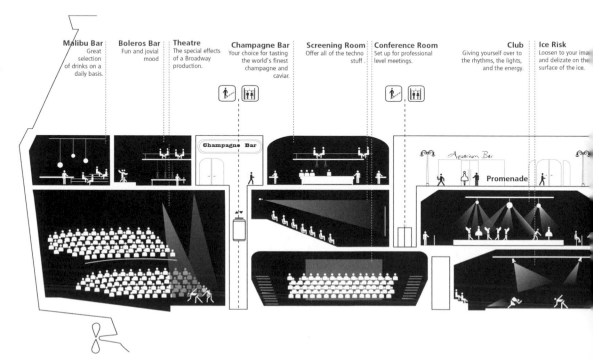

**Malibu Bar** Great selection of drinks on a daily basis.

**Boleros Bar** Fun and jovial mood

**Theatre** The special effects of a Broadway production.

**Champagne Bar** Your choice for tasting the world's finest champagne and caviar.

**Screening Room** Offer all of the techno stuff.

**Conference Room** Set up for professional level meetings.

**Club** Giving yourself over to the rhythms, the lights, and the energy.

**Ice Risk** Loosen to your ima and delizate on the surface of the ice.

Supersudaca Team: Stephane Damsin, Martin Delgado, Félix Madrazo, Max Zolkwer, Fiorella Galvalisi, Javier de Paepe, Andrea Silvestre, Ana Rascovsky.

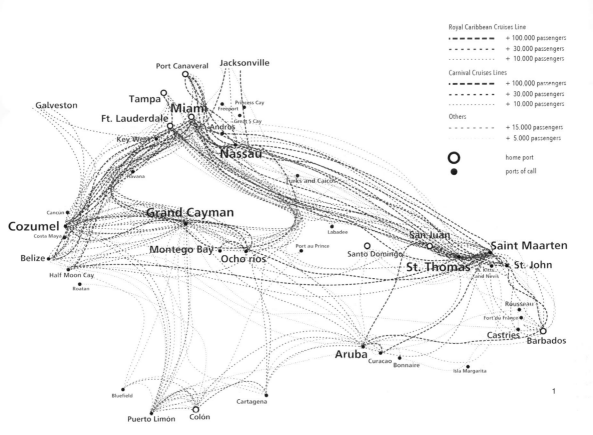

Legend:

Royal Caribbean Cruises Line
- – – – – – + 100.000 passengers
- – – – – + 30.000 passengers
- ......... + 10.000 passengers

Carnival Cruises Lines
- – – – – + 100.000 passengers
- – – – – + 30.000 passengers
- ......... + 10.000 passengers

Others
- – – – – + 15.000 passengers
- ......... + 5.000 passengers

○ home port
● ports of call

1

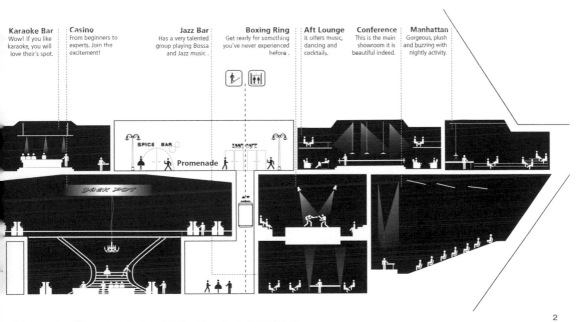

**Karaoke Bar**
Wow! If you like karaoke, you will love their's spot.

**Casino**
From beginners to experts. Join the excitement!

**Jazz Bar**
Has a very talented group playing Bossa and Jazz music .

**Boxing Ring**
Get ready for something you've never experienced before .

**Aft Lounge**
It offers music, dancing and cocktails.

**Conference**
This is the main showroom it is beautiful indeed.

**Manhattan**
Gorgeous, plush and buzzing with nightly activity.

2

1 Supersudaca, "From where to where." Cruise ship routes in the Caribbean. From "Al Caribe" project. Courtesy of the author.

2 Supersudaca, "Cruise ship section through entertainment." From "Al Caribe" project. Courtesy of the author.

Supersudaca, "Fun Day at Sea." From "Al Caribe" project. Photograph by Carlos Weeber. Courtesy of the author.

**New Value**

Benjamin Reynolds and Valle Medina (Pa.LaC.E)

Nestled between fairway condominiums and kidney pools is a data center that stores the massive and shapeless stuff of digital production. For the leisure-suit-clad retired bankers of Palm Springs, CA, this country club spans two worlds.

*Above:* spaces that exploit tired bodies through games where play is celebrated and illusions temporarily dislocate realities. Every metaphor is swiftly realized through precise technology.

*Below:* excreted wax once used as a coolant for servers mixes with the ashes of deceased bankers, a glutinous burial ground, dripping explanations of artificial and natural processes. Where a data center cleans up concepts, below is the domain of physical superabundance—error, excess, death—across time and through strata of materiality, a reified .csv file.

The building's likeness to a body—wrinkles / inflatables, pits / pools, hair / cables—is no coincidence. The total creation of information is the sum of human effort. The building becomes where information came from. The bankers are libidinous college kids; youthful splendor is restored and is floating as a desert oasis of information.

Benjamin Reynolds and Valle Medina (Pa.LaC.E), "New Value," 2012. Courtesy of the authors.

# Heālthcạŕė Ṭoǔřışm
## in Dubai

Discourses on health care often concern the role of the state in social welfare programming as part of the government's duty to its citizens. But as globalization facilitates the movement of people around the world, new care systems operate within the logics of tourism, providing treatments for the "global citizen." The Dubai Healthcare City (DHCC) was established in 2002 as a free economic zone occupying four million square feet in the heart of the city. This real-estate operation was intended to make Dubai a hub for "medical tourism."

Architecture and urbanism play a role in this venture. As the chief executive officer of the American Academy of Cosmetic Surgery Hospital states, "the aura [is] just as important as the quality of care." A particular aesthetic regime permeates DHCC, from the design of wallpapers to the rhetoric of media campaigns and scientific credentials. Operating rooms are combined with VIP rooms, seven star hotels, and florid interiors with views to a system of open spaces. These architectures are conceived to attract a high-end clientele, and seen as having a therapeutic function, with color schemes and interiors chosen to aid the healing process.

While Dubai targets overseas patients (offering packages that include treatment, accommodation, a visa, and insurance), local residents travel abroad for healthcare, as state services are far below the level of private care.

In its mediation of a transformed logics of tourism and the circulation of patients in search of treatments, the DHCC allows us to inspect the prominent role given to architecture in the production of imaginaries meant to attract a global audience.

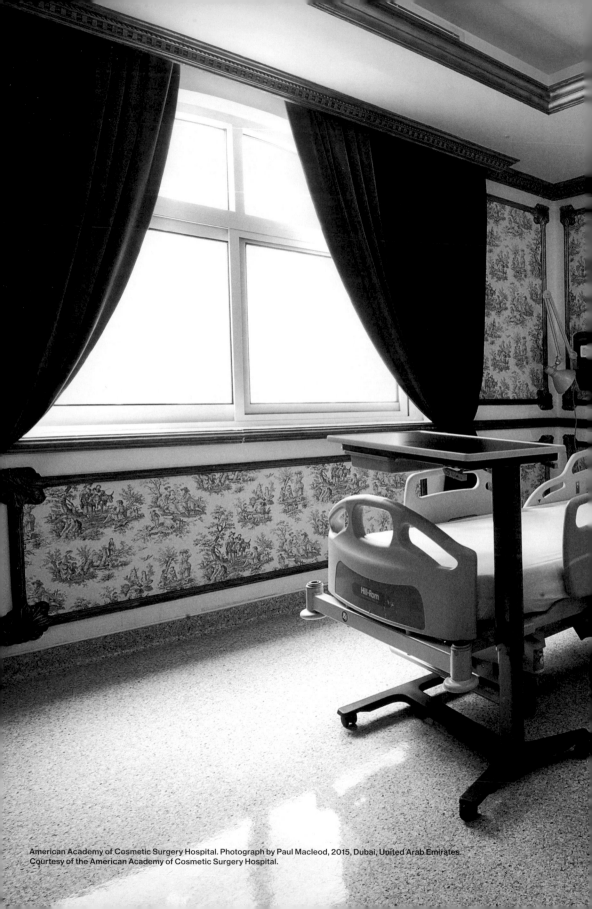

American Academy of Cosmetic Surgery Hospital. Photograph by Paul Macleod, 2015, Dubai, United Arab Emirates. Courtesy of the American Academy of Cosmetic Surgery Hospital.

Façades

THE STATE (Rahel Aima, Ahmad Makia,
Deepak Unnikrishnan)


We continue to be fascinated by the in-progress and on-going narratives about what Dubai and other swaths of the Khaleej (aka The Gulf) are expected to be. We are also wary. This hesitation may be because some of us are from this place. At the same time, we are unable to absolutely claim ownership of the place because narratives other than ours exist, something we accept. Then, from what vantage point could or should we dissect Healthcare City or speculate on healthcare tourism? Inhabitant? Resident? Observer? Reporter? Patient? We were not sure, so we turned to Paul Macleod's photograph of the recovery room at the American Academy of Cosmetic Surgery Hospital for inspiration, simply because the picture was there. We needed a prompt: the photograph provided it. Soon, the photograph began to dictate the search. We wondered why. Macleod is based in Dubai, like some of us. He was commissioned to take the picture, just as we have been commissioned to report on Healthcare City. Macleod photographed a room and what it contained, but we wanted to explore what was not on display: the individuals who built, used, and maintained the room. Two problems presented themselves: how to acknowledge the people responsible for building and maintaining Healthcare City, if we were going to address the vibe of the place; and how to talk about its inhabitants—or visitors, if patients and their dear ones can be called that—while respecting and maintaining their privacy. Our solution: fiction— an anomaly in a *report* we have to admit, but one that frees us to speculate. Our imagining, rendered in the form of a video installation featuring invented people, is, we would argue, an important and necessary tool to examine a place with an architectural footprint that is enormous, in plain sight, yet invisible and difficult to access: a space that, in theory, values the body, and is about the body, details of which are normally (and perhaps should be) private, unless one wishes to share or divulge them. We were not interested in voyeuristic displays of the real, pictures of patients in pre and/or post-op, or why they—irrespective of nationality—were there. It is then possible to negotiate and speculate on the moods the space creates in the eyes of the observer/visitor/worker, the myths—subtle and/or hyperbolic—on display and those invented simply because the space is there, to be speculated about.

Deepak Unnikrishnan, "Hospital Toolkit," stills from fictional work "Pravasis ["Expatriate" or "Emigrant"]," included in THE STATE's video filmed in 2015 in preparation for the 2016 Triennale. © Deepak Unnikrishnan, courtesy of the author.

PRAVASIS

Expat. Worker.
Guest. Worker.

Guest Worker. Worker.
Foreigner. Worker.

# Teċhnōlŏġieš fòr a Ĺife ıṇ Tranšit
## Texts

# Architectures of Position

## John Harwood

1 John Ruskin, *The Stones of Venice*, abr. and ed. J.G. Links (New York: Hill and Wang, 1960), 40.

2 See Marshall McLuhan's lasting evaluation of Ruskin's ambiguous concept of the grotesque in the concluding section of *The Gutenberg Galaxy: The Making of Typographic Man* (London: Routledge & Kegan Paul, 1962).

3 Ruskin, *The Stones of Venice*, 40.

Towards the beginning of *The Stones of Venice*, John Ruskin neatly divided architecture in two. Buildings were intended either "to hold and protect something," which he called the "Architecture of Protection," or they functioned to "place or carry something," which he named the "Architecture of Position."[1] Readers of even the twentieth-century abridged American edition of Ruskin's nearly 500,000-word travelogue will recall that he had much more to say about the former than the latter. The architecture of protection, he held, was the greatest properly architectural achievement, provided that it was produced with the proper moral orientation and sound rationality required to produce *art* as opposed to *convenience*. Yet, it is plain, even in the most florid passages describing the landscapes through which he traveled by locomotive and stage-coach on his "arduous" transalpine journey to the eponymous monuments described through the most microscopic tactics of metonymy and parataxis yet committed to print,[2] that he was writing (and drawing) the architecture of protection from the privileged vantage point of the architecture of position. It is easy enough to imagine the moralist, art and architectural theorist, armchair socialist, and latter-day evangelical epistle writer scrawling the notes and phrases that would eventually form the volumes of *Stones* in the architecturally "impoverished" confines of a modest depot in Ticino or Lombardy, perched amongst the foot lockers and dunnage.

One has to peruse the text carefully, but it turns out that Ruskin did spare some words for the architecture of position:

> This is architecture intended to carry men or things to some certain places, or to hold them there. This will include all bridges, aqueducts, and road architecture; lighthouses, which have to hold light in appointed places; chimneys, to carry smoke or direct currents of air; staircases; towers, which are to be watched from or cried from, as in a mosque, or to hold bells, or to place men in positions of offence, as ancient movable attacking towers, and most fortress towers.[3]

The theme reappears in the tenth chapter of book one, in a tantalizing passage on towers (in which he promises the reader a free-standing study on the subject that is one of the few things Ruskin never wrote), and in several other passages both before and after the partition. With each of these passages, however, it is possible to detect the logic of Ruskin's forceful and artificial division of architecture into two kinds — one worthy of a theory, the other bound by mere practicalities.

For example, in discussing the basic elements of the architecture of protection, Ruskin defined the wall as "an even and united fence of wood, earth, stone, or metal. Metal fences, however, seldom, if ever, take the form of walls, but of railings; and, like all other metal constructions, must be left out of our present investigation."[4] At first, it is difficult to make out why, indeed, metal architectural elements *must* be omitted from his text; after all, iron tie rods and chains had been helping to keep the Venetian buildings he so admired above the waves for centuries, even if he bemoaned the city's collapse into a moral depravity so severe that nothing but "gray dust" remained in the eddies of the Adriatic.

Yet, by the time the first volume of *Stones* had appeared in print, the notion of the architecture of protection had already neared its technical horizon of total anachronism. As his French contemporary Eugène Emmanuel Viollet-le-Duc detailed in his children's novel and masterpiece of military theory *Annals of a Fortress* (1872), the advent of modern artillery and automatic weapons had rendered the fortress hopelessly obsolete. As he relates in the "Conclusion" to the book, in the voice of a memorandum from a "Captain Jean" written in the wake of the Prussian victory over France:

> Attack implies a shock or onset; defence is a resistance to this onset. Whether a piece of ordnance discharges a ball against a plate of iron, or a casing of masonry, or an earthwork; or an assaulting column climbs a breach, the problem is substantially the same; in either case we have to oppose to the impulsive force a resistance that will neutralise its effect.
>
> When there were no projectile weapons, or their range was inconsiderable, only a normal resistance had to be opposed to the shock—a man to a man—or if the effect was to be rendered certain, two men to one. But when projectile arms acquired a longer range, the *position* of the attack and defence became a question of importance.[5]

Captain Jean goes on to analyze the theoretical basis for fortification over its entire history up to the present day, and comes to a startling conclusion:

> [I]n the art of fortification we are exactly at the same point as were the men-at-arms of the end of the fifteenth century, who heaped plates on plates to protect themselves from artillery. It is time the art of fortification should be modified.
>
> It will be objected that a vessel or a horseman can move about, but that a fortress is immovable, and that consequently passive force cannot here be replaced by active force or agility. This is a mistake. Though a fortress cannot be moved, the defensive system of a district can and ought to be studied, in view of various contingencies. In future warfare the plan of temporary fortification ought to play a principal part and may be made to do so. In other terms, *an army ought to be able to fortify itself everywhere, and take advantage of every position.*[6]

In short, the only possible defense is a good offense, and a good offense depended upon movement—the logistically complex, mechanized movement of materiel, weapons, and troops no longer protected by an *enceinte de préservation*, but provisionally protected by virtue of their positions within a now universalized *enceinte de combat*. Viollet-le-Duc himself struggled to

4 Ruskin, *The Stones of Venice*, 45.

5 Eugène Viollet-le-Duc, *Annals of a Fortress* [1872], trans. Benjamin Bucknall (Boston: James R. Osgood and Company, 1876), 357.

6 Ibid., 379–80.

imagine the precise technical and architectural nature of this new militarized environment (although he did look to the steam-powered line-of-battle ship as a model for a new mode of terrestrial warfare), yet his insistence that conventional architectures of fortification had to yield to an architecture reconceptualized around the notion of position echoes Ruskin's awareness of the changing nature of modern architecture as something to be moved through, and even something that itself could move.

For Ruskin and the more sanguine Viollet-le-Duc alike, the interpenetration of spaces engendered through the industrialization of warfare and transportation—the literal penetration of architecture not by Albertian windows and doors but by iron, steel, and copper—raised the specter of an architecture no longer governed by the rule of human beings. One can detect at the edges of their texts the sneaking suspicion that an architecture of position, an architecture that serves as an infrastructural framework for the machinery of logistics, perpetually threatens to overtake architecture as a preserve of humanism.

Architectural historians have been slow to take up the challenges posed by these great nineteenth-century theorists and reluctant modernists. As Reyner Banham and later Robert Bruegmann showed decades ago, the transformations wrought on architecture in the nineteenth century were not in essence formal or "stylistic." Rather, they were responses to "advances in central heating and forced ventilation, innovations in structural systems, lighting, water delivery, and waste disposal."[7] One might add to this list the various transportation networks then interlacing urban and rural areas, telecommunications technologies, and weapons; and one could also push the boundaries of an architectural-technical history back past the nineteenth century and into the early modern period or beyond.[8] In short, to borrow a term at secondhand from Sigfried Giedion, the "constituent facts" of nineteenth-century architecture are very much that conventional buildings became shot through with *media*.

The difficulties with regarding architecture from a mediatic perspective are well known. In a discipline—art and architectural history—that has at its very core a need to secure the conventional ontological distinctions of aesthetics (subject/object), and in which the term *medium* has long been used to describe the material substrate of the work, it is a challenge to change the basic categorical distinctions in order to consider, as Friedrich Kittler wrote in introducing and defending his own methods, "coupling" the fine arts and technics in a configuration that might ignore conventions of authorship and objecthood in favor of a rigorously materialist and bloody-minded technical account of informatics.[9] The problem becomes an even thornier one when one recognizes that the main lines of architectural theory that have been canonized in printed treatises, journals, and anthologies over the past six centuries have a tendency to subordinate technical matters as mere instruments in service of a higher ideal.

Despite these difficulties, the architecture of position has moved closer to the center of architectural discourse over time; however, its movement towards that particular zero is quite strictly asymptotic. As a generation of architectural historians and critics noted in the period stretching from 1945

**7** Robert Bruegmann, "Central Heating and Forced Ventilation: Origins and Effects on Architectural Design," *Journal of the Society of Architectural Historians* 37, no. 3 (October 1978): 143–166. Quotation on p.143. See also Banham, *The Architecture of the Well-tempered Environment*, 2nd ed. (Chicago: University of Chicago Press, 1984), and Michael Osman, "Regulation,Architecture and Modernism in the United States, 1890–1920," (Ph.D. Dissertation, MIT, 2008).

**8** For a fascinating account of the transforming role of the architect as a technical expert in the late eighteenth century, see Robin Middleton and Marie-Noëlle Baudouin-Matuszek, *Jean Rondelet: The Architect as Technician* (New Haven and London: Yale University Press, 2007), especially the passage on Guillaume-Abel Blouet's attempt to update Rondelet's *Traité*, 348–9. See also Robert Bork, ed., *De Re Metallica: The Uses of Metal in the Middle Ages* (Aldershot and Burlington: Ashgate, 2005).

**9** Friedrich Kittler, "Unpublished Preface to *Discourse Networks*," trans. Geoffrey Winthrop-Young, *Grey Room* 63 (Spring 2016): 90–107, especially p. 98.

to 1960, the horizon over which the architecture of position cannot cross is protected by the strength—one is tempted to consider it a "tower" in a Ruskinian sense—of *analogy*.[10] As long as one does not stray too far into *metaphor*, the *likeness* of architecture proper to the vast buildings and "infrastructures" that disqualify the architecture of position from every being *actually architecture*, it remains not only possible but probable for hierarchical distinctions to be enforced between high and low, between is and is not, in the canon of admissible objects that *belong* properly. Thus, a mediatic architectural history risks violating architecture's *value* as part of what Jean Baudrillard once called "the system of objects."

World's Columbian Exposition, Machinery Building, Chicago, IL, 1893. Peabody & Stearns, architects. T. H. McAllister, photographer. Historic Architecture and Landscape Image Collection, Ryerson and Burnham Archives, The Art Institute of Chicago. Digital File #80036.

Yet as a contemporary generation of architectural thinkers now recognize, the crux of the ontological problem that continues to haunt architectural historical writing can actually be located within the very canon that the architecture of protection produced. Writer after writer—architect and historian alike—signals the death or at least the crisis of architecture at the hands of technics. Not only would the book kill the building; consider John Summerson, who in the wake of World War II, boldly declared that "[a]rchitecture is no longer required to give symbolic cohesion to society. Cohesion is maintained by new methods of communication."[11] Writing decades earlier with his trademark bombast and withering tragic irony, the great and frustrated Louis Sullivan would locate the precise time and location of the death of architecture at the World's Columbian Exposition in Chicago in 1893. It is to this moment and place that I propose to return in this short essay, in order to demonstrate the blind spots of our historiography as it relates to the problem of the architecture of position, and to point out the possible merits of a renewed historical engagement with it.

The birthday-cake neoclassicism and staff-and-spray-paint fakery of the exhibition is familiar enough to readers of modernist architectural histories,[12] as is the fire that eventually destroyed most of the temporary buildings less than a year after the closure of the exposition. Also familiar to such readers is the fact that these bombastic exteriors concealed—behind the sculptures (many by the Boston sculptor Robert A. Kraus) and gigantic classical columns—complex steel structures of trusses, girders, and gantries. Yet a closer look into the architecture of the exposition—perhaps some of the most literally and logistically minded works of architecture of position ever constructed, housing millions of unique objects that placed wildly divergent technical demands upon the buildings—reveals more than the crypto-Hegelian moral archaeology that Sigfried Giedion performed on the industrial "Architecture?" of the nineteenth century.[13]

The Palace of Mechanic Arts, more familiarly known as "Machinery Hall," was—once a necessary annex was added to accommodate some of

10 John Summerson, "The Mischievous Analogy" [1945], republ. in Summerson, *Heavenly Mansions and other Essays on Architecture* (New York: Norton, 1963): 195–218.

11 Ibid., 209.

12 Adler & Sullivan's exceptional design for the Transportation Building at the exposition is often cited by contrast as evidence of the backward nature of the pompous neoclassical architecture favored by Daniel H. Burnham and his deputies such as Peabody and Stearns; however, it is interesting to note that in the conclusion of his memoir *The Autobiography of an Idea* [1924] (New York: Dover, 1956), Sullivan's criticism of his colleagues was so sweeping as to include his very own design as part of the grand demise of architecture and democratic culture; see pp. 317–330.

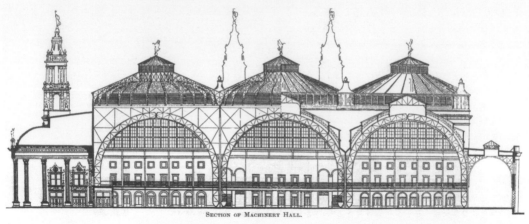

SECTION OF MACHINERY HALL.

"Machinery Hall, World's Columbian Exposition, Chicago, 1892–93, Peabody & Stearns architects."
Section, published in *The Wonders of Machinery Hall: World's Columbian Exposition-Chicago 1893*
(Bradley, IL: Lindsay Publications, 2012).

**13** See Giedion, *Building in France, Building in Iron, Building in Ferroconcrete*, trans. J. Duncan Berry (Santa Monica, CA: Getty, 1995), 90–91: "The concept of architecture is linked to the material of stone. Heaviness and monumentality belong to the nature of this material, just as the clear division between supporting and supported parts does…. It seems doubtful whether the limited concept of 'architecture' will indeed endure. We can hardly answer the question: What belongs to architecture? Where does it begin, where does it end?
Fields overlap: walls no longer rigidly define streets. The street has been transformed into a stream of movement. Rail lines and trains, together with the railroad station, form a single whole. Suspended elevators in glazed shafts belong to it just as much as the insulating filling between the supports. The antenna has coalesced with the structure, just as the limbs of a towering steel frame enter into

the seven hundred exhibition applications that could not be housed in the original structure—the largest pavilion at the fair. (The other major pavilions were dedicated to agriculture, mines, electricity, transportation, and commerce in general in the Manufactures and Liberal Arts Building.) In addition to being supervised by Daniel H. Burnham as Director of Works for the fair as a whole, the construction and organization of the building was overseen by Lewis W. Robinson, the Chief Engineer of the US Navy, who had previously been the Assistant Chief of the bureau that installed the machinery at the 1876 Centennial Exposition in Philadelphia, and who was a widely respected expert in planning complex industrial activities.[14]

Planning for the "seventeen acres of palpitating iron and steel"[15] in the main hall of the building began in 1891, with the architecture firm of Peabody and Stearns left to figure out how to elevate such a massive footprint over the swampy and quicksand-ridden site. This feat was accomplished by driving timber piles into the ground, allowing for a timber foundation several feet above the ground that could safely support 200 pounds per square foot. Three massive trusses spanned the entire width of the hall, dividing the building into three "great halls." These trusses were designed to be demounted at the end of the exposition, either to be reused in other buildings or sold for railroad iron. The interstitial circular-arched trusses, each with a radius of 57.5 feet, were lofted 22 feet into the air and attached by expansion and pivot joints to a lightweight steel girder system. Eventually, the architects were forced to concede that the original 17-acre footprint was inadequate for the purpose, and an annex of more than 6 acres was added at the rear of the building, along with a basement for "the largest boiler house in the world" and lofted galleries for administrative offices, visitor services, and a restaurant. In order to aid visitors in traversing this deafeningly loud, vast space, three "cranes" or gantries were installed on rails running along the galleries. These gantries held wide viewing platforms that could carry more than a hundred visitors apiece, gazing down at the whirring models of industry below from a safe distance.

"Largest Boiler Room in the World. Machinery Hall, World's Columbian Exposition, Chicago, 1892–93, Peabody & Stearns architects."
View of basement of annex, published in *The Wonders of Machinery Hall: World's Columbian Exposition-Chicago 1893* (Bradley, IL: Lindsay
Publications, 2012). The original photographs were published in the pages of *American Machinist Magazine.*

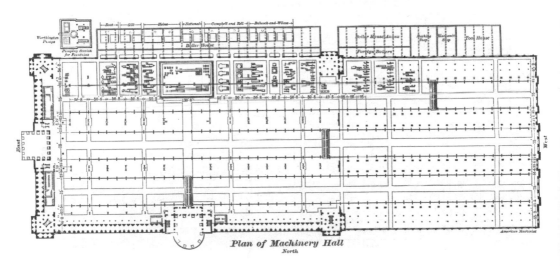

"Machinery Hall, World's Columbian Exposition, Chicago, 1892–93, Peabody & Stearns architects." Plan of main level, published in
*The Wonders of Machinery Hall: World's Columbian Exposition-Chicago 1893* (Bradley, IL: Lindsay Publications, 2012).

World's Columbian Exposition, electrical subway, Machinery Building, Chicago, IL, 1893. Peabody & Stearns, architects. C. D. Arnold, photographer. World's Columbian Exposition Photographs by C. D. Arnold, Ryerson and Burnham Archives, The Art Institute of Chicago. Digital File #198902_140619-E20994.

a relationship with city and harbor. Tall buildings are bisected by rail lines. The fluctuating element becomes a part of building."

An excellent example of the kind of cheap historiography to which Giedion (surely unwittingly) gave license is François Loyer, *Architecture of the Industrial Age, 1789–1914* (Geneva: Skira; New York: Rizzoli, 1983).

**14** "Excerpts from Shepp's World's Fair Photographed," republ. in: *The Wonders of Machinery Hall: World's Columbian Exposition–Chicago 1893* (Bradley, IL: Lindsay Publications, 2012), p. 171.

**15** James W. Shepp and Daniel B. Shepp, *Shepp's World's Fair Photographed, Being a Collection of Original Copyrighted Photographs Authorized and Permitted by the Management of the World's Columbian Exposition…* (Chicago and Philadelphia: Globe Bible Publishing Company, 1893), 188.

For all of the effort at economy and ephemerality in constructing the building, the hall nonetheless required 10,500,000 feet of lumber and 11,000,000 pounds of steel, not including the machinery, generators, or infrastructural connections. The latter were perhaps the most sublime infrastructural accomplishment of the entire exposition. In order to power the 24,000 horsepower worth of engines that drove the leather belts animating the multitude of machines ranging in size from one-half ounce to massive force-pumps spraying a "cataract" into an indoor reservoir, the entire building needed to be designed as a complex framework of chases and hollows that allowed millions of miles of water, steam, and oil pipes; electrical wires; and pneumatic conduits to be threaded into the exhibition halls. To power the largest generator, oil was piped over 300 miles directly from a field and refinery in Ohio.

It is beside the point here to enumerate all of these systems—the curious reader can refer to the regular articles on the progress made and setbacks suffered that appeared in the pages of the professional journal *American Machinist Magazine* from 1892 through 1893[16]—and they are the subject of past and future histories. What is significant for the purposes of inquiring about the methods proper to historicizing an architecture of position such as Machinery Hall is the extent to which the architecture of the building is at once subject to the most diverse array of technical demands that determine so many aspects of its form, *and* a wholly novel architectural articulation of the sum total of machinery and technical systems then operating in the world. In other words, Machinery Hall is a vast aggregation of cultural techniques on a wholly unprecedented scale, in which the conventional architectural elements of enclosure—floor, ceiling, and wall, but also window and door[17]—are radically perforated and covered over by technical systems that define the spatial and temporal matrix of the building.

In the face of this monstrous architecture of position, the position of the spectator became redefined. As the Shepp brothers marveled in the heady prose of their *World's Fair Photographed*:

> One does not need to be a mechanic to be interested in the machinery before us. Each part is performing some wonderful task, as though possessed of intelligence. Man seems a weak being beside these forceful servants of his, which obey his slightest touch. In one place we see printing-presses busily at work: "The Daily Columbian," which gives all the news of the Fair, is printed here, and other works also. One press can turn out 48,000 papers in an hour, and is said to be the fastest in the world. It also prints in five colors, and is constructed in a succession of rolls, one above the other, which may be added to at will, and each representing a separate machine.

"Machinery Hall, World's Columbian Exposition, Chicago, 1892–93, Peabody & Stearns architects." View of an installation of various belt-driven machining tools in the US section, published in *The Wonders of Machinery Hall: World's Columbian Exposition-Chicago 1893* (Bradley, IL: Lindsay Publications, 2012). The original photographs were published in the pages of *American Machinist Magazine*.

What is a source of sublime wonder to the jingoistic publicists of the fair, and is plainly uncomfortable for any humanist, is the fact that the most important architecture of the age—so important that Sullivan could imagine it literally *killing* architectural culture altogether—had only the space to house the whirring movement, sublime power, and irreducible complexity of machines and a belittled audience of human beings servicing them and consuming their products as passive spectators. Walter Benjamin reminded us that we cannot hope to understand film by watching it on a screen, but by taking up the very techniques that produce it and reassembling the apparatus;[18] Heidegger explained that unlike the work of art, "the production of equipment is finished when a material has been so formed as to be ready for use. For equipment to be ready means that it is released beyond itself, to be used up in usefulness."[19] The architecture of Machinery Hall, itself rendered into apparatus for housing equipment, bent to the purpose of, in Ruskin's words, "carry[ing] men [and women] and things to some certain places" in a constant renegotiation of positions and relations—is far from being the death of architecture. It just isn't art anymore.

16 Many of these articles are republished in *The Wonders of Machinery Hall: World's Columbian Exposition—Chicago 1893* (Bradley, IL: Lindsay Publications, 2012).

17 See Bernhard Siegert, "Doors: On the Materiality of the Symbolic," trans. John Durham Peters, *Grey Room* 47 (Spring 2012): 6–23.

18 Walter Benjamin, "The Work of Art in the Age of Its Technical Reproducibility: Second Version," trans. Edmund Jephcott, in: Benjamin, *The Work of Art in the Age of Its Technological Reproducibility and Other Writings on Media*, ed. Michael W. Jennings, Brigid Doherty, and Thomas Y. Levin (Cambridge, MA and London: The Belknap Press of Harvard University Press, 2008), 19–55.

19 Martin Heidegger, "The Origin of the Work of Art," in: Heidegger, *Basic Writings*, 2nd ed., trans. David Farrell Krell (New York and San Francisco: Harper Collins, 1992), 143–212. Quotation on p. 189.

# Smart/Borders

Louise Amoore

### Scene One: The Vision-Box

1 www.vision-box.
com/solutions/
bordercontrol

2 www.icao.int/
security

3 ABC4EU.com

4 Interview conducted
October 24, 2013.

5 Anne Friedberg, *The
Virtual Window: From
Alberti to Microsoft*
(Cambridge, Ma.: MIT
Press, 2006), 242.

6 Louise Amoore, *The
Politics of Possibility:
Risk and Security Beyond
Probability* (Durham,
NC: Duke University
Press, 2013), 157.

Welcome to the world of Vision-Box.[1] The row of automated border gates gleams, holding out a glass-and-steel promise of biometrically-secured transit. The promise is a world of easy mobility—"security and facilitation"[2]—where even the acronym of automated border control is ABC.[3] Every sixteen seconds of stillness experienced inside the e-gate is also a time of teeming data streams and algorithmic risk calculation, as the software "reaches back into enriched databases" to calculate the border-crosser's claim to mobility.[4] This computational event engenders the apparent smartness of the smart border: a machine-readable travel document, with its biometric template data, communes with a risk assessment engine of advanced analytical algorithms in order *to make a sovereign decision*. It is not only the data that is in transit, circulating and crossing domains for new deployment, but rather mobility itself which is reconfigured as associations and correlations between past patterns and future possibilities of transit. Fragments of my past pattern of transit enter an intimate correlation with yours, these elements recombining to calculate our possible future mobility, and its degree of risk. The work of the smart border renders what would otherwise be imperceptible to human vision, nonetheless perceptible and amenable to action: stop, detain, submit to secondary scrutiny, assess the claim, question, profile, defer, deport.

"Automated authorizations," October 24, 2013, Montreal, Canada. Photography by Louise Amoore. Courtesy of Vision-Box.

What does it mean for the automated gate to claim to "reach back" to enhanced databases to make a decision at the border? As Anne Friedberg has written in her compelling history of the screen, "the 'postcinematic' viewer has new forms of ever-virtual mobility—new speeds of access to deep histories of images and text, newly mobilized screens."[5] Yet, the smart border's extraction algorithms cut out pieces from across an array of different data sources and types, stitching them together in a curious composite of multiple data elements. In this sense, the technology is not virtual at all, but rather works to actualize all data elements into possibilities to be acted upon.[6] The smart border composite not only flattens political subjects so that they become computable, it also entangles the sixteen seconds of the e-gate with the violence of refusal and disavowal of today's Mediterranean crossings. Among many other data sources, the EU databases of VIS, EURODAC, and the Schengen Information System act like relays across which recognition at the shiny e-gate correlates to a refusal to recognize a political claim made elsewhere. Through the correlated patterns of our mobilities, we are all associated—ethically implicated—one with another.

"At the e-gate," October 24, 2013, Montreal, Canada. Photography by Louise Amoore. Courtesy of Vision-Box.

## Scene Two: The Predictive Perimeter

In a darkened corporate film screening room, a security software company demonstrates its "event-driven architecture" and "how it can be used in border security and counter-terrorism." Pattern recognition algorithms are deployed across the seams of past, present, and future, allowing the "fusion of information from historical databases" with what are described as "real-time, in-memory sensor data and events." The software is presented as the information architecture of a "predictive perimeter"—a border that acts to anticipate what crossings might take place in the future. Here, the border line is written spatially, not only in the sovereign techniques at the edge of territory, but in and through the correlative spaces of predictive analytics. Just as the spaces of the border crossing are extended into the future through the analysis of past data, so, also, the temporality of the border folds future possible infractions into the present moment of decision. At the predictive perimeter, it is no longer possible for someone to arrive who is not already anticipated within the data architecture. What happens, then, to the many political claims (to asylum, to refuge, to find hospitality) that are not already anticipated by the calculations of the predictive perimeter?

The analysis of the datastream becomes the only recognizable way to perceive the arrival of an as-yet-unknown subject. As fragile boats founder in the seas of the Mediterranean and the English Channel, the border authorities respond to say that these are the most intensively monitored and sensed stretches of water anywhere in the world. So, all data must be available to be sensed and analysed by the smart border, and if nothing is sensed then there can be no response, no ethics, no responsibility. The predictive perimeter appears to offer an enhanced version of perception and to capture a complete totality of data, data that would otherwise exceed human perceptibility. Yet, notwithstanding the aggregation of multiple and heterogeneous datasets, the predictive perimeter acts to reduce the multiplicity to one. The "event-driven architecture," once appearing as risk scores on the screen of the border guard or on the mobile device of the FRONTEX officer, filters what can be perceived of the world. The so-called "decision support tool" has, in effect, become the arbiter of an automated decision. As the twenty-first century's smart border becomes the sovereign decision tool par excellence, the radical heterogeneity of forms and experiences of border crossing is diminished and disavowed.

The patterns of life that generate the world captured at the e-gate or in the algorithms of the smart border are more accurately thought of as durational, multiple, continuous, embodied, violent, experienced. Consider what a "data point" might be: a past failed visa application from a turbulent time; a previous journey to a place now deemed a high-risk geopolitical space; a money transfer sent by a migrant worker in Berlin to his or her family in Lebanon; a past association with someone who is now a "listed" individual. The data points are contingent singularities arising from real, embodied, and complex life stories. That is, until they become algorithmic association rules defining all future risks in the "rules based" security device.

While the smart border claims to afford a vantage point on risky patterns of life, in practice it flattens the border into a form that can be amenable to computation, as demonstrated through a scenario involving the predictive perimeter software at the US-Mexico border:

> The alert was triggered by a pattern of events that matched a pre-defined pattern in a complex event processing system—a sophisticated software that consumes streams of real-time data and converts them into actionable information and decision patterns. In this case, the events of interest were sensor input from face recognition software; flight, bus, and rail information into Mexico; satellite pictures of license plates; thermal activity from the road near the border. With event processing software, more movements can be monitored without human intervention.[7]

The fraught borders of our world are being governed as "patterns of events" that may, or may not, match a "pre-defined pattern." As Europe seeks to delineate and discriminate—Syrians from Afghans, Libyans from Eritreans, political from economic migrants—the capacity to make a political claim is reduced to the pattern. As Jacques Derrida wrote nearly twenty years ago: "[W]e proceed to bolt the external borders of the European Union tightly. Asylum seekers knock successively on each of the doors of the EU states and are being repelled at each one of them."[8] In the era of the smart border, even the capacity to knock at a door is curtailed, so that the condition of hospitality Derrida describes can never be met, and the stranger either does not arrive or is detained upon arrival.

## Scene Three: Life Patterns – Bani Abidi

In her work "Security Barriers A-L," Pakistani artist Bani Abidi arrays an alphabetical series of digital prints of the many security barriers on the streets of Karachi. In an interview, Abidi explains that she wants to bring back to the surface of perception the exclusionary architecture of borders that otherwise fall beneath the visible threshold.[9] The barriers are diverse, ranging from a truck-bomb-proof planter outside the British Deputy High Commission, to the shipping containers of the American Consulate and the concrete barriers of the Iranian Embassy. Abidi's drawings are produced as ink-jet prints on a stark white background. The use of inkjet printing as a technique echoes the aesthetic of abstracted scientific illustrations, classified and ordered alphabetically, infinitely reproducible, flattened and digitized. And yet, the arrangement of the prints in a grid of horizontal and vertical lines—tabular rows and columns, like a database—invites the observer to enter the space anew, to consider the border architecture of their daily lives, to make the border a peculiar curiosity. Beneath and within the ink-jet data points and digital halts of the border, another life pattern teems with the circulations of the city streets.

7 Tibco Software Inc, *The Predictive Perimeter* (Palo Alto, Ca., 2010).

8 Jacques Derrida, *On Cosmopolitanism and Forgiveness*, trans. Mark Dooley and Michael Hughes (London: Routledge, 2001), 13.

9 Bani Abidi, "Interview with Bani Abidi," *Asia Art Archive* (February 10, 2010).

Bani Abidi, "Two of Two," photographic work part of the series *Section Yellow*, 2010. The works in *Section Yellow* are about people who are going elsewhere; an anatomy of preparation, anxiety and anticipation. © Bani Abidi, courtesy of the artist.

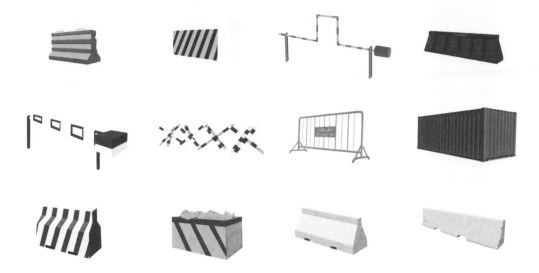

Bani Abidi, "Security Barriers A-L," 2008. A design survey of security barriers on the streets of Karachi, Pakistan. © Bani Abidi, courtesy of the artist. [First row left to right] *Security Barrier Type A*: Iranian Embassy, Shahrah-e-Iran, Clifton, Karachi. *Security Barrier Type B*: Near the American Consulate, Abdullah Haroon Rd, Karachi. *Security Barrier Type C*: 47th St, Block 6, PECHS, Karachi. *Security Barrier Type D*: Pakistan Naval Base, Karsaz, Karachi. [Second row left to right] *Security Barrier Type E*: Jinnah International Airport, Karachi. *Security Barrier Type F*: Jinnah International Airport, Karachi. *Security Barrier Type G*: Traffic Police, Karachi. *Security Barrier Type H*: Near the American Consulate, Abdullah Haroon Rd., Karachi. [Third row left to right] *Security Barrier Type I*: American Consul Generals Residence, F. Jinnah Rd., Karachi. *Security Barrier Type J*: British Deputy High Commission, Shahrah-e-Iran, Karachi. *Security Barrier Type K*: Near the American Consulate, Abdullah Haroon Rd., Karachi. *Security Barrier Type L*: Varied Locations, Karachi.

In her video work "The Distance from Here" (2010), Abidi dramatizes the mundane acts of waiting in line for an immigration assessment, interrupting the time of the sovereign decision. Abidi displays on her screens the stilling and pausing of the movements of border crossers as they wait in line for the authorization of their papers. The assessments take place under a canopy in the parking lot of the British High Commission, the line winding through the quotidian space divided by yellow lines painted on the asphalt. The people waiting seem to occupy a durational time in which their stories are carried in the documents, proofs of identity, and certificates they carry with them. The material weight of the documents, and the categorization and verification that takes place in this improvised space, seems to defy the lightness and the easy facilitation of the automated and apparently smart border. Abidi was denied access to the actual British High Commission parking lot because her film would breach the prohibition of recording devices in this sovereign scene. Yet, in her careful reproduction of the space—complete with the notary typing documents slowly on an old typewriter—Abidi's literal fiction tells a truth about the border. There is very little that is "smart," or indeed digital, about the daily routines of checking and verification on which the geopolitics of border controls rests. Here, in Bani Abidi's scenes of waiting, stilling, anxiety, and disappointment, is the embodied scene of a human in transit. In this scene, one can never know finally and definitively what the "life patterns" of people are in their data, what their associations may be, at what personal cost and risk they seek to cross the border.

Bani Abidi, "Two of Two," photographic work part of the series *Section Yellow*, 2010. © Bani Abidi, courtesy of the artist.

## Of Borders and Belonging

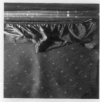

Bani Abidi, "Two of Two,"
photographic work part
of the series *Section
Yellow*, 2010 © Bani Abidi,
courtesy of the artist.

10 Mark Hansen, *Feed-Forward: On the Future
of Twenty-First Century
Media* (Chicago:
University of Chicago
Press, 2014), 39.

11 Katherine Hayles,
*How We Think: Digital
Media and Contemporary
Technogenesis* (Chicago:
University of Chicago
Press, 2012), 179.

The circulation and analysis of data has become the contemporary condition for the movement of people and things. What Mark Hansen has called the historical "transition to the paradigm of mobility" has witnessed a move from the cinematic age of sequential frames to "the service of connection," where the emphasis is on "information that is practically oriented, at levels of technical operation beyond human awareness."[10] And so, the connections between people, and between people and place, are made amenable to computation. To connect or to associate is rendered as a means of governing circulation. All connections are possible correlations.

What kind of relation of mobility is a correlation? One in which all mobilities are implicated in the setting of the gauge of risk analysis. The data traces of my sixteen seconds at the e-gate commune with those of others, whose wait in line at an offshore visa application outpost results in a rejected claim. Such data traces, aggregated with the traces of countless others, also feed the curve of normalities from which some future anomaly will halt the movement of some as yet unknown future person. As Bani Abidi so compellingly reminds us, though, the data traces of the border do not capture the narrative of the life stories of those who dwell and belong in bordered places. "Database and narrative are different species," writes Katherine Hayles, since "databases must parse information according to logical categories that order the different data elements," whereas "narratives gesture toward the inexplicable, the unspeakable, the ineffable."[11] The data-driven border technologies we have seen in scenes one and two above, parse data in ways that reduce the inexplicable to the calculable. As the predictive perimeter analyses the vast quantities of data at the US-Mexico border, the "real time" decision of border guard or security analyst is unable to encounter the unspeakable or the ineffable. As the analysis of data is offered up as the solution to a "migration crisis," we must ask what kinds of narratives the smart border reduces to logical categories. What has to be forgotten and disavowed?

Seemingly unable to confront the full consequences of its own past patterns of war and violence, the state is seduced by the appeal of the smart border. With data analytics, even the most turbulent and violent of situations must surely be rendered tractable. As the past patterns of circulation become correlated to the data points of social media networks, biometrics, and other transactional data, what chance is there that the waiting and the weight of Bani Abidi's lines can be felt and expressed? What kind of claims to mobility can be made in a world where the risk scores of each move are always already known in advance? How can the thing that would otherwise be imperceptible to the database be retold in the narrative so that another political claim can be spoken?

# Junktime

**Troy Conrad Therrien**

If "Junkspace is what remains after modernization has run its course," then Junktime is the mess digitization has made of temporality.

Junkspace was Rem Koolhaas's early twenty-first century moniker for the architectural detritus—the "fallout"—of modernization: air-conditioned mega malls in the desert, instantly crumbling concrete housing blocks in urban peripheries, glinting dust-covered post-modern acrobatic atrocities in countries yet to develop to a modernism worthy of disowning. Junktime is the equally dehumanizing overthrow of empty calendrical time—modern time—by an occult clock of interpolated events. It is the discretization of time into a succession of interruptions and nothing more. Junktime drowns out the old drone of homogeneous ticks with a new cacophony of heterogeneous pings: updates, notifications, reminders, alerts, alarms, more updates. It is the temporality of the "CNN effect," an always-on deluge of information that offers no time for thoughtful reaction. It is the ravenous chain-smoking cadence of a Netflix binge, the grammar-bashing blitzkrieg of a tweetstorm, the apish mechanical swiping ritual of Tinder. As the natural cadence of machines, it lobotomizes humans. It requires your full attention but only a fraction of your brain. If ".Junkspace is like being condemned to a perpetual Jacuzzi with millions of your best friends," Junktime accounts for the incongruous restlessness.

Junktime comes from Japan. Building upon multiple generations of experimental industrial acumen beginning with automated looms and exacerbated by a post-WWII urgency to either catch up or capitulate to the Americans in the automotive industry, the Toyoda family concocted a cocktail of protocols, infrastructure, and mantras for eliminating waste in the production of cars. The aim was to only make precisely what was needed, when it was needed, and in the amount needed. Toyota called this process just-in-time manufacturing. Amongst its many inventions, *kanban* were perhaps the most significant: index cards that traveled with each set of parts, they formed a physical feedback loop that regulated speed by pegging each process to the previous one in a deterministic chain of causes and effects. Toyota factories exacerbated Ford's assembly line into miniature mechanical Laplacian universes—each was a game of Mouse Trap with its own internal clock, divorced from absolute time.

Junktime is Californian slang for just-in-time. Picked up and adapted by the software industry around the turn of the century, the atom-constrained

Japanese war on waste evolved into a Californian cult of leanness. Scrum, the development management methodology, transmogrified *kanban* from orders for physical parts to orders for code that could implement idealized stories: "User can log in with unique ID and password"; "User can see the current USD-Bitcoin exchange rate." Scrum boards track the progress of each story as it migrates across states of completeness during "timeboxed" sprints, fixed-duration coding sessions that chip away at a backlog of stories that sum to the features deemed good enough to release as an update. Scrum is a principal mechanism of leanness, the dogmatic adherence to micro-improvements directed by big-data feedback loops, responding immediately to changing user behavior, technological breakthroughs, or competitive threats with the least possible capital investment. Leanness is the sacrificing of perfection for minimum viability. Perpetual beta is the objective, a strategy born of the belief that the market is tempestuous and the best way to deliver a product is through regular recalibrations based on which way the wind is blowing. Planning is anathema to leanness; the long-term is eschewed. What counts most is the speed of pivot, the ability to quickly change tack based on new information. Leanness is a managerial ballet that elevates agility to become a master competency.

Whereas the rhythm of the just-in-time pipeline is quarantined to the factory, insulated by the dominant cycles of car shows, advertising campaigns, container shipping latency, technological progress, and input material sourcing, the Internet as distribution channel disintermediates this distance by bringing consumers directly into the production pipeline itself. Users—half of the human population and counting—are unwittingly tapped directly into the temporal vibrations of agile development. Leanness takes the Toyota mantra of *kaizen*, continuous improvement, to its logical conclusion: continuous integration. Rather than becoming the downstream recipients of technological emancipation, we become just one more layer in the technology development stack, buzzing at the same frequency of ever-tighter release cycles. With the Californication of the workplace—from "casual Fridays" to the "new professional" apparatus of flatter hierarchies, more flexible hours, and telecommuting, to the "gig economy" atomization of the workforce into task rabbits, mechanical turks, and Uber drivers—the tools of continuous integration are naturalized into the productive apparatus of cognitive capitalism. Google Docs was the gateway drug for Trello, Asana, Github, Slack, and a host of other existing and forthcoming instruments of agility to go mainstream like the very social platforms they were built to help create. The true effect of continuous integration is the temporal harmonization of work and leisure. Liberated from the factory, life itself takes on the rhythm of an assembly line.

Junktime is only junky for humans. Our identities were not built to handle such a blistering refresh rate. McLuhan's diagnosis of numbness from the electrification of media seems twee in light of the socio-psychic pathologies that accompany technologically-advanced societies today. South Korea has the

SPEEDISM (Pieterjan Ginckels), "TRUMP L'OEIL," billboard piece for the 7th Bucharest Biennale, 2016.
© Pieterjan Ginckels, courtesy of the artist.

highest rate of connectivity in the world and one of the highest suicide rates, the leading cause of death for those under forty. In the US, 11% of children, also among the most digitally connected, are now diagnosed with attention deficit hyperactivity disorder (ADHD). One in ten Americans over the age of twelve regularly take anti-depressants. Are these the ailments of Junktime? Have you seen a thirteen-year-old use Snapchat? Yik Yak? Kik? The electrification of the American high school popularity contest has turned adolescence into a psycho-social war of attrition measured in raw throughput and scored in likes. The young-est, most malleable brains are being overclocked by direct interface with the machinic phylum in a historic experiment with epigenetics. The neuroplastic effects of Junktime immersion will not be registered for years, but Ritalin sales may be an indication of their magnitude. The great irony of Junktime is that while it is the tempo of productivity, its greatest product is stress.

Junktime is a subset of Garbagetime. In computing, garbage is useless data. Computers are garbage-in-garbage-out (GIGO): ingesting garbage only produces more garbage. No valid inference can be made from garbage; no information about the future can be interpolated. Garbagetime is when all information turns to noise. It is a moment when no clear signal about the future can be spotted on the horizon, no matter how faint or how near. It is a confluence of maximum volatility and maximum possibility, wherein complexity dominates causality and anything can happen. Garbagetime sits at the nexus of venture-funded and military-backed fault lines, each of which may erupt at any time and entirely change the course of history. In Garbagetime, prognostication is futile. All predictions made in Garbagetime are equally worthless, equally embarrassing eventually. Because anything is possible, radical change is the only certainty. Garbagetime is the savage transcience of system change. It spawns new social forms, new cultural norms previously thought settled.

There are many registers of Garbagetime. Finance is an obvious domain. High frequency trading has turned much of the stock market into a mystical game of technical analysis and algorithmic dogfighting clocked at light speed and far removed from the underlying assets. Quantitative easing (the unremorseful printing of troves of money by central banks to paper over the depths of the financial crisis) further fuels the abstraction into garbage of financial data floating precariously on a bubble of hype and mutually reinforced speculation.

Prometheanity, the Californian church of techno-deterministic progress, thrives on Garbagetime. Prometheanity's code is a pastiche of Moore's Law, the Tao of Steve [Jobs], and the interplanetary prophecy of Elon. Its ideology is a seemingly impossible mix of entrepreneurial zeal with hippie liberation. Innovation is its Eucharist. Its spirit animal is the unicorn, the billion dollar private company. Its social politics are various shades of libertarianism. Prometheanity feeds on globalization but dreams of seasteads, startup cities, Martian colonies, alternative currencies, algorithmic governance, and other exits. Burning Man reveals its techno-pagan underpinnings. It does not technically discriminate about gender but is almost entirely male.

Prometheanity is anti-fragile to useless information. As less and less can be assumed about the future, the practices of Prometheanity are bolstered more and more. It achieves this hegemony through a vertical hierarchy whereby venture capitalists place a sea of bets on an army of entrepreneurial hackers: twenty-first century digital miners who chip away at institutions calcified in centuries of analog use and ripe for disrupting—Promethean code for retrofitting old infrastructures for the new technosphere and the attendant financial windfalls of the new monopolies that are created. Because the wins are so big, a low hit rate is acceptable. A shotgun strategy prevails. Prometheanity's colonization of the future is admirably puritanical: rather than predicting it, Prometheans invent it. The process is a self-fulfilling prophecy codified by the mantra of Netscape co-founder and venture capitalist Marc Andreessen: "Software is eating the world." Like capitalism, the Promethean epistemology is tacit and always evolving, often open source. It is the organized mastery of agility.

Acceleration is the Promethean alibi. After decades of ambling up the slowly-then-all-at-once exponential cliffs of technological development, the prophecies of Prometheanity are materializing on their vertical asymptote in a sublime magical realism with the capacity to bend common sense. The spectacular wonders of driverless cars, reusable rockets, 3D-printed organs, nootropics, biosynthesis, gene doping, and weather manipulation legitimize a Faustian tethering to the Dark Enlightenment, the various Promethean sub-cultures that have become disenchanted with democracy. Bayesian rationalists, anarcho-capitalists, neoreactionaries, accelerationists, singularatians, and a host of others make up the wide and varied spectrum of skeptics placing bets on new world orders while fixing the outcome. Promethean clergy like Google chairman Eric Schmidt argue that democracy is now too slow to make effective policy in times of technological acceleration. It should be left to technology companies in a deregulated wild west of innovation adventurism.

The stakes of Prometheanity are rendered in the shape of society. According to Thomas Piketty, the twentieth century American middle class was less the logical product of human progress than an accidental blip in the ongoing, violent human story of radical inequality. This middle-class-centric life—politics, economics, culture, and the like—drew a social distribution best captured by the normal curve, the nineteenth century cipher of social physics. Prometheanity skews this symmetry with its own dynamics: the power law. The power law describes the winner-take-all monopolies of zero-marginal cost digital economies operating at global scale. It is the basic tenet of venture capital. It describes both the hockey stick growth of successful startups and the typical distribution of their users: 80% of the engagement, content, or value comes from 20% of the users. It is the portrait of the One Percent. Unleashed on society, the power law inverts the normal curve, exacerbating the extremes at the expense of the middle. Prometheanity separates a spectral society into a dichotomous emulsion of winners and losers.

Prometheanity does not only reshape society; it is a full stack ecosystem for rebuilding institutions, transaction infrastructures, and value systems. Not just a survival strategy for the viciousness of Garbagetime, Prometheanity is using its competitive advantage to terraform the world to outlast it. If architecture is the process of consciously ordering the world, then the ambitions of Prometheanity are fully architectural. And if the Promethean telos is to eat the world, then there is no room for competing regimes. The injunction is clear: Prometheanity must do away with Architecture.

Prometheanity's preferred weapon uses the formula for Architecture kryptonite hinted at in the breathlessness of Koolhaas's text: hardwiring Junkspace to Junktime. Junkspacetime is as ungainly as the moniker itself. The Internet of Things is one potential avenue to the Junkspacetime universe: stupid architectural objects—locks, thermostats, smoke alarms, and the like—smartified by a battery of cheap sensors and cheap microprocessors connected to the Internet to achieve cheap tricks like dimming the lights or ordering milk. But while this Jetsons futurism may appear imminent to techbloggers and CES-goers, more impressive are the Junkspacetime wormholes that already exist. Take Chinese "memeufacturing." Tightly packed into China's first Special Economic Zone (SEZ), Shenzhen, memeufacturing is the natural evolution of the just-in-time Toyota factory: a superorganism of independent assembly factories and electronic parts wholesalers interlinked through supply chains, distribution channels, and an insolent intellectual property policy of mutual cannibalization with the agility to reinvent product categories at the speed of Internet memes. From drones to e-cigarettes to selfie-sticks to hoverboards, the offerings of these plants pivot and ramp with the same speed that a Kardashian Instagram video goes viral. They are Junkspaces programmed by Junktime to produce, simply, junk. The product of an international alliance of Promethean interests, they are a shot across the bow of Architecture.

Architecture did not pick this fight, but it cannot ignore it. In fact, this battle may be the spur Architecture needs to wake up from its limiting condition: its psychology of scarcity. Architecture, the original Promethean enterprise—suffocated slowly by modernization, Utopian hysterics, and professionalization—is now bound by the arithmetic calculus of bricks. Bricks pile to make brick walls that are precisely the sum of their parts. Bricks add up. Prometheanity draws its perspective from the geometric calculus of bits. Bits are non-rivalrous. A line of code can be used over and over, shared, and congealed into open source libraries, frameworks, and platforms that become an intellectual commons for even the most novice coder to quickly cobble together impressive cathedrals of digital functionality. Bits teach non-zero-sum thinking. Bits scale. The Promethean mindset they inform is one of abundance. Abundance, perhaps even more than agility, is the ultimate Garbagetime anti-fragile trait. The Promethean challenge prods Architecture to escape the gravitational pull of scarcity.

The principal fount of Promethean abundance is its self-annulling ethos concocted from the hacker ethic of sharing, openness, decentralization, free information, and making the world a better place, with the latter twisted by a Randian libertarianism that says looking out for number one is the best way to do it. This shady coalition of beliefs admits an elasticity of persuasive convictions: a catch-all strategy that Andreessen calls "strong beliefs, weakly held." This ethical agility inexhaustibly provides a rationale for whatever best serves the immediate Promethean interest, whether lobbying users, funders, or congress. This agility also admits all adherents. There is no Promethean licensing exam. Its army is voluntary. If we are truly living a moment of Garbagetime, when the outcome of major currents of human history are simultaneously in flux and entirely unknowable in advance, Architecture should similarly open its borders. Defined by an ethical compass rather than a tribalist coterie of incompatible localized codes that landlocks architectural intelligence and severs the possibility for a global trade, Architecture could become a discipline able to both become and support technologies for lives increasingly lived in transit.

The brick-think disciplinary border patrol of schools, blogs, magazines, exhibitions, awards, lecture series, and the rest of the apparatus of Capital-A filtration coupled with the licensing exams, standardized contracts, and liability insurance of the profession becomes a debilitating weight in Garbagetime. Why limit the field? Like garbage-time in sports, when time is left on the clock after a decisive blowout victory, Garbagetime is a moment that beseeches experimentation: new figures, new moves, new ideas. Taking a cue from the playbook of the blogger Venkatesh Rao—to be fair, this entire text is littered with them—in situations where no new information is presented, looking at old information with and for new perspectives is a way forward when swimming in garbage. In Architecture, going back to the beginning of the modern fall is one such avenue to recover abundance.

Alberti left two clues in his biases. The first is the topic he covers in the first book of *De Re Aedificatoria*: "The Lineaments." Alberti wrested the architect from the building site into the drawing room by trading know-how for a formalized epistemology based on design. Shaping lineaments—the characteristic invisible vectors of a building—rather than directing bricklayers was to be the province of Architecture. Lineaments are non-scarce. Not only do they extend infinitely, they have no material bias: lineaments can apply to ideas as much as they do to bricks. Lineamental thinking implies an explicit architecture of decision-making: mental models for making sense of an illegible world. In the deluge of digital information, such models reduce the processing anxiety by moving much of the conscious thinking to the background. Critical Architecture is scarce lineamental thinking, a defensive sorting mechanism for limiting the interior of the discipline. The architecture of mental models, like those constructed by Rao, support abundant lineamental thinking. They do not run out of gas or bump up against historical lines in the sand. They can be applied to any information, even garbage. This is not a "post-critical" apology: it is an argument for abundance that does not make a meal out of the petty disciplinary trysts that render Architecture increasingly irrelevant.

The second clue is in the first architectural type that Alberti mentions: the thermal bath. While he goes on to speak of the role of the architect in connecting the world with infrastructure, winning battles, and creating healthy cities for thriving societies, he begins with individual corporeal effects. If the factory runs down the human motor, the bath charges the human battery. As Junktime proliferates, we need more intelligence about baths. Junktime is the product of commingling with machines in some places, in others, it spawns from the interminability of camps or the uselessness of prison life. Baths need to take different forms in each of these places to sustain humanity in inhumane conditions. Baths are technologies for making-due in Junktime, for outlasting Garbagetime. A bath in Finland, one of the most digitally connected places on Earth, might look like the Kulttuurisauna, a contemporary architecture for primordial nourishment. What might one look like in an asylum seeker's center? Or a detention center? Neither will be designed or built by architects, unless the discipline opens its doors.

# The One, the Binary, the One-to-One, and the Many

Keller Easterling

It is the first global digital teenage war—a war in which, not nations, but members of an age-group living anywhere on the planet are enticed to travel to the cradle of civilization by the tens of thousands to annihilate each other. Among the distinguishing factors of the ISIS jihad are its dream to establish a caliphate, its significantly younger adherents, and its global digital reach. This magic cocktail composed of the teachings of monomaniacal clerics, sexual repression, violence, adventure, love, duty, and a yearning to belong mixed with the accelerant of social media seems to be especially potent and effective on the teenage mind. While millions stream away from Syria and Iraq, young people are traveling in the other direction to be part of an epic, lethal dream. And the numbers are doubling. In 2014, there were 12,000 foreign fighters from 81 countries. By the end of 2015, there were between 27,000 and 31,000 from 86 countries.[1] They are recruited through cells in cities around the world or contacted online. Some fit an expected profile while the stories of others are met with surprise and disbelief.

Contemporary culture finds it unfathomable that teenagers who seem to be cheerful, accomplished, and fully engaged in Western consumerism would be willing to trade their lives to engage with the grisly activities of ISIS.[2]

A young man in Cairo—a body builder and fun-loving friend and family member—began following commandments of a cleric who declared not only sexual behavior but even sexual thoughts to be a sin. Drifting further and further into solemn dress, resolute behavior, and strict adherence to more and more demanding Islamic practices, he became ripe for ISIS recruitment. The smiling pictures of him in the gym with newly sprouted muscles were replaced by smiling pictures of him in Syria with bloody weapons.[3]

Three young women from Bethnal Green in London—two aged fifteen and one aged sixteen—captured global media attention because their story seemed to defy all reason. As if reclaiming them from the dark side by pointing out identifying features of normality, the press and their families emphasized that they were straight-A students who liked to shop, hang out, listen to music, and dance. One of the girls, it was often mentioned, wore Lacoste perfume. Around six hundred women from around the world have joined in the ISIS jihad.[4]

Jihadi recruitment manuals—eerily simple, practical, and enthusiastic guides like "A Course in the Art of Recruiting"—describe the targets. The manual states that the best candidates are: "Any religious people who do not

1 "Foreign Fighters: An Updated Assessment of the Flow of Foreign Fighters to Syria and Iraq," The Soufan Group (New York, December 2015); R. Barrett, "Foreign Fighters in Syria," The Soufan Group (New York, 2014)

2 Two popular clerical authorities are Ahmad Jibril and Musa Cerantonio. J.A. Carter, S. Maher, and P.R. Neumann, "#Greenbirds: Measuring Importance and Influence in Syrian Foreign Fighter Networks," The International Centre for the Study of Rad-ical-isation and Political Violence (London, 2014)

3 http://www.nytimes.com/video/world/middleeast/100000003517767/fit-for-isis.html

4 Steven Morris, "British woman who joined Isis is jailed for six years," The Guardian, February 1, 2016; and Kimiko de Freytastamura," Teen-age Girl Leaves for ISIS Others Follow," New York Times,February 24, 2015. February 24, 2015.

نشرة دورية
تعنـــى
بالعمليات
العسكرية
للدولــة
الإسلامية
فـي العراق
والـشـام

النبأ
السنة الخامسة

العمليات
العسكرية
للدولة
الإسلامية
لسنة ١٤٣٤ هـ
فــي العراق

2013 annual report from The Islamic State of Iraq and Syria (ISIS). Cover.

2012 annual report from The Islamic State of Iraq and Syria (ISIS). Number of explosive devices the group detonated and the weaponry it had in its possession.

have the 5 following (negative) characteristics can be recruited: a. The coward b. The excessively talkative person c. The person who has hostile ideas against the Mujahideen d. The stingy person e. The loner." The person who talks too much asks too many questions about things out of sequence, and the stingy person does not recognize that "money is the backbone of Jihad." The loner, potentially the most independent of the possible recruits, is not promising because he or she does not really need a group. This sort of character is vilified as someone whose "life is traditional, i.e. boring, he can't make great changes. If he is absent from a gathering, there is no effect, whatsoever (no one misses him). Also, he has cold emotions." The manual also states: "The youths who live far from the cities" have "a natural disposition for the religion and it is easy to convince them and to shape them." Students over fifteen years of age are good candidates, although the guide cautions that university students might be spies.[5]

Like many evangelical texts, the guide is a gentle, almost selfless, call of salvation to a brotherhood and sisterhood. Like a management course that begins "in the next few meetings we will see," it is arranged as a holistic program with steps, checklists, and grades, all with the intent of addressing the problem of acquiring "money, men and weapons." Delivering the da'wa or religious call to Allah on the internet, the techniques exploit one-to-one contacts while social media enhances their potency and intimacy in isolation. For as long as necessary, relentlessly friendly contact, a strictly regimented schedule of daily activities, and exposure to webinars and videos gradually polishes the candidate until Jihad is inevitable. Finally, checklists, charts, surveys, and questionnaires score the performance of the candidate and trainer as if they were taking part in quality management self-evaluation. One chart, for instance, assigns seven points to practical means, three points to theoretical means, seven points to audio/visual media, and nine points to "Your own creative ways" for a total of twenty-five points.[6]

Whatever the assertions of this bureaucratic guide, the undeclared messages embedded in "Your own creative ways" may have special powers. Candidates tracked by research groups argue that the recruitment works because candidates feel isolated and uncertain of their identity in Western culture. They consistently feel that Muslims are persecuted around the world in the full view of an international community that does nothing. And they are drawn to the adventure, the humanitarian duties, and the sense of belonging to the sisterhood and brotherhood of a utopian caliphate.[7] But there are also simple kindnesses and love expressed by the recruiters—people who devote hours and hours to communicate in the middle of the night, describe an appealing form of heroism, and send gifts like candy or pictures of fighters in Raqqa gently holding kittens.[8] Analysts speculate that all of these approaches are designed to make recruits feel that they will be a more "compelling person."[9] Insanity is spoken by the voice of sanity, and the cadence of the argument mimics that of criticality.

One powerful female recruiter, Aqsa Mahmood, is something like a ring leader in high school—the smart, honest girl who mixes popularity with good grades, bossiness with inclusiveness, and religious devotion with Western worldliness and savvy. Surpassing irony, she has had amazing success with

5 Abu Amru Al Qa'idy, ed., "A Course in the Art of Recruiting." https://archive.org/stream/ACourseInTheArtOfRecruiting-RevisedJuly2010/A_Course_in_the_Art_of_Recruiting_-_Revised_July2010_djvu.txt

6 Ibid.

7 Erin Marie Saltman and Melanie Smith, 'Till Martyrdom Do Us Part' Gender and the ISIS Phenomenon. (PDF). Institute for Strategic Dialogue (London, 2015). p. 4, retrieved February 25, 2016.

8 R. Barrett, "Foreign Fighters in Syria;" Rukmini Callimachi, "ISIS and the Lonely Young American," New York Times, June 27, 2015.

9 R. Briggs and T. Silverman, Western Foreign Fighters: Innovations in Responding to the Threat, (PDF), Institute for Strategic Dialogue (London, 2014).

**10** Kimiko de Freytastamura, "Teenage Girl Leaves for ISIS Others Follow."

**11** R. Briggs and T. Silverman, *Western Foreign Fighters: Innovations in Responding to the Threat.*

**12** Joby Warrick, *Black Flags: The Rise of ISIS* (New York: Knopf Doubleday Publishing Group, 2015). Kindle edition.

**13** Rukmini Callimachi, "ISIS and the Lonely Young American."

**14** Shiv Malik, "The ISIS Paper: Behind 'Death Cult' Image Lies a Methodical Bureaucracy," *The Guardian*, December 7, 2015. See also R. Barrett, "Foreign Fighters in Syria;" J.A. Carter, S. Maher, and P.R. Neumann, "#Greenbirds: Measuring Importance and Influence in Syrian Foreign Fighter Networks;" and R.Briggs and T. Silverman, *Western Foreign Fighters: Innovations in Responding to the Threat.*

**15** Vikram Dodd and Nadia Khomami, "Two Bethnal Green schoolgirls 'now married to Isis men' in Syria," *The Guardian*, July 3, 2015.

**16** Erin Marie Saltman and Melanie Smith *'Till Martyrdom Do Us Part' Gender and the ISIS Phenomenon.*

**17** Carolyn Hoyle, Alexandra Bradford, and Ross Frenett, *Becoming Mulan? Female Western Migrants to ISIS*, (PDF), Institute for Strategic Dialogue (London, 2015).

**18** Kathy Gilsinan, "The ISIS Crackdown on Women, by Women," *The Atlantic*, July 25, 2014, retrieved February 25, 2016.

an "ISIS as girl power" message, and she was the one believed to have recruited the Bethnal Green trio. The successful recruiter counters the global cultural assumption that the Muslim woman is a victim. Teenagers who are given the sense that they have intelligence that no one else has or teenagers who actually are more intelligent than the parents or adults in their life may, in the absence of any other measure, feel they are exercising mature power and leadership.[10] The exceptional student and the perfect daughter may feel even more bullet-proof.

The social media delivery mechanism also has special powers to make individuals feel included or excluded, and other media forms amplify its power. Recruiters have used Go-Pro footage from the front that excites a mind accustomed to gaming.[11] The professionally-edited propaganda films suggest to teenagers that their intelligence will finally be recognized. They will finally be given the keys to a hyperbolic adulthood in a superior world. The films of beheadings or a film like the one in which the Jordanian fighter pilot Muath al-Kasasbeh was burned alive in a cage are carefully staged with computer graphics and Hollywood production values.[12] A teenager is offered a starring role—a hero's role—in the ultimate movie.

The power of the one-to-one contact is intensified with the dreams of "the one" caliphate. No longer an abstract desire, Abu Musab al-Zarqawi called for an implementation of the caliphate, and, in June 2014, Abu Bakr al-Baghdadi declared it to exist. Arrival on Syrian soil is a moment of rapturous euphoria for recruits who have been told that it is a sin to dwell outside the Muslim land. A woman from the United States, who first became curious about ISIS because of beheadings depicted in the media, was heavily recruited but did not travel to Syria. She said in an interview, "I think that they brought stability to the land. I think that it might be one of the safest places to live in the Middle East."[13] The caliphate is territorial and funded by oil revenue and confiscated property. But since it is also conceived as a universal condition, Raqqa is the center of the universe. Alongside other ghastly practices of killing and destruction, its administration strikes a remarkably bureaucratic, managerial tone, with a branded identity in stationery and logos, contracts, infrastructure and agricultural initiatives, elaborate rules and regulations, and even a corporate-style annual report.[14]

Once in Raqqa, the female recruits live communally and most are soon married. The Bethnal Green girls were married to men in their twenties within months of arrival.[15] Largely confined indoors, the female recruits do housework under difficult conditions and in fear of widowhood. But in this position, they are closer to god and share their stories of love, sisterhood, and brotherhood on encrypted sites.[16] The recruits share opinions about the need to cleanse the world of the PKK, Shia, and Jews, and about the beauty of beheadings and other forms of violence.[17] They tend to associate with those who speak the same language, and there are segregations between those who volunteered and those who were kidnapped. A story surfaced about a kidnapped woman who, as cover, became part of a brigade to enforce proper behavior and observance among the women. After escaping to Turkey, she spoke of beatings for small infractions.[18]

The story of ISIS is stupefying, and it makes no sense because no sense has been built around it. Conventional histories about the teenager at war—whether in the Crusades or the Spanish Civil War—usually fan the flames with narrative structures that draw on violent conflict and universal dreams. Enter the stories of ISIS recruitment, with their pictures of conscientious students and totems of modernity or consumerism, and our misaligned logics cannot deliver a satisfying explanation. Try to profile the recruit, and there is nothing that can be named. Teenagers themselves resist or exceed the capacities of cultural stories. Since the things they do are often shoved aside as non-conforming information, their behavior seems to come from nowhere, or it twists and inverts into paradox. Teenagers then seem to ironically engage in the most extreme behaviors to conform. They rebel against the conservatism of their parents who they see as "joiners" by even more desperately and completely pledging allegiance to a group.

But consider a story that focuses not on the names of religions or the brackets identifying age, but rather on the underlying dispositions—the one, the binary, the one-to-one, and the many. Cybernetician Gregory Bateson provided

2013 annual report from The Islamic State of Iraq and Syria (ISIS). Group's operations in 2013.

a model for this inquiry when he studied alcoholism and twelve-step programs. He contended that culture does not easily comprehend the apparently contradictory systems regarding alcoholism because of inadequate theoretic constructs to explain them. Bateson often looked past what people were saying to focus on the chemistry or circuitry of the organization. He frequently analyzed what he called "binary" organizations where two entities were either in a "symmetrical" binary with oppositional escalating tensions (alpha dog versus alpha dog), or a "complementary" binary in which one party was submissive to another (alpha dog and beta dog). The symmetrical condition described the ongoing competition with drugs or alcohol that led to escalating tensions. This fight of willpower against drugs is relieved by assuming a complementary posture—actually relaxing and giving in to an episode of using. Or alternatively, in a seeming paradox, the only moderately successful treatment involves, not a war against drugs and alcohol, but a submissive acknowledgement of powerless in the face of drugs and alcohol that is at the center of AA fellowship.[19] For Bateson, addiction offered a chance to demonstrate that a cybernetic orientation was a more appropriate model, one that could more easily process what would otherwise be regarded as inadmissible evidence. Cybernetic theory and holism aside, Bateson identified organizations where exchanges flowed freely and with less tension in a more information-rich network.

19 Gregory Bateson, *Steps to an Ecology of Mind* (Chicago: University of Chicago Press, 2000), 68.

20 https://www.youtube.com/user/abdullahx

21 R. Barrett, "Foreign Fighters in Syria."

22 http://www.dispatch.
com/content/stories/
local/2015/09/17/
refugees-impact-on-
community.html;
Suzanne Hall, "Migrant
Infrastructure:
Transaction economies
in Birmingham and
Leicester" (2016) Urban
Studies http://eprints.
lse.ac.uk/65328/; Suzanne
M. Hall, Julia King,
Robin Finlay, "Envisioning
Migration: Drawing
the infrastructure of
Stapleton Road, Bristol,"
New Diversities, accepted
12 April 2016; Dirk
Hoerder, "Flexible Spaces
or Demarcated Turf: Young
People's Views of Their
Lives and Belongings
in Two Neighbourhoods in
Hamburg, Germany" in Dirk
Hoerder, Yvonne Hebert,
and Irina Schmitt, eds.,
Negotiating Transcultural
Lives (Göttingen: V&R
University Press, 2005).

Similarly, to counter ISIS, deradicalization techniques perhaps do not work on content but rather on disposition. In other words, they do not try to refute the teachings of Islam or the politics of ISIS, nor do they try to substitute the values of Western culture. Rather, they approach with a one-to-one connection, offering the same fellowship and love as a threshold not to a monistic universal or a bloody battle but to the expansive platforms of difference that critical thought generates. One of the deradicalization programs is actually called *One2One*. Similarly, *Abdullah X* uses a YouTube channel and graphic novels to divert attention from radicalism with a sympathetic, critical voice devoted both to Islamic principles and to simply asking questions rather than making declarations.[20] Even defense strategies recognize that while binary battles only fuel the ISIS narrative, multiple splinter groups and rivals like Jabhat al-Nusra potentially confuse and, perhaps, partially diffuse ISIS power.[21] There is no single profile for a community that induces or rescues from radicalization, just as there is no single profile for radicalized individuals, but surely a successful community in any form possesses a disposition that eases tensions by being information rich. Finally, perhaps, there can be a story about the untold power of the fresh teenage mind that, by way of the one-to-one, leads adults and their ingrained cultural stories away from the one or the binary and on to the many.[22]

1 Exit Fondation
Cartier EXIT-Virilio,
Diller Scofidio + Renfro,
Hansen, Kurgan, Rubin,
Pietrusko, Smith-
2008–2015, https://
www.youtube.com/
watch?v=kyMbF2uuSIw

2 http://www.iata.
org/pressroom/pr/
Pages/2013-12-30-01.
aspx

3 http://www.ilo.
org/global/topics/
labour-migration/
lang--en/index.
htm. "Today, migrant
workers account for 150
million of the world's
approximately 244
million international
migrants."

4 http://www.unhcr.org

Fast forward through millions of years of constant migration—wandering, sailing, marching, exploring, and conquering. Arriving at the present, the tracings of these movements speed up and thicken.[1] Every year, three billion people, or almost half the people on earth, fly around in the atmosphere—even sometimes halfway around the world and back in the same day for business or pleasure—and tens of millions sail around on big cruise ships as tourists.[2]

Of all the technologies pushing, pulling, and conveying these streams of humanity, spatial technologies are among the most powerful. While spatial products composed of time and commodified experiences circulate consumers, giant installations of logistics and trade circulate hundreds of millions of people as cheap labor. Spatial networks have even created whole cities as repeatable formulas in a global network of free zones—an extra-state supernode of urbanism that offers incentives like no taxes, cheap labor, and the deregulation of labor and environmental laws. The sovereign states that exist to stabilize and defend territory and political property rights with war are ironically eager to sanction these extra-state spaces and partner with their market players. Nearly a quarter of a billion people are international migrants and 150 million of these are migrant workers who move through these networks.[3]

The atomized technologies of contemporary militarization also allow war to be waged everywhere over ideological tensions that may even be several degrees removed from place or national identity. The diaspora of war as distributed terrorism sets off a buckshot of multiple diasporas. In this scatter, currently sixty-five million people—more than at any other time in history—are displaced or locked out, their movements halting or precarious.[4] And while infrastructure space has managed to perfectly streamline the movement of billions of products, goods, and services, it somehow cannot manage to move several million people away from a global atrocity like Syria. This problem is simply one that cannot be solved.

Viewed from a distance, the migrating figure—floating on a rubber dinghy in the ocean or trapped in compounds and holding pens—is graphically caught between layers of the nation-state's false or contradictory logics. The nation-state cannot resolve the image of the refugee and, like a closed loop, behaves as if its only repertoire is to grant or deny citizenship. It is "the one." And given the desire for autonomy or supremacy when confronted with extrinsic or contradictory information, the nation-state often retaliates with a binary stance that declares the other to be an enemy. The nation-state circles the wagons, tightens its closed loop, and increases its security against further contradiction. As Jacques Rancière has written, "the immigrant appears as at once the perpetrator of an inexplicable wrong and the cause of a problem calling for the round-table treatment. Alternately problematized and hated, the immigrant is caught in a circle, one might even say a spiral: the spiral of lost political otherness."[5] While there have always been some obstacles to migration, the sovereignty of the nation-state abruptly stalls movement to achieve legal compliance. For extended periods of time, there can be no exchange, no place, no work, but only waiting and detention in a legal and cultural lacuna.

But as the same migrating figures come into closer view, they are immediately recognized. The press makes a point of mentioning the smartphones they hold in their hands. The migrant speaks all the shibboleths and displays all the accessories and stripes of belonging to multiple overlapping global social and commercial networks that selectively conquer terrains and territories. But this sense of digital connectivity, often falsely portrayed as something like a global demos, benefits global corporations more than individuals. It will not help now.

Besides, in this latest Syrian-European migration the information passing through smartphones or by word of mouth is information about the old nation-state. Even though national citizenship is not always what the members of a migrating population ultimately want, they are sifting through information about which nations will be most welcoming or provide the most sustaining health and education resources. At a moment when an individual should be surrounded by the most information about jobs, education or aid, the logic of inclusion and exclusion cancels out information.

The IGOs and NGOs that rush in at this juncture, unlike the global commercial networks, do not create their own reality, but rather exist immediately outside of national law or in the remaindered leavings of the nation. They inhabit the logical outcome of national law or the negative condition of the sanctioned state of citizenship—the place of exception and emergency that is the camp. These refugee camps have become permanent settlements that have been in operation for decades, with an average detention of seventeen years. They are strange inverted cousins of the free zone—that privileged entity that is somehow exempt from all the quaint restrictions of national bureaucracy. In some cases these antithetical entities even meet or cluster in extra-state conurbations like those in the Jordan Qualifying Industrial Zones (QIZ) where the free zone, in its quest to find the cheapest labor, hires women from the

5 Jacques Rancière, *On the Shores of Politics* (London: Verso, 1995), 105.

6 UNHCR, "Protracted refugee situations: the search for practical solutions," in *The State of the World's Refugees*, http://www.unhcr.org/4444afcb0.pdf; "Quest Means Business," interview with Guy Ryder, February 4, 2016, https://www.youtube.com/watch?v=1vFUo55AEzc

nearby refugee camp. And, behaving as if migrants threaten jobs that nations have in finite quantities, the International Labor Organization (ILO) recently proposed as a possible solution the employment of Syrian refugees in jobs at these very installations, some of them well known for labor abuse.[6]

In this blinkered historical absurdity, the migrant makes no sense because no sense has been built around them. Ingenuity to serve something other than a national/military/commercial story is somehow inconceivable. The nation is frequently reluctant to admit to all its other forms of sovereignty deployed in dealings with international networks or transactions across its borders. The migrations that have been constantly in progress for millennia are treated as aberrations, emergencies, or surprise events—footnotes to the histories in which nations and old-fashioned wars are the darlings.

Old anthems about protecting place and those who belong to that place continue to be sung, and authority continues to be given to conventional organs of design and governance even when they are spectacularly unimaginative. In mid-chorus, the voice should waiver and stray given the overwhelming evidence of the true nature of scattered and multifarious belonging. But banging away with blunt tools, the full-throated refrain of country, place and jobs defends against threats from the outside and is regarded as comforting and fortifying. This song is the anthem of a history that records finite events, declares boundaries, and chooses sides.

But turning the sound down on the anthem, imagine a history in which undeclared organizational dispositions are in the foreground rather than bombast about names, territories, and declarations. Beyond what nations are saying, their organizational constitution dooms them to oscillation between the one (or the monistic loop) and the binary. This oscillation is not the violence of warfare, but the deadly violence of remaining intact. If this oscillation between the closed loop and its binary remedy is structurally incapable of addressing the real material of the problem, what macro-organizational moves might shift the field of play without engaging the tragic logics of inclusion and exclusion?

What if this history on the flip side of conventional histories put five thousand years of migration at the center of the story. The moments of unrest and warfare around the world might be tragic, but the moment when people move away from them might be moments of celebration. Not only would human resources be streaming towards the rest of the world, but the contested subject of the fight would be walking away from the fight and starving it of the attention it craves and requires to exist. If history is usually enthralled with binary fights, this history would focus on those organizational shifts that ease tension. If the evacuation of people and resources—both disabled and able-bodied—were as carefully engineered and thoroughly financed as the invasion of territory, war mongers could routinely find themselves in a tussle over an empty box or throwing themselves against an open door. Replacing the national anthems might be songs about arrival and the diffusion of fear.

Not a crisis, but rather a constant, the refugee situation has no *solution*, and beyond an initial need to escape, each refugee has different needs and desires. Rather than trying to work solely through the state, the NGOcracy, or the market, perhaps it is possible to slither in between as social/political entrepreneurs who adjust disposition in space and offer spatial urban variables that change the terms of the problem. In the failure of both the commercial and the political is an opportunity to trade physical and labor resources in another way. Is it possible to exploit or hijack the powers of large infrastructural systems with protocols offering a branching set of options that are both more practical and politically agile?

Any macro-organizational shift would make time a more instrumental variable in migration. Displaced persons must wait a crushing amount of time to belong again or begin to exchange their talents and work with the world—a period of travel or quarantine that may last for years. The mobility to move and match their situation to their changing needs or to an opportunity for repatriation, is a better fit. An approach to passage—the first increment of time—might replace the current untenable model of storage for a refugee population. This model of passage might convert shipping/cruising/military logistics, the twenty-six billion dollar annual smuggling trade, and a portion of the budget for the maintenance of refugee camps into new options.[7] The passage away might be not only the moment to recover but also to engineer a branching itinerary composed of blocks of time—a fixed destination, a series of temporary stopovers, or a respite and return.

Another macro-organizational move overrides a binary deadlock with dominant national sovereignty in favor of one-to-one links between a refugee in one country and a personal financial or cultural sponsor in another. Sponsorships have long structured the most successful migrations. This sort of rewiring that multiplies one-to-one relationships changes the disposition of the political field—breaking the impasse and creating cascading changes in public opinion. For the refugee, if the one-to-one linkages are related to talents and resources from either party, they become even sturdier and more nuanced. But even the simple act of linkage potentially strengthens security and redoubles the possibility that information can be exchanged and released rather than contained in isolation. The one-to-one leads away from "the one" towards the many.

Aging nations consider refugee populations as a resource because of their relative youth, but few other assets of these populations are recognized and placed in productive interplay with other opportunities and problems in this one-to-one exchange. The sharing economy has linked millions of people in over 190 countries. Products and preferences in the market are endlessly tracked to individual needs and tastes. Might some of the same ingenuity be applied to problems of migration? More than the need for citizenship, migrating refugees often share with migrating labor the need to work or continue their studies. There is work to be done everywhere, and places with problems and opportunities that call for human capital. A super-rich network of information might be deployed to link the talents and resources of immigrants with global needs, scouring data to foreground jobs which require the special recruitment of talent and labor, if only for blocks of time. Countries not only have timed employment needs, but also housing that serves different populations at different stages of life, and territories that shrink and expand with the changing fortunes of the market.

As a process of evacuation, education, and linkage, these slow resettlement voyages might engage one-to-one indexes, or evaluate educational

7 http://www.aljazeera.com/programmes/countingthecost/2015/09/billion-dollar-business-refugee-smuggling-150913113527788.html; The budget to care for about a million refugees in Jordan in 2015 was set at USD 404.4 million, with the largest portion devoted to the emergency response for Syrian refugees. http://www.unhcr.org/pages/49e486566.html

needs, matching the needs and opportunities of a new location to the needs and talents of a migrating population. Some initial work, education, or accreditation might even be accomplished over the course of the journey. For some, a fixed destination or even a typical refugee installation is appropriate. For others, there is only certainty about the next ten years of their child's education, or the next four years of college, or a need for professional reaccreditation. For still others there might be a chance to design a global life for fifteen years of changing locations and educational opportunities. The university attended by anyone in the world anywhere in the world for four years or more has long been the first step in a branching global journey, and it has often served both a need to escape as well as a university's desire for diversity. The space-time of passage could facilitate that connection or convert the camp to the campus.

This sort of passage might seem to be a hopelessly complicated process with far too many unexpected, even dangerous outcomes. The Philippine Overseas Employment Agency (POEA) finds jobs (1,687,831 in 2011) for millions of its citizens, but it has often put those citizens at risk in difficult or poorly paid jobs.[8] And while shipping and cruising logistics are expertly scheduled to meet quotas, tightly organized materials-handling logistics and complex supply chain networks, they are themselves sources of labor and environmental abuse.[9] Still, some forms of productive passage may be just complicated enough and with enough players to be robust and self-sustaining in various forms. Nothing could be less productive and more information-free than the indefinite extra-state storage of migrating populations in camps.

Might it even be possible to imagine inverting the impossibly unjust status of the refugee as rejected and victimized? Migrating individuals who trade their intelligence and willingness to engage in a global network of endeavors and exchanges have already earned a special status in the world. Just as Dean MacCanell speculated that the tourist is the new social scientist, perhaps the migrants engineering a more sustained passage through the world are trusted to be the new global leaders, diplomats, and strategists.[10] The migrating population is primarily composed of young people, and there are great fears about a lost generation or about the cruel processes of migration fueling the fires of radicalization. But perhaps migration is instead the adventure of learning that attracts and nourishes growing minds, and the experience of being a refugee is the special credential of those who know multiple languages and cultures as well as techniques to ease tensions and violent dispositions. The story of this passage can capture a global imagination as a story about being released from the conflicting logics of sovereignty. It is a story not about those who belong nowhere but those who belong everywhere—who use the one-to-one to move away from the one and binary towards the many.

8 http://www.poea.gov.ph/

9 For instance, the experience economy has created luxury products like Residensea and the Freedomship International. Freedomship, the so-called "City at Sea," would allow for constant movement around the world. Carrying 100,000 people, the ship—4500 by 750 feet—would move constantly around the world and even allow for a global children's soccer league. The promoters of the ship argue that it will make money and create jobs. http://freedomship.com/.

10 Dean MacCannell, The Tourist (Berkeley: University of California Press, 1976), 1–16, 91–107.

# Teçhņò-Rēļįgiōuš Cŏmmūnĩtieš
## in Lagos

Communication technologies have a central role in the redefinition of daily life in Lagos, Nigeria, pervasively inflecting the spaces of the city, its urban landscape, and its architectures. The increase of bandwidth and the massive use of mobile phones and tablets in Sub-Saharan countries has resulted in new expectations for the region, and a growing enthusiasm that has been mobilized for a diversity of goals, including religion. These technologies have been appropriated by religious congregations as a tool of both dissemination and gathering, in the hope of addressing growing transnational communities. Updating the operations of religious belonging, certain communities have proceeded to utilize technology to maximize the effects of big ceremonies as events of spiritual mediation in their own right, as well as to broadcast these ceremonies as messages to be heard and seen through different technological media.

Among these religious affiliations, Charismatic-Pentecostalism (an international movement within the Christian faith), has witnessed an unparalleled growth, and has exponentially expanded its presence in Sub-Saharan countries in the last two decades. From huge interiors hosting celebrations for thousands and small garages adapted with decorative curtains and lighting fixtures to temporary tent structures, spaces of worship repurpose existing buildings and pop-up as new constructions as well. The architectures of congregation hosting these events are not only transforming the physical landscape of the surrounding city, but might now also be understood as transmission platforms.

From videotapes and sound recordings of ceremonies, to online streaming and televangelism, technology is being increasingly mobilized to foster spiritual and social congregation.

The Redeemed Christian Church of God annual convention campground near Mowe, on the outskirts of Lagos.
Photograph by Robin Hammond, ca. 2013. Courtesy of Robin Hammond and National Geographic.

Lagos

Emeka Ogboh

Nigeria has thousands of registered churches, with Lagos—the nation's most populous city and its major commercial hub—hosting the majority. These churches are fast springing up in many different corners of Lagos, and this phenomenon is also being transmitted through the city's visual and sound scapes. Sermons, prayers, and worship songs are becoming part and parcel of the urbanism of the city, often broadcast from the private spaces that serve as the privileged locations for religious gatherings.

Many of these new places of worship result from the conversion of residential homes (from living rooms to garages) and commercial spaces (such as shops) into places of worship and fellowship. Given the small number of followers who establish these constantly germinating congregations, this conversion has proven to be a cheaper solution than renting entirely new spaces. The location of these venues affects the soundscapes of their surrounding urban areas. Particularly on Sundays, prayers, religious sermons, and live vocal and instrumental performances—both in English, and in various Nigerian languages—are channeled through loudspeakers and public address systems into the surrounding areas. These religious sounds merge with the noise of the city, human and vehicular traffic, and the ubiquitous sound of power generators.

The twenty-first century expansion of churches is not just limited to physical spaces. Aiming to spread the gospel far and wide, the churches are rapidly expanding online and on television to accommodate remote spiritual fellowship. Their worship expand across countries and media formats in the form of apps like iOpenHeavens, Facebook pages, Twitter handles, YouTube channels and even in architectural projects like *Mount Carmel,* a Prayer Village located in Osun State, Nigeria. Religious organizations are focusing on the increasing value of digital technology, which enables them to fulfill their mission, using tele-evangelism, social media, and other online platforms to reach the multitude that awaits in the digital space.

All photographs by Jeremiah Ikongio, 2015, Lagos.

# Tèchṇolōgĩĕs fōř a Lifę įń Tranŝĭť
## Works

## Uncharted

Folder (Marco Ferrari, Elisa Pasqual, Pietro Leoni)
with Alessandro Mason

Cartographic representations and geographic information databases are used daily by millions of people to move across familiar environments, plan long-range trips, cross national borders, reach shores of unknown countries in hope of a better life, and search oceanic seabeds for untapped resources. Once directly linked to a physical activity on a territory, the action of topographic measurement necessary to produce a map now has been replaced by the real-time observations of various geospatial technologies orbiting the planet. Land surveying has been transformed from a concerted parade of military and state presences into the invisible monitoring of natural features and human activities from the infinite distance of the satellite.

Even if spatially disconnected from the fate of our earthly surroundings (and bound to an almost-eternal life outside of the harsh conditions that constantly reshape the ground being monitored), these systems are owned by nation-states, managed through an intricate network of ground stations, their data routed through fiber-optic cables and distribution servers. This monitoring infrastructure is designed to conceal its different agendas—and the dialectics between the different national supremacies at play.

On the screen where the information is delivered and experienced, all that counts is a smooth navigation experience. We can go everywhere—and we belong anywhere—on the evenly accessible surface criss-crossed by GPS-calculated paths. Along with global search engines for flights that aggregate thousands of airline databases to find the cheapest combination of stopovers for reaching virtually any airport on Earth, portable positioning devices are the most striking evidence of the profitable rhetoric of a borderless world. Political and natural features are erased under the uniform roaming of a GPS positioning dot.

The northenmost regions of Earth are also its ultimate undermapped territories—where accurate geographic information decays into algorithmically interpolated satellite scans—and, at the same time, the best location to download information from the polar-orbiting satellites that are used for earth-mapping, reconnaissance and intelligence tasks, and climate and environmental studies. By observing the current transformations within these regions and the corresponding evolution of mappingtechnologies, we can take a snapshot of the production chain of contemporary geographic knowledge, and the interaction between the different national agencies that control this global orbiting infrastructure.

1 Bernt Rostad, "Platåberget," March 23, 2015. Svalbard Satellite Station (SvalSat), located at 78°N on Spitsbergen, Norway. SvalSat and TrollSat—its Antarctic counterpart—are the only ground stations in the world able to provide all-orbit support to polar-orbiting satellites. © Bernt Rostad, courtesy of the author.

2 Rick Bajornas, "Approaching Svalbard Satellite Station (SvalSat) on July 8th, 2015." SvalSat is located at at 78°N, close to Longyearbyen and is recognized as the best-located ground station in the world for satellite observations. © UN Photo/ Rick Bajornas, courtesy of the author.

1

2

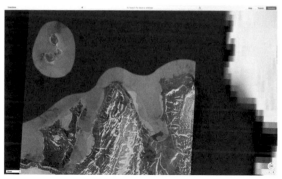

"Satellite image of the Svalbard archipelago from Apple Maps," images captured by DigitalGlobe, accessed May 24, 2016. Each of the four active satellites (WorldView-1, 2, 3 and GeoEye-1) maintain a sun-synchronous low-earth orbit. The sensors circle the earth's poles every ninety minutes, transmitting each image to the SvalSat base station. Courtesy of DigitalGlobe.

Femke Herregraven

*Sprawling Swamps* is a digital installation that proposes a series of speculative infrastructures that operate on a technological, legal, and social level and which are placed on a number of unstable territories. These infrastructures are dispersed within the cracks of the contemporary financial geography that is shaped by the rat race for speed, loopholes in international law, and financial regulation. As loopholes within loopholes, these speculative infrastructures are located on unstable territories such as swamps, ice, and shifting shorelines. Within these territories, the binary presumption of land or water is ineffective, as well as theories of territories and laws: it is unclear what is to be governed when territories can melt, drown, or erode. The dynamic nature of matter itself—and therefore its territory—complicates legal framing but also matter's absorbance into infrastructures, whether legal, physical, or social. It is from this ambiguous condition that *Sprawling Swamps* explores new infrastructures and geographies for reevaluating, reinventing, and transmitting "value." Could exhaustion, sleep, intimacy, loneliness, and empathy be starting points for value and infrastructures?

Flat, rectangular objects made out of translucent materials once floated in the ocean. Much like uninhabited islands these mysterious blocks were never really noticed and no attention was paid to them. That is, until they drifted ashore to capture our imagination. *Malleable Regress* comprises a series of tiles of polyurethane rubber, which reappear as props in *Sprawling Swamps*. They are archeological remnants in a fictional scenario in which platforms were strategically placed in the ocean based on a set of specific coordinates. These locations were calculated as mid-colocation points where communication nodes would connect to make for an optimal planetary-scale high-speed trading infrastructure. The sculpture itself derives from the recent discovery of 100-year-old gutta-percha blocks from Indonesia that have been mysteriously washing up on beaches in Europe. This rubber-like tree gum was originally used in the nineteenth and first half of the twentieth centuries to insulate the All Red Line, a network of telegraph submarine cables of the British Empire.

*The All Infrared Line* is an ongoing research project that focuses on the historical and contemporary construction and geography of the telecommunications infrastructure, which serves as the backbone of today's financial markets.

Femke Herregraven, "Sprawling Swamps." Digital installation screen capture, 2016. All images courtesy of the artist.

2

3

1

1 Femke Herregraven, "The All Infrared Line,"
2012 – ongoing, film still, cable landing point
Mauritius.

2 Femke Herregraven, "Malleable Regress," 2016,
original objects.

3 Femke Herregraven, "Malleable Regress," 2016,
ten polyurethane sculptures.

All images courtesy of the artist.

## Immaterials at Home

### Einar Sneve Martinussen and Jørn Knutsen

Our environment is comprised not only of the physical, visible architecture and infrastructure that we can see and touch, but also of immaterial and invisible technological structures that have a profound impact on how we experience the world. WiFi, GPS, streaming technologies, and mobile networks are among the invisible materials which enable contemporary digital culture. As we increasingly inhabit technical systems, and enact society and culture through them, it seems dangerous to have so little idea about how these things work. Our inability to see these systems hinders our capacity to critically understand and evaluate their importance across contemporary life.

*Immaterials at Home* seeks to investigate commonplace technologies of contemporary networked living, with a focus on domestic spaces. Contemporary homes consist of an increasing number of networked objects, including phones, tablets, TVs, stereos, and lightbulbs. Data is being streamed in and out of homes across these objects. The processes and protocols that make these circulations possible are both mundane and obscure. What does the networked landscape of a contemporary home look like? *Immaterials at Home* is a work-in-progress in which we are creating instruments and visualizations for making this technological, domestic landscape accessible as a cultural phenomena.

1

1  Martinussen, Arnall, and Knutsen, "Light painting WiFi," 2011. The *Immaterials* project has previously used light, design, and photography to visualize the spatial characteristics of WiFi networks (seen here in 2011). Martinussen and Knutsen, with their latest project, explore the complex behaviors within such a network. Courtesy of the authors.

2  Knutsen and Martinussen, "The complex minutia of networked life," Screenshot, 2016. Today, domestic wireless networks have become remarkably complex, with data streams flowing in and out of our homes through a growing ensemble of devices and applications. Here, we see the network activity and sources/destinations for information from a few seconds of browsing Instagram on a smartphone. Courtesy of the authors.

```
192.168.2.2 -> 31.13.72.53 | 1398 | Ireland
192.168.2.2 -> 31.13.72.53 | 1398 | Ireland
192.168.2.2 -> 31.13.72.53 | 675 | Ireland
192.168.2.2 -> 31.13.72.53 | 1398 | Ireland
192.168.2.2 -> 31.13.72.53 | 675 | Ireland
192.168.2.2 -> 31.13.72.53 | 0 | Ireland
192.168.2.2 -> 31.13.72.8 | 31
192.168.2.2 -> 31.13.72.8 | 0 | Ireland
192.168.2.2 -> 31.13.72.8 | 0 | Ireland
192.168.2.2 -> 31.13.72.8 | 0 | Ireland
192.168.2.2 -> 31.13.72.53 | 490
192.168.2.2 -> 31.13.72.53 | 1398
192.168.2.2 -> 31.13.72.53 | 1398
192.168.2.2 -> 31.13.72.53 | 1398
192.168.2.2 -> 31.13.72.53 | 1398
192.168.2.2 -> 31.13.72.53 | 53
192.168.2.2 -> 31.13.72.53 | 0
192.168.2.2 -> 31.13.72.53 | 0
192.168.2.2 -> 31.13.72.53 | 0
192.168.2.2 -> 31.13.72.53 | 0
192.168.2.2 -> 31.13.72.8 | 31 | Ireland
192.168.2.2 -> 31.13.72.53 | 1398 | Ireland
192.168.2.2 -> 31.13.72.53 | 1398 | Ireland
192.168.2.2 -> 31.13.72.53 | 1398 | Ireland
192.168.2.2 -> 31.13.72.53 | 53 | Ireland
192.168.2.2 -> 31.13.72.53 | 1398 | Ireland
192.168.2.2 -> 31.13.72.53 | 490 | Ireland
192.168.2.2 -> 31.13.72.53 | 0 | Ireland
192.168.2.2 -> 31.13.72.53 | 0 | Ireland
192.168.2.2 -> 31.13.72.53 | 0 | Ireland
192.168.2.2 -> 31.13.72.53 | 0 | Ireland
192.168.2.2 -> 17.252.108.34 | 0
192.168.2.2 -> 17.252.108.34 | 0
192.168.2.2 -> 17.252.108.34 | 0
192.168.2.2 -> 17.252.108.34 | 0 | Cupertino, United States
192.168.2.2 -> 17.252.108.34 | 0 | Cupertino, United States
192.168.2.2 -> 17.252.108.34 | 0 | Cupertino, United States
192.168.2.2 -> 66.220.146.163 | 37
192.168.2.2 -> 66.220.146.163 | 0
192.168.2.2 -> 31.13.72.53 | 0
192.168.2.2 -> 31.13.72.53 | 0
192.168.2.2 -> 31.13.72.53 | 0
192.168.2.2 -> 66.220.146.163 | 0
192.168.2.2 -> 66.220.146.163 | 0
192.168.2.2 -> 66.220.146.163 | 0
192.168.2.2 -> 66.220.146.163 | 0
192.168.2.2 -> 66.220.146.163 | 0
192.168.2.2 -> 66.220.146.163 | 37 | Menlo Park, United States
192.168.2.2 -> 31.13.72.53 | 0 | Ireland
192.168.2.2 -> 66.220.146.163 | 0 | Menlo Park, United States
192.168.2.2 -> 31.13.72.53 | 0 | Ireland
192.168.2.2 -> 31.13.72.53 | 0 | Ireland
192.168.2.2 -> 66.220.146.163 | 0 | Menlo Park, United States
192.168.2.2 -> 66.220.146.163 | 0 | Menlo Park, United States
192.168.2.2 -> 66.220.146.163 | 0 | Menlo Park, United States
192.168.2.2 -> 66.220.146.163 | 0 | Menlo Park, United States
```

## Red Silk of Fate—Tamaki's Crush/Teshima 8 Million Lab
## Sputniko!

Red String of Fate is an East Asian mythology in which gods tie an invisible red string between those who are destined to be together. Sputniko! collaborated with scientists in genetically engineering silkworms to spin this mythical "Red String of Fate" by inserting genes that produce oxytocin—a social-bonding "love" hormone—and the genes of a red-glowing coral into silkworm eggs. In the past, science challenged and demystified the world of mythologies, from Galileo's trial to Darwin's theory of evolution and beyond; but, in the near future, perhaps, science could recreate our mythologies.

The film *Red Silk of Fate—Tamaki's Crush* unravels a story around the protagonist Tamaki, an aspiring genetic engineer, who engineers her own "Red Silk of Fate" in the hope of winning the heart of her crush, Sachihiko. She sews the "Red Silk of Fate" into her favorite scarf in order to win the love of her dreams,

but strange, mythical powers start to inhabit her creation....

*Teshima 8 Million Lab* is the first Shinto shrine worshipping a genetically engineered life form— a silkworm created for Sputniko!'s work *Red Silk of Fate—Tamaki's Crush*. In the Shinto religion, "Yaoyorozu" (which literally means "8 Million") is a word used to describe the myriad of gods believed to reside in almost anything—such as the wind, the ocean, trees, and animals. *Teshima 8 Million Lab* sets out to create new members of Yaoyorozu, forming a mythology by merging science and art. Far from the big city and located on a site blessed with an abundance of nature, the facility invites the exploration of alternative perspectives on the future of nature and beliefs, as science continues to move forward.

Project Team: *Red Silk of Fate* is a project by Sputniko!. *Teshima 8 Million Lab* is a project by Sputniko! with architecture by Naruse Inokuma Architects, and curated by Yuko Hasegawa. *Teshima 8 Million Lab* is supported by Fukutake Foundation.

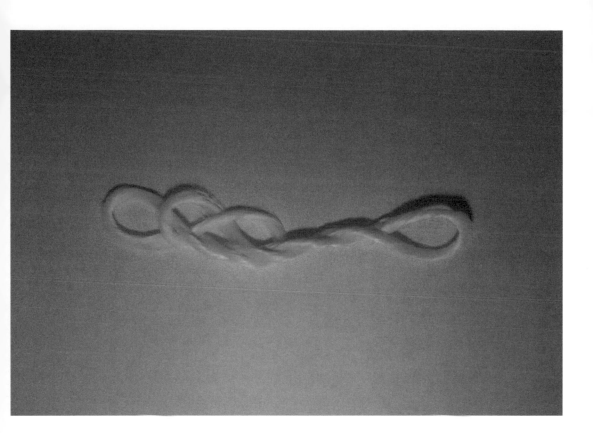

Sputniko!, "Red Silk of Fate—Tamaki's Crush," 2016.
All images courtesy of the artist and SCAI The Bathhouse, Tokyo.

## Pornified Homes

### Andrés Jaque / Office for Political Innovation

1

Joseph Bory Latour-Marliac's 1890 genetic hybridizations can be seen as the origin of a replacement. With his innovations, the three-step technique to bring home and exploit the findings of European colonial states—expedition, displacement, and resettling of the exoticized—was then replaced by a precious capacity to recompose genes as a means to render bodies and plants pornified, multimedia, and ready-to-be-taken-home: a shift from an expansive Europe, with an exoticized periphery, to daily co-habitation with layers of sexy exotics.

The 2014 snapshot of the sex-worker Rogerio dos Santos being entertained by MP Mark Menzies in the Houses of Parliament was perceived as evidence of the pair's improper intimacy. The pornified profile of dos Santos, self-labeled as a "Brazilian hunk," in the number-one UK male-escort directory sleepyboy.com, rendered him as displaced in a circulation fueled precisely by the way he was tagged to the "Brazilian" demarcation.

The 1849 publicizing of a *Victoria amazonica* blossoming for the first time in the UK, months after having been plucked from the Esequibo Region in Amazonia, is sleepyboy.com's foundation. The construction of the Lily Hothouse at Chatsworth to provide *Victoria amazonica* with a capsule of tropical habitat was part of the equation by which tropical entities were resocialized through displacement + encapsulated environment + transmedia iteration.

In 1890 Joseph Bory Latour-Marliac succeeded in producing the first hybrid water lilies, crossing US specimens with European *Nymphaea alba*. The composition of transnational subjectivities was coupled with President Harrison's desire to render US waterfronts as infrastructures for transnational circulation. Based on Latour-Marliac's technique, online directories such as internationalwaterlilycollection.com mediate in the transnational manufacturing and relocation of water lilies always perceived as exotic, but constituted so distributed networks of collectors can acquire them by dragging their fingers across the smooth-to-the-skin potassium-coated ion-strengthened glass of their iPhones.

As Parliamentary Private Secretary to the Minister of State for Housing Mark Prisk, Menzies promoted the reinforcement of the "Bedroom Tax," a policy that has resulted in the massive eviction of social tenants from their homes within the UK, the displaced being simultaneously reconstructed as unrooted and as attached to the "social-benefit receptor" label, forced to compose their domesticity in the journey from shelters to the temporary occupancy of public space. Sleepyboy.com, internationalwaterlilycollection.com, and the "Bedroom Tax" are all technologies contributing to exoticize contemporary subjects, setting them in displacement, detached from fixed permanent environments while displaying them to be perceived as the vernacular of a demarcation of other.

**SUNDAY** £1.10 MARCH 30, 2014 HAPPY MOTHER'S DAY
# Mirror
## Michelle Collins
'My pills overdose'

### EXCLUSIVE: NO 10 ROCKED BY CRISIS

# TORY MP QUITS IN DRUGS & RENT BOY SCANDAL

**SUNDAY Mirror INVESTIGATION**

2

3

4

1 "Gabriel at his home in Chelsea, London." Production stills from the video installation "Pornified Homes" by Andrés Jaque / Office for Political Innovation, with direction of photography by Jorge López Conde and Eduardo López Rodríguez, London, 2016. Courtesy by Andrés Jaque / Office for Political Innovation.

2 "Top Tory MP quits over rent boy scandal," *The Sunday Mirror*, March 30, 2014. Newspaper Cover.

3 "Marcos and his dog Eros at their home in Kensington, London." Production stills from the video installation "Pornified Homes" by Andrés Jaque / Office for Political Innovation, with direction of photography by Jorge López Conde and Eduardo López Rodríguez, London, 2016. Courtesy by Andrés Jaque / Office for Political Innovation.

4 "The Gigantic Water-Lily (*Victoria Regia*), in flower at Chatsworth" from *Illustrated London News*, November 17, 1849, 328.

1 Online directories of Brazilian escorts.

2 *"Victoria Regia* at Royal Botanical Gardens Kews, London." Production stills from the video installation "Pornified Homes" by Andrés Jaque / Office for Political Innovation, with direction of photography by Jorge López Conde and Eduardo López Rodríguez, London, 2016. Courtesy by Andrés Jaque/Office for Political Innovation.

3 "Bedroom Tax" covers in the press.

4 Hybridization Process of *Victoria Amazonica*. www.victoria-adventure.org/waterlilies/make_your_own.html

5 Online directories for manufacturing and relocating (exoticizing) water lilies and contemporary subjects.

All photo-collages and manipulated images: Andrés Jaque/ Office for Political Innovation, "Pornified Homes."

1

2

3

4

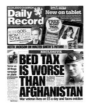

# PatchWork

## Martti Kalliala

Inside ≠ Outside

Total Freedom

We live in an age of #exit. Wherever one looks, one sees individual and collective escapes—or escape attempts—from systems and situations interpreted as broken, obsolete, and/or hopeless.

Exit, insofar it requires a habitable space to escape to, poses a fundamental question: Where to? If none of the existing alternative destinations are satisfying or possible—if one is vying for an *ultimate* exit—where can one find *terrae incognitae?*

Many believe that the answer is to be found in technological "disruption" through digitalization.

The processes which made huge numbers of textile workers obsolete after the invention of the Jacquard loom in the early nineteenth century, and transformed and overthrew a number of industries two hundred years later, are now ready to take on the "legacy source code" of government itself.

PatchWork explores the spatio-/ideo-/techno-logical foundations of a variety of exit trajectories found across the world today as well as their collective logical conclusion: the world as a layered patchwork.

Thanks to Katja Huhmarkangas.

# Hŏme Shaŗĩñg Platformš
in Copenhagen

Home sharing platforms are becoming increasingly popular around the world, leading to new forms of cohabitation that challenge the relationship between commerce, residency, and ownership. For a city like Copenhagen that was a pioneer in shared inhabitation models beginning with the introduction of co-housing communities in the 1970s, the flourishing of home sharing companies such as Airbnb may be seen as the market-oriented version of the Scandinavian culture of communal living.

Airbnb provides access to a distributed network of privately-owned residential spaces and domestic interiors, from spare rooms and couches, to entire houses and apartments. Unknown "guests" pay to live amongst the belongings of others, simultaneously challenging traditional ideas of homeliness and tourism. Domestic artifacts are, in this context, potential revenue streams. What "guests" are seeking to rent is not simply the bed itself but the "authentic" experience of temporarily being a local.

The transformed conditions of tourism and habitation that Airbnb's promise embodies provide an opportunity to connect strangers and expand the economic benefits brought by travelers beyond traditional touristic areas. However, some reports point out that the service exacerbates housing shortages and masks how rental prices have risen so high that many people cannot afford to pay them without, paradoxically, the supplemental income from renting out their own homes. Airbnb hides a controversial reality behind the welcoming and inclusive rhetoric of the company's commercial slogan: "Belong anywhere."

Reaching from the inflatable mattress to the city, the various scales of these phenomena highlight a questioning of the role of architectural expertise in defining documents, visualizing processes, and intervening in the architectural logics triggered by the so-called sharing economy.

# Classic Apt near the Lakes and City

København, Hovedstaden, Denmark ★ ★ ★ ★ ★ (17)

Entire home/apt

2 Guests

1 Bedroom

## $137

Digital Platform, 2015. Courtesy of Airbnb.

Check in                    Check out                    Gues

Selling Dreams

Ila Bêka and Louise Lemoine

Imagine yourself telling a friend a few years ago: "Could I crash on your couch tonight? A couple is sleeping in my bed." She would most probably have thought something was wrong with you....

And yet, today, it is common to rent your apartment—or even your bed— for one night or more to a complete stranger. You will even sacrifice your own time, be kind and welcoming, and let them have access to anything they might need in your apartment during their stay: your food, your books, your computer, your personal beauty products....

Your bedroom is now ready to welcome these strangers who will sleep in your bed, covered by your bed linen, leaning on your pillow. Wasn't this bed your ultimate refuge? Your place to relax, love, dream, and confide? The one and only place that really belonged to you? Are you not disturbed by the fact that tonight this couple will sleep where your dreams lie, and will make love over the shape of your body impressed in the mattress?

I understand. You need money. It's indeed an easy way to earn some money to pay your rent or to go on holiday. You are probably right, after all.

But what I would like to know and understand is what happens deep down within you when you hand your keys over to this young couple after giving them access to your intimacy and say to them with your usual kind and appealing smile: "Have a great stay, and enjoy!"

**Storyboard sketches. Ila Bêka and Louise Lemoine,**
**"Selling Dreams," 2016.**

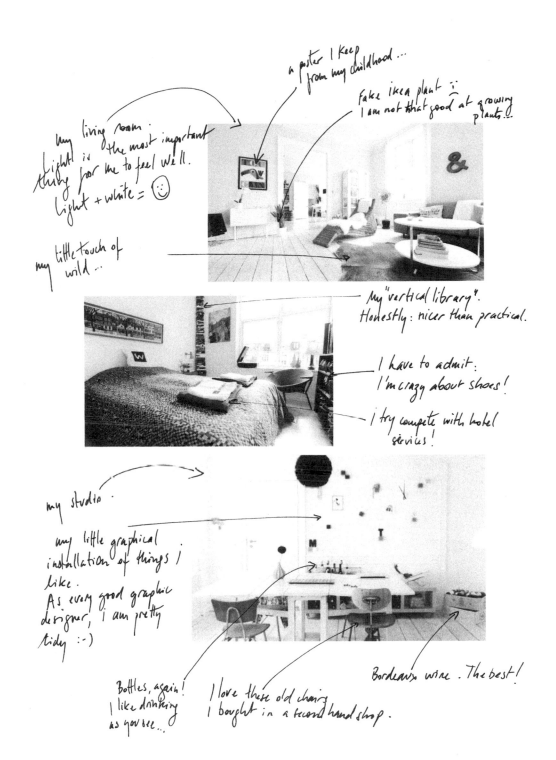

a poster I keep from my childhood...

Fake ikea plant :.
I am not that good at growing plants..:.

my living room :
Light is the most important thing for me to feel well.
Light + white = ☺

my little touch of wild...

My "vertical library".
Honestly: nicer than practical.

I have to admit:
I'm crazy about shoes!

I try compete with hotel services!

my studio

my little graphical installation of things i like.
As every good graphic designer, i am pretty tidy :-)

Bordeaux wine. The best!

Bottles, again!
I like drinking as you see...

I love these old chairs I bought in a second hand shop.

Film Stills. Ila Bêka and Louise Lemoine, "Selling Dreams," 2016.

# Markets and Territories
# of the Global Home
## Texts

# The One / The Other: Mass Media Identity Constructions in Architecture between Mexico and California, 1915–1951

Cristina López Uribe

When Juan O'Gorman and Juan Legarreta built some of the first modernist houses in Mexico City around 1930, the European references were clear. Le Corbusier's ideas, books, and images had traveled to a post-revolutionary Mexico where they found a fertile ground for development, especially the local reading of the chapter "Architecture or Revolution" in *Vers une Architecture* (1923). Facing the threat described by Le Corbusier, the young architects idealistically aimed to address the problems of the country through low cost housing and educational buildings supported by the State. The architects utilized an architecture comprised of bare concrete-frame structures devoid of aesthetic intentions or superfluous expenses—or so they claimed. Three large housing developments for workers were built in Mexico City based on a design prototype by Juan Legarreta, and twenty-five new elementary schools were erected under the direction of Juan O'Gorman as the head of the construction department of Mexico City's Public Education Ministry between 1932 and 1934. O'Gorman also designed houses for intellectuals in tune with this conception of modernism.

But the architecture of this Mexican avant-garde, unlike the structures being built by avant-gardes elsewhere at the same time, was never conceived as "universal." The Mexican Revolution (1910–1920) raised many nationalist sentiments that made the global search for a "national identity" inescapable within the Mexican context.

In contrast to the new state-sponsored architecture that recreated the highly ornamented colonial architecture of the seventeenth and eighteenth centuries—the Neocolonial style—Juan O'Gorman and Juan Legarreta, the "radical functionalists" as they were called, incorporated multiple references to popular architectures from rural Mexico into their otherwise avant-garde mechanically-produced architectural expressions.

One of the most striking features of their functionalist practice was the use of color. Unlike Le Corbusier's abstract use of color in the Pessac housing development (1925), O'Gorman and Legarreta employed color in place of baseboards and window and door casings to highlight these junctions in a contrasting way—as was the practice throughout the towns and old cities of Mexico. Furthermore, the rough finish of the construction and the hand-brushed finishing coat of paint on the walls appealed to folk art and traditional crafts that were similarly present in the interior furnishings of the functionalist houses. In addition, the designs of the landscapes were carefully planned to look as if they were not designed, mimicking those found in rural settings. One example of these seemingly accidental plantings was the cactus fence used to delimit the properties—a feature used in many of the small towns around Mexico City.

All these strategies, however, were not enough for this architecture to be read at the time as a Mexican expression—if that was the intention in using them rather than an intention to utilize the dislocating strategies of the avant-garde.

By 1933, radical functionalism was condemned and opposed by the guild of architects, considered as a misstep in the search for a "correct" path to develop a modern Mexican architecture. This rejection of functionalism was due to a number of reasons, some political, others aesthetic—or, rather, what was understood as the lack of aesthetics. However, the one reason of particular importance was that the radical functionalists were accused of doing "non-Mexican" architecture. As was clear during the 1933 conferences organized by the Society of Architects with the intention of criticizing the radical use of functionalism in Mexico:

> [T]oday,... European modernist architecture has been imported.... Further-
> more, it is truly sad to say but true: we have to state that what has been
> done is a cartoon of the foreign architecture. We must take into consider-
> ation that this architecture does not adapt well to our way[s].... [I]t does
> not answer, no matter what they say, to our Mexican way of life.[1]

Nonetheless, the relationship of the Mexican avant-garde with anonymous popular architecture—instead of educated Spanish colonial—would later prove to be a less troubled connection. As O'Gorman himself explained some decades later, the inspiration for this interest came not directly from Mexico, but rather from California:

> After the Mexican Revolution of 1910, architects began to interest them-
> selves in folk architecture provoked in part by the popularity in the United
> States at that time of the Mexican Ranch Style, introduced by California
> architects and subsequently re-introduced into Mexico, where it was
> accepted by the Academy. This was our first attempt to express Mexico in
> its popular aspect, and was soon abandoned.[2]

In this case, O'Gorman was writing about the Neocolonial style which, contemporary to functionalism, obviously shared some of the same influences.

**1**

In the 1950s, the Gardens of El Pedregal suburban residential development designed by Luis Barragán was broadly publicized by the media and was surrounded by several myths. As scholars have shown, a cleverly designed advertising campaign was manufactured to sell real estate which linked the volcanic landscape of the subdivision with the profound sense of what was considered, at the time, the "Mexican spirit."[3]

The abstract and surreal photographic images of the landscape taken by Armando Salas Portugal were central in conveying this message and thus

Juan O'Gorman, "Cecil O'Gorman House and Studio." 1929. Pencil and watercolor on tracing paper. Museo Casa Estudio Diego Rivera, INBA, Mexico.

1 Silvano B. Palafox, "Ideas sobre arquitectura moderna en México," in Alfonso Pallares, ed., *Pláticas sobre arquitectura: México, 1930* (Mexico City: Lumen, 1934), 67.

2 Juan O'Gorman, "Statement," *Arts & Architecture* (March, 1955), 30.

3 See Alfonso Pérez-Méndez, "Conceptualization of the Settlement of El Pedregal: The Staging of the Public Space in the Master Plan of Ciudad Universitaria," especially the sub-chapter "Second conceptualization: the landscape regionalism of Diego Rivera and Luis Barragán," in Salvador Lizárraga and Cristina López Uribe, eds., *Living CU 60 years* (Mexico City: UNAM, 2014) 46–59. Also see the subchapter "The Landscape of Nationalism" in Keith Eggener, *Luis Barragan's Gardens of El Pedregal*, (New York: Princeton Architectural Press, 2001), 106–110; and Alfonso Pérez-Méndez and Alejandro Aptilon, *Las casas del Pedregal, 1947-1968* (Barcelona: Gustavo Gili, 2007).

**Alfonso Pallares, "El Pedregal y Barragán,"** *Espacios* **1 (January 1950), 111.**

4 *Espacios* 1
(September, 1948).

5 Alfonso Perez-
Mendez and Alejandro
Aptilon, *Las casas
del Pedregal*, 14.

convincing people that this place was a nice one to live in despite the fact that the area had been considered inhospitable for centuries.

In January of 1950, in the first issue of *Espacios* magazine, the architect Alfonso Pallares presented the project—as it would be presented for years to come—by highlighting the possibilities of the wild landscape in a poetic language. Then, suddenly changing his tone, he noted:

In this unique topographic and plastic condition, so far not valued by our original and colonial cultures, it is clear that the pioneers of this residential area of El Pedregal have derived the imperious need of an architectural regulation that prevents this gem of our valley from becoming, by the esthetic ignorance of the dwellers, an emporium of a sample of houses or opulent palaces, ones that show absurd and degenerated forms like "colonial," "maison," or the unacceptable "Californian."[4]

This rejection of the "Californian" would need further elaboration. In the end, paradoxically, El Pedregal was a place where Californian architecture and ideas were experimented with in Mexico, but a Californian architecture of a different kind. Both California and Mexico, and their architectures, took different forms and valences throughout the period reaching from the 1910s to the 1970s.

Luis Barragán—and Diego Rivera before him—wanted the architecture in El Pedregal to use a modern language, while others after them used Californian architecture for that same purpose.

In fact, by the 1950s modernism was already very well accepted in Mexico, especially in large state-promoted projects like public hospitals and schools and in private enterprises where the low cost of the "naked" language of modernism was a convincing factor. But just as in the US, the large majority of private houses built in the 1930s and 1940s were eclectic even though they were built with concrete frame structures. The popular taste of the people—when it came to their homes—was not modern and, as such, "the coordinated battle of convincing hundreds of clients of the middle or upper-middle class in the voluntary use of this architecture for their own houses was not, by far, won in advance."[5]

## 2

As the Mexican film *María Eugenia* (1943) starring María Felix shows, the urban landscape of Mexico City, especially in new developments, was dominated until the middle of the 1940s by a style of domestic architecture known locally as *colonial californiano*. Despite not even being Californian but rather a local expression, the style's name referred to specific influences: contemporary media images read collectively. Architectural magazines, travel posters, and Hollywood films portrayed the Spanish Colonial Revival architecture that was popular in California, and the images that surrounded this style spoke—also to Mexicans—of a manufactured and idealized atmosphere of a romantic Spanish past.

Scholars in Mexico have said that the Mexican Revolution was the starting point for modern architecture in the country. Thousands of *colonial californiano* houses, where politicians and presidents of the Revolution preferred to live, prove this to be wrong. Not only politicians but also movie stars and, above all, the emerging middle class—the new rich—favored this style if the choice concerned their own homes.

The *colonial californiano* style, in a similar way to the Spanish Colonial Revival in California, nourished the vanity of the new rich with an invented lineage for families that did not have one to show off. But the Mexican expression went much farther and borrowed ornaments from eighteenth century Churrigueresque churches and coats of arms from medieval castles. Paradoxically, while the houses were made of modern materials like concrete, their expression was conservative.

Manuel Ortiz Monasterios, "González de Cossío House." *El Arquitecto* XII (December, 1926), 12.

# 3

Since the 1890's Southern Californian architects traveled to Mexico in the same way that architects from the French Beaux-Arts Academy travelled to what was named "the Orient" in the nineteenth century. For them, Mexico was, similarly, an exotic adventure and source for inspiration, the only difference was that this place was very close due to newly-laid railroad tracks. After the Mexican revolution, these travels increased. Southern Californian architects, in the 1920s, went in search of architectonic details that they carefully sketched, drew, measured, and photographed. Some of these architects travelled with the idea of making books to be used in the design of what they called Spanish—rather than Mexican—architecture.

The reasons for naming the style Spanish are many and often complicated, but the architects and promoters naturally did not want to name a style after a country that their forebears had battled against in 1846–1847. Their identity needed to be differentiated from that of the territory across the border. The name also reflected the bad image of the Mexican in the United States. Western movies and newsreels projected in theaters north of the border portrayed a country of strange, uncivilized people at war: the Mexican Revolution was being filmed on a regular basis, and the battles that were filmed mostly took place in rural settings. When architects were able to travel to Mexico, they also documented a place where they believed that the Spanish colonial monuments were doomed to disappear.

Palmer Sabin, "Dickey Ranch House." 1929, Ojai, California. *Architectural Record* 36 (November, 1930), 362.

A new identity for California was needed to lure dwellers from the East, and the romantic idea of a world that was exotic but part of the U.S. proved to be ideal. In the creation of this image, the Mexican identity was instrumental. The Spanish past of the formerly Mexican territory was useful in creating an image that provided the singularity needed. Even though no big monuments remained in the area, leaving only the simple Franciscan monasteries—the missions—and some civil adobe structures, details and elements of the

Mexican baroque churches of other Mexican cities were copied to design the 1915 Panama-California Exposition in San Diego.

But the very successful domestic architecture of California made in this so-called Spanish Colonial Revival style was, for the most part, unornamented and inspired by the vernacular architecture of small towns rather than the heavily ornamented examples of the colonial city houses in large colonial cities. The most famous architects who developed this style were not originally from California and were not Spanish or Mexican. However, and in spite of this lack of personal links with these regions, they designed simple, romantic houses that recaptured the atmosphere of towns in Mexico and of places like Andalusia in Spain or even of small towns in France and Italy. The Mexican past was an open door that allowed these architects to make use of the whole Latin world or even Spanish Moorish forms in the search for romantic scenery. For many years, this image defined California's identity and traveled everywhere through the media.

## 4

While architects from California traveled to Mexico, all the most prominent Mexican architects had subscriptions to American architectural magazines. Even though a few of them could not read English — French was more the rule for Beaux-Arts educated architects — they saw images of houses in the old Mexican towns of their own past being recreated as modern expressions through the Spanish Colonial Revival Style. The Mexican magazine *Cemento* highlighted on the cover of its January 1925 issue the possibilities of the use of cement in a "Beautiful Mexican style patio in a residence made with concrete in the United States," and often provided examples of small "Spanish" houses to be built with concrete frame structures.

Furthermore, images in the media—advertisements used to promote modern travel to the U.S. Southwest and later to Mexico, the early Hollywood films (Westerns, for the most part, especially with the prominent Mexican/Spanish character of "El Zorro"), and celebrity magazines that featured the houses of the Hollywood movie stars — led to the strong popularity of this use of Hispanic forms and romantic images in architecture among the people of the middle class and the new rich of post-revolutionary Mexico who wanted to be part of the glamour that was inspired by their own heritage.

All this led to the invention of the *colonial californiano* style of architecture. An observer in 1945 wondered about the strong popularity of this style, built mostly by engineers or real estate promoters in Mexico, when almost every educated architect agreed that modernism (not radical functionalism, but modernization within Beaux-Arts training) suited the "spirit of the times." Cesar Novoa explained that "even with a cartoonish language, those shapes of the *colonial californiano* are the only ones so far that had spoken to the

# CEMENTO

Tomado de *The Architectural Record*

**ENERO DE 1925**

Bellísimo patio estilo mexicano de una residencia de concreto en los Estados Unidos.
El aplanado es de estuco de cemento Portland.

*Cemento* (January 1925), magazine cover.

Mexican about his Spanish heritage.... even when its splendors arrive in the consciousness of the Mexican in a very confusing way due to the systematic work of denial carried out by whole generations."

He attributed this development to the fact that "the basic features of the Hispanic in our cultural training have not yet found their adequate architectural expression for today, meanwhile the shapes of the *colonial californiano* seem to be the only ones that in the middle of the universal confusion of today make the Mexican feel the reality of his being, which is his only grip and the true path to the encounter of himself." Other factors that the author considered were the inferiority complex that—according to contemporary philosopher Samuel Ramos—was part of Mexican psychology, acting in a self-affirmative reaction with an exaggerated nationalism that "fit like a glove with the ridiculous ostentation of the *colonial californiano*."[6]

Not only the Spanish Colonial Revival style, but also modern architecture traveled from California to Mexico even if, up until World War II, modernism was far more pervasive in the urban territory of Mexico City than in American cities. Still, this expansion of modernism did not apply to the new ways of occupying the territory—the suburban reality—as in the Gardens of El Pedregal.[7]

## 5

In July 1938, the ninth issue of the Mexican magazine *Arquitectura y Decoración* opened a new flood of California modernist images into Mexico. The entire issue was dedicated to the renowned California architect Richard Neutra. Published by the Society of Mexican Architects and edited by architect Luis Cañedo Gerard, the magazine was modernist in its scope; the president of the society was then the young architect Mauricio M. Campos. The magazine often published the work of O'Gorman and other modernists like Barragán and Enrique del Moral with construction details and work costs that promoted the principle of "maximum benefit for minimum cost." The fact that this publication was so early—only a year after the first issue of a magazine ever dedicated to Neutra's work, the July 1937 issue of *Pencil Points*—speaks to the huge influence that Neutra had in Mexico.

Architects in Mexico have always been very cautious when speaking about foreign influences. This cautiousness was even more the case with modernism given the explanation that the Mexican Revolution was the source of the general revolution in art, especially for architects like Barragán who explained modern architecture as an abstraction of popular buildings like ranchos and convents. Nevertheless, none of these architects had any problem admitting—and they were even eager to explain—that Neutra had had a profound influence on their work.

The special issue of *Arquitectura y Decoración* was published after Neutra's "particularly refreshing" trip to Mexico in late 1937, just after one of his severe psychological depressions. In his own words, "I came to learn myself and to receive impressions of one of the most interesting regions of the world."[8] He visited Diego Rivera and Juan O'Gorman, both of whom he had long admired.[9] He wrote to his wife:

**6** César Novoa Magallanes "El colonial californiano" *Arquitectura y lo demás* 7 (December 1945–January 1946), 16–17.

**7** Alfonso Pérez-Méndez, *Las casas del Pedregal*, 29.

**8** Richard Neutra, "Lecture," *Arquitectura y Decoración* 9 (July 1938), 91–95.

**9** Thomas S. Hines, *Richard Neutra and the Search for Modern Architecture* (New York: Rizzoli, 2005).

*Arquitectura y decoración* 9 (July 1938), 128.

[O]n the sunny street, I meet the immense, the colossus Rivera and soon afterwards his diminutive, black-haired doll, his wife. Later I meet O'Gorman.… [The Riveras] drive me in their car through the endless metropolitan region.… I see the Piazza del Duomo, old palazzi. Finally we drive to Guadalupe where thousands of Indians are on a pilgrimage from December 12th to observe the yearly Fiesta of the Holy Virgin.… On the way I see an excellent housing project as well as the Aztec villages unchanged from a thousand years ago. Finally we reach the… fantastic pyramid encircled by granite stone snakes. Night falls as we carefully climb higher, not wanting to break our necks on this steep incline. Then a long drive back in the darkness. We have a good time together.… The diminutive Mrs. Rivera lays her manicured hand on my knee or her elbow on my shoulder.[10]

10 Cited in Thomas S. Hines, *Richard Neutra and the Search for Modern Architecture*, 205.

The "excellent housing project" he saw must have been Legarreta's San Jacinto housing complex of 1935.

On Christmas Day in 1937, Neutra addressed a crowd of Mexican architects in the Palacio de Bellas Artes—the most important venue in the country—with an (unusual for him) improvised conference. Apparently, he had no time to prepare a formal presentation. The invitation may have taken him by surprise. (There was no announcement in the November issue of the magazine which had, however, announced his presence in the country.) Also, he had been travelling with "super-American speed" through the country for two weeks. After detailing Neutra's biographical data, the 1938 issue of *Arquitectura y Decoración* opened with a transcript of the conference (in both English and Spanish). Neutra shared his impressions of the country with the audience:

The cultural stratification of the country is the most stimulating and also one of the most confusing things that a foreigner observes. It transforms an observer into a philosopher.… My impression is that this country, in spite of all strange influences, has at all times, had its own cultural fate. The expression 'colonial' does not well fit.

He spoke about the standardization and industrialization of materials and construction techniques warning that Mexico could become a colony again "if she does not produce and create a building material market." He defended the massive use of domestic technologies and the broadening of consumption to improve the living standards of the masses. He invited the Mexicans to follow the example of California where "the lack of communal enjoyment is replaced by the enjoyment of one's own dwelling." Then, he advocated for suburbs, almost announcing the architectures of El Pedregal:

The automobile has brought about a new type of modern architecture, a new possibility for city layout. A psychological accentuation of the dwelling is the consequence, which a city of the character of Mexico City does not possess, but which its future suburbs may acquire.

He also spoke against the false use of styles from the past, highlighting as an example "the Mexican Ranch houses which are seen in Hollywood and which belong to the motion picture producers and the semi-Churrigueresque store fronts in Wilshire Boulevard in L.A."

His knowledge of the Hispanic styles in California made him speak in a language that Mexicans were familiar with, as where his ideas for architecture, developed in a similar climatic and stylistic tradition.

From the conference, we know that Carlos Contreras discussed the planning of Mexico City's downtown with Neutra. He also met Luis Barragán during the trip, as Barragán remembered in 1962: "The other friendship that I had, although before El Pedregal, was with Richard Neutra because he was here and I joined him on many excursions around Mexico City. I had many conversations with him."[11] He wrote on a piece of paper:

> I like very much what Neutra is doing and what we have talked about. I have learned a lot from him even though I have my discrepancies in human aspects. Life is different in all places: customs, religions, weather, everything. For example, you cannot compare the idiosyncrasy of someone from the capital with that of someone from Veracruz, much less that of a Californian. We need to make some revisions, above all for the new needs of the modern life. The new architecture cannot be separated from this analysis. [...] Neutra wants commissions here because he wants to apply his knowledge—and he has a lot—here. He tells me that the freedom we have here is enviable. I took him on trips, and he wants to return. He liked the surroundings of the capital; he was surprised by the urban feeling of the pyramids.[12]

It could be argued that influences traveled both ways.

According to the publication, Neutra himself sent the images and explanatory texts in June 1938, six months after his trip. And from the special issue of 1938 of *Arquitectura y Decoración* until the final one of October 1943, he was credited as collaborator on the masthead. The projects included in the special issue were the most up-to-date and showed a variety of typologies and scales. Three of the projects included aluminum-clad surfaces in the façades. Jorge González Reyna's Van der Graaff Pavilion of 1952 in Ciudad Universitaria would later have its external walls covered with the same material.

The plurality of examples and the different solutions showed a number of issues discussed by the guild of architects in Mexico: enclosed or open patios, small dwellings, elegant residences, apartment buildings, etc. Neutra's clever designs integrating the interior with the landscape, characteristic of his work, resonated in a country of patios and life spent outside. What Neutra defended and called "the old California tradition of a home life half in-doors and half (the better half!) out-of-doors,"[13] was part of Hispanic traditions in both California and Mexico. Gardens and flowers were very often portrayed as the essential element of domestic life in Mexico.[14] Maybe Mexican architects saw themselves reflected in some way in Neutra's arguments, which could be an explanation of his huge influence in the country and the willingness of architects to acknowledge their debt.

After 1938, other publications followed. Probably following the advice of his dear friend Neutra, Raphael Soriano published his Los Angeles Dodie Piver House I (1937) and Luckens House and Studio (1940) remarkably early, in the July 1941 issue of *Arquitectura Mexico* edited by architect Mario Pani.[15] In January 1942, the magazine also published the work of Mario Corbett and Graham Harnden.

**11** "Los jardines de Luis Barragán," Alejandro Ramírez Ugarte interview with Luis Barragán, November 1962. Cited in Antonio Riggen Martínez, *Luis Barragán escritos y conversaciones* (Madrid: El Croquis, 2000), 81.

**12** Luis Barragán, "Reflexiones sobre la arquitectura moderna en México DF y EEUU." Dated September 1938. Cited in Antonio Riggen Martínez, *Luis Barragán escritos y conversaciones*, 20–21.

**13** Richard Neutra, article announcing the opening of the Museum of Modern Art's traveling "Modern Architecture: International Exhibition,"*California Arts & Architecture* (July-August, 1932).

**14** See the various Verna Cook Shipway and Warren Shipway books on Mexican houses from the 1960's and 1970's.

**15** "Dos casas en California, Raphael Soriano Arq.," *Arquitectura México* 8 (July, 1941), 43–47.

*Arquitectura México* 30 (February, 1950), 277.

That Neutra's work was featured in Mexican publications is not surprising given his talent as a skilled publicist, but there were other, less predictable, California modernists published in Mexican magazines. *Espacios* published "6 Houses in Los Angeles, California" in 1952 that included the almost unknown private work of Campbell & Wong, Henry L. Eggers, Mario Corbett, R. Summer, Carl Louis Maston, and the not entirely unknown Gregory Ain.[16]

## 6

16 "6 casas en Los Angeles Cal.," *Espacios* 11/12 (October, 1952), 95–109.

17 Mauricio Gómez Mayorga, "La casa en el desierto de Richard Neutra," *Arquitectura México* 30 (February 1950), 276–280.

With the end of World War II in 1945, mass media images traveled both ways with increasing speed. In 1950, architecture critic Mauricio Gómez Mayorga wrote about Richard Neutra's "House in the Desert" accompanied by "one of modern architecture's most brilliant and famous photographs," Julius Schulman's twilight photograph of the 1946 Kaufmann house.[17]

Gómez Mayorga took advantage of the task—and a text by Neutra— to express a couple of things he had on his mind. By 1950, Diego Rivera was building the Anahuacalli Museum and his home on the lava bed of El Pedregal in Coyoacán, and Juan O'Gorman had bought a lot and started to build his own "cave" house adjacent to the Gardens of El Pedregal subdivision. Both of them had been formulating a discourse in favor of a particular, local reading of Frank Lloyd Wright's organic architecture. For them, this architecture was a realist architecture, as opposed to the International style, which they called abstractionist. Inspired by the landscape and pre-Columbian cultures, these two buildings were unique handcrafted works of art not reproducible or even possible in another geographical or cultural location. Gómez Mayorga was very much opposed to this turn away from modern architecture and, instead of critiquing the Kaufmann House, complained about the "irrational" and "eccentric" architecture that was becoming "the personal style" and "fixation" of some.

> Under the remote influence of the lessons of Frank Lloyd Wright, "organic" or regionalist architecture is now in fashion…. and it is the case that some recently built works, which emerge from the soil and landscape with a truly telluric boost, have in fact very little to do with architecture.

The author then explained that Neutra himself had not turned to organicism despite what others might say, and that Neutra's still modernist approach to architecture could be better explained by his own words. Indeed, Neutra's explanation moved away from Wright's ideals. Neutra started by saying that the desert allowed him to build in a place with no previous historical associations, that is, "outside tradition," and that the intention of this project was to

Juan O'Gorman, "Juan O'Gorman house in San Jerónimo." 1956. Juan Guzmán photographer. Archivo Fotográfico del Instituto de Investigaciones Estéticas de la Universidad Nacional Autónoma de México.

experiment with a possible extension to other habitable regions of the planet. He almost described El Pedregal when he spoke of the

> entirely new cities with schools, hospitals, dwellings, theaters, and churches that are being built in burned rocky places that the original habitants used to describe as the devil's playground.... The designer of the future will perhaps face the need and the means to extend the range of his projects to places devoid of any cultural precedent such as a crater in the moon.

He then continued, explaining that the house in the desert was not rooted in the soil it sat on, and that the building was not "local" but instead "an artificial artifact" prefabricated elsewhere and transported there, and that even the plants were also "imports." Neutra noted that "even though not rooted in the desert, the building does, however, absorb the scenario of the desert, take part in its events, and enhance its character."

In these words, we can see the distance between the ideas of Neutra and those of Wright. The Kaufmanns had hired Wright to design Fallingwater and their decision to hire Neutra to design their Palm Springs residence was a source of tension. Wright's Boulder House drawing (1951), made in response to a later request by the Kaufmanns, illustrates how Wright might have designed the house according to his organic ideals. This conflict is the reason why the house was known as the "House in the Desert" and its location was given as the ambiguous "Colorado desert."

CASA No. 140 DE LA AV. DE LAS FUENTES

**"JARDINES DEL PEDREGAL DE Sn. ANGEL"**
*El lugar ideal para vivir*

El Pedregal advertising, *Arquitectura México*
35, magazine back cover. Armando Salas
Portugal photographer.

**18** The German-born
architect Max Cetto had
worked for a year in
Neutra's office since
1938 before arriving
to Mexico in May 1939.
Neutra could have
suggested him to travel
to Mexico where he
stayed for the rest of
his life.

**19** Simon Niedenthal,
"'Glamourized Houses':
Neutra, Photography,
and the Kaufmann
House," *Journal
of Architectural
Education* 47/2
(November, 1993):
101–112.

**20** See the chapter
"Photographic
architecture" in
Keith Eggener, *Luis
Barragan's Gardens of
El Pedregal*, 61–93.

Neutra's approach was in tune with the type of architecture being built at the moment in El Pedregal—such as the first Max Cetto and Luis Barragán designed houses—which stood in contrast to the excesses of O'Gorman and Rivera.[18]

## 7

Shulman's enigmatic twilight photograph of the Kaufmann house was a huge success, adding to the mystery of the name and location; in the shot there is a strange atmospheric effect and the presence of an observer is unsettling. Neutra usually preferred interior "objective" photographs where the image could better illustrate his architectural design intention of a close indoor-outdoor relationship.[19] However, he widely disseminated this particular photograph in the mass media knowing that it had other qualities that could support his pro-modernist publicity campaign.

The images that have illustrated El Pedregal since 1945 share some characteristics with Shulman's photograph. Some commentators have argued for the similarities between the architectures of Barragán and Neutra. Although they did share general ideas about architecture, they are not that similar from a formal standpoint. Nonetheless, there is a strong similarity in their use of photographs: both the original impact of the Kaufmann house photograph and the success of the advertising campaign for El Pedregal were the result of carefully orchestrated publishing campaigns.

Barragán had a strong relationship with the photographer Armando Salas Portugal, who was responsible for the images for the Gardens of El Pedregal advertising campaign.[20] These images seem to intentionally stimulate the viewer's imagination by always leaving something out of the frame. Salas's abstract, appealing compositions provided little architectural information: they consisted of fragments, distant blurry volcanoes, and dramatic skies.

Barragán was very fond of surrealism and some of the photographs by Salas Portugal have the magic of De Chirico paintings. This same magic is what Schulman's photograph brought to the foreground with the blurry image of Mrs. Kaufmann blocking the pool's light.

In both cases, there is an interesting dissonance between the architecture and the manner of its representation; the photographic image made a familiar image strange and mysterious in order to increase the interest in the architecture and landscape. El Pedregal was led by the goal of convincing people to live in a rough landscape, and the Kaufmann house, according to Neutra's words, was an experiment on how to do the same.

Other Mexican architects like Francisco Artigas, Antonio Attolinni, and José María Buendía followed the formal language of Neutra when they started their careers building houses in El Pedregal. The scale and the construction technology, however, were very different. They knew Neutra's work from consuming Shulman's photographs in architectural magazines and books. Shulman was very fond of using wide-angle lenses, and Neutra used to paint the wooden structures silver to get people accustomed to the look of industrial materials: these images suggested architecture always built of steel or concrete. When the Mexican architects tried to follow Neutra's designs, the scale of the details was changed (in their translation for the new context) and the surfaces of the Mexican concrete structures were very distant from Neutra's wooden interiors. Neutra's regular size houses seem very small when compared to their Mexican counterparts, the ones designed and built by the three most popular architects at El Pedregal.

# 8

In 1951, while Barragán was giving his famous speech in Coronado, California and speaking of "the fine and valuable influence in Mexico of the good Californian architects like Neutra," Esther McCoy, the most notable critic of California modernism, was in Mexico organizing the August issue of *Arts & Architecture* magazine on Mexican architecture.[21] Irvin E. Myers was also in Mexico preparing his book, *Mexico's Modern Architecture* (1952), for which Neutra wrote a short introduction. Neutra was back in Mexico that very year and, at some time, provided his opinions for the design of the new Ciudad Universitaria in El Pedregal. The urban planner Carlos Contreras, who constantly made reference to Neutra in his Sunday column in the newspaper *Novedades*, published the translation of Neutra's 1951 book *Mysteries and Realities of the Site*.

In her article on Mexican architecture in *Arts & Architecture*, Esther McCoy cited the architect Enrique Yáñez and seemed to agree with him that a new decorative sense was being applied to the use of native materials, like volcanic rock, wood, and brick, which were "all rich in architectural qualities, texture and color." She seems to have been convinced by the discourse of Mexican architects arguing for a modernity based on the vernacular:

> The popular house of Mexico is the only truly native style. [It] has always been restrained, in contrast to the embellished house of Mexico City.... In the popular house the art of building was reduced to its simplest and plainest forms. Indeed the International Style… that gripped Mexican architecture after the fall of Díaz was in its clean surfaces closer to the Mexican spirit, as revealed in the popular house....
>
> Mexico has long been a borrower of architectural styles from Europe, but today she turns seriously to her own past for her inspiration. The architects have shown a willingness to revalue their own culture and learn a lesson in design and construction from indigenous building. Mexico, for the first time, faces itself.

JARDINES DEL PEDREGAL DE SAN ANGEL

*"El lugar ideal para vivir"*

PIDA INFORMES EN LA OFICINA DE VENTAS DEL FRACCIONAMIENTO O EN LAS OFICINAS

AVENIDA DE LOS INSURGENTES SUR, 453 EDIFICIO "LAS AMERICAS", PRIMER PISO

El Pedregal advertising, *Arquitectura México* 50, magazine back cover. Armando Salas Portugal photographer.

21 Luis Barragán, Address to the California Council of Architects Convention and Sierra Nevada Regional Conference in the Hotel del Coronado, Coronado, California in October 6, 1951. Published as "Gardens for Environment" *Journal of the American Institute of Architects* 17 (April 1952) 167–172.

*Arts & Architecture* (August, 1951), magazine front cover. © David Travers. Used with permission.

**"El Pedregal is one of the most beautiful places in the planet" Richard J. Neutra. *Espacios* 8 (December, 1951) magazine cover.**

One could wonder what could she grasp of that so-called "Mexican spirit" during her short trip, and even if there was anything unified or stable to be grasped.

When it came to speaking about Mexico, the modernist critic showed a flexibility with incorporating local traditions in modern architecture that she did not embrace in the architectures of her home region, California. At the time, some architects in California like Cliff May were using an approach similar to the one endorsed by McCoy for Mexico — a modern architecture inspired by the California vernacular, gaining great popular acceptance — but these architects were not published with the select modernists in *Arts & Architecture* magazine.

Featured in the August 1951 issue were the three renowned architects who were doing what was considered to be the "correct" Mexican modern architecture: Luis Barragán, Max Cetto, and Enrique del Moral. Juan O'Gorman was included as a representative of an eccentric and critical position. Also appearing were the young Luis Rivadeneyra and Jaime López Bermudez who were more in tune with the modernist ideals of California — as portrayed in the Case Study House Program — with their small, low cost houses made of standardized industrially-produced materials. Victor de la Lama and Ramón Torres were left to the end of the publication and were the perfect synthesis of the two approaches. The texts highlighted the fact that in the work of De la Lama and Torres, modern materials combined well with ancient materials and that adobe walls and enclosed gardens were considered characteristically Mexican.

In *Arquitectura Mexico*, the elegant, talented work of Victor de la Lama, Ramón Torres, and Héctor Velázquez, who designed houses of steel structures and almost floating sheets of glass in combination with adobe walls, was published right next to the houses and buildings with steel structures of Raphael Soriano in California.[22] These Mexican architects had achieved the apotheosis of the integration of outdoor spaces with domestic interior spaces and of the union of tradition and modernity. The fact that the projects of these three Mexican architects were published next to Soriano's work could not have been a coincidence; it showed clearly that experimentation with steel was being made at the same time in both places. Mexicans wanted to make that fact very clear.

By this point, the source of nationalism had changed in a series of cultural shifts from the earliest Spanish past, to the landscape and soil, and then, finally, to a nationalism of essences that was unattached to any specific place or time. The "love affair" that McCoy had with Mexico was based on the recognition of her own California traditions and experimentations being reflected in Mexican architecture.

**22** "Tres casas en California, Raphael Soriano Arq.," *Arquitectura México* 42 (June, 1953), 87–98. Projects featured were the Curtis House (Experimental House) of 1950, the Soriano 1950 Case Study House, and the early Katz House of 1947.

**9**

The members of Mexican society in the postwar period—especially the main beneficiaries of the economic boom of this period who were among the first inhabitants of El Pedregal—had a specific way of understanding nationalism. After the war, economic relations were stronger between Mexico and the U.S. They had to be: the cold war secured understanding between neighbors. The search for *Mexicanidad* became related to the landscape, the land, and to the essence of the Mexican. Finding that essence meant an escape from the city, to be close to a rural Mexico where traditional values were kept— as Mexican ranchero movies of the 1950s portrayed—but, at the same time, within a modern "American way of life." In those years, to be Mexican also meant to be cosmopolitan.

Ideals associated with modernity moved from the turn-of-the-century metropolis to the ranchos in an idealization of rural life. This image was more appealing for the people than that of design based on mass-produced and standardized materials and construction techniques. Neutra's influence in architecture was strong for a couple of decades because his house designs stood in between the cosmopolitan use of new materials and an attach-ment to a natural site, outside the city. The very basic idea of Neutra was to heal the neurosis of people from the metropolis with a healthy psychological environment. A very similar idea is what was sold in El Pedregal: in Barragan's discourse, a quiet and peaceful domestic life with private "emotional" gardens.

In spite of his flattering comment at the 1951 conference, Barragán was very critical of the use of glass—as in California modernism—when transplanted to Mexico, despite the fact that climatic conditions are very similar. "Even though I consider Neutra a first-class architect who has exerted a decisive influence, I think his glass walls—badly understood—have been very dangerous in the history of architecture."[23]

Barragán smiled when he remembered the hours he had spent talking with Neutra about the semidarkness (penumbra) when he stayed at Neutra's home, the VDL house, for a week.[24] For Barragán, it was a necessity for human beings—as mammals—to have darkened, somber spaces to feel the coziness of a home. The psychological effects of the buildings and the environment on the people who inhabited his houses were also one of the main concerns for Neutra. He often spoke of biological responses to the environment. The emotional architecture of Barragán was aimed at a very similar experience.

Critics of the modernist architecture of El Pedregal described its "extravagance" and its being to "the liking of foreigners."[25] Despite these criticisms, the architecture was never, however, judged as "non-Mexican." Still, what was Mexican and foreign had in fact been shaped (and not merely represented) for many years in the exchanges and meaningful associations and through the very different approaches to architecture within and between Mexico and California.

23 "Luis Barragán. Entrevista," Elena Poniatowska interview, November, 1976 in Antonio Riggen Martínez, *Luis Barragán escritos y conversaciones*, 115.

24 "Luis Barragán. Entrevista" Elena Poniatowska interview, November 1976 in Antonio Riggen Martínez, *Luis Barragán escritos y conversaciones*, 118.

25 Carlos Obregón Santacilia, *50 años de arquitectura mexicana 1900-1950* (Mexico City: Patria, 1952).

# Transborder Belongings of the International Retirement Migrant

Deane Simpson

1 The term "Retirement Home of Europe" came up frequently during expert interviews, and in the author's interviews with residents along the Costa del Sol.

2 The phenomenon of European retirement migration to Spain has been addressed by geographers and sociologists such as Andreas Huber, Karen O'Reilly, Russell King, Tony Warnes, and Allan Williams. See Andreas Huber and Karen O'Reilly, "The Construction of Heimat under Conditions of Individualized Modernity: Swiss and British Elderly Migrants in Spain," *Ageing and Society* 24 (2004): 327–51; Andreas Huber, "Retirement Settlements in the Spanish Coastal Regions: A New Kind of Non-place?," unpublished paper, 2004; Karen O'Reilly, *The British on the Costa Del Sol: Transnational Identities and Local Communities* (London: Routledge, 2000); Russell King, A.M. Warnes, and Allan M. Williams, *Sunset Lives: British Retirement Migration to the Mediterranean* (Oxford: Berg, 2000).

Just as Florida and Arizona have performed as migratory sunbelt destinations for American retirees, Spain's Costa del Sol and Costa Blanca have functioned as corresponding destinations for the retirees of Western and Northern Europe, popularized as "the retirement home of Europe."[1] [2] While both the North American and European forms of retirement migration involve moving large distances to experience more favorable climatic conditions and lower costs of living (although the latter condition has diminished in recent years), an important contrast in the European case involves the crossing of national cultural and linguistic borders—with the partial reconstitution of those cultural and linguistic borders as micro-Britains or micro-Germanys at an urban scale within the Spanish context. The spatial conditions which buttress this form of transborder and transcultural "belonging" involve the tension between the desired cultural exoticism of the (permanent) vacation destination, on the one hand; and the cultural and social familiarity of the permanent home, on the other. "Home" in these terms constitutes not only spaces of domesticity, but spaces of a social, collective, or public nature, such as pubs, restaurants, shops, supermarkets, banks, clubhouses, golf courses, streets, highways, squares, etc.—defining a spatial scaffold for "belonging" based upon what Mary Yoko Brannen has described as "modified exoticism," experienced by an elastic subject positioned between the Spanish resident living in Spain and the Briton living in Britain.

With the arrival to Spain of international mass tourism in the 1950s and the growth of all-inclusive package tourism in the 1960s and 1970s, followed by Spain's admission to the EU in the mid-1980s, and the expansion of low-cost airlines in the mid-1990s,[3] the popularity of the Costa del Sol as a tourist destination expanded rapidly from 51,000 yearly visitors in 1959, to 925,000 in 1968, to 2.5 million in 1975, and to 9.4 million in 2015.[4]

On the Costa del Sol, the conditions supporting tourism—which include the attractions of climate and landscape, and the common infrastructural and social requirements such as airport connectivity and leisure attractions—proved highly suitable at a regional scale in supporting immense growth in international retiree-occupied residential areas, a transformation that has led to a more or less continuous carpet of exurban development stretching across the coastal landscape. This diversification—from purely touristic space to one that also supports international retirement migrants—was triggered in the 1980s, when local and central governments in Spain attempted to offset the destabilizing effects of the seasonal economic fluctuations typical of the tourism industry by promoting foreign investment in land and property in the coastal areas. This new focus would in turn attract international retirement migrants to spaces already socially constructed by the tourist industries as sites of "holiday, escape, leisure, fun, liminality, fecundity and new beginnings."[5]

The exact scale of the resulting migratory phenomenon has been difficult to quantify as it consists of what has been referred to as a "veiled population" of predominantly unregistered foreign residents.[6] Official numbers for registered foreign residents on the Costa del Sol document 251,942 out of a total official Málaga province population of 1,619,497 (2014), while estimates of actual foreign residents are considerably higher, ranging up to 600,000, of which Britons are the largest single nationality represented.[7]

The resulting "solar utopia" may be understood as an index of particular forces of globalization on the field of population aging: most notably, improved international transport and accessibility, diminishing institutional and legal barriers to foreign living, and increased familiarity with foreign destinations. These transformations, among others, have supported a form of "cultural and economic convergence" that has increasingly enabled the successful negotiation of everyday life for international retirement migrants in foreign cultural contexts. These changes are detailed by Russell King et al. in the book *Sunset Lives*:

> Today, if a person knows how to make an international telephone call…, to do their weekly shopping in a supermarket, or to draw money from their bank account through a "cash machine," they rarely have trouble doing the same things in any part of Western Europe—which was not the case twenty years ago. These activities reflect a general process of "cultural and economic convergence" which has involved the standardization of product ranges, and simplification of the "customer interface" in many convenience, telecommunications and financial services.[8]

It is necessary to register the role of language in addition to the more tangible objects of "cultural and economic convergence" —especially in the key role that language plays in touristic and therefore retirement migration infrastructure. In particular, this convergence is enacted through the internationalization of English, and its subsequent domination of the touristic and retirement milieu of the Costa del Sol. A further contributor to the speed of development has been a form of governance characterized by informal and innovative alliances between the public and private sector at the boundaries of legality.[9]

The spatial territory of Costa del Sol is to a large extent comprised of three components—"historical towns," "tourist resorts," and "retirement *urbanizaciones*." This spatial condition is evident in the territorial demarcations of each of these three "ecologies" common to maps of the coast,[10] which simultaneously articulate the key phases of the historical growth of the region. The most numerous of the "bubbles" on the map are *urbanizaciones*;

**3** O'Reilly, *British on the Costa Del Sol*, 31–32.

**4** King et al., *Sunset Lives*, 59. 2013 statistics from "International Tourists in Andalucía," Andalucia.com, http://www.andalucia.com/spain/statistics/tourism.htm (accessed June 20, 2016).

**5** O'Reilly, *British on the Costa Del Sol*, 106.

**6** The term "veiled population" has been used by José Maria Romero to described this phenomenon. Romero estimates that the territory of ZoMeCS is occupied by 12,000,000 inhabitants. This figure includes of the range of additional constituents including unregistered resident tourists (foreign residents), tourists, and business travelers. See José Maria Romero, *Territory ZoMeCS: Urban Attributes* (Granada: 2004), 3.

**7** "Población de Andalucía por provincia de residencia, nacionalidad y sexo," Junta de Andalucía, Instituto de Estadística y Cartografía de Andalucía, http://www.juntadeandalucia.es/institutodeestadisticaycartografia/padron/avance/tab/padron2014_prov_t2.xls (accessed May 25, 2014). O'Reilly, *British on the Costa Del Sol*, 49. The 600,000 figure, presented in 1999, refers to the south of Spain.

**8** King et al., *Sunset Lives*, 201.

**9** In this particular context, these alliances have been focused on the production of economic win-win situations on both sides of the public-private divide. The public sector gains, however, have been largely limited to improved economic conditions for administration officials.

Aerial view over Benalmádena toward Torremolinos and Málaga, Costa del Sol, 2009. Photography courtesy of the author.

New green "coastlines," golf course *urbanizaciones* near Estepona, Costa del Sol, 2009. Photography courtesy of the author.

**10** See for example the *Guía Oficial* map: Producciones GeoGraphic, *Guía Oficial Map of Costa del Sol Urbanizaciones*, Málaga, 2009.

**11** Huber, "Retirement Settlements," 2-3.

described by Andreas Huber as "fully planned and structured settlements of various sizes that lie outside the historical boundaries of towns and villages. They are often initiated by a single "promoter" (builder or building and general contractor), who buys a large area of land, which he transforms into building land by a series of legal procedures. This transformation allows the investor to implement the necessary infrastructure later and to "urbanize" the land, in order to sell the building plots or build on them himself.[11]

The *urbanizaciones* represent a form of hybrid urbanity lodged in the space between the vacation resort and the American gated community, and between the Andalusian pueblo and the colonial outpost. They are to a large extent based on the mutation of the temporary leisure typology of the leisure resort toward full-time leisure use. The format of the vacation resort is, thus, the most influential model in the realization of *urbanizaciones*, one that produces and supports a private form of social space through an array of communal leisure infrastructures such as golf courses, swimming pools, tennis courts, clubrooms, and bars. Collectively, the *urbanizaciones* contribute less to a coherent connective urban fabric than to a field of fragmented entities distinct from much of their surroundings both in organizational and sociocultural terms. Organizationally, the Costa del Sol may be understood as a linear form of exurban development, forming a post-metropolitan condition without a clear organizational or productive center of gravity — apart perhaps from the role the Málaga-Costa del Sol Airport plays in facilitating the transnational mobility necessary for the realization of such a condition.

Socio-culturally, the *urbanizaciones* of the Costa del Sol may be characterized by their tendency toward domination by single nationalities — most apparent in terms of displaced microcultures constructed by language, media, and consumer environments and programmatic sites of communal life. In *urbanizaciones* such as Miraflores Golf, for example, within which the vast majority of residents are British retirees, English is spoken almost exclusively. Stores and supermarkets are British-owned and sell British products. Kiosks stock every major British daily newspaper; and streets, stores, bars, and restaurants deliberately evoke the "homeland" with names such as Churchill's Bar, Cornish Pride, The Scots and Irish, and The London Pub. Interiors of local pubs and restaurants follow the British script word for word, producing a form of cultural displacement that extends to familiar cultural events ranging from "quiz nights" to "Sunday roasts" — all undeniably British in their make-up.

A similar level of national coherency can be experienced in German *urbanizaciones* located most frequently to the east of Málaga, near settlements such as Torrox. Instantly perceptible is a language shift from English to German, a hospitality shift from Guinness and fish and chips in cluttered dark wooden interiors to Löwenbräu and currywurst in beer gardens. While suggesting a melting pot, or "rainbow culture" at the scale of the territory — in the terms of King et al. — the Costa del Sol appears at the scale of the *urbanización* to be dominated more by discrete areas of national identity, a situation most evident in the micro-Britains and micro-Germanys of the *urbanizaciones*.

The nearly continuous carpet of *urbanizaciones* laid out between the punctuated semicircles of the historical towns, and the water-front line of tourist hotels and resorts may be framed as an index for a contemporary form of cultural and territorial neo-colonization. According to King et al., the realities of linguistic and cultural barriers, combined with the importance of climate and lifestyle in determining the choice to move to the Costa del Sol, reinforces the prioritization of the feeling of "being at home" ahead of integrating into a foreign culture. This highlights "the attempt to fashion their own cultural environment within their new home—the fully carpeted Essex bungalow on the Costa del Sol.... [T]he tourist resort, or even the cosmopolitan countryside of Tuscany, with its confusion of cultures and manners, allows everyone the illusion of being 'at home' and the freedom to 'be themselves.'"[12] While the national cultural concentrations of the *urbanizaciones* therefore limit integration between the British retirement migrant and the local Spanish culture, they are understood to be highly effective in supporting strong social integration among the British migrants themselves. For King et al., "The *urbanización*, with its inward-facing cul-de-sacs and residents' committees, is in effect a miniature village, within which virtually every permanent resident is known. One of the characteristics of such small communities is that new arrivals tend to find themselves quickly incorporated into the local social networks."[13]

Such an interpretation suggests a form of colonization distinct from that of the nineteenth century—which was based on the explicit top-down imposition of the political (and economic) will of the foreign imperial nation-state—and distinct from the neocolonialism of the twentieth century—based on the subtle or not so subtle imposition of the economic will of the multinational corporation. Rather, this form of colonization represents a contemporary, perhaps late twentieth- or early twenty-first-century form of neocolonialism based on the imposition, in bottom up rather than top down terms, of the demographic will of a collective of consumers, meeting the speculative offerings of a collection of developer-suppliers. In other words, this form of neocolonialism functions as a result of the coincidence of bottom-up forces—that is, the almost unintended collective effect of the concentration of tens of thousands of micro-environmental (and therefore *demographic*) colonizations taking place at the intersection of forces of globalization, individualization, and the market. O'Reilly introduces another definition of colonization—an ecological one—as a spatial or environmental expansion of a "species into a new habitat, such as a freshly cleared field, a new motorway verge, or a recently flooded valley." She acknowledges that the *urbanizaciones* conform to this form of environmental appropriation, but she warns against accepting this label based upon the "dangerous assumption" of defining the British as a separate "species" of non-integration.[14] Nevertheless, as O'Reilly outlines, "the British in Spain can be described as a strongly ethnic group: [they] are essentially British."[15] While differentiating themselves from the Britons of Britain, they are still remarkable for their lack of integration.

Golf course *urbanizaciones*, Costa del Sol, 2014. Photography courtesy of the author.

12 King et al., *Sunset Lives*, 162–63.

13 Ibid., 150.

14 O'Reilly, *British on the Costa Del Sol*, 142.

15 Ibid., 86.

In terms of the social life they construct, the language they speak, and the media and products they consume, they function as another "subspecies," another ethnic group to the local Spaniards. In this context it is difficult to deny the appropriateness of the ecological understanding of colonization to the English in their new Mediterranean habitat and, in turn, particularly within the understanding of a collective bottom-up behavior of individual actors that results in a form of spatial (and economic) domination that is not related to a single consciously coordinated political or corporate will but is the product of a swarm, and the anticipation of that "swarm," occupying a new habitat.[16]

Just as touristic infrastructure, such as an airport, is highly suitable for retirement migration at a regional scale, it is at the scale of the individual *urbanizaciones* themselves that the organizational and programmatic framework of the foreign vacation resort has an equally important influence. As a leisure rather than work-focused environment in which a form of pseudo-communalism is organized around common leisure facilities such as swimming pools, lawns, tennis courts, and golf courses, the vacation resort is typically arranged within a demarcated perimeter of national occupation, defining a world distinct from the local indigenous context around it.

The distinct environment of the resort engages in a dialogue between local and global conditions, articulating the exotic local destination (Spain) to the (British) visitor/resident, while at the same time operating according to familiar protocols of global convergence. Within the context of the vacation resort, the iconography of this "exotic" context operates as a form of appliqué to the substructure of the generic shell. The expansion of these approaches into environments for retirement migration has seen the increasing application of theming techniques from the entertainment-industrial complex applied to both the architecture and landscape design of the *urbanizaciones*. These techniques play out in architectural terms, according to a dominant "stylistic" form—consisting of a set of representational devices that have become known in local real estate parlance as Pueblo Mediterráneo (PM) or "Mediterranean Village" style, characterized as relatively dense assemblages of two-story to four-story-tall dwelling complexes with clay tile roofs and walls of white, beige, or earth-toned stucco. Freestanding villas are less frequent but tend to follow the same material palette as the apartment or townhouse dwellings. The hillside village of Mijas is often presented as the model for this form of architecture, despite its architectural authenticity being compared by some

Golf as branding strategy across *urbanizaciones*, Costa del Sol, 2009. Photography courtesy of the author.

critics to that of Málaga's airport. While the color of the stucco finishing among the various *urbanizaciones* ranges from a standard off-white to tints of terracotta, ochre, or apricot, the basic formula exhibits a remarkable level of stylistic standardization. This uniformity relates to Dean MacCannell's concept of staged authenticity, which according to Huber "applies not only to tourists, but to long-term holidaymakers who spend the winter on the Spanish coast, as well as permanent residents. They are also guided by a yearning for authenticity in the realization of a desire nurtured over many years for a house in Spain in which to spend their twilight years. The house cannot

**16** It would be possible to advance this discussion with reference to the nonhierarchical forms of network organization described in Antonio Negri and Michael Hardt, *Multitude: War and Democracy in the Age of Empire* (New York: The Penguin Press, 2004); or Eric Bonabeau, Marco Dorigo, and Guy Theraulaz, *Swarm Intelligence: From Natural to Artificial Systems* (New York: Oxford University Press, 1999).

be any old house, but must conform to their picture of a 'Spanish' house."[17] The Spanish architect Carlos García-Delgado Segués describes the problematics of a similar condition with respect to the collective construction of touristic environments at the intersection of two cultures.

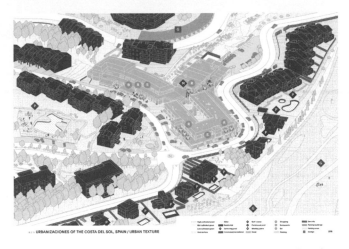

URBANIZACIONES OF THE COSTA DEL SOL, SPAIN / URBAN TEXTURE

*Urbanizaciones* of the Costa del Sol, Spain, urban texture, 2015. Drawing by the author.

> The inhabitants of places specialised in sun and sand tourism learn very quickly—especially if they retain the memories of an economy of scarcity—that their mission is to offer the visitor what the visitor hopes to find. They then set about replacing their cultural values—richer than their personal economy—with a saleable simulacrum of these values. The perversion inherent in this process is obvious, for in reality what is offered is not what the host actually has, nor even what the visitor expects to find, but what the host believes the visitor expects to find…. One often hears it said, in these places: "what the Germans want is…" and there follows some fabrication, thought up by someone who is trying to recreate on his own the most profitable representation of himself and his country.[18]

The delivery of this "authentic" and exotic Spanish-ness is rather specific in its extent—a situation that may perhaps best be described by Mary Yoko Brannen's notion of modified exoticism, based on maintaining a tension between making the exotic familiar, while keeping the exotic *exotic*.[19] The stylistic role of Pueblo Mediterráneo, particularly on the building's exterior envelope, is to represent an image for a local "authentic" Spanish village settlement—one that must be sufficiently exotic to foreign retirees that it does not feel like they are living in their home country. At the same time, the architecture is necessarily made familiar through common contemporary amenities and infrastructure that perform almost exactly the same way as those found in Britain or Germany—both in an interior architectural sense and at an urban scale. The production of a retirement lifestyle equivalent to that experienced in Britain is realized demographically, programmatically, and, to a large extent, culturally on the Costa del Sol, but the equivalency is necessarily denied and camouflaged in stylistic terms by the aesthetic construct of Pueblo Mediterráneo—produced by a relatively limited number of effects, such as a thin layer of paint and stucco over a brick or masonry wall, a slight difference in roof tile profile, and the removal of rain guttering from roof edges.

The typical British or Irish pub located inside or close to the larger enclaves is one of the most socially active of the private social spaces of the *urbanizaciones*. This building form is notable in architectural terms for the level of schizophrenia between what is conventionally a Spanish Pueblo

17 Huber, "Retirement Settlements," 10.

18 Carlos García-Delgado Segués, "Living from Tourism, Dying from Tourism," in *La Arquitectura Del Sol / Sunland Architecture* (Barcelona: Collegi d'Arquitectes de Catalunya, 2002), 176.

19 Mary Yoko Brannen, "Bwana Mickey: Constructing Cultural Consumption at Tokyo Disneyland," in *Re-made in Japan: Everyday Life and Consumer Taste in a Changing Society*, ed. Joseph J. Tobin (New Haven: Yale University Press, 1992), 219; cited in Sarah Chaplin, "Authenticity and Otherness: The New Japanese Theme Park," *Architectural Design* 68, no. 1/2 (January/February 1998): 77 (my italics).

Recurring signage on the A-7 highway, Costa del Sol, 2009. Photography courtesy of the author.

Uppa Crust Cafe, Fuengirola, Costa del Sol, 2009. Photography courtesy of the author.

20 O'Reilly, *British on the Costa Del Sol*, 140–66.

21 Margarita del Cid, "Golf makes our destination 100 per cent attractive throughout the year," *Andalucia Golf*, no. 223 (2014): 74.

22 Estate Agent for Valle Romano, interview with the author, April 4, 2009, Estepona, Spain.

23 Ibid.

Mediterráneo-themed exterior (albeit with a typical British or Irish pub sign and name), and an Olde British or Irish pub interior. This disjunction forms a fitting parallel to O'Reilly's description of the form of subjectivity that characterizes the British retirement migrant—betwixt two cultures and two locations. As documented in interviews, permanent residents tend to pride themselves on their ability to "fit in" to the Spanish environment through not looking like British tourists, while at the same time socializing almost entirely with fellow British retirement migrants.[20]

Organizationally, the *urbanizaciones* function as spatial products with the mobility and reproducibility of neocolonial formats. In the most recent decades, the landscape of golf has played a central role as a major conceptual and organizational armature for the development of the urban landscape. In an effort to exploit areas of land more distant from the overheated coastal real estate market, and as an attempt to even out the seasonal occupation of the Costa del Sol with the promotion of year-round golf to attract tourists in the winter months, a collective regional branding ploy was initiated, expanding the original name of Costa del Sol to the double moniker of *Costa del Sol–Costa del Golf*.[21] The number of golf courses expanded rapidly starting in the 1990s, reaching approximately sixty by 2009, and representing the highest concentration of golf courses in Europe.[22] Based on the ongoing ambition toward exclusivity evident in a location such as Marbella, it is perhaps not surprising that the majority of the Costa del Sol's golf courses are located within its vicinity. According to one real estate agent interviewed on the Costa del Sol, "The majority of retirees don't play golf, but they love living next to courses. Golf is getting very trendy in Spain."[23] Insofar as golf has been associated with a desire for status and prestige, it has become an essential tool in the branding of *urbanizaciones*. This effort extends to the naming of streets ("Calle del Golf"), houses ("Balcon del Golf" or "Golf Gardens"), *urbanizaciones* ("Estrellas del Golf"), and even geographic features ("Monte del Golf"), in many cases despite their being neither related to the activity nor in the vicinity of a golf course.

The ease of redeployment of these protocols is evidenced by the rapid emergence of new *urbanizaciones* in places such as Greece and the Balkans based on variations in relative currency values and the expanding borders of regional alliances both before and after the 2007 crisis. Retirement lifestyles resemble package holiday products in terms of both the tropes of desire they employ and the formulation of a product capable of collapsing the "exoticism" of destination and the familiarity of "home" into a single space.

The *urbanizaciones* therefore produce a kind of third culture between Britain and Spain, and in turn produce a third type of subject, between the Briton and the Spaniard, empowered as a curator to select, edit, and recombine the most desirable aspects of each culture and each identity. For the British on the Costa del Sol, such an experimental curatorial project is largely underwritten by the security offered by the national cultural solidarity of fellow British retirement migrants living closely together in this foreign lifestyle laboratory.

# Before Belonging

Iver B. Neumann

Can it be that we're all exiles? Is it possible that all of us are wandering
strange lands?
—Roberto Bolaño[1]

The first *Homo sapiens* to reach what we now call Europe came from Africa
45,000 years ago, via the Arabian Peninsula. They were hunters and gatherers,
who typically lived in bands of between twenty and two hundred people. Each
band engaged in regular gatherings with other bands, characterized by partner
swapping, partner shopping, and barter trade. The scale was very small; when
glacial ice was at its thickest, about 19,000 years ago, no more than five thousand individuals were left. Then, 6,000 years later, the temperature fell again,
and, once more, the local detachment of *Homo sapiens* barely pulled through.
Europe remained populated by small bands, for whom attachment to a community was a question of proper primary socialization in their respective groups.

As the ice began to melt, the first humans to reach what now we call
Norway arrived about 12,000 years ago. They quickly settled by the coast,
where marine resources were plentiful enough for them to remain for extended
periods. Interestingly enough, the first humans to live in these lands had dark-
pigmented skin. The aboriginal population of Europe, that is the hunters and
gatherers who populated the area alone until 9,000 years ago and remained
dominant for a millennium, retained the skin color of their African ancestors.
Until recently, we assumed that their skin pigmentation had been lost as a
result of the lack of sunshine. However, DNA tests of surviving ancient skin
have demonstrated that this change was not the case.[2]

The members of this group were not the only ancestors of later
Norwegians. The groups being small, their numbers only began to climb
sig-nificantly with the coming of agriculture. Early agriculturalists reached
the Balkans from the Caucasus around 9,000 years ago, bringing their cattle
and settling in villages. About three thousand years passed before agricultural practices arrived in Norway. Once established in villages, groups of people
would split off and go in search of places to found new villages. They would
keep contact with the mother village, to which the new colonies would feel
a sense of connection. Agriculture spread north at a steady pace.

There is no evidence about whether agriculture was actually brought to
Norway by new people, or whether it was copied by people already there. What
we do know was that the spread of agriculture was a collaborative effort
between old-timers and newcomers. We also know that, for two thousand

1 Roberto Bolaño,
"Exiles," in *Between
Parentheses: Essays,
Articles, and Speeches,
1998–2003* (New York:
New Directions, 2011).

2 Kate Manco, *Ancestral
Journeys: The Peopling
of Europe from the
First Venturers to the
Vikings* (London: Thames
& Hudson, 2013). The
meat-rich diet of this
population provided
enough vitamin D, so
mutations that reduced
pigmentation did not
provide an advantage.

**3** We know that every single steppe empire was multi-lingual and multi-ethnic. Up until and including the Scythians (from the Indo-European word *skodr*, that is, "shot," referring to those who use a bow), the leading strata were Indo-Europeans. The dominant empires— Huns; Alans; Turkic peoples like the Pechenegs, the Bulgars and the Seljuks; the Mongols; and then the Ottomans who overran Constantinople in 1453—were the direct heirs to the social and political steppe tradition forged by the Indo-Europeans. Of course, there were also other influences at work, not least of all religious ones, but the basic matrix belonged in the first place to the Indo-Europeans. The Huns may even, as archaeologist Lotte Hedeager has maintained, have been present in Scandinavia. See Lotte Hedeager, *Iron Age Myth and Materiality: An Archaeology of Scandinavia, AD 400–1000* (London: Routledge, 2011).

years, agriculture spread out and replaced hunting and gathering. Relations between villages tightened. Population numbers shot up.

Some 4,000 years ago, yet another major wave of immigrants arrived in Norway. These were the last of three great out-migrations from the Eurasian steppe, which consisted of peoples who spoke languages that evolved into the Slavic and Germanic languages. The backstory of these peoples is fascinating. Around 6,000 years ago, the invention of the wheel made possible the construction of wagons which could be used to transport water into the Eurasian steppe. These early or proto Indo-Europeans were organized in clans under a leader. Attachment to a group would not only be a question of the immediate cluster of households, but also of loyalty to the leader, who typically gathered as many such clusters as he could under his command. From their bases in the Pontic Steppe, the resulting amalgamated groups raided and traded with sedentary peoples to their west and south on an ongoing basis. At irregular intervals, groups of Indo-Europeans would reach Europe and establish control over the local populations, becoming themselves sedentary. This process characterized Norway from around 2000 BCE onwards.

By the time Indo-Europeans began invading Europe—first in the south and then in the north—they represented a western detachment of a loosely knit population present throughout the steppe. The superior military technology of the Indo-Europeans established them as a ruling population from India via Anatolia to Europe. There were even Indo-European elements amongst the Hsiung-nu, that is, the barbarians who harassed the sedentary Han Chinese during the first millennium BCE. So, the arrival of descendants of the Hsiung-nu at Europe's doorstep in the fourth century AD in the guise of the Hun was a homecoming of sorts for some of them.[3]

European textbooks still tell the story of how the Indo-European Greeks colonized the Mediterranean. They certainly did, but from the very beginning, they did so in competition with Semitic peoples that came out of cities in the East Mediterranean, like Tyre. The Romans knew these vanquished peoples as Carthaginians. In Norway, the Jewish community was formed much later, in the nineteenth century; and Norway only really developed a Muslim community with the arrival of what were then called "guest workers" in the late 1960s. In a world-historical perspective, the Indian and Pakistani populations in today's Europe are simply distant Indo-European cousins who have done what our common ancestors did all the time: decamped for greener pastures.

These brief chapters of the origins of Norway as a nation-state show how migratory processes have been always present. They are more intense in some periods, like the present one, but have characterized European life since the beginning of human settlement. According to the received version of the origins of Norway, the roots of the country lay with the hard-working, sturdy, uncontaminated peasants who lived in the Norwegian interior, as far away from foreigners and their civil servant lackeys as possible. The doctrine of nationalism—based on the idea that people who are culturally similar should share a state—has become naturalized to such a degree that we still have difficulty with thinking about the past in any other way. That resistance is our loss, for the situation in Europe before the formation of the Roman empire had little room for nations, understood as homogenous entities. So does the situation today. The world is yet again on the move.

# Belonging and Neoliberalism

**Michel Feher, in conversation with James Graham[1]**

**James Graham** I thought we might begin with the news. It's May 31, 2016, and over the past five days, over seven hundred migrants have drowned in three shipwrecks on the crossing between Libya and Italy.[2] This route has generally been the preferred one for migrants from Sub-Saharan Africa, though it's also expected that many Syrians and Iraqis will resume using the route now that several Eastern European countries are tightening border controls. The EU and Turkey, meanwhile, have struck an agreement—though it might be unraveling—which includes a somewhat remarkable quid pro quo: that Turkey will help stem the flow of refugees, provided that Turkish citizens receive the privilege of visa free travel within Europe. It's hard to imagine a much clearer diagram than that of how "belonging" is negotiated and constituted at the state administrative level.

**Michel Feher** Widespread Euro-skepticism notwithstanding, there is arguably such a thing as a "European project," which involves turning Europe into a gated community for aging white asset holders. Utopian as it may seem, the achievement of such a project is a pretty brutal process, especially near the edges of the EU territory. The vast majority of refugees and migrants trying to reach European shores do not match the desired profile, which means that they can't be let in, while others who are already in Europe must be expelled for the same reason. Of course, the EU will never be fully gated and xenophobic policies are not going to make most of its white citizens more affluent—quite the contrary. But for European institutions, what matters is that they convey that they'll do what they can to keep Europe safe for native rentiers and their savings.

European governments have long been brandishing about the threat of uncontrolled and thus massive migration. Since their own economic policies (namely flexible labor markets, regressive taxation, and spending cuts, all with the purpose of making the territory under their care "attractive" to investors) leave many of their constituents in an increasingly precarious condition, they are eager to show that they can still protect their citizens from *something*, to wit the impending invasion of allegedly poor and culturally alien immigrants. Though utterly fictitious until 2011, the prospect of substantial immigration has gained a modicum of credibility with the tragic outcome of the so-called Arab Springs, thereby encouraging European leaders to fan anxieties about immigration so as to stake their own leadership on the promise of tighter border control.

However, toward the close of the summer of 2015, this trend of fearmongering tactics were briefly put to rest by none other than Angela Merkel, arguably Europe's most powerful politician. Confronted with an increasing number of Syrian refugees seeking asylum in Europe, the German chancellor not only claimed that taking them in was an undisputable *moral* duty, but also broke with the long-standing official line that claims that immigration is unbearably costly for host nations, arguing instead that welcoming asylum seekers was a good *economic* idea.

Angela Merkel's *Wilkommenskultur* moment proved short-lived, due to the very unfavorable reactions it provoked among her European colleagues and the members of her own Christian Democratic party. Realizing that she could not resist mounting international and domestic pressure, Merkel also did not want it to appear that she was reneging on her commitment to welcome Syrian refugees, at least. Thus, she looked for a middle ground and found a perverse albeit familiar solution, namely that of using so-called transit countries to act as a buffer zone and stem the flow of migrants. Hence the deal with the Turkish government: to the extent that Ankara's regime commits to keeping most Syrian asylum seekers within Turkish borders, Merkel can continue to say that those refugees who manage to get to Germany are still welcome.

But from Recep Tayyip Erdoğan's perspective, the appeal of the agreement with the EU is not only about getting Schengen visas for Turkish citizens or even about resuming negotiations for a future Turkish membership in the EU. Probably more crucial for him, in the short run at least, is the insurance that that Europe will turn a blind eye to his dirty war in Turkish Kurdistan and to the human rights abuses perpetrated by his government.

The current agreement between Turkey and the EU is in many ways reminiscent of the deal that the EU, and more specifically Silvio Berlusconi's Italy, had with Libya under Qaddafi at the turn of the millennium. At the time, the Italian prime minister poured money into Libya— to develop infrastructures, bolster border policing, and build detention camps—and he even apologized for past colonization.

In exchange, Qaddafi committed to take in migrants expelled by the EU, regardless of their nationality, and to limit sub-Saharan migration to the EU by detaining people transiting through Libya in EU-funded camps. Sometimes, when the camps filled up, the Libyan police would just drive migrants to the desert and let them die there.

**JG** Was there resistance to the Libyan arrangement when it was taking place, or is something changing about how these sorts of actions are being perceived?

**MF** The point of these agreements is for Europe to conceal—by virtue of subcontracting and outsourcing—the dirty underside of its immigration policy. So these agreements were hardly publicized. Human rights organizations denounced them of course, but immigration issues rarely cause widespread outrage. What is truly frightening and perhaps different about the current agreement with Turkey is that European governments and institutions don't even try to hide it from public view. They seem to be sure that whatever is done to stem the inflow of refugees will be well received. This puts into question the efficacy of the "naming and shaming" approach that has always been at the heart of human rights and humanitarian activism, for what is the point of exposing the discrepancy between the actions of a government and the principles that it claims to uphold, when appearing to abide by these principles ceases to be a concern for that government?

**JG** One of the places you've written recently about the EU–Turkey question is the web publishing platform you've begun with Zone Books, called "Near Futures Online."[3] It's a great title, in that the "near future" is also the preferred time horizon of the speculator, as you've argued in your ongoing work on the idea of neoliberalism— a term you deploy very strategically, in that we have to name a thing to take action on it. The near future is neither about present value nor long-term sustainability, but the kinds of short-term gains that drive our current economy. So your project is clearly a kind of counter-speculation, in that you're adopting the temporalities of neoliberal investment as your arena of political intervention.

**MF** Near Futures Online, which falls somewhere between an online journal and an online book series, is the digital companion of our print series with Zone Books entitled *Near Futures,* edited by Wendy Brown and me.

The "near future" designates the privileged timeframe of the current mode of governing firms, nations, and individual selves. It constitutes the horizon of the speculative bets upon which several forms of value are predicted: the shareholder value of a corporation, but also what Wolfgang Streeck aptly calls the "bondholder" value of a state, and, increasingly, the reputational value or capital of an individual. In other words, we live in a world where gambles on tomorrow's presumptive profits are given precedence over the mending of today's social woes as well as the prevention of after-tomorrow's ecological disaster.

Politically, however, to challenge the current capitalist regime—alternatively analyzed through the lenses of neoliberalism and financialization—it may not be sufficient to expose that regime's effects either on the present or the more or less distant future. Challenging financialization on its own turf requires us to reclaim the near future, to occupy not only public spaces— the Puerta del Sol, Zuccotti Park, Gezi Park, and most recently the Place de la République—but to occupy the timeframe in which speculative gambles exercise their hegemony. So, the twofold ambition of the Near Futures series is to gather books that provide a clear picture of our current

neoliberal and/or financialized condition but also explore activist venues in the realm of this kind of counter-speculation.

**JG** Obviously the most architectural site of this kind of speculation is real estate, and it interests me how real estate asks individuals to adopt and internalize the practices of the neoliberal economy. The forces that seem somehow abstract at the scale of states and corporations percolate into our own behaviors. I was reading an article recently about Sweden's ongoing privatization of real estate. Because of the sharply limited supply of housing and the competitive nature of obtaining both financing and an available apartment, people are obliged to document what's known as a "housing career"—the idea that in accruing your architectural belongings, if you will, whether owned or rented, you're developing a form of self that can acquire credit.[4] This is just one of many ways that regimes of real estate demand new kinds of self-management, touching on Foucault's idea of the *homo oeconomicus,* in that we become entrepreneurs of our own personal histories.

**MF** I agree, but we must also consider what type of *homo oeconomicus* we're talking about. Foucault already historicized the *homo oeconomicus* when he distinguished between the subject of exchange or trade proposed by classical economists (Adam Smith in particular) and what he saw as the neoliberal subject of competition, epitomized by the Chicago School's idea of the entrepreneurial self.

My contention would be that the type your Swedish example refers to is still a different character than the entrepreneur of his or her own life that Foucault drew from the work of Gary Becker. For while the plan of early neoliberal economists was to incite everyone, whether entrepreneur or not, to act and think like an entrepreneur—to make decisions based on cost/benefit calculations and the optimization of profit—the actual implementation of their program instead produced a society in which individuals are enticed to act and think like asset managers. In such a regime, one makes decisions based on a speculative assessment of how conducts and practices are currently rated, so as to maximize credit.

In the case you mention, potential homeowners and even renters are not only required to have the financial means to buy or rent the place they covet (and are of course required to refrain from unlawful conduct that could get them evicted); they are also expected to attend constantly to their creditworthiness in the eyes of lenders and other agents involved in the real estate market. That is what the so-called "housing career" you mention refers to.

Under the neoliberal regime, all but the higher salaries tend to be stagnant at best, so people increasingly stake their livelihoods not on the income they make but on their ability to borrow—hence the primacy of credit, even over profit, that characterizes both natural and artificial persons in the era of financialization. The latest incarnation of the *homo oeconomicus* can be considered a "rated agency." In the realm of consumer credit, the algorithmically produced FICO credit score (which is operative in numerous countries) is the paradigmatic device that not only supplies the rating but also provides the guidelines of conduct that purport to help individuals enhance their creditworthiness. Yet some people in the rating industry find the FICO credit score, which is exclusively based on the individual's credit history, too reductive—especially considering that in the age of big data, it is possible to construct rating devices based on an almost infinite range of personal information. So the twofold trend is both toward a multiplication of ratings and rating devices pertaining to the various regions of a person's existence and, ultimately, toward the construction of a consolidated score that would combine those various regional ratings of a person.

JG This connects to things you've said about the concept of leasing. The relationship between landlord and renter is the most familiar form of leasing, but you've argued that with the transition to an economy that we might characterize as neoliberal, the mechanism of the lease spreads to other areas. We lease time—something like a third of Americans are now considered private contractors rather than employees, and that's on the way up.[5] And with the rise of the so-called sharing economy, we even lease objects—"belongings" in the other sense, I suppose. Anything within our capital assets becomes a possible avenue of monetization. It seems to me that operating under the idea of the lease also breeds distinct ways of structuring our relationship to the object world that surrounds us.

MF That's right. This is the flip side of the rated agency: assets are both sources of income and collaterals that enable the *homo oeconomicus* as credit-seeking asset manager to borrow. As social benefits dwindle and jobs become more precarious, the private contractor, often glorified as a "free agent," gradually takes over from the relatively well-protected wage earner of the Fordist age. Rather than selling their labor power, as did the salaried classes of yore, private contractors try to reap revenues from their assets—their skills (from computer programming to assembling Ikea furniture by way of platforms like TaskRabbit), their cars or the extra rooms in their flat, (respectively through Uber and Airbnb) or even some of the durable consumer goods they own, such as cameras and vacuum cleaners, which they "share," that is to say, rent (through consumer-to-consumer platforms that specialize in the facilitation of such deals).

Even more than the actual revenues generated by his or her various assets, what matters to the rated agency is the estimated capital value of his or her portfolio, just as the CEO of a company is more concerned with shareholder value and the firm's creditworthiness in the eyes of investors than with the commercial income generated by the sales of the firm's commodities. Having very little protection with regard to health care, retirement plans, or welfare benefits, the private contractor is largely dependent on the estimated worth of the assets he or she can draw on. In other word, rated agencies largely depend on the *reputational* value of their assets—which is precisely what the so-called "sharing" platforms are supposed to provide and measure, hence the importance of the "reviews" that are such a central component of these platforms.

So what differentiates the contemporary *homo oeconomicus* from its predecessor includes this transition from a commercial, profit-based economy operated through trading markets to a reputational, credit-based economy operated through "sharing" platforms.

Of course, the two kinds of institutional settings still operate alongside each other and are intricately entwined. My contention is that the process of financialization that neoliberal policymakers more or less unwittingly unleashed involves a gradual subordination of the former to the latter. In a world ruled by speculating investors, firms and individuals are both less motivated to manage their capital so as to optimize its long-term yield than to manage their income so as to maximize the short-term value of the capital that generated it. (This is why, for instance, corporations use such a large share of the liquidity at their disposal to buy back their own stock—though commercially absurd, such a practice makes perfect sense if what you are after is the share value of your stock.)

JG   You've described a similar process at work at the scale of the state, or at the scale of the European Community, which is to maximize capital value by displacing the category of person you've termed "the discredited." Here, the qualifications of "belonging" are really replaced with something like bankability.

MF   As I mentioned earlier, Wolfgang Streeck has eloquently shown how the governments of the developed world have become primarily concerned with the "bondholder" value of their public debt—that is to say, with the propensity of investors to hold their Treasury bills and bonds. More generally, the art of governing nations in the age of credit is about maximizing the reputational value per capita of its population, so as to make the territory in which they reside as attractive as possible for investors.

Now, the maximization of human capital value per capita can be achieved in two ways. The first one, which could be called neoliberalism with a human face, involves enhancing the capabilities of the resident population. This is the course of action promoted by OECD [Organization for Economic Cooperation and Development] reports that urge their members to invest in education, open their borders to skilled and eager migrants, and balance the ever-increasing flexibility of the markets with re-training programs. The second one, on the other hand, is about raising the average worth of the population by either getting rid of, or not letting in, those endowed with a low reputational capital. Though governments have generally resorted to both methods, disposing of the people deemed un-creditworthy has clearly been the approach of choice since the 2008 financial crisis.

In the European Union in particular, disposing of the discredited involves (1) deporting migrants as well as barring them from accessing European territory, even if it means letting them drown in the Mediterranean; (2) encouraging European citizens to emigrate—more than 10% of both the Irish and the Portuguese population, most of them young and college educated but without many prospects of enhancing their bankability in the near future, has been forced to leave their country since 2008; and (3) tightening the conditions of eligibility for welfare or disability benefits, for the sake of making public deficits look less unattractive to bondholders.

**JG** Within the history of architecture, particularly that of early twentieth-century socialist movements, the speculator was an essentially villainous figure, and that remains the case in many discussions of contemporary real estate.[6] So as a matter of contrast, I find it notable that for you, speculation and credit are not negatives on their own, but the issue is rather how we attach cultural values to those things we speculate on behalf of. To the extent that architecture participates in the making of cultural values, it seems that understanding more a more progressive role for speculation might reflect back into how architects participate in the world of finance and real estate.

**MF** Keynes has a famous passage about how speculation is innocuous when it is limited to "bubbles on a steady stream of enterprise," but becomes a serious problem when enterprise "becomes the bubble on a whirlpool of speculation." For Keynes, the point was to issue a warning, to convey that having financial markets rule the economy would be like having "the capital development of a country become a by-product of the activities of a casino."[7]

In the last decades, however, what Keynes presented as a frightening possibility has become a reality—and a pretty resilient one at that, given that a shock of the magnitude of the 2008 crisis did not act as a wake up call. In other words, the world of credit is now ours, which means that those of us who find it objectionable must find a way to fight it on the very turf where its beneficiaries exercise their hegemony, instead of longing for the return of postwar welfare capitalism and centering our activism on the preservation of its remains. Insofar as credit, or creditworthiness, is the central stake, social struggles should be about the conditions of accreditation, the conditions under which credit is given, just like how the main struggle in the age of industrial capitalism and commercial profit was about the allocation of income.

**JG** Thus your call to minimize the "self-depreciating effects of left melancholy," which is always a fundamental political risk but feels especially poignant at the moment, given the cycles of optimism and disappointment that have afflicted so many movements globally. So if another valence of speculation is possible, what might it be? What are some ways we might reorient this idea of accreditation that would help move things toward a more—let's say—equitable, tolerable situation?

**MF** To get an idea of the kind of activism that would be capable of challenging the hegemony of financial capitalism, we might recall how earlier labor movements succeeded in challenging the hegemony of industrial capitalists. In Marxian parlance, "exploitation" refers to the conditions of employment under capitalism: the supposedly "free" workers, whose labor is constituted as a commodity that they seek to sell, are exploited insofar as their wages are inferior to the exchange value of the wealth they produce, thereby enabling their employer to make a profit. In keeping with this Marxian definition, labor activists of the industrial era identified salaried work as the social institution responsible for their exploitation. Practically, however, instead of simply rejecting the condition of salaried workers that was forced onto them, they formed unions based on the shared experience and interests of wage earners. As a coalition of salaried workers united and strengthened by the recognition of their common lot, they managed to challenge their exploitation in the labor market. Thus, while denouncing the "free worker" selling his or her labor as the subjective formation enabling capitalist exploitation, the labor movement also embraced it, strategically at least, as the collective identity from which the working class would draw its power.

Reenacting this dual strategy— exposing and yet appropriating the subjectivity predicated by capitalist relations of production—is what must be done today, but this time vis-à-vis the power of investors. It involves *identifying* the subjective formation that is constituted by financial markets, i.e. the "successor" of the free worker constituted by the labor market in the era of industrial capitalism, as well as *embracing* it in order to challenge investors on their own turf.

In the labor market, the free laborers identified by Marx are merchants selling the only commodity in their possession, namely, their labor power. To put it differently, the labor market is constructed and represented as a place where individual agents, guided by their interest, negotiate in order to buy or sell a commodity called labor at the best possible price. Employers, who buy labor in the labor market, use their purchase for the manufacturing of commodities that they sell in the market of goods and services. Meanwhile, workers, who sell their labor to employers in the labor market, use their income to buy commodities from employers in the market of goods and services. In the liberal world constituted by the articulation of these two markets, both workers and employers are thus merchants, that is to say owners of tradable commodities, who are equally free to negotiate the price of the commodities they seek to acquire and sell.

In contrast, the subjects that investor-driven capitalism both presuppose and construct are no longer salespeople trying to make a profit by means of maximizing the price of what they sell and minimizing the cost of what they need to purchase. What investors contemplate are "projects" trying to attract financing, or, more generally, trying to bolster their credit. Such projects range from the provisional budgets of national governments and the business plans of corporations to the applications of job seekers, statements of purpose by prospective students, and, of course, the credit scores of loan seekers. From the standpoint of financial markets, any such company, state, or person is not perceived as a legal or natural entity seeking to profit from mutual commerce but as a legal or natural entity to be *invested in*, or better still, to be considered worthy of investment.

To counter the exploitation that was enveloped in the representation of workers as "free" labor merchants, labor unions did not encourage their members to discard their alienated identity but to embrace it, albeit strategically: they went to the labor market as a coalition of labor merchants and used their solidarity as leverage in order to raise the price of the commodity they were selling. From their perspective, assuming the liberal condition of free worker was necessary if employers were to be challenged in the labor market.

Once again, if they are to follow in the steps of the labor movement that arose in the nineteenth century, current social movements should also appropriate the condition is assigned to them. To confront investors as efficiently as labor unions confronted employers, they cannot simply refuse to be perceived as more or less bankable projects. On the contrary, today's activists can only be faithful to the winning strategies of the past if they identify as credit seekers. For it, it is by embracing their "invested" condition— by identifying as "investees"—that they will be able to turn financial markets into a contested field: a field where the stakeholders of a firm—its workers, its consumers, the taxpayers financing the infrastructures that it relies on, the neighbors affected by what it does to its environment—will be able challenge the hegemony of its shareholders, and where the users of public services and beneficiaries of social benefits will be able to challenge the hegemony of the bondholders of the State's debt.

To pursue the same analogical reasoning, it can be argued that, while labor unions mirrored the mode of operation of the bosses' cartelslabor unions mirrored the mode of operation of the bosses' cartels—name that of an alliance of producers intent on "fixing" the price of the commodity they are selling—then investee activists may be well advised to mirror the mode of operation of a rating agency—namely, that of an alliance of stakeholders intent on modifying the criteria that preside over the allocation of credit to companies, governments, and individuals.

JG This idea of leveraging financialization to produce change, rather than waiting on legislative channels, speaks to your work on nongovernmental politics. I'm thinking here of the book you edited with Yates McKee and Gaëlle Krikorian in 2007, and especially the section on what you termed "stakeholder activism."[8]

MF What we tried to get at with the notion of nongovernmental politics was a domain of activism that identifies the specific workings of a mode of government—how it operates, what type of characters and expectations it seeks to produce in order to sustain itself—and checks its noxious effects on its own terms. Stakeholder activism, whereby labor unions, consumer groups, and environmentalists would act together to weigh on the ratings of corporations and states, is certainly one instance of such nongovernmental activism. The essence of many new forms of activism being built right now is to recognize and counteract the kinds of power that finance is able to assert.

1 This conversation took place in Paris on May 31, 2016.

2 See, among many others, https://www.theguardian.com/world/2016/may/29/700-migrants-feared-dead-mediterranean-says-un-refugees.

3 "Europe at a Crossroads," Near Futures Online 1 (March 2016), http://nearfuturesonline.org.

4 Hélène Frichot and Helen Runting, "The Promise of a Lack: Responding to (Her) Real Estate Career," Avery Review 8 (May 2015), http://averyreview.com/issues/8/the-promise-of-a-lack.

5 In September 2014, the Freelancer's Union published a survey indicating that 53,000,000 U.S. residents—34 percent of the workforce—worked as private contractors.

6 Among the historical voices in this debate one finds Ludwig Hilberseimer's programmatic call for "an end to the metropolis that is based on the principle of speculation." See Hilberseimer, Metropolisarchitecture, ed. and trans. Richard Anderson (New York: GSAPP Books, 2012).

7 This passage comes from Chapter 12, "The State of Long-Term Expectation," in John Maynard Keynes, The General Theory of Employment, Interest, and Money (London: Palgrave Macmillan, 1936).

8 "Stakeholder Activism," in Nongovernmental Politics, ed. Michel Feher with Gaëlle Krikorian and Yates McKee (New York: Zone Books, 2007), 196–281, esp. 198–199.

# Rēmįțtançe Arćhitecturēs
## in Risaralda

The coffee-growing region of Risaralda is one of the most relevant areas in Colombia in which to investigate how remittances have transformed the spaces of residence. Remittances—transfers of capital from migrants to family members staying in the home country—involve not only economic exchanges, but also affect the design, production, and commercialization of objects and architectures in both regions of origin and regions of destination.

Due to migratory trends starting in the second half of the twentieth century, Colombia is the country in South America with the largest emigrant population. These flows result in robust commercial, social, and cultural networks: four billion dollars of remittances were received in Colombia in 2015, benefitting approximately 10% of its inhabitants. This influx of money has fostered the proliferation of new larger buildings and the renovation and vertical expansion of preexisting family houses. The augmented dimensions of these constructions provide the possibility of dividing the units into separate spaces for different family members or for rental, as well as to include new businesses on the ground floor as an additional source of revenue. These variations of scale and typology manifest the different social dynamics of transnational families. But these constructions are also a consequence of the circulation of technical expertise and new understandings of luxury and success, making extensive use of mirrored glass, bright colors, and pronounced balconies and cornices.

This case questions architectures resulting from international economic transactions and labor fluctuations, their effects on the urban landscape, and their impact on the affections, desires and aspirations of transnational families and communities.

House built with remittances in El Salvador. Photograph by Andrés Asturias, 2010. Courtesy of the author.

Interfaced Remittance Urbanisms: Mediating the Forces
of Love, Work, and Translocal Microfinance

Husos Architects (Camilo García, Diego Barajas,
Marta Correal, María García)

The coffee producing region of Colombia is a hotspot for receiving remittances,
which make up almost 13% of the regional GDP. It is estimated that one in every
five families in Risaralda and the surrounding area receives support from family
members living abroad.

In what way do these flows generate new kinds of urbanism? What role does
architecture play in those processes? There are two main urban trends relating
to remittances in Colombia.

One is associated with neighborhoods configured by self-developed houses.
These constructions, constructed over time, adapt to the micro-realities and economic
fluctuations of those sending the remittances and those receiving them. Their
basic typology consists of a multifunctional productive unit which houses more
than one dwelling, and either includes shops at the street level, or businesses
on the upper floors, all with separate access. These buildings are associated
with residential communities that make intensive use of the street as a public
social space.

By contrast, there is also a form of urban development very much based on housing
inscribed within the commercially-financed production system. These neighborhoods are both advertised and supported by large agents in Colombia and in those
cities in Spain and the United States with large concentrations of Colombian
migrants. These houses are bought as finished products, with few possibilities
for extension or transformation, and thus, a limited capacity to absorb workplaces.
These constructions are usually grouped in gated developments, separated from
public streets. This type of real estate usually qualifies for government subsidies.

Both models are, to a great degree, managed from a distance. For this reason, the
large number of agents that act as mediators between the globalised workforce
and their loved ones—whether they be currency exchanges, technologies, banks,
migrants' shops in receiving countries, or advertising media—take on a particularly
key role. Through these agents and the architectures themselves, family ties are
remotely constructed and maintained.

The two different city models mentioned above are related to two different economies
and modes of production. It is currently impossible to procure help from the state
for self-developed houses, so they are frequently financed outside the conventional financial system, as their inhabitants are often shopkeepers or small businessmen.
The owners of the second type of home are usually associated with the current,
growing shift to a service economy in the region which allows their inhabitants to
receive a more stable income that permits them to pay a mortgage.

How do each of these models respond to a national context in which 40% of
jobs are concentrated in small businesses such as these neighborhood micro-
establishments? How do they relate to the life plans of migrants and to society
as a whole? This scenario renders the urgency of reflecting on the long-term
implications of each of these urban dynamics, and identifying elements that could
lead to alternative scenarios which respond to the interests of their particular
inhabitants and their collective lives.

1 Hangout for the migrant community from Risaralda at the entrance of the Colombian Bakery Jose Pan. Amongst the advertising stickers, there is one from Union Andina, one of the financial companies offering mortgages to migrants and mediating between banks and future creditors. Photo by Husos (Camilo García), in Usera (Madrid), 2016.

2 Paquito Colombiano is a small business owned by migrant entrepreneurs. This advertising image offers courier delivery service of goods to Colombia and other Latin American countries with important migrant communities in Spain. Published in "Latino" a local newspaper for the Latin American community in Madrid.

(Previous spread) Left: Self-built, remittance-driven urban model — Kennedy neighborhood. A productive home financed by remittances. The house has three entrances, making it possible to rent out one apartment and a shop on the ground level. Right: Residential gated community — Cuba neighborhood, Pereira. Built by a Spanish construction company, advertised for investing remittances. Photographs by Husos (María García and Marta Correal). Risaralda, 2016.

1 Still from promotional video by Bancolombia. One of the biggest banks in Colombia, it now offers mortgages to Colombians living abroad so that they can purchase homes in Colombia while still living in other countries.

2 Fieldwork in the San Camilo neighbourhood in Pereira. In San Camilo, a large percentage of families receive money from relatives abroad. In the picture, Gober, now living back in his neighbourhood, explains the self-managed building process of his house built with remittance money sent during his period living and working in Spain. Photograph by Husos (María García and Marta Correal), in Pereira, 2016.

3 Real Estate fair in Madrid. This fair specifically targets Colombian migrants as potential investors in new housing projects in Colombia. Stalls include builders, financial institutions both private and public, airlines, and other Colombian products. Photograph by Husos (Diego Barajas), in Madrid, 2016.

# Mârķĕțș and Térrıtòrïeš of the Glŏbaḷ Ħòmė
## Works

# A Secular Cosmology

## Adrian Lahoud

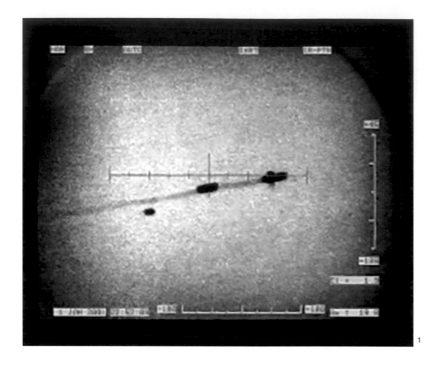

1

In the Warburg Library in London, there is a folio of plates from lectures given by the art historian Fritz Saxl. In one of the lectures devoted to the evolution of cosmological diagrams from the medieval period to the renaissance, Saxl introduces a rather remarkable image referenced simply as: *Microcosm. Germany, 15th Century. Vienna, Nat. Bibl, Cod. 5327, fol. 160r.* The mandala-like image presents a series of concentric circles indicating the orbits of various astrological constellations. Rays piercing parts of the human body indicate the celestial bodies responsible for their fate. As if from nowhere, lines of force arrive in every direction to make their demands. Unlike the more familiar images that conclude Saxl's lecture like Da Vinci's *Vitruvian Man* or even Durer's *Melancholia,* in this image and as a result of the of the conflict between forces, the body is in torsion rather than repose. Nonetheless, what the image tries to resolve is a certain crisis: to explain the way distant forces make intimate and ultimately contradictory claims on the soul.

It is more difficult than ever to disentangle microcosms from macrocosms, archaisms from modernities, and intimacies from abstractions. The paths of aerosols through the atmosphere and the paths of a diaspora seeking refuge in Europe perforate the partitions that divide existing systems of knowledge and belief. The small is brought into contact with the very large, and the heavens once again make their contradictory claims on the soul. The sense of immersion in a field of conflicting forces lends our experience of the climate an aura that—though it is no longer perceived as religious— has all the same effects: we are simply subject to its vagaries like the polytheistic combat between gods of old. But unlike the cosmological image cited above, what emanates from the macrocosm toward the microcosm is more like a field of uncertainty than a line of causality, a limit within systems of quantification and calculation.

Project team: Adrian Lahoud with Michaela French, Robert Walker (Royal College of Art, Full Dome Research Group); Spyros Efthymiou, Fanos Katsaris, Necdet Yağız Özkan, Hilmi Dalkir (Dome development and fabrication).

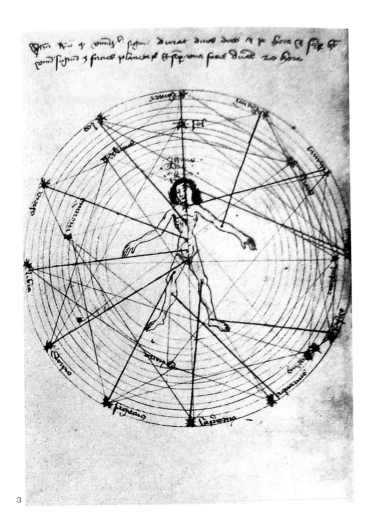

3

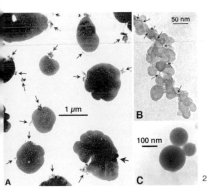

2

1 Refugee boat tracked using drone. A screenshot from the thermal camera of a Schiebel camcopter shows two boats carrying hundreds of migrants, as well as a smaller smuggler speedboat guiding them, in the central Mediterranean, August 10, 2015. © Migrant Offshore Aid Station (MOAS) Schiebel.

2 Aerosol Particles Size and Morphology Comparison. Researchers used an electron microscope to capture these images of black carbon attached to sulfate particles. The spherical structures in image A are sulfates; the arrows point to smaller chains of black carbon. Black carbon is shown in detail in image B. Image C shows fly ash, a product of coal-combustion, that's often found in association with black carbon. While black carbon absorbs radiation and contributes to warming, sulfates reflect it and tend to cool Earth. Peter Buseck, Arizona State University, August 2009.

3 Microcosm. Vienna, Nat. Bibl, Cod. 5327, fol. 160r. 15th Century, Germany © Warburg Institute.

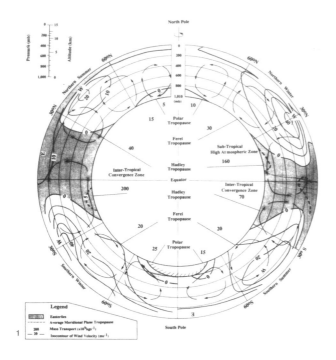

1 Schematic global circulation and tropopauses,
*United Nations University Report on Sustaining
Global Life-support Systems*, December 2006.
Courtesy of the United Nations.

2 Adam surrounded by the winds. Bibl. Vaticana,
Cod. Vat.Lat.645, fol.66r, 9th Century
© Warburg Institute.

## Split Waters: Forty Installations for Disputed Islands

**Luis Callejas and Charlotte Hansson**

"Geographers say there are two kinds of islands. This is valuable information for the imagination because it confirms what the imagination already knew. Nor is it the only case where science makes mythology more concrete, and mythology makes science more vivid. Continental islands are accidental, derived islands. They are separated from a continent, born of disarticulation, erosion, fracture; they survive the absorption of what once contained them. Oceanic islands are originary, essential islands. Some are formed from coral reefs and display a genuine organism. Others emerge from underwater eruptions, bringing to the light of day a movement from the lowest depths. Some rise slowly; some disappear and then return, leaving us no time to annex them. These two kinds of islands, continental and originary, reveal a profound opposition between ocean and land. Continental islands serve as a reminder that the sea is on top of the earth, taking advantage of the slightest sagging in the highest structures; oceanic islands, that the earth is still there, under the sea, gathering its strength to punch through to the surface."

—Gilles Deleuze, "Desert Islands" in *Desert Islands (and Other Texts, 1953–1974)* (Los Angeles, CA: Semiotext(e) / Foreign Agents, 2004)

Japanese landscape. Photograph by Luis Callejas, 2016. Courtesy of the author.

## Pacific Aquarium

### Design Earth (El Hadi Jazairy and Rania Ghosn)

The *Pacific Aquarium* portrays the overlapping concerns of ecology and economy in the Pacific Ocean, where the projected one million square meters of deep-sea mining in the Clarion-Cliperton Zone could constitute the greatest footprint of human activity in what is considered the largest continuous ecological unit on Earth. The project appropriates the object of the aquarium to take aim at the abysmal distance between our selfish economic worries and the great scales of the Earth. Rather than an image of the ocean that lies outside of human activity, the aquarium channels our sense of wonder to stage environmental externalities as an intimate part of the political constituency of the Earth. Each aquarium constructs a section of the world in which the externalities of resource exploitation and climate change are weaved into spatial scales, temporalities, and species beyond the human. Collectively, the nine aquariums reinsert the productions of nature into public controversies by connecting political ecology with speculative design and collective aesthetic experience.

1

Project Team for the Design Phase: Design Earth (El Hadi Jazary and Rania Ghosn) with Reid Fellenbaum, Ya Suo, Jia Weng, Shuya Xu, and Saswati Das, with initial contributions by Rixt Woudstra.

1 Over Mining

2 Below the Water Towers

3 Classified Sediments

Design Earth, "Pacific Aquarium."
Drawings, 2016. Courtesy of the authors.

2

3

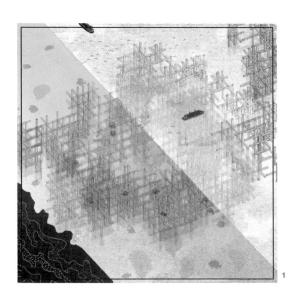

1

5

4

6

1 Jellyfish Maze

2 Marine Landfill

3 Parliament of Refugees

4 Iron Tower

5 Robot Fish Colony

6 Climate Sanctuaries

Design Earth, "Pacific Aquarium."
Drawings, 2016. Courtesy of the authors.

## Conflict Urbanism: Colombia

### Center for Spatial Research (Laura Kurgan, Juan Francisco Saldarriaga, Angelika Rettberg)

Over the course of the last thirty years, almost 7 million Colombians have left their homes and towns in a search for safety. Concentrated in the regions around Medellín, Buenaventura, Sincelejo, and Santa Marta, much of this displacement occurred in the areas where the conflict between the guerrillas, the Colombian armed forces, and right-wing paramilitaries was the most intense.

This mass migration, with its dense network of specific and often hyper-local causes, forms one part of the much larger global story of human beings on the move, mostly from countryside to city. But this movement of people also underlines the fact that the massive urbanization of the planet is born out of conflict. Who has not heard that by 2050, more than 66% of the world's population will live in cities? Behind this seemingly inevitable transformation lay battles of all sorts: military, political, social, economic, ethno-religious, imperial, ecological….

In Colombia, the armed conflict, if not the movement, might be nearing its end. After more than three years of negotiations between the government and the FARC—and following a controversial demobilization process by the paramilitaries in 2005—Colombian citizens might soon vote on a referendum to approve a historic peace accord between the two parties.

In this project we plot the trajectories of these Colombians in conflict, thanks to one dataset: the Registro Unico de Victimas, a massive project undertaken by the Unidad para la Atención y Reparación Integral a las Víctimas as part of an effort to allocate reparations in the peace-building process. As of May 1, 2016, 8 million Colombians were registered in the database and more than 6.2 million of them were "subjects of aid and reparation." The data reflects their stories—not simply the ones that will lead to aid, but the thick, complicated and often contradictory narratives of an extended and multi-sided conflict, an archive of the memories of millions of people.

How has this war affected cities? And how has the conflict played out in the countryside? How have cities—small, medium and large—coped with these massive influxes of displaced people? Can spatial analysis—indeed spatial memory—figure into discourses of cultural and historical memory? And what relationships can we discover between land use and conflict or the built environment and war?

Government agencies have led data collection efforts designed to inform policy; cultural and civic groups have led extensive efforts to document cultural and historical memory with the intention of furthering transitional justice. Our work is situated between these two realms: it introduces spatial memory into the discourse of transitional justice, and provides insights that might inform nuanced transitional justice policies that are responsive to local needs and cognizant of socio-spatial phenomena.

Our map shows an overview of the routes of internally displaced people in Colombia from 1985 to 2015. Depending on thickness, each line represents between 50 and 40,000 displaced people. The color white marks origins, while orange represents destinations. Zooming in and zooming out, we highlight specific events, places, and people that offer interpretations of the conflict, its traces, its memory, its impact, and its future.

Colombia's reported internally-displaced people. Forced displacement routes. Registro Único de Víctimas – Red Nacional de Información, Colombia 1985–2015. Conflict Urbanism: Colombia. Center for Spatial Research, Columbia University and Masters in Peace Building, Universidad de los Andes.

Project team: Laura Kurgan, Juan Francisco Saldarriaga, Angelika Rettberg with Research Assistants Dare Brawley, Anjali Singhvi, Patrick Li, Stella Ioannidou.

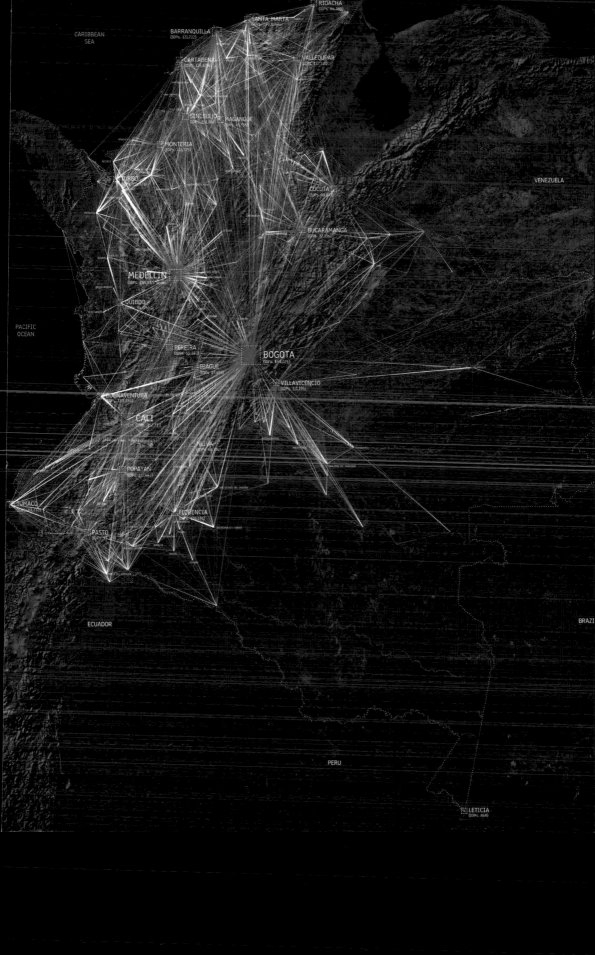

CARIBBEAN
SEA

RIOACHA
(IDPs: 64,369)

SANTA MARTA

BARRANQUILLA
(IDPs: 121,722)

CARTAGENA
(IDPs: 128,428)

VALLEDUPAR
(IDPs: 137,110)

SINCELEJO
(IDPs: 121,860)

MAGANGUE
(IDPs: 11,556)

MONTERIA
(IDPs: 143,105)

CUCUTA
(IDPs: 99,653)

VENEZUELA

TURBO

BUCARAMANGA
(IDPs: 72,150)

MEDELLIN
(IDPs: 456,917)

QUIBDO

PACIFIC
OCEAN

PEREIRA
(IDPs: 55,583)

IBAGUE
(IDPs: 97,454)

BOGOTA
(IDPs: 619,075)

BUENAVENTURA

VILLAVICENCIO
(IDPs: 111,195)

CALI

NEIVA
(IDPs: 74,745)

POPAYAN
(IDPs: 117,443)

TUMACO

FLORENCIA
(IDPs: 122,997)

PASTO
(IDPs: 78,681)

ECUADOR

BRAZIL

PERU

LETICIA
(IDPs: 869)

## Isle of Pleasures

Ana Naomi de Sousa, Paulo Moreira, Pétur Waldorff

The Ilha de Luanda is the oldest settlement of Angola's capital, a curious spit of land that is layered with history and myth. It has also long represented a haven, a place where the residents of Luanda go to drown out the stresses of daily life.

In the first decade of the new millennium, the Angolan economy boomed and international migrants poured into the country — many of them fleeing recession and unemployment in the former colonial power, Portugal. Luanda became the most expensive city in the world for foreign "expatriates," most of whom ended up living in the luxurious condominiums that pepper the city-scape, while working in the lucrative construction, retail and oil sectors.

On the Ilha, surrounded by the waters of the Atlantic Ocean, there is something for Luandans from all walks of life: they come here to enjoy the beaches and open-air fish restaurants and bars, though rarely crossing paths. But as the relentless regeneration of the city continues, bringing with it the chaos of evictions and demolitions—and the logic of gated developments— Luanda's last pleasure resort is changing dramatically and risks becoming another gilded cage.

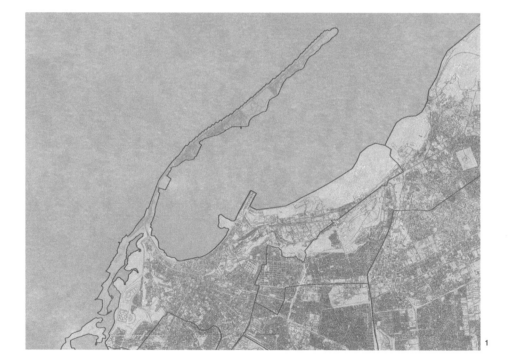

1

1  Paulo Moreira, Plan of Luanda, Angola, with Ilha de Luanda highlighted. Paulo Moreira, 2016. © The author.

2  Barracuda restaurant on the Ilha de Luanda. Photograph by Fernando Moura Machado, 1970s. ©The photographer.

3  Sunbathing in Chicala on the southern side of the Ilha. Photograph by Daniel Quintã, 1971. ©The photographer.

*Isle of Pleasures* is additionally supported by PanoramAH!

2

3

## PANDA

### OMA and BENGLER

In the early 2000s, the democratic spaces of the web were greeted as an alternative to a centralized commercial and social structure; and, later, after the financial landslide of 2007, the sharing gospel gave hope to those struggling to make a living.

The booming "sharing platforms" instrumented the private sphere with powerful market mechanics, enabling a fluid commodification of life. Flexible, web-scale human resourcing drew "app freelancers" into the gig economy—an unprecedented economic reactivation of latent human assets. A new labor force emerged, one obliged to hire itself out for ever-smaller jobs with no safety net, as companies profited handsomely.

While sharing platforms employ organizational tools of savage power, masses are atomized—strong-armed into unorganized negotiation.

Crowds attack taxis and block streets as services are banned in countries around the world. Unrest is staged against app-based, short-term accommodation platforms and the conversion of entire buildings into de facto hotels, tangible manifestations of a common resistance against unregulated digital competition and uncontrolled working conditions.

PANDA is a counter-organizational platform, providing a distributed toolkit of tactical disruption-as-a-service, empowering app workers with the means to mediate terms with the platforms and their algocrat masters.

That the service materialized out of Kinshasa is probably a fabrication. Skirting traditional venture capital cycles, the platform nevertheless emerged as a distributed, open source network of for-profit tactical nodes, untraceable and decentralized, a system of vast data and self-regulating algorithmic control.

PANDA is at once an act of resistance and a business opportunity, conceived within the cultural framework and space of new economic digital realms. It is the antibody for metastasizing platform capitalism.

Within mere months, PANDA experienced dramatic expansion, crystallizing the masses in tactical just-in-time action groups: from intangible interventions to exaggerated physical transformations.

As software eats the world, as everything solid melts into air, PANDA recasts technologies of oppression into a machinery of individual empowerment. By providing tools to actively navigate the turmoils of new digital regimes, PANDA fosters a new sense of belonging and purpose.

OMA Team: Ippolito Pestellini Laparelli, Paul Cournet, Giacomo Ardesio, Giulio Margheri, Laurence Bolhaar.
BENGLER Team: Simen Svale Skogsrud, Even Eidsten Westvang, Øyvind Rostad, Kristoffer Sivertsen.

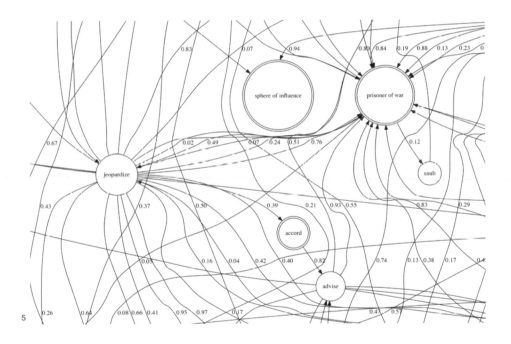

1 PANDA, a tool for counter-organizational empowerment: Logo.

2 Anti-Sharing Economy demonstrations: Taxi-drivers protesting against Uber in Paris, January 2016 ©ANP/AFP PHOTO/ Thomas Samson.

3 Cover of The Economist: The Sharing Economy, March 2013. © The Economist Newspaper Limited, London March 9th 2013.

4 App freelancers: Microworkers reply to the $0.50 question "Why do you turk?" for the project The Faces of Mechanical Turk. © Andy Baio, Waxy.org

5 PANDA actions: A tactical network alignment.

6 App freelancers: Helping advertisement, their "community workers."

1 A three-bedroom apartment converted by
the tenants into ten bedrooms to be rented on
Airbnb, New York City, 2015.

2 PANDA actions: Flash barricades.

3 Start-up incubator, Facebook office working
space. © Martin Schoeller / August Image /
Hollandse Hoogte.

4 Anti-sharing economy demonstrations signs
plastered by activists: "Warning! The apartments
in this building have been illegally converted to
hotel rentals," San Francisco, July 2014.

# Mąnụf̄āćtūŕįnğ Ašsembĺageš
## in Prato

The district of Prato is one of the engines for the manufacturing of "Made in Italy" labeled products, which the industry proudly markets globally as a trademark of quality based on "local" standards of production. However, the Italian textile industry depends on networks that cannot be confined within the Mediterranean country. Historically developed as a textile center, Prato grew throughout the second half of the twentieth century around a characteristically Italian model of small family-owned business. Major migration influxes, coming first from the south of the country and in recent decades from China, have supported this growth. The Chinese-led industries of the Italian city are currently mostly subcontractors for other Italian and European firms, participating in networks that are totally integrated in the productive fabric of the continent.

Located in the vicinity of Florence, Prato currently has one of the biggest Chinatowns in Europe, with more than 50,000 inhabitants (more than half allegedly without work permits). The social dynamics of this population are complemented by sustained links to the municipality of Whenzou, and by very strong networks internal to the dispersed ethnic community. The daily activities of the employees are often confined to workshops where they not only work, but also eat and sleep. This socio-architectural assemblage has uncritically resulted from a hybridization between the factory house and the factory town, adapted for global free-market regimes.

Nation-branding projects are not always calibrated with the labor that sustains them. Focusing on the architectures of production and their imbricated social relations can help to question the global circulation of goods in the market, and the attendant systems of valorization.

Textile factory in Prato, 2013. Copyright Fabrizio Giovannozzi/Afp/NTB Scanpix.

Sewing machines, dragoons, and firecrackers
Matilde Cassani

The buildings of the city of Prato and the surrounding area only partially reveal the complexity of their interiors.

Long series of warehouse buildings, inherited from a past focused on heavy industry, host a textile business which still survives in a new, reinvigorated Chinese-driven version. The articulated reality which lies behind apparently run-down facades, closed doors, and infrequent, darkened signs can be perceived only by an attentive passerby. These seemingly somnolent build- ings reveal themselves as reverberant the moment one approaches them. The repetitive, constant sound of sewing machines echoes, night and day, as the large Chinese community in Prato plays its role in a globalized market of clothes design, production, and sale from these modest local units.

Yet, there is one day when the sewing machines stop, the community takes a break from the incessant production process, and the world-famous Chinese dragon runs through the streets of the historic city center, and then through the surrounding industrial towns. A red carpet is placed outside each ware- house, and a small altar with offerings of food is set up inside. Finally, millions of clothing items, only partially hidden by large tarpaulins, pop-up. The noise is overwhelming when long lines of firecrackers and fireworks explode in the daytime sky. Following the path of the dragon, you can actually get a sense of the dimensions of the productive area, which starts in the city center and extends to its periphery and to the small towns surrounding Prato: Cantagallo, Carmignano, Montemurlo, and Poggio a Caiano, among others.

During the Chinese New Year, a completely closed territory is suddenly reveal- ed and accessible, offering a landscape of fireworks, festivities, and one million clothing items open to the city and its surroundings. The celebration signals a break in the tensions that result from the still extremely problematic process of integration between the Chinese and Italian communities. All the actors and institutions are there to collaborate: mayors, monks, business- men, and workers. Each of them has a clear role in the organization, and the feast is, ostensibly for a moment, part of the Pratese calendar at large. Rather than peaceful, the atmosphere is powerful and explosive. The crisis of the Italian textile market has found the perfect opportunity for continuity with the new Chinese "pronto-moda" method of production. In a delicate stasis, the Chinese presence holds the future of the textile past.

Prato offers the basic infrastructure needed to operate within the logics of the empire: a bunch of run-down factories, the proximity of traditional local manufacturing skills, and a cheap labor force. Together with these, the cultural network revealed by the Chinese New Year makes possible the comforting "Made in Italy" tag on clothes: a paradoxical manifestation of identity.

All images: Chinese New Year festivities. Photographs by Delfino Sisto Legnani. Prato, February 21, 2016. Courtesy of the author.

Project Team: Matilde Cassani with Martina Motta, photographs by Delfino Sisto Legnani, graphic design Bianca Fabbri, video editor Antonio Buonsante.

# Intervention Strategies

# Nature, Labour, Land: A Forum for Collective Arctic Governance

**Nabil Ahmed and Dámaso Randulfe**

*Nature, Labour, Land* operates on three negotiations in the region: the melting of Arctic ice (Nature), the expected pro-liferation of global shipments along the Northeast Passage (Labour), and the indigenous conception of the territory (Land). These three areas serve as a starting point to inter-rogate Kirkenes as a global model and reference point for a potential "transnational eco-political citizenship."

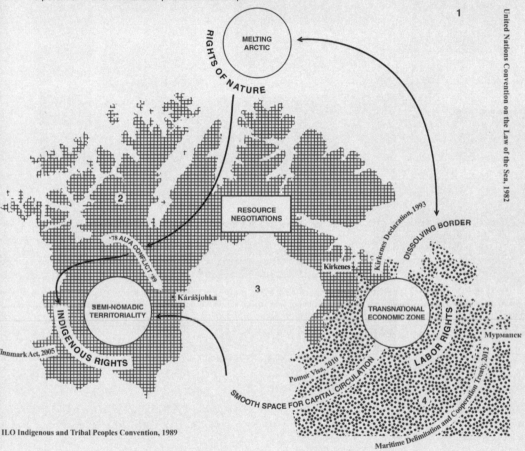

1. Barents Sea 2. Finnmark, Northern Norway 3. Finland 4. Russia. Nabil Ahmed and Dámaso Randulfe, "Nature, Labour, Land. Diagram for Action" (detail).

**I**

On January 13, 1907, almost one thousand Norwegian, Swedish, Finnish, Russian, and Sámi workers gathered on the outskirts of the copper mine in Sulitjelma, Northern Norway. The congregation was a response to a new regulation that forced workers to wear an identification label around their necks, a controversial measure which turned out to be the last straw in an atmosphere already inflamed by poor working and living conditions. Named "slave tags" by the miners, the identification medals provoked strong opposition and raised awareness about the need for coordinating strike actions. However, in addition to the question of how to organise them-selves, workers faced the problem of where to do so.

At the time, the village of Sulitjelma was entirely under the
control of the company, who owned not only the mines
and the processing plants but also the railway, the tunnels,
the houses, the infirmary, and the public spaces of the
town. Lacking a site to gather, workers had to congregate
alongside the waters of Lake Langvatn, the only place which
was not owned by the company. Once there, those in favour
of starting a trade union were asked to take a step forward.
Attendees responded by moving as one from solid ground

Nabil Ahmed and Dámaso Randulfe, "Collection of pictures of Arctic encounters, 1979–2012." April 2016.

onto the frozen lake. By standing on the ice, the workers were
laying the foundation for the Nordic trade union movement
while, at the same time, defying a spatial order to which they
did not belong.

The story of Sulitjelma's ice was told to us by Henning
Bråten, former leader of the mining union Nordens Klippe.
Founded in 1906 in Bjørnevatn near Kirkenes, the history of
Nordens Klippe runs in parallel to that of the town's iron mine,
both having played a determining role in the life of Kirkenes.
When we first met Bråten in early April 2016, the mine had
just shut down for the second time in two decades as a
result of low global iron ore prices. Today both the mine and
the union remain dormant, temporarily frozen in the hope
of better times to come.

II
The story of the Sulitjelma's icy union is instructive as it
tells us about the material and spatial conditions that allow
for the political enunciation of collectivities. This need for
defining and governing spaces has also characterised the

Sydvaranger open-pit mine after its closure. Photograph
by Nabil Ahmed and Dámaso Randulfe. Bjørnevatn, Kirkenes,
March 2016.

Russian and Norwegian vessels docked in the port of Kirkenes, March 2016. Photograph by Nabil Ahmed and Dámaso Randulfe.

recent history of the Sámi people and, by extension, of the Arctic indigenous communities. After centuries of discriminatory laws and forced assimilation, the second half of the twentieth century unfolded for the Sámi as a continuous struggle in favour of the recognition of their collective land and political rights. This struggle reached its peak during the 'Alta conflict', which originated in the mid-1970s around plans for the construction of a hydroelectric power plant in the Alta-Kautokeino river system in Northern Norway. What had begun as a protest that exclusively concerned environmental organizations and the state, suddenly acquired a radically different dimension when Sámi activists joined the opposition movement.

By framing the proposed damming as an infringement of their land rights and autonomy, the Sámi were able to position their demands on the political agenda in Oslo. Their strategy, which combined civil resistance at the front line of the protest and negotiations with the Norwegian state, turned out to be successful. While the dam was eventually built in 1987, the outcome of the Alta affair proved a strategic victory. Direct consequences of the conflict included not only the construction of the Sámi Parliament in Kárášjohka (1989), but also the ratification by Norway of the ILO Indigenous and Tribal Peoples Convention (an explicit recognition of indigenous rights to natural resources), and the passing in 2005 of the Finnmark Act by means of which the Sámi Parliament acquired a decisive role in the management of land use. Likewise, the Sámi victory was instrumental in the organizing of forums such as the World Council of Indigenous Peoples.

Whereas the recent history of the Sámi provides a highly effective model for bringing together environmental mobilisation and struggles for the recognition of collective political rights, the ancestral modes of production and territoriality of the Sámi might offer some valuable lessons on the dynamics of global capitalism. Sápmi—the land of the Sámi—is a

A popular allegoric representation of the Alta conflict in which Oslo's Storting takes the place of the dam. The painting was used as the poster for Bredo Greve's documentary drama "La elva leve!" (1980). Rolf Groven, "La elva leve." 1980. Oil on Canvas. Sámediggi, Kárášjohka. © Rolf Groven.

borderless nation which pre-dates and indeed crosses the state borders of Norway, Finland, Sweden, and Russia. For centuries, the culture of the Sámi people has been related to reindeer herding, a semi-nomadic, seasonal way of life that refuses fixed places and stable identities. Traditional Sámi cosmologies offer both an alternative Arctic imaginary around global commons, and a model for reading the transnational legal alliances that — in blurring state jurisdictions throughout the contemporary Barents region — seem to mimic the indigenous semi-nomadic conception of the territory.

Dámaso Randulfe, "Nature, Labour, Land: A Forum on Arctic Governance." Event poster, May 2016.

Norwegian-Russian border crossing point located 15 km east of Kirkenes, March 2016.
Photograph by Nabill Ahmed and Dámaso Randulfe.

A Forum on Arctic Governance, public meeting. May 26, 2016, Kirkenes. Photograph by Samfundshuset.

### iii

As an environment-making species, humans are transforming global nature. Nowhere is this impact more evident than in the Arctic, where the glaciers and sea ice are retreating at extraordinary speed. While dissolving the formerly stable boundaries between land, ice, and sea, global climate change produces not only new conditions for resource exploitation and navigation, but also northward claims for sovereignty, frustrated legally and politically by the complex materiality of the Arctic.

Many new questions present themselves: How does the melting of Arctic ice complicate the legal protocols of the UN Convention on the Law of the Sea with regard to claiming seabed rights beyond the limit of Exclusive Economic Zones? What do the circumpolar peoples of the Arctic have at stake in negotiating the ocean floor and subsoil, and how successful are Arctic indigenous organizations in negotiating with the states in intergovernmental forums? How can international law on sovereignty and national territorial claims address the geophysical reality of the Arctic, and the transnational workforce extracting its riches?

*Nature, Labour, Land* is a forum of thought and action that seeks responses to pressing questions by considering these three actors together, cutting across scales, disciplinary boundaries, and the politics of forgetting imposed by

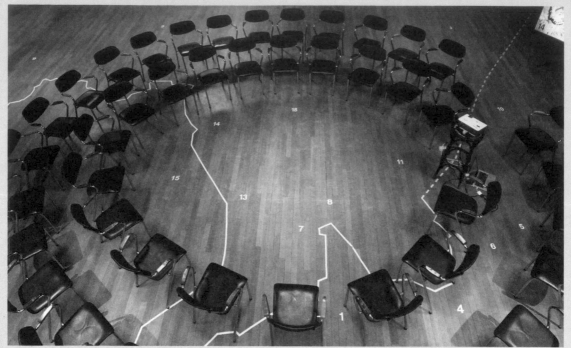

A Forum on Arctic Governance, public meeting, Kirkenes, May 26, 2016. Photograph by Dámaso Randulfe.

integrated world capitalism. In parallel, *Nature, Labour, Land* addresses the challenges and potentials of the dialectic conflict that emerges when bringing together environmental, labour, and indigenous rights, aiming to produce a synthesis which is not centralized but distributed among things. Historical experiences of trade unionism and indigenous struggle in Northern Norway provide us with transverse models for future action. Operating from the peripheries of sovereign power yet overflowing the space of the sovereign, we aim to rethink contemporary Kirkenes as a pivot for eco-political change, a site of pure potentiality in the construction of a collective Arctic governance.

Indre Finmark District Court, Tana Bru. May 2016.
Photograph by Dámaso Randulfe.

# OPEN transformation

## Elisabeth Søiland, Silje Klepsvik, Åsne Hagen

*OPEN transformation* explores alternative ways of meeting asylum seekers' needs through new notions of adaptability and hospitality, in order to overcome the narrative of "us" and "them." The project aims at intervening in the larger process of displacement derived from global migration, including real-estate market forces and housing solutions, taking the transit center Torshov Transittmottak in Oslo as a point of departure for a multiscalar and multilayered intervention.

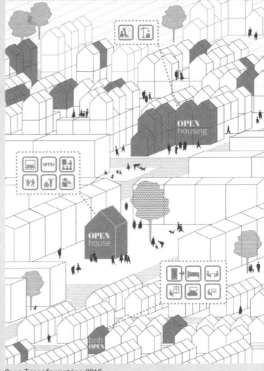

Open Transformation 2016.

Open Transformation, "Two reception houses," February 26, 2016, Torshov Transittmottak, Norway. Courtesy of the authors.

Open Transformation, "Welcome," February 26, 2016, Torshov Transittmottak, Norway. Courtesy of the authors.

The intervention strategy consists of three parts: *bnbOPEN*, *OPENhouse*, and *OPENhousing*.

*OPEN transformation* will enable those who arrive to find ordinary housing as an alternative or supplement to reception centers. To test this plan, the project will develop the app *bnbOPEN*, facilitating access to offers of accommodations from the inhabitants of Oslo.

Simultaneously, *OPEN transformation* will conceive of shared arenas of encounter for locals and the newly arrived. The spatial prototype, called *OPENhouse*, will become a meeting point for local communities.

Furthermore, with *OPENhousing*, the project will seek to challenge the hegemony of market forces in the housing provision process in Norway by investigating alternatives to current real-estate dynamics. The project adds to the public debate by presenting the arrival of migrants and asylum seekers as an opportunity to re-imagine housing policies and regulations in Norway.

**Minutes of Meeting, Hack for Humanity,
February 19, 2016**
For Hack for Humanity: Adam and Sinan
For OPEN transformation: Åsne and Elisabeth
Tilfluktshjem.no are also developing an app.

Tilfluktshjem.no got in touch with Hack for Humanity (HfH)
and was a case during a hackathon organised by the latter.
Some people from HfH have worked a lot on the project
"Et hjem" ("A home") and developed a digital platform, but ran
into some bureaucratic obstacles. Will OPEN transformation
be able to move the idea forward?

    HfH are able to contribute by designing and developing a
prototype, concept or digital solution which can be applied or
developed further after the exhibition. At this stage, a digital
platform or solution is preferable to an app (easier to make
adjustments, less coding involved).

Open Transformation, "Activity
leader Shwan Karem Wahed showing
one of the dining halls," February
26, 2016, Torshov Transittmottak,
Norway. Courtesy of the authors.

Open Transformation, "Bunk
beds provide sleeping space,"
February 27, 2016, Torshov
Transittmottak, Norway.
Courtesy of the authors.

Open Transformation, "Work meeting OPEN transformation and Hack for Humanity,"
(left to right: Elisabeth Søiland, Silje Klepsvik, Sinan Softic, Adam Gullerud
Haeger, Amra Softic), May 5, 2016. Courtesy of the authors.

**Process:** HfH recommends testing
real life interaction before developing an app. Use experience from
encounters between guests and hosts
to develop the digital communication.
Present digital solution as sketches
on paper first to get reactions from
stakeholders. Use web page to share
experiences — the HfH network
offers to make one. Possible to have
a new hackathon on site, at Torshov?
Combine this with stakeholder
workshop?
**Places on Torshov:** Trikkestallen,
close to the park Torshovparken.
**Progress:** We will talk again next
week. HfH will send a presentation
from the "Et hjem" project. OPEN
transformation will get in touch
with Tilfluktshjem.no and the local
reception centre operator Norwegian
People's Aid to establish connections.

**Mapping at Torshov,
February, 2016**
Questions:
1 Do you live here?
2 Where do you usually meet friends?
  Can you show us on the map?
3 What kind of activities do you
  associate with Torshov?

Open Transformation, "Mapping
at Torshov," February 27, 2016,
Torshov, Norway.
Courtesy of the authors.

Open Transformation, "Mapping at Torshov," February 27, 2016, Torshov, Norway.
Courtesy of the authors.

**Interview with psychologist Svein Ramung, April 5, 2016**

1 At an early stage of the reception phase, asylum seekers receive information on everything from the house rules of the reception centre to medical checkups and return schemes. Could you give examples of experiences that make it difficult for the individual asylum seeker to absorb and use information at this early stage?
2 What practical, external obstacles to receiving and processing information are inherent in the reception situation itself?
3 Does it make a difference in what sort of context the information is given, whether the group is big or small, in a new or familiar place, etc.?

Open Transformation, "Messages left by inhabitants." February 27, 2016, Torshov Transittmottak, Norway. Courtesy of the authors.

**Excerpted notes from interview**

To address the living conditions of reception centers in Norway requires several distinctions: first, between individuals in transit reception centers, and ordinary, more long-term reception centres; and, second, between asylum seekers who arrive on their own and those who arrive grouped in different family structures.

Open Transformation, "Shared bedroom at reception centre," February 27, 2016, Torshov Transittmottak, Norway. Courtesy of the authors.

Open Transformation, "Torshov resident 2," February 27, 2016, Torshov, Norway. Courtesy of the authors.

Open Transformation, "Torshov resident 1," February 27, 2016, Torshov, Norway. Courtesy of the authors.

**Excerpted notes from interview**

Asylum seekers normally show high rates of psychological stress, caused by the violence to which they have been submitted. These pressures might affect their ability to recount memories. Many are economically pressured due to obligations to send money to family back home and pay debts to smugglers. Ramung also pointed to the inefficacy of the current welcoming protocols, which overwhelm them with information—also known as "carpet bombing." This procedure does not consider the different backgrounds, ranging from illiterate to highly educated, does not ensure that the information has been correctly absorbed given the states of distress, and implies a constant provision of the same information.

Open Transformation, "Torshov resident 4,"
February 27, 2016. Torshov, Norway.
Courtesy of the authors.

Open Transformation, "Torshov resident 6,"
February 27, 2016, Torshov, Norway.
Courtesy of the authors.

Open Transformation, "Meeting place 2,"
February 27, 2016, Torshov, Norway.
Courtesy of the authors.

**Excerpted notes from interview**

Asylum reception centres are often placed in buildings not specifically designed for this purpose. In them, families are usually placed in a single room, while unaccompanied individuals share a room. In this second case, the different hygiene standards and sleep patterns of each inhabitant can lead to conflicts and daily living disruptions. This sharing interferes with opportunities for individual seclusion, medically recommended for individuals in states of high psychological stress as "it could be beneficial to have the opportunity of withdrawing rather than being constantly exposed to others."

Open Transformation, "Books in Arabic and Persian at local library branch," February 27, 2016, Deichmanske bibliotek, Torshov, Norway.
Courtesy of the authors.

Additional credits: Hack for Humanity (Sinan Softic, Amra Softic, Adam Gullerud Haeger, Natale Hugvik). Advisers: Svein Ramung, Nuray Yıldırım, Kawa Gharji, Susanne Bygnes, Marwan Hudery, Tellef Grønlie, Per Kristian Nygård. Thank you to: Shwan Karem Wahed, Else M. E. Abrahamsen, Makers'Hub, Ketil Blinge, Christine Annexstad, Linn Landro, Eli Støa, Anne Sigfrid Grønseth, Ida Helen Skogstad, Arild Eriksen, Joakim Skajaa, Nhu Diep, Jan Olav Ryfetten.

Open Transformation, "Torshov resident 7,"
February 27, 2016. Torshov, Norway.
Courtesy of the authors.

Open Transformation, "Traces
of home: a door at Torshov
Transit Reception Centre,"
February 26, 2016, Torshov
Transittmottak, Norway.
Courtesy of the authors.

**E-mail from Tellef Grønlie, UDI, April 12, 2016**
---------- Forwarded e-mail ----------
From: Tellef Kristofer Grønlie
Date: April 12, 2016, 10.10 AM
Subject: RE: Project on alternative lodging for
asylum seekers
To: OPEN transformation
<opentransformation@gmail.com>

Hi.
Will look into the dates further.
Confirming that lodgers in transit may be granted
leave by approval from the Directorate of Immigration. This concerns potential agreements and
logistics. In ordinary reception centres I think
they may have up to a week of leave without our
approval, more if approved.

Open Transformation, "Written in red on the board of the library room: HJEM = HOME," February 26, 2016, Torshov Transittmottak, Norway.
Courtesy of the authors.

# Managing Dissidence

## Bollería Industrial / Factory-Baked Goods
### (Paula Currás, Ana Olmedo, Enrique Ventosa)

*Managing Dissidence* operates on the fabricated experiences of the airport. Departing from real stories in which airport regulations have been exposed and contested, the project seeks to produce a set of devices which question the airport's homogenizing rituals and configure a platform for criticality. By means of boredom, oddly familiar scenarios, and the climate-controlled atmospheres of in-transit buffers, the spaces and technologies of the airport relax our sensory spatial apprehension to camouflage the control parameters to which passengers are submitted.

In contrast to the individualizing rules of the airport, interactions among users — killing time during delays, sharing inconveniences, being in close proximity — create micro-communities based on temporary alliances. These interactions can develop into indirect, unsophisticated forms of dissidence. This project is a form of soft activism which re-codifies existing airport rituals, and provokes new social conventions.

The proposal analyzes the highly-designed sequence that airport passengers must follow to depart and arrive. This sequence is divided into eight sections in a passenger's promenade through the airport:

1. Oddly Familiar; 2. Prohibited Items; 3. Security Control Failures; 4. Delays and Boredom; 5. Duty-Free Issues; 6. Baggage Carousel; 7. Warm Welcome... or Not; and 8. Secondary Effects.

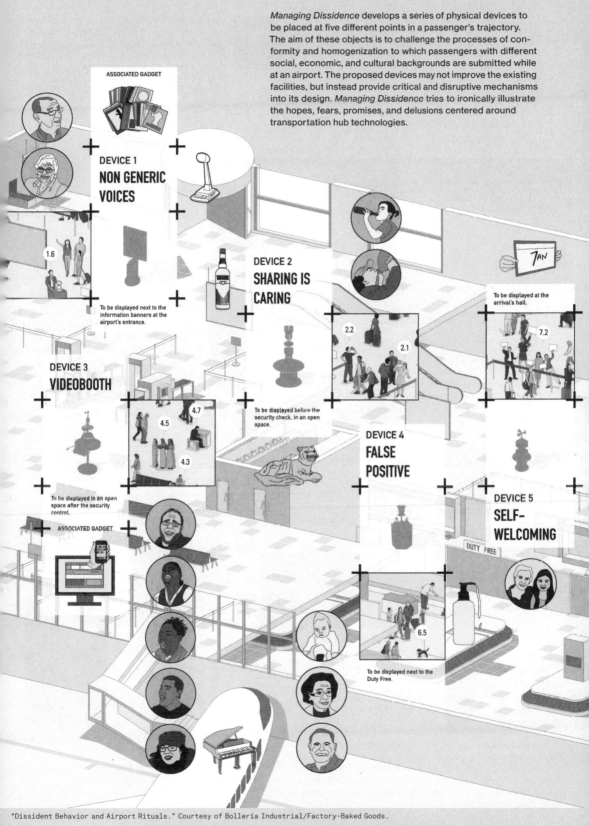

Managing Dissidence develops a series of physical devices to be placed at five different points in a passenger's trajectory. The aim of these objects is to challenge the processes of conformity and homogenization to which passengers with different social, economic, and cultural backgrounds are submitted while at an airport. The proposed devices may not improve the existing facilities, but instead provide critical and disruptive mechanisms into its design. Managing Dissidence tries to ironically illustrate the hopes, fears, promises, and delusions centered around transportation hub technologies.

ASSOCIATED GADGET

**DEVICE 1**
**NON GENERIC VOICES**

1.6

To be displayed next to the information banners at the airport's entrance.

**DEVICE 2**
**SHARING IS CARING**

2.2

2.1

To be displayed before the security check, in an open space.

7AN

To be displayed at the arrival's hall.

7.2

**DEVICE 3**
**VIDEOBOOTH**

4.7

4.5

4.3

To be displayed in an open space after the security control.

ASSOCIATED GADGET

**DEVICE 4**
**FALSE POSITIVE**

**DEVICE 5**
**SELF-WELCOMING**

DUTY FREE

6.5

To be displayed next to the Duty Free.

## 1  Oddly Familiar

Despite the efforts of designers to render each airport as a unique nation-, region- or city-branding symbol, the globally-shared operational logics of these facilities' interiors end up providing a highly antiseptic experience to their heterogeneous body of users. Ultimately, the repetition of protocols and the placement of similar technological apparatuses submits travellers to a strange familiarity which results in the memory equalization of all these buildings.

1.2

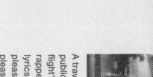

Carolyn's voice has been used for announcements a more than two hundred airports and transportation hubs. Her perfect English diction can be heard at multiple latitudes, from the New York City Subway system to Paris-Charles de Gaulle Airport.

A traveller decided to use the public address system at his flight's boarding gate to recite rapper Eminem's well-known lyrics 'May I have your attention please? Will the real Slim Shady please stand up?'

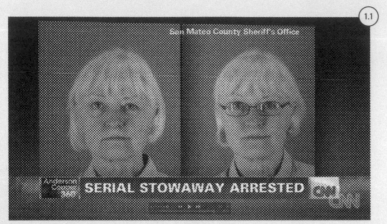

1.1

Following three failed attempts to board a flight without a ticket, 62-year-old Marilyn Jean was finally able to board a plane to Los Angeles after slipping through the check-in point at San Jose International Airport. Marilyn was immediately arrested upon landing.

1.10

35-year-old Spaniard Juan is one of the twenty inhabitants of Barcelona Airport's Terminal 2 listed in the national census. According to Juan, the two major inconveniences of living in the airport are the never-turned-off white light, and boredom.

1.4

In 2015, a man was arrested in the Jorge Chavez Airport in Peru after a dog discovered that his average-size carry-on suitcase hid a man trying to illegally enter the country.

1.11

57-year-old German René has been living for more than four years in Palma de Mallorca Airport. He refuses to leave.

1.8

Once expelled from Iran, his home country, Mehran was finally awarded refugee status in the United Kingdom in 1977, after proving the existence of British relatives. Mehran departed for London, but when his documentation was lost, he was forced to return to France. With no country of residence, Mehran ended up settling at Paris-Charles de Gaulle Terminal 1.

1.9

While walking from Madrid to Zaragoza in 2013, Edu encountered Barajas Airport, where he decided to settle down. Living in the airport ever since, Edu has described on several occasions the more comfortable conditions of these kind of facilities in comparison to street living. Camouflaged among everyday transportation users and utilizing the same resources, his presence in Barajas is hardly noticeable.

(1.3)

...ensive experience on voice-overs, ...mmercials, and audiobooks led Louis-...radio announcer and disk jockey Jack ...nter the airport security announce-...nt business, becoming one of the most ...iliar voices for travellers worldwide.

**...naging Dissidence Workshop**
**... vice 1 — Generic Voices**

...the development of this associated gadget, ...ctory-Baked Goods collaborated with Universidad ...opea de Madrid to organize a workshop during ...*Handsthinking–Festival de Arte, Arquitectura ...iseño*, on April 18, 2016. Along with fifteen ...dents, the architecture office addressed the ...rils of voice homogenization and generic voice ...ndards establishing a heterogeneous *Archive ...Non-Generic Voices* that would serve to desta-...ze any attempt at voice and idiom normalization ...ransportation-hub announcements. The idea ...s to collect the maximum number of samples to ...used when Device 1 is installed in Gardermoen ...port. Based on the technology of public address ...tems, the installation would allow passengers to ...ransmit flight announcements in real time.

**The airport voice: An Interview with Jack Fox and Bollería Industrial.**
Jack Fox is a professional voice-over artist for radio and TV. His voice is heard in airport announcements in over one hundred cities around the United States, as well as in the New York Subway, the Mayo Clinic, various Capitol buildings, and the Kennedy Space Center.

BI  Why do you think that you were selected to be the public-address-system voice in so many locations?

JI  My voice was selected because "an authoritative yet friendly male voice" was desired. I seemed to meet those desired needs.

BI  How would you describe your accent? Have you learned to avoid it?

JF  My accent is a typical "Middle America" style that has been developed to avoid most extremes.

BI  There are several videos showing airport voices struggling to pronounce non-English names, Have you ever had any similar problems? How do you think that they could be solved?

JF  The way I try to solve it is to have the names written phonetically and, if possible, have a person of that language pronounce it for me.

BI  Do you believe that your voice produces the sense of a friendly atmosphere to the people who travel?

JF  Yes. My voice has a warm, calm, clear, and friendly quality. I also mentally picture people in the situation I am addressing, and I believe that affects the tone of the announcement, as if I am speaking to a person or persons rather than just recording words on a written notice.

BI  If your voice can also be heard in other places like the subway or a train station, do you change your voice register depending of the situation?

JF  Not usually. Again, I picture mentally the audience and that may change the pitch or tone of the announcement.

"Generic Voices" Starting Kit. Photograph by Bollería Industrial/Factory-Baked Goods.

"Generic Voices," Workshop at Universidad Europea de Madrid during Handsthinking Festival, July 22–23, 2016. Photograph by Bollería Industrial/ Factory-Baked Goods.

Sample Kit of the "Generic Voices" Archive.
Photograph by Bollería Industrial/Factory-Baked Goods.

A cat named Felix went missing when his crate collapsed after a foureen-hour flight from Abu Dhabi to New York. Lost for more than two weeks, Felix spent his time wandering around the airport until he was finally found and returned to his owner.

After his flight was delayed, Wu decided to use the rice cooker in his hand luggage to prepare himself a meal in the middle of Hong Kong's Airport. Jiayong used water from the restroom facilities and plugged his cooker into one of the airport's power outlets.

1.5

After finding an alligator underneath an escalator at the O'Hare International Airport in Chicago, the Transit Authority released photos of the animal being held by its owner. She received a misdemeanor indictment for cruel animal treatment.

Due to the lack of technological equipment to read his identification microchip, American puppy Buddy remains detained at Barcelona Airport.

1.12

## 2 Prohibited Items

The continual increase in the number of objects forbidden in the plane cabin, and the variation in the regulations from one airport to another, require the user to be well-informed about the specific carry-on policies applying to the origin and destination of their flights. Food and beverages, medication, weapon-shaped items, and the chemical components contained in many cosmetics are some the most controversial issues that figure in security control.

2.1

When asked at security control to surrender a 300€ Cognac purchased at the duty-free store from her previous flight transfer, 40-year-old Chinese citizen Miss Zhao decided to drink the whole bottle. Due to severe intoxication, Zhao required medical assistance and missed her flight.

2.3

Two Chinese siblings hid a bottle of wine in a tiger costume to slip it through security control. After arguing that the bottle actually contained a male fertility solution, the brothers ended up consuming all the wine before passing through security.

2.2

A 64-year-old German traveller decided to drink a whole bottle of vodka rather than surrender it to the security officers at the Nuremberg Airport control. After suffering alcohol poisoning, he was obliged to reschedule his return flight.

2.4

Well aware that carry-on rules specify that 'no liquids' are permitted on flights, scientifically-correct Simon was denied access to the airport security area with a frozen, 'solid' Diet Coke.

## 3 | Security Control Failures

Despite attempts to transform passengers into "universal, safe travellers" using security technology systems ignorant of social or economic background and age, these protocols are constantly disturbed, as are their homogenizing considerations of subjects, bodies, and lifestyles.

James had to hand over the brightly-coloured plastic gun spotted in his luggage by X-ray machines, as the item was considered an in-flight

28-year-old Haisong entered the security area at the Newark Liberty International Airport to kiss his girlfriend one last time before her departure. The breach in the security system forced the terminal to shut down for several hours, causing major flight delays.

Kate and her kids became extremely upset when officers at the security control in Heathrow Airport in London confiscated the board game they had chosen for their vacation. The game, called 'Pass the Bomb,' was considered a security threat even though rated for children of age five and above.

At the suggestion of the Transportation Security Administration, Levi was forced to surrender his favorite toy, a Buzz Lightyear figure, to the security guards at the Lauderdale-Hollywood Airport who considered the toy a security menace.

Dancer Abdur-Rahim was forced to perform in front of security staff members at Israel's International Airport in order to prove his identity. Jackson's Arab first name led him to be considered a possible terrorist threat.

As reported via Twitter, Shadi was asked to pass through the scanner several times to ensure her gender. Minutely inspecting her crotch through the body scanner, the long duration of this process nearly caused her to miss her flight.

## 4 | Delays And Boredom

Amongst the most common images associated with airports are those of people stuck in flight delays. Although generally seen as a waste of time, delays constitute routine-disrupting breaks in which the boredom-born creativity of passengers can lead to unexpected events.

Frequent long-distance traveler Tyler is responsible for a blog compiling detailed instructions on how to take a refreshing shower in airports to always stay clean.

During a flight delay, the University of Pittsburgh basketball team shot music videos of popular songs. Their fans have already requested extended versions.

Liverpool musician Matthew teamed up with a singing police officer, who used his gun as a "guitar," in order to entertain passengers at Manchester Airport's Terminal 2. The recording of the performance immediately went viral.

The suspension of flights due to the presence of fog at the Dalian international Airport in China stranded more than five thousand passengers for hours at the facility's main lobby. The airport administration decided to hire a team of cheerleaders to entertain and, thus, calm the angry passengers.

During a peak period at the Chiang Mai Airport, a Chinese tourist decided to hang her wet under-wear across six seats in order to lie down, a widespread technique to mark one's "seating territory." The tourist was immediately asked to put her clothes away.

After finding a piano at 6:00 am in the lobby of Amsterdam Airport, Russ and Kate attracted a huge audience while improvising Adele songs. Their performance was widely shared on social media.

During a flight delay at the Atlanta Airport, a religious chorus decided to entertain the waiting passen-gers using the public address system.

During a six-hour flight delay, the casts of the Lion King and Aladdin musicals performed a free, improvised concert to entertain the other passengers.

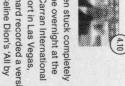

When stuck completely alone overnight at the McCarran International Airport in Las Vegas, Richard recorded a version of Celine Dion's 'All by Myself' and dedicated the clip to his wife, a video now watched more than eleven million times.

During a connection at the Frankfur Airport, professional pianist Jesus was rewarded with free coffee by th Bechstein Restaurant after playing the piano located on its terrace.

## 5   Controversial Cosmetics

Have you ever thought about the chemical composition of soaps and creams or duty-free items? Their ingredients may actually provoke unexpected consequences.

North Carolina web deve-loper and self-proclaimed security expert Evan proved how several lethal weapons could be assembled using only duty-free items.

After a false positive which detected the presence of explosives on her body, Linda was accused of carrying explosives by TSA agents at an Ohio airport. The traces were actually hand lotion.

An NBC 5 employee reported live from the Dallas Airport on the too-highly calibrated sensitivity of the Explosive Trace Detection system after his body lotion signaled the presence of explosive material on his body.

Controls utilized by the Transportation Security Agency employ the highly sensitive Explosive Trace Detection system. This technology can detect the presence of any substance used in the making of explosives on any surface, including human skin. Photographer Ned Levi was on the verge of a nervous breakdown when his bag was continuously flagged as a false positive for explosives at all the airports he would visit: his baggage had been washed with a soap solution containing the kind of glycerin utilized in the production of explosive mixtures.

Eva's hand scan tested 25% positive for gunpowder at Pearson International Airport in Toronto. An internet search proved the high frequency of this situation, caused by the generalized use of common glycerin hand cream.

The food of baby Bruce was declared suspicious when its container gave a positive reading for explosive substances, which was actually caused by the chemical composition of the soap used to clean it.

## Baggage Carousel

The baggage carousel has become one of the most attractive devices for airport users. While waiting for their luggage, unusual items rolling on its surface —ranging from a kid or a rock star to pieces of fruit— can surprise passengers.

Rock group frontman Wes was arrested at the Denver airport for riding the baggage carousel. His trip, recorded by the CCTV system, spread widely in the media.

Air India passenger Rajkumar, a first-time flyer, was observed going through an X-ray machine of the baggage handling system at Delhi Airport.

The pants of a teenager were ripped by the luggage carousel of Las Vegas Airport while he was resting on the apparatus.

A pornographic movie was broadcast on the information screens of the Lisbon Airport while passengers were waiting for their luggage at 3:00 am. The movie remained on the screen for several minutes before flight arrival information could be restored.

**6.9** After noticing a coin glued to the baggage carousel, a group arriving at the Palma de Mallorca Airport recorded the reactions and hesitations of passengers in their attempts to get the money.

**6.5**

Russian 6-year-old boy Leon was spotted by the CCTV system travelling via the baggage conveyor belt through restricted facilities in Sheremetyevo Airport in Moscow. Bogdanov was safely rescued before entering any dangerous areas.

**6.3**

Sherlock is a beagle that aids in the return of lost items at the Amsterdam Airport. After smelling the forgotten luggage, Sherlock surveys the facility searching for the similar smell of its owner.

**6.6** To celebrate its 172nd anniversary, the staff of Thomas Cook Airlines amused the passengers retrieving their belongings by singing the song "Sunny Heart" while standing on the baggage carrousel.

**6.7** The Thrilling Cities collective decided to welcome passengers upon their arrival at the Vilnius Airport in Lithuania by placing fresh fruit between the pieces of luggage on the baggage carousel.

## 7 Warm Welcome... Or Not

The welcoming area for arrivals at an airport can host heartwarming moments. Yet, if no one is there to welcome the passengers, these places can also turn into the coldest, loneliest area of the facility.

**7.1** When stepping off her return flight after a month-long teaching program in Costa Rica, Lindsay encountered a lip-sync performance organized by her boyfriend in order to propose marriage to her.

While waiting for a friend at the arrivals gate at Heathrow Airport, Alexander was surprised by a small a cappella group hired by his girlfriend Alexandra, who joined the performance displaying hand-written cards.

**7.2**

## 8 Secondary Effects

The field of action of airports is not restricted to its interior. The behavior and the survival politics of people and animals in the surrounding areas are also affected.

**8.2**

The owners of a restaurant located near the Schiphol Airport in Amsterdam incorporated traditional Dutch goose and pigeon recipes into its menu in order to utilize the birds culled to prevent them from interfering with aircraft engines.

**8.1**

More than 150 turtles crossed runway 4 at New York's JFK Airport looking for the perfect spot to breed. In order to guarantee the safety of these animals during this unique process, the airport administration decided to delay the flights departing from this runway.

# Modes of Movement

**Ruimteveldwerk (Pieter Brosens,
Brecht Van Duppen, Sander Van Duppen,
Lene Beelen, Pieter Cloeckaert)**

*Modes of Movement* explores the potential of asylum seekers to participate in the cultural, social, and economic life of the city. The project invites refugees to find niche spaces within Oslo's public sphere which are useful or appealing to them. Through the collection and dissemination of information about these spaces and experiences, *Modes of Movement* aims to have asylum seekers occupy the city and make their presence visible within its spaces.

© Ruimteveldwerk.

Ruimteveldwerk.
Entrance of
the center.
May 2016,
Torshov transit
center, Oslo.
Courtesy of
the author.

The idea is manifested in a series of "public spaces" selected by asylum seekers: shelter/housing, health/administration, and culture/sports. This array of spaces will be collected in a guide, a platform by refugees for refugees. The project aspires to activate the voice of asylum seekers within the city who are in the process of receiving refugee status even while potentially being transferred between different centers. A Travel Guide will be presented that collects *Modes of Movement* ranging from primary needs to elements of interest. This citizen's manual will be an instrument for asylum seekers to find their way in Oslo and to help them identify particular answers to short term or perennial questions. Norwegians and earlier generation migrants are also asked to contribute in complementary ways to the guide. In addition to these *Modes of Movement*, the guide will also bring together existing volunteering initiatives in Torshov, information about services, functional data, and practical focal points.

The Travel Guide is not only a collection of physical and practical modes of navigating the city, it can also be a register of 'personal stories.' Experiences, memories, and narratives become attached to places in the guide. *Modes of Movement* operates as an instrument to absorb and (re)present the city through a subjective reading and becomes a platform that not only (re)produces interactions between the asylum seekers and the citizens of Oslo, but also facilitates these connections.

By means of two architectural incentives, the model and the map, space-related agencies are proposed in workshops where the material for the guide is gathered and discussed. Both incentives establish a communication tool between the different agents involved, in particular between groups with different backgrounds. These representations of the city become the common language for people participating in the project. Diverse types of information are collected as layered maps within the interpretative city model: objects, drawings, pictures, writings, etc. The model and the map are not seen as final products but as interactive and participatory platforms.

Ruimteveldwerk. Workshop with asylum seekers.
May 2016, Torshov transit center, Oslo.
Courtesy of the author.

The model has been under preparation from the first workshop, where all contributors have been asked to explore their connections to the city and to pinpoint on a map their places of meaning and interest. The spaces can be a meeting place, a shop, a park to relax, or a place that is somehow linked with their homeland. Conversations between participants are intended to lead a discussion of similarities and differences, looking for a mutual understanding. The central idea of the workshops is to establish participation and connection between asylum seekers, volunteers, and local citizens. Through activity and dialogue, a sense of community can be established among these agents.

Ruimteveldwerk. Asylum seekers' guides
(Russian, Somali, Tigrinya and Arabic)
versus tourist guides (Norwegian, Spanish,
German and English). Courtesy of the author.

The Travel Guide to the city—an interpretation
and synthesis of the model—is an ongoing
adaptive tool that provides alternatives for
newcomers, long-term Torshov residents, and
others. Above all, this guide aims to result in
a sustained dialogue among the residents of
Oslo and to facilitate their interaction, connection, and integration in the public sphere.
Furthermore, the guide—in the format of a
booklet or foldable map—can be seen as a
template for future projects throughout other
European cities.

**Minutes of Torshov staff interviews (report 1)
— early March**
**Important findings Visit 1**
× The number of residents will increase up to 200, of which
90% will be relocated by the end of July
**Short stay of residents**
    Most of them are Dubliners and stay for 2–8 weeks
    maximum (come from other centers)
× Not everyone is sent back
    *Conclusion: during the project there won't be continuity of
    residents; we have to focus on different short trajectories/
    workshops with different residents*
**Transportation of residents**
× Asylum seekers in Torshov get no (pocket) money, only food
and clothes
    *Conclusion: main transportation to activities (city
    center – central station: +/- 3.5 km), should be covered by
    organizers. Alternatives: public transportation, bike (looking
    for sponsorship together with Shwan Khaled-Torshov)*
**Communication with residents**
× Various members of the Torshov staff speak all languages
× Interpreters are only used for official interviews
× Information / notice board outside the entrance of the
administration building (activity announcements, personal
messages, etc)
**Daily schedule in the center**
× Activities (organized by volunteers and/or staff): 10am–5pm
× The center is open, but residents are asked to be back inside
at 10pm
× 3×/day food served in the canteen (food prepared outside
and brought to the center)
**Privacy & protection of residents**
× Pictures from and personal information about the Torshov
residents are not allowed to be shared without personal
(written) permission + permission of the UDI
    *Conclusion: RVW has to find out legal possibilities to share
    and make information public (social media, digital archive,
    etc.): make residents anonymous in texts and images*

Ruimteveldwerk.
Presentation by RVW
at the Arrival City Bar,
organized by Eriksen-
Skajaa. May 2016,
office Eriksen Skajaa
Arkitekter, Oslo.
Courtesy of the author.

## Existing initiatives & activities by volunteers

Already several initiatives and collaborations exist in the Torshov center

**e.g.:** activity and contact list from Shwan Khaled, 20th of June: International refugee day, workshops by Makers'Hub Oslo, every season happenings are organized with neighbours, etc.

*Conclusion: RVW will look how to connect and maybe participate in existing and planned activities, how to integrate these into the guide*

## Space in the center

Every building (4 in total) has a living room and an activity room, these rooms are well used

*Conclusion: is there a more permanent space (central/visible?) available to locate the model? (RVW is still waiting for an answer from Torshov, we are looking into different scenarios)*

Ruimteveldwerk. Information board with activities for the asylum seekers. April 2016, Torshov transit center, Oslo. Courtesy of the author.

## Communication with Torshov staff — early April

Fra:
Sendt: 6. april 2016 16:08
Til:
Kopi:

Emne: RE: Project Oslo Architecture Triennale
[...]
We have very few people living here and they all have Dublin cases. They are waiting to be deported from Norway to that first European country where they landed or the first country where they had their fingerprints scanned.

Fra:
Sendt: 6. april 2016 15:57
Til:
Kopi:

Emne: RE: Project Oslo Architecture Triennale
Answers in CAPS.
From:
Sent: 6. april 2016 15:04
To:
Cc:
Subject: Project Oslo Architecture Triennale
Dear ,
I hope this e-mail finds you well.
[...]

Also, the team plans to do interviews with the residents in the center, and to take pictures for their project. They would like to know which authorizations they need to apply for in order to do this. They will of course start to ask permission from the individuals they will be in contact with, but do they also need to get an official authorization in addition?
WE ARE NO LONGER A CAMP FOR MINORS. WE NOW HAVE RESIDENTS THAT LIVE HERE WHILE THEY WAIT FOR DEPORTATION. I AM NOT SURE THAT THEY ARE THE RIGHT GROUP TO CONTRIBUTE TO THIS PROJECT? THERE IS LOT OF DESPAIR AND FRUSTRATION WITH THE SYSTEM, THE COUNTRY AND THE GOVERNMENT. WE USE MOST OF THE TIME ON LONG CONVERSATIONS IN ORDER TO KEEP CONFLICT AND AGGRESSIVE BEHAVIOR FROM HAPPENING.
[...]
Thank you in advance for your help.
Best Regards,



On Wed, Apr 6, 2016 at 8:57 AM, wrote:
Hi Pieter
Torshov is in a big transition. We have very few people living here now. We have a huge building project from UDI coming our way. We have new people we have to train. All in all a very stressful period.
[...]

Ruimteveldwerk. Translated emergency messages in case of fire, asylum seekers' housing units. April 2016, Torshov transit center, Oslo. Courtesy of the author.

**Report on Torshov event**
**Folkemøte — early May**
Organized by Makers'Hub on Sunday
May 8 at Torshov Transittmottak

**Preparation:** The abandoned
rooftop of a garage that gives an
overview of the terrain of the center
is transformed by Makers'Hub into
a green rooftop garden. Citrus
trees, flowers, and grass carpets
transform a leftover space into a
central reception and meeting place
at Torshov. The recuperated plants
on the rooftop, which once served
as decoration for a stand at a fair for
the reception of clients and expats,
now serve for the reception of asylum
seekers.

Ruimteveldwerk. Presentation by RVW at Folkemøte, event organized by Makers'Hub.
May 2016, Torshov transit center, Oslo. Courtesy of the author.

Makers'Hub. Poster/flyer Folkemøte event. Courtesy of the author.

**Workshop:** One of the asylum seekers stressed how
important interaction with locals is to move on with their
lives, living in different places, always meeting other
people. For him the local sports club, like a boxing club, is
a stimulant for interaction, something to look forward to.

**End of the day:** Makers'Hub invited us and some of the
residents of the transit center for a bbq on one of the
islands in front of the city hall of Oslo. This spontaneous
event was an opportunity to explore part of the city as
non-locals, together with asylum seekers. It was also
a beautiful initiative to circumvent mobility problems
because we were brought there by locals. Being
outside the center, in a place well-known by locals,
created a relaxed and friendly atmosphere.

**After presentation:** Difficulties to make contact with the
center. Who should we contact: UDI, the operator of the
center, the asylum seekers themselves, the staff?

The staff does not have the capacity to coordinate this.
They are occupied with their daily tasks.

Potential volunteering and social interaction between
asylum seekers and locals gets lost.

The folkemøte brought people together and opened up a
network to find an easier way to get in contact with asylum
seekers. Some people are waiting for projects to participate. Also, Makers'Hub has a trustful relationship with the
center that can play an important role for this.

**After presentation:** For some of the neighbors, the
presence of asylum seekers is an opportunity to reflect
on their own society. Cultural questions of asylum seekers
can open up discussions, reflecting not only on the difficulties of contact with locals, but also between locals.

**Workshop:** Gathering information on the map by inter-
viewing asylum seekers was much easier when a local was
involved. Describing places and finding them on a map
was much easier with three parties around the map.

# Cher

**Caitlin Blanchfield, Glen Cummings, Jaffer Kolb, Farzin Lotfi-Jam, Leah Meisterlin**

## TERMS AND CONDITIONS

### IMPORTANT
For those who seek a couch for cuddling, for those with a homesick thirst to quench, for those who need an overhang for huddling, for those who'd like to share a bench... There's Cher.

### A. PLATFORM OPERATIONS
Cher is a digital platform—a prototype-as-provocation, allowing visitors and users to offer or reserve objects by the minute. Produced through community-driven methods of research, Cher identifies untapped opportunities and existing controversies within sharing-economy social platforms for changing urban environments.

Responding to home-sharing and short-term rental apps, Cher foregrounds their broader social and economic consequences: the marketed reinterpretation of one's personal belongings, incrementalized subdivisions of time, and the delicate but unearned trust between strangers. Following these trends, Cher exploits their logics: a frictional platform unapologetically connecting individuals through things and the scripted language of exchange.

### B. CONDITIONS OF EXCHANGE
Cher connects city-dwellers to one another through the listing and sharing of domestic objects and local landmarks: just as private owners advertise their objects for use on the platform, a city's public objects are advertised for "reservation" to others by its citizens. Weaving interior and exterior space through the isolation of these items, the platform is a mechanism to advocate for local public space, learn about a city and its constituencies, and retool interior architecture for social encounters at a humble scale.

### C. MONITORED NEGOTIATIONS
The project's intervention is as much its process as its platform. Through workshops, walking tours, and interviews, the design process amasses a rich taxonomy of Copenhagen's object landscapes, generating an intricate understanding of how these differ by community, and organizing public conversations around social exchange, peer-to-peer place-making, latent tensions in the sharing economy, and material culture. Spinning object-oriented narratives, Cher tells the many, plural stories of a city and its citizens through things, addressing publics and counterpublics by advocating for common space. Copenhagen, as a city facing a nascent market of home-sharing in a country with a well-developed and widely used social housing system, lends urgency and specificity to the questions of residence raised by Cher.

### D. INTELLECTUAL PROPERTY
Cher is and will remain the intellectual property of Caitlin Blanchfield, Glen Cummings, Jaffer Kolb, Farzin Lotfi-Jam, and Leah Meisterlin.

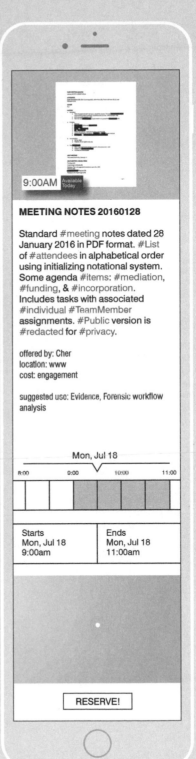

9:00AM  Available Today

**MEETING NOTES 20160128**

Standard #meeting notes dated 28 January 2016 in PDF format. #List of #attendees in alphabetical order using initializing notational system. Some agenda #items: #mediation, #funding, & #incorporation. Includes tasks with associated #individual #TeamMember assignments. #Public version is #redacted for #privacy.

offered by: Cher
location: www
cost: engagement

suggested use: Evidence, Forensic workflow analysis

Mon, Jul 18

8:00     9:00     10:00     11:00

| Starts | Ends |
| --- | --- |
| Mon, Jul 18 | Mon, Jul 18 |
| 9:00am | 11:00am |

RESERVE!

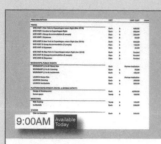

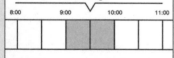

9:00AM Available Today

## ONE-OF-A-KIND PROPOSAL BUDGET

Cost estimate from #openCall for #InterventionStrategies. **PDF file** summed in #MicrosoftExcel, **styled in #AdobeInDesign. Exhibits clear** #evidence of gross #uncertainties in #figures **and** #feasibility. **Includes** #rare **and** #special 50% #InKindDonation **of suspect technical delivery by graphic-design-not-app-development studio MTWTF. Serves as a** #historicalRecord **of** #collective #seduction **overpowering reality.**

offered by: Cher
location: www
cost: engagement

suggested use: When nonsensical detail conveys feasibility over unattainable reality

Mon, Aug 8

| 8:00 | 9:00 | 10:00 | 11:00 |
|------|------|-------|-------|
|      |      |       |       |

| Starts | Ends |
|--------|------|
| Mon, Aug 8 | Mon, Aug 8 |
| 9:00am | 10:30am |

RESERVE!

Sample Chers listing essential process documents from the project.

Caitlin Blanchfield
New York, NY, USA

Maybe Accepting Guests

NOT VERIFIED

OVERVIEW

9:00AM Available Today

## SHARING SITE USER PROFILE

Very unsuccessful profile for attempted use on #homeSharing website Couchsurfing to infiltrate #onlineNetwork of #likeMinded, #socially #generous #community of #kindredSpirits. #UserProfile includes #photos, fairly #honest #personalStatements, & sincere attempts at #likability, #relatability, and #nonthreatening appeal. Rent for #LoginDetails.

offered by: Cher

cost: engagement

suggested use: Learn what to not
course of on-the-ground, in-the-tr
through-the-milieu research

Wed, Sep 7

| 8:00 | 9:00 | 10:00 |
|------|------|-------|
|      |      |       |

| Starts | Ends |
|--------|------|
| Wed, Sep 7 | Wed, S |
| 8:30am | 11:00a |

## *VINTAGE* THUMBS UP

9:00AM Available Today

Great for showing digital #support and #agreement among #friends. This #vintage Thumbs Up can also be used for #ride #sharing and #traveling from one #place to another as a 20th century tool once...

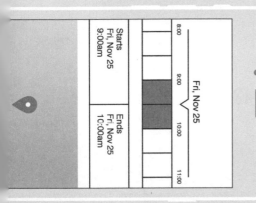

Fri, Nov 25

| 8:00 | 9:00 | 10:00 | 11:00 |
|---|---|---|---|

Starts
Fri, Nov 25
9:00am

Ends
Fri, Nov 25
10:00am

Sample Chers communicating conceptual framework of project.

12:00PM Available Today

### COVERED FORECOURT ENTRY

Do you need a spot that's not #public and not #private? This clean and covered entry to forecourt parking can be used as an extended #threshold between the #city and the #home. You can #share a little of the #outside on the #inside. Or vice versa.

offered by: Anders Andersen
location: Amagerbro
cost: free!

suggested use: Blurring lines, Keeping dry in the rain, Loitering

Fri, Jun 24

| 11:00 | 12:00 | 13:00 | 14:00 |
|---|---|---|---|

## ZONE DENMARK KITCHEN TIMER

12:00PM Available Today

#Stylish little helper. Usually for the #kitchen, but great for not cooking too. Rent it and watch #minutes (up to an hour) pass. Or rent it with something else, and this red kitchen timer will alert you. Also, it has a great #ding!

offered by: Anders Andersen
location: my kitchen
cost: 1 DKK per minute

suggested use: Keeping track of time, "Dinging" repeatedly

Fri, Jun 24

| 11:00 | 12:00 | 13:00 | 14:00 |
|---|---|---|---|

Starts
Fri, Jun 24
12:00pm

Ends
Fri, Jun 24
1:00pm

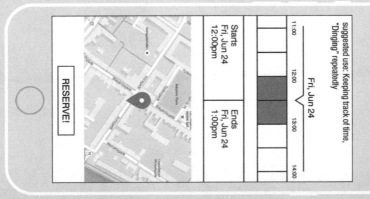

RESERVE!

8:30AM Available Today

## RESERVED PARKING

YOU CAN NEVER FIND A PLACE TO PARK YOUR *$&#$-ING BIKE. #Reserve a slot at this #handy #rack so you'll never again have to lock up to a tree (you monster) or to a free-standing signpost (you idiot) or to another bike (you jerk). Out jockey those #nonReserving cyclists, and get to work #OnTime without losing twenty minutes wandering the #streets.

offered by: Anders Anderson
location: That side street near Copenhagen University
cost: free!

suggested use: Convenience, guaranteed space, services that should be easy but are

Starts
Wed, Sep 7
8:30am

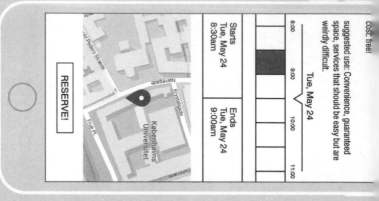

cost: free!

suggested use: Convenience, guaranteed space, services that should be easy but are weirdly difficult.

Tue, May 24

| 8:00 | 9:00 | 10:00 | 11:00 |

| Starts Tue, May 24 8:30am | Ends Tue, May 24 9:00am |

RESERVE!

Sample Chers identifying sites and use scenarios unique to Copenhagen.

7:00AM Available Today

### "GOOD MORNING FELLOW ANARCHISTS!"

Sturdy new #Christiana Bike (it's not a F*ck*ng Amsterdam bike!) in earnest dark tone with cheerful blue cargo box and cover. Pedal around like a #local. Shop for expired veggies like a local. Bring the kids, like a local. If you're #NewToTown and want to blend in, or test the low-carbon footprint #lifestyle before committing, this is the #ride for you.

offered by: Anders Andersen

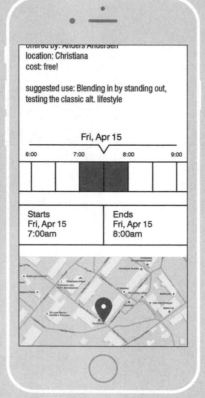

offered by: Anders Andersen
location: Christiana
cost: free!

suggested use: Blending in by standing out, testing the classic alt. lifestyle

Fri, Apr 15

| 6:00 | 7:00 | 8:00 | 9:00 |

| Starts Fri, Apr 15 7:00am | Ends Fri, Apr 15 8:00am |

RESERVE!

**5:00PM** Available Today

**AIR RAID SHELTER STAGE**

Perfect for a short recital, poetry slam, or 1-man concert. Speak your mind, or #share your feelings standing on these #historic #safehavens. Multiple units #available (see related postings).

offered by: Anders Andersen
location: Around the Copenhagen Castle
cost: free!

suggested use: Poetry Slam, Public Speaking, Rocking in the Free World

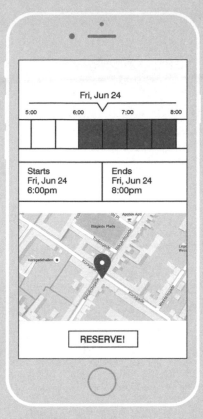

Fri, Jun 24

| 5:00 | 6:00 | 7:00 | 8:00 |
|------|------|------|------|

| Starts | Ends |
|--------|------|
| Fri, Jun 24 | Fri, Jun 24 |
| 6:00pm | 8:00pm |

**RESERVE!**

Available Today

Sample Chers listing exemplary examples of application of the app.

**BACK DESK DRAWER IN SARI STORE**

Enter this #Nørrebro storefront & find the desk in the back. In it is a drawer ideal for stashing small items. Talk to owner/drawer-proprietor. If you've got an #airbnb upstairs she'll produce an envelope with your name handwritten. Reciept of envelope with key and instructions spares both you and host the efforts of interaction. The shopkeeper offers a piece of #advice, and even in a #strange #place, you're more at #ease.

offered by: Anders Andersen
location: Nørrebrogarde near Assistens
cost: open to negotiation

suggested use: safe storage, general hand-offs, avoiding host-guest relationship

Tue, Aug 16

| 2:30 | 3:30 | 4:30 | 5:30 |
|------|------|------|------|

| Starts | Ends |
|--------|------|
| Tue, Aug 16 | Tue, Aug 16 |
| 3:30pm | 4:30pm |

3:30PM Available Today

## HANDMADE LAMP

I made this fixture out of a #recycled #street #lamp and think it gives off both great light and a #funky #vintage vibe. Hand wired and fitted out with Edison bulb, it truly is one of a kind and a #labor of #love. I like to #browse the morning paper underneath or use its light to work on other wiring projects.

offered by: Anders Andersen
location: Gråbrødretorv
cost: 1DKK per minute

suggested use: Bringing the outside in, sharing a light, shining a light

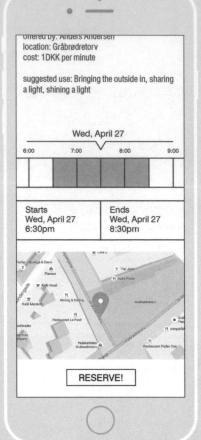

offered by: Anders Andersen
location: Gråbrødretorv
cost: 1DKK per minute

suggested use: Bringing the outside in, sharing a light, shining a light

Wed, April 27

6:00    7:00    8:00    9:00

| Starts | Ends |
|--------|------|
| Wed, April 27 | Wed, April 27 |
| 6:30pm | 8:30pm |

**RESERVE!**

**Additional Credits**
Research assistants: Daniel Cooper, Joachim Hackl, Matthew Lohry, S. Tola Oniyangi, Iara Pimenta de Mello, and Violet Whitney. Thank you to Columbia University's Graduate School of Architecture, Planning, and Preservation, the Danish Architecture Center, and the International Federation of Housing and Planning Copenhagen Chapter for their generous support.

## PLUSH TOWEL PUMPKIN SPICE

Headed #home after a night on the #town and need to do a little clean up? Stop in to use this 30 x 58 inch, 100% Egyptian cotton #towel in a unexpected beautiful color. This towel is freshly machine-washed and air-dried in the sun. Perfect for touch-ups between clubs or to dry off when caught in the rain. Ask me about #shorterTimes—and #groupRates—they are both definitely available.

offered by: Anders Andersen
location: Korsgarde
cost: 1DKK per minute

suggested use: Drying, Touch-ups

The Embąssy
The Acadēmy
Ťhē Aftēŕ Belongĭnĝ Çőnfeŗençe

# The Embassy

**New World Embassy: Rojava**
**November 2016**
**Democratic Self-Administration of Rojava and Studio Jonas Staal**

The *New World Embassy: Rojava* is a temporary embassy that will be built in Oslo, representing the political ideals and vision of the autonomous region in northern Syria known as "Rojava." The embassy consists of a large-scale oval-shaped architectural construction, designed as an "ideological planetarium" covered with the universalist symbols of rainbows, stars, and suns from the flags of the Rojava autonomous region.

The Rojava region declared itself autonomous in 2012 in the wake of the Syrian Civil War. Despite continuous threats by the surrounding Assad regime and the Islamic State, the Rojava region has been able to develop a new political model described as "Stateless Democracy." This ideal is based on local self-governance, communal economy, and gender equality on all levels. Through broad coalitions between the Kurdish, Assyrian, and Arab peoples of the region, new parliaments, universities, and cultural centers modeled after the ideal of stateless democracy have been realized across the region.

The *New World Embassy: Rojava* will operate in Oslo for three consecutive days, bringing representatives of the Democratic Self-Administration of Rojava together with politicians, diplomats, academics, journalists, students, and artists. Through public deliberation, the *New World Embassy: Rojava* will involve a broad public in understanding the struggle of Rojava, not only in terms of the humanitarian crises it faces due to attacks by the Islamic State and the difficulties of acquiring international recognition as a non-state entity, but also by communicating the ideals and practice of stateless democracy, the successes of building a new civil society in a war-torn region, and the po-litical alternative that Rojava proposes in confronting the crises of democracy that we witness all over the world.

The *New World Embassy: Rojava* deepens and expands the history of alternative models of diplomacy developed in Norway, not only by using the domain of art to provide a platform for an unrecognized political entity, but also by questioning the very concept of the embassy. For if Rojava is a state-less democracy, then its embassy must be a stateless embassy: a space of assembly that belongs not just to Rojava, but to a new world and a new democratic ideal in the making.

1

*New World Embassy: Rojava* is supported by KORO (Public Art Norway).

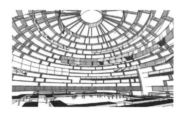

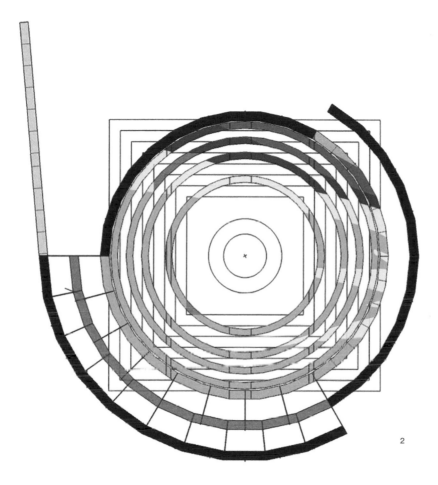

2

1  Jonas Staal, "*Anatomy of a Revolution: Rojava*. Special forces of the Women's Defense Units
   (YPJ) look out over their training camp situated near Qamişlo." 2015.

2  (All Drawings), Democratic Self-Administration of Rojava and Studio Jonas Staal, "*New World
   Embassy: Rojava*. Preliminary design of the temporary embassy of Rojava, surrounded by the
   universalist symbols of stars and flags from the autonomous Rojava region." 2016.

   All images courtesy of the author(s).

# The Academy

**September 9–16, 2016**

*The Academy* is a forum organized by the Oslo School of Architecture and Design (AHO). It will bring schools from around the world into a global dia-logue and knowledge-sharing experiment, reflecting on issues related to the topics explored in the Oslo Architecture Triennale 2016, *After Belonging,* including new forms of residence, contemporary states of transit, and the ways in which architecture and design are responding to new forms of belonging and belongings.

    *The Academy* includes a full program of events, including workshops, roundtables, and lectures, among others. The forum will operate in three phases—an analytical phase, a critical phase, and a production phase—which will be distributed over a period of eight days. The aim is to produce a collective project—be it an ephemeral structure, a performance, a publication, an action, an exhibition, or a combination of these things. *The Academy* will project the concerns of the Triennale into the future by introducing long-lasting academic conversations and collaborations between multiple universities around the world, which are intended to have an impact on architectural education and practices.

# The After Belonging Conference
September 9, 2016

*The After Belonging Conference* will bring together architects, thinkers, decision-makers, and local experts in order to dissect the architectures entangled in the contemporary reconfiguration of belonging.

## Participants

Amale Andraos
Work Architecture Company
Columbia GSAPP

Yoshiharu Tsukamoto and Momoyo Kaijima
Atelier Bow-Wow

Negar Azimi
Bidoun

Simen Svale Skogsrud and Even Westvang
Bengler

Gro Bonesmo
Space Group
Oslo School of Architecture and Design

Grete Brochman
University of Oslo

Thomas Hylland Eriksen
University of Oslo

Michel Feher
Cette France-Là

Per Heggenes
IKEA Foundation

Juan Herreros
Estudio Herreros

Yasmeen Lari
Heritage Foundation of Pakistan

Reinhold Martin
Buell Center for American Architecture
Columbia GSAPP

Ippolito Pestellini Laparelli
OMA

Karl Otto Ellefsen
The Oslo School of Architecture and Design

Kjetil Trædal Thorsen
Snøhetta

Andreas G. Gjertsen
TYIN Tegnestue Architects

Ann-Sofi Rönnskog and John Palmesino
Territorial Agency

Eyal Weizman
Center for Research Architecture
Goldsmiths

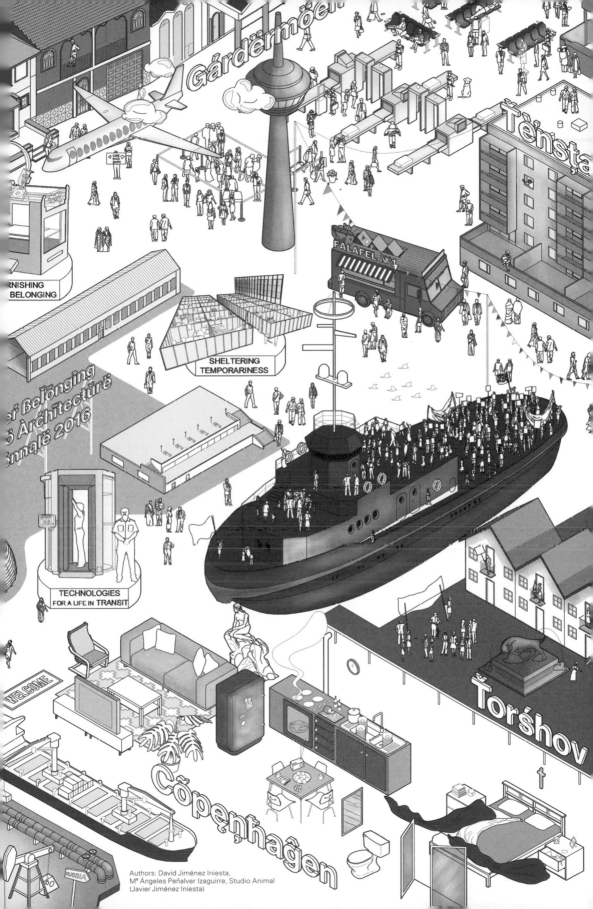

Gárdermöe

Tênsta

FALAFEL Nº1

FURNISHING
BELONGING

SHELTERING
TEMPORARINESS

of Belonging
s Architecturë
nnalë 2016

TECHNOLOGIES
FOR A LIFE IN TRANSIT

WELCOME

Torshov

Cöpenhagen

RUSSIA

Authors: David Jiménez Iniesta,
Mª Ángeles Peñalver Izaguirre, Studio Animal
(Javier Jiménez Iniesta)

# Contributors

### Editorial and Curatorial Team

LLUÍS ALEXANDRE CASANOVAS BLANCO is a New York based architect and scholar. He is chief co-curator of the OAT 2016. He is currently a PhD Candidate at Princeton University. Casanovas was trained as an architect at ETSABarcelona and the Edinburgh College of Art, and graduated from the MSc in Advanced Architectural Design at Columbia GSAPP. Casanovas has co-curated the lecture series "Margins and Hyphens" at Princeton SOA, and the symposium "Conflict of Interests" on architectural research at Columbia GSAPP. He has collaborated with different design offices and research institutions such as the Buell Center for the Study of American Architecture and the GSAPP Global Africa Lab. Casanovas has taught studios at Barnard College, Princeton University, and ETSA Barcelona. His current interests include the aesthetic agendas of the architectures resulting from institutional practices (such as the New York's network of homeless shelters or Radio Televisión Española), and the relationship between the history of the senses and architecture.

IGNACIO G. GALÁN is a New York based architect and scholar. He is chief co-curator of the OAT 2016, and the Principal of [igg—office for architecture]. He was trained at ETSAMadrid and TU Delft, and graduated as a Fulbright Scholar from the MArchII program at Harvard GSD. He has been a Fellow at the Spanish Academy in Rome, and is completing a PhD Candidate at Princeton University. His work concentrates on the architectures articulating modern and contemporary societies, particularly addressing their relation to process of material and cultural circulation, and the mediations transforming their occupations. His designs have been awarded in competitions including the First Prize for the New Velodrome in Medellín, and he was nominated to the 2014 Iakov Chernikhov Prize. His work has led to the production of several publications and exhibitions including the installation Cinecittá Occupata for the 2014 Venice Biennale by invitation of the general curator Rem Koolhaas. Galán has taught studios and seminars at Columbia GSAPP and PennDesign, and is currently Term Assistant Professor in the Department of Architecture at Barnard+Columbia Colleges.

CARLOS MÍNGUEZ CARRASCO is a New York based architect and curator. He is chief co-curator of the OAT 2016, and Associate Curator at Storefront for Art and Architecture. In 2014 he was Assistant Curator of OfficeUS, the U.S. Pavilion at the 2014 Venice Biennale. Previously, he co-founded PKMN, an internationally renowned architecture collective based in Madrid. Trained as an architect at ETSABarcelona and TU Delft, he graduated from the MSc in Critical, Curatorial and Conceptual Practices in Architecture at Columbia University GSAPP. Mínguez has organized a wide range of exhibitions, events and competitions with a particular focus on how social, cultural, and pressing political issues influence contemporary architecture, including Cáceres Creates Cáceres (2008), Interpretations (2010), Storefront's 30th Anniversary exhibition and conference BEING (2013), Letters to the Mayor (2014), and the platform World Wide Storefront (2014). His work has been published in different journals such as Domus and Código and he is editor of two forthcoming publications; OfficeUS Manual and Sf30 (Lars Müller Publishers). Mínguez has been Adjunct Assistant Professor at Columbia University GSAPP and lectured at different universities including Columbia University GSAPP, Harvard GSD, Princeton University SoA, and RISD.

ALEJANDRA NAVARRETE LLOPIS is a New York based architect. She is chief co-curator of OAT2016. Navarrete was trained at ETSAMadrid and IUAVenezia, and graduated from the MSc in Advanced Architectural Design at Columbia University GSAPP, where she has been Adjunct Assistant Professor. She is the principal of NaMi, an architecture design and curatorial office working on public and private projects in Europe and the US including the exhibition design for the Iberoamerican Art Museum of Alcalá de Henares University. Previously, she co-founded PKMN, a research based architect's collective, focused on the role of art and architecture to articulate how the citizen transforms the contemporary urban environment. PKMN has been widely awarded, published and exhibited in locations such as Fresh Latino and Storefront for Art and Architecture, New York. She has also collaborated with different design offices including Solid Arquitectura, receiving several prizes including the first prize for the Performing Arts Center International Competition in Seoul, and for the "Aguila-Alcatel" Apartment Building in Madrid, exhibited in the Spanish Pavilion at the 2014 Venice Architecture Biennale.

MARINA OTERO VERZIER is an architect based in Rotterdam. She is chief co-curator of OAT2016, and Head of Research at Het Nieuwe Instituut. Previously, she was Director of Global Network Programming at Studio-X, and Adjunct Assistant Professor at Columbia University GSAPP. Otero studied architecture at TU Delft and ETSAMadrid, where she is a PhD candidate. In 2013, as a Fulbright Scholar, she graduated from the M.S. in Critical, Curatorial and Conceptual Practices in Architecture at Columbia University GSAPP. Her work, recently awarded by The Graham Foundation and Fundación Arquia, has been published in different publications including sqm: The quantified Home, Arquitectura Viva, and Domus. Otero is co-editor of Promiscuous Encounters and Unmanned Architecture and Security Series, and has co-curated exhibitions at The 2013 Shenzhen Bicity Biennale and the 2014 Istanbul Design Biennial. Her current research is concerned with how changing notions of privacy and safety, and their articulation with global circulatory regimes, have an effect on the spaces of residence.

### Authors

LOUISE AMOORE researches and teaches in the areas of global geopolitics, security, and political theory. She has particular interests in how contemporary forms of data, analytics and risk management are changing the techniques of border control and security. Louise is currently Leverhulme Major Research Fellow (2016–18), working on a book project Ethics of Algorithm. In this work she is investigating the limits of accountability in an age of algorithmic decisions. Louise's most recent book, The Politics of Possibility: Risk and Security Beyond Probability (2013) is published with Duke University Press.

ARJUN APPADURAI is a contemporary social-cultural anthropologist recognised as a major theorist in globalization studies. He is the Goddard Professor in Media, Culture and Communication at New York University, where he is also Senior Fellow at the Institute for Public Knowledge. He serves as Honorary Professor in the Department of Media and Communication, at Erasmus University, Rotterdam, Tata Chair Professor at The Tata Institute for Social Sciences, Mumbai and as a Senior Research Partner at the Max-Planck Institute for Religious and Ethnic Diversity, in Gottingen. He was previously Senior Advisor for Global Initiatives at The New School, where he was the Provost and Vice President for Academic Affairs. He was formerly the William K. Lanman Jr. Professor of International Studies, Professor of Anthropology, and Director of the Center on Cities and Globalization at Yale University.

MERVE BEDÍR graduated from METU, Department of Architecture (2003). She is a phd candidate at TU Delft Faculty of Architecture and partner of the Rotterdam/Istanbul based Land and Civilization Compositions (L+CC). Her recent work focuses on urban transformation and migration. She was a curator for the Netherlands Architecture Institute (Rotterdam, 2012), producer of Agoraphobia (2013), curator of Vocabulary of Hospitality (Istanbul, 2014), One Architecture Week (Plovdiv, 2015), and Aformal Academy (Shenzhen, 2016). L+CC's projects have been exhibited in Bucharest, Istanbul Design and Shenzhen Urbanism Biennale's. She has published in MONU, Volume, Zivot, Site, Docomomo, uncube, and Quaderns. Vocabulary of Hospitality will be published by Dpr Barcelona (2016).

KELLER EASTERLING is an architect, writer and professor at Yale University. Her most recent book, Extrastatecraft: The Power of Infrastructure Space (Verso, 2014), examines global infrastructure networks as a medium of polity. Other books include Subtraction (Sternberg Press, 2014), Enduring Innocence: Global Architecture and its Political Masquerades (MIT, 2005) and Organization Space: Landscapes, Highways and Houses in America (MIT, 1999). Easterling's research and writing was included in the 2014 Venice Biennale, and she has been exhibited at Storefront for Art and Architecture in New York, the Rotterdam Biennale, and the Architectural League in New York. Easterling has lectured and been published widely in the United States and abroad.

HU FANG is a fiction writer, co-founder of Vitamin Creative Space in Guangzhou and The Pavilion in Beijing. His recent books include fiction Dear Navigator (2014) and Towards a Non-intentional Space (2015), which reflects upon the research and thinking process of building Mirrored Gardens, a project space seeks to merge with its environment to construct a "nature" where contemporary art practices, daily life and farming-oriented life practices can be nurtured and cultivated in tandem.

DIDIER FASSIN is Professor of Social Science at the Institute for Advanced Study in Princeton and Director of Studies at the École des Hautes Études en Sciences Sociales in Paris. An anthropologist, sociologist and physician, he has carried out research in Senegal, Ecuador, South Africa, and France. He recently conducted an ethnography of the state, through a study of urban policing as well as the justice and prison systems in France. His current work is on punishment, asylum, inequality, and the politics of life, and he is developing a reflection on the public presence of the social sciences. He occasionally writes for the French newspapers Le Monde and Libération. His recent books include Enforcing Order: An Ethnography of Urban Policing (2013), At the Heart of the State: The Moral World of Institutions (2015), and Prison Worlds: An Ethnography of the Carceral Condition (2016).

MICHEL FEHER is a philosopher who has taught at the École Nationale Supérieure, Paris, and at the University of California, Berkeley. He is the publisher and a founding editor of Zone Books, NY (in 1986) as well as the president and co-founder of Cette France-là, Paris (in 2008), a monitoring group on French immigration policy. He is the author of Powerless by Design: The Age of the International Community (2000) and the co-editor of Nongovernmental Politics (2007), with Gaëlle Krikorian and Yates McKee. He co-authored, with Cette France-là, Xénophobie d'en haut: le choix d'une droite éhontée and Sanas-papiers et préfets: la culture du résultat en portraits (2012). He most recently co-edited "Europe at a Crossroads" (with William Callison, Milad Odabaei and Aurélie Windels), the first issue of Near Futures Online (Zone Books, 2016).

JAMES GRAHAM is a historian, editor, and architect. He is the Director of Publications at Columbia University's Graduate School of Architecture, Planning, and Preservation, where he also teaches seminars on architectural history and publicatory practice. He has edited and co-edited several books on the Columbia Books on Architecture and the City imprint — including the recent Climates: Architecture and the Planetary Imaginary (2016) and 2000+: The Urgencies of Architectural Theory (2015), and he is the founding editor of the Avery Review, a monthly periodical of critical essays on architecture. He is completing his dissertation on applied psychology, occupational therapy, and architectural pedagogy between and during the world wars in Germany, the Soviet Union, and the United States.

JOHN HARWOOD is Associate Professor of Architecture at the Daniels Faculty of Architecture, Landscape and Design at the University of Toronto. He is the author of The Interface: IBM and the Transformation of Corporate Design, 1945–1976 and is currently working on two books: Architectures of Mass Media: Telephony, Radio, Television, and Corporate Architecture, 17th to 20th Centuries. His articles have appeared in Grey Room, JSAH, AA Files, Perspecta, Art Forum, among others. He is a founding member of the architectural history collaborative Aggregate, has taught at Oberlin College, Princeton University and Columbia University, and received fellowships from the University of Queensland and the Center for Advanced Study in the Visual Arts at the National Gallery of Art.

CHARLES HELLER and LORENZO PEZZANI are both Research Fellows at the Centre for Research Architecture, Goldsmiths, University of London. In addition, Heller is currently conducting a postdoctoral research supported by the Swiss National Fund (SNF) at the Centre for Migration and Refugee Studies, American University, Cairo and the Centre d'Etudes et de Documentation Economiques, Juridiques et Sociales, Cairo. Pezzani is currently post-doctoral fellow at the Kent School of Law. Together, since 2011, they co-founded the WatchTheMed platform and have been working on Forensic Oceanography, a project that critically investigates the militarized border regime and the politics of migration in the Mediterranean Sea. Their collaborative work has been exhibited internationally and has been published in several edited volumes as well as in journals such as Cultural Studies, Postcolonial Studies, New Geographies, ACME, and in the Revue Européenne des Migrations Internationales.

THOMAS HYLLAND ERIKSEN is Professor of Social Anthropology at the University of Oslo and the author of many books in English and Norwegian. In his academic work, he has a sustained interest in the implications of global modernities for the dynamics of culture and identity, and he has published widely on nationalism, ethnicity, cultural creolisation and identity politics. He has also written several widely used and translated textbooks in anthropology, such as Small Places – Large Issues and Ethnicity and Nationalism. A different strand of Eriksen's work is evident in his Tyranny of the Moment, an exploration of cultural acceleration seen through the lens of information technology. His latest book, Overheating: An Anthropology of Accelerated Change, brings many of these interests together in an attempt to write a global history of the early 21st century seen from a multitude of local perspectives.

PAMELA KARIMI is Associate Professor of Art History at the University of Massachusetts Dartmouth. Her primary field of research is art, architecture, and visual culture of the modern Middle East. Her second field of specialization is design and sustainability in North America. Karimi is the author of Domesticity and Consumer Culture in Iran: Interior Revolutions of the Modern Era (Routledge, 2013), and co-editor of Images of the Child and Childhood in Modern Muslim Contexts (Duke, 2012) and Reinventing the American

Post-Industrial City (Sage, 2015). Her essays and reviews about the modern and contemporary art of the Middle East have appeared in Ibraaz, ArtMargins, Jadaliyya, Art Journal, Bidoun, Honar-e Farda, and the Arab Studies Journal, among others. She has held fellowships from Iran Heritage Foundation, American Council of Learned Societies, the Social Science Research Council, the American Association of University Women, and the Society of Architectural Historians. She has been the recipient of the University of Massachusetts Creative Economy Fund twice and in 2014 she earned the University of Massachusetts Dartmouth Green Award. Co-founder of Aggregate Architectural History Collaborative and a former member of the editorial team of the International Journal of Islamic Architecture, Karimi currently serves on the board of the Association of Modern and Contemporary Art of the Arab World, Iran, and Turkey.

THOMAS KEENAN teaches media theory, literature, and human rights at Bard College, where he directs the Human Rights Project and helped create the first undergraduate degree program in human rights in the United States. He is the author of Fables of Responsibility (1997) and, with Eyal Weizman, Mengele's Skull (2012). He is co-editor of New Media, Old Media (2006), and The Human Snapshot (2013). Flood of Rights, co-edited with Suhail Malik and Tirdad Zolghadr, is forthcoming in 2016. He curated Antiphotojournalism (2010–11), and Aid and Abet (2011), and was part of the research group behind Forensis (2014). He has served on the boards of a number of human rights organizations and journals, including WITNESS, Scholars at Risk, the Crimes of War Project, and the Journal of Human Rights, and Humanity.

JESSE LeCAVALIER is an award-winning designer, writer, and educator. His research and design work focuses on the architectural, urban, and spatial implications of contemporary logistics. His book, The Rule of Logistics: Walmart and the Architecture of Fulfillment, is forthcoming from the University of Minnesota Press in 2016. LeCavalier is assistant professor of architecture at the New Jersey Institute of Technology and was the recipient of the 2015 New Faculty Teaching Award from the Association of the Collegiate Schools of Architecture (ACSA). His research has been supported by the Graham Foundation, the New York State Council for the Arts, the BMW Foundation, and the ETH Future Cities Laboratory.

CRISTINA LÓPEZ URIBE is an architectural historian who specializes in twentieth-century Mexican architecture. She graduated as an architect from UNAM (Universidad Nacional Autónoma de México) in 2001 and holds an M.A. in Art, Architecture and City Planning History from the Universitat Politécnica de Catalunya, Barcelona, where she is currently a PhD candidate in Theory and History of Architecture. She also teaches History of Architecture and Architectural Design at UNAM, and is the editor-in-chief of Bitácora Arquitectura magazine and co-editor with Salvador Lizárraga of Living CU: 60 Years (Mexico City: UNAM, 2014). She is the author of "Reflections of the 'Colonial': Between Mexico and Californiano" which was published in Patricio del Real and Helen Gyger, Latin American Modern Architectures: Ambiguous Territories (New York: Routledge, 2012), among other publications. She is currently an advisor for LACMA's forthcoming exhibition Lost in Translation: Design in California and Mexico 1915–1985.

IJLAL MUZAFFAR is an Assistant Professor of Modern Architectural History at the Rhode Island School of Design. He holds a PhD in architectural history from MIT, a Masters in Architecture from Princeton, and a BS in Mathematics and Physics from the University of Punjab in Lahore, Pakistan. His work has appeared in numerous edited volumes and peer reviewed forums including Grey Room, Future Anterior, and Aggregate, the architectural collaborative of which he is also a founding member. He is currently working on a book titled, The Periphery Within: Modern Architecture and the Making of the Third World, which looks at how modern architects and planners played a critical role in shaping the discourse on Third World development and its associated structures of intervention in the postwar era.

JEFFREY SCHNAPP is the founder/faculty director of metaLAB (at) Harvard and faculty co-director of the Berkman Center for Internet and Society. At Harvard, he serves as Professor of Romance Literatures and Comparative Literature, and is on the teaching faculty in the Department of Architecture at Harvard's Graduate School of Design. Effective June 2015, he assumed the position of Chief Executive Officer and co-founder of Piaggio Fast Forward, a Cambridge-based company devoted to developing innovative solutions to the transportation challenges of the contemporary world.

FELICITY D. SCOTT is Associate Professor of Architecture, Director of the Ph.D. program in Architecture, and Co-director of the Critical, Curatorial and Conceptual Practices in Architecture program at Columbia GSAPP. Her work as an architectural historian and theorist focuses on articulating genealogies of political and theoretical engagement with questions of technological and geopolitical transformation within modern and contemporary architecture, as well as within the discourses and institutions that have shaped and defined the discipline. She has published Architecture or Techno-Utopia: Politics After Modernism (MIT Press, 2007), Living Archive 7: Ant Farm (ACTAR, 2008), Outlaw Territories: Environments of Insecurity/Architectures of Counter-Insurgency (Zone Books, 2016), and Disorientation: Bernard Rudofsky in the Empire of Signs (Sternberg Press, 2016).

DEANE SIMPSON is an architect, urbanist, and educator. He is associate professor at the Royal Danish Academy of Fine Arts, Copenhagen where he leads the international masters program Urbanism and Societal Change with Charles Bessard. He was formerly unit master at the Architectural Association, London, professor at BAS Bergen, associate at Diller + Scofidio, New York, and faculty member at the ETH Zürich. His research addresses thematics in contemporary architecture/urbanism including: demographic change, securitization and sustainability. He is author of Young-Old (Lars Müller, 2015), and co-editor of Atlas of the Copenhagens (Ruby Press, 2016) and The City between Freedom and Security (Birkhäuser, 2016).

TROY CONRAD THERRIEN has been Curator of Architecture and Digital Initiatives at the Guggenheim Museum since 2014. Initially trained as a computer engineer, and later in architecture design, history, and theory, he has held positions as an architect, creative technologist, innovation consultant, and scholar. His current work focuses on the relationship between architecture, communication technology, and political economy through exhibitions, writing, and teaching. He received an MA in Architecture History and Theory from the Architectural Association in London and an MArch from Columbia University.

MABEL O. WILSON's design and scholarly research investigates space, politics and cultural memory in black America; race and modern architecture; new technologies and the social production of space; and visual culture in contemporary art, film and new media. As a professor at Columbia University's GSAPP she teaches architectural design and history/theory courses, is a Research Fellow at the Institute for Research in African American Studies (IRAAS) and co-directs the Global Africa Lab (GAL). She is also part of the research collaborative Who Builds Your Architecture? which advocates for fair labor practices worldwide.

On Residence Exhibition Participants

AIR DRIFTS research group is an interdisciplinary team of practitioners and educators in architecture, anthropology, film studies and astronomy, including: Kadambari Baxi, architect and professor of practice in architecture at Barnard + Columbia Colleges, Columbia University; Janette Kim, architectural designer and assistant professor at California College of the Arts; Meg McLagan, film-maker, anthropologist and visiting professor in film studies at Barnard College; Mark Wasiuta, director of exhibitions and co-director of the graduate program in critical, curatorial and conceptual practices at the Columbia Graduate School of Architecture, Planning and Preservation; David Schiminovich, astronomer and associate professor in astronomy at Columbia University.

NORA AKAWI is the director of Studio X Amman, Columbia University GSAPP, where she is also teaching; NINA VALERIE KOLOWRATNIK is practicing as architectural researcher and currently teaching at Vienna University of Technology and Columbia University GSAPP, New York; JOHANNES POINTL is an architect and urban designer, working as a project manager in Vienna and teaching at the Vienna University of Technology; EDUARDO REGA CALVO is a PhD candidate in Architectural Design at ETSA Madrid and teaching at PennDesign Philadephia and Pratt Institute New York. Together they investigate and visualize movement across borders as the central element that defines contemporary territories and geopolitical terrains.

LUIS CALLEJAS and CHARLOTTE HANSSON work at the intersection of architecture, urban design and landscape architecture. LCLA was founded in 2011 by architect Luis Callejas, and since 2014, he has been partnering with the Swedish architect Charlotte Hansson on exhibitions and spatial experiments that involve unconventional cartographies, representations, and interventions in tropical and Nordic landscapes. The studio focuses on the interaction between buildings and landscapes, often relying on art and mixed media to bridge gaps between disciplines.

THE CENTER FOR POLITICAL BEAUTY is an assault team that establishes moral beauty, political poetry and human greatness while aiming to preserve humanitarianism. The group's basic understanding is that the legacy of the Holocaust is rendered void by political apathy, the rejection of refugees and cowardice. It believes that Germany should not only learn from its History but also take action. The Center for Political Beauty engages in the most innovative forms of political performance art—an expanded approach to theatre: art must hurt, provoke and rise in revolt. In one basic alliance of terms: aggressive humanism. The Center's exhibitions and plays were shown at Gorki Theatre, the 7th Berlin Biennale, ZKM Karlsruhe, Steirischer Herbst, NGBK, and HMKV, amongst others.

THE CENTER FOR SPATIAL RESEARCH was established in 2015 as a hub for urban research that links design, architecture, urbanism, the humanities and data science. It sponsors research and curricular activities built around new technologies of mapping, data visualization, data collection, and data analysis. LAURA KURGAN is an Associate Professor of Architecture at the Graduate School of Architecture Planning and Preservation at Columbia University, where she directs the Visual Studies curriculum, and the Center for Spatial Research. She is the author of Close Up at a Distance: Mapping, Technology, and Politics (Zone Books, 2013). ANGELIKA RETTBERG has a Ph.D. from

Boston University and leads the M.A. Program on Peacebuilding at Universidad de los Andes in Bogotá (Colombia). JUAN FRANCISCO SALDARRIAGA is a Mellon Research Scholar at the Center for Spatial Research and an Adjunct Assistant Professor of Architecture and Urban Planning at the Graduate School of Architecture, Planning and Preservation at Columbia University.

COOKING SECTIONS (DANIEL FERNÁNDEZ PASCUAL & ALON SCHWABE) is a London-based duo of spatial practitioners. They explore the systems that organize the world through food. Using installation, performance and mapping, their research-based practice operates within the overlapping boundaries between visual arts, architecture and geopolitics. They were part of the U.S. Pavilion, 2014 Venice Architecture Biennale. Their work has also been exhibited at the Neue Nationalgalerie and HKW, Berlin; Storefront for Art & Architecture New York; dOCUMENTA(13); Peggy Guggenheim Collection; CA2M, Madrid; Het Nieuw Instituut, Rotterdam; Fiorucci Art Trust, London; 2014 Kortrijk Biennale; Victoria & Albert Museum, London; UTS Sydney; Glasgow International; and have been residents in The Politics of Food at Delfina Foundation, London.

DESIGN EARTH is led by El Hadi Jazairy and Rania Ghosn. The practice engages the geographies of technological systems to open up aesthetic and political concerns for architecture and urbanism. Their work involves the coupled undertakings of writing about the earth and also writing on, or projecting again a world. DESIGN EARTH has been recognized with several awards, including the 2016 Architectural League of New York Young Architects Award, the Jacques Rougerie Competition, and an ACSA Faculty Design Award for Geographies of Trash (Actar, 2015). Ghosn and Jazairy hold doctor of design degrees from Harvard Graduate School of Design, where they were founding editors of the journal New Geographies.

ENORME STUDIO is an architecture office based in Madrid, co-founded by Rocío Pina, David Pérez, and Carmelo Rodríguez. The office focuses on three interconnected aims of research. First, Enorme addresses architectural and design preoccupations, dealing with notions of industrialization, typology, urban environments, local identities, heritage, and the implementation of tools for territorial and public space re-activation. Second, the office works on what they call social innov-action: the development of participation dynamics based on performance and action. And third, Enorme concentrates on pedagogy and research, investigating and building up new methodologies and learning formats based on direct experience and experiment.

FRIDA ESCOBEDO is head of an architecture studio based in Mexico City. The projects produced at the studio operate within a theoretical framework that addresses time not as a historical calibration but rather a social matter. This expanded temporal reading stems directly from Henri Bergson's notion of 'social time' and is evocative of conceptual works such as Split Subject, the Civic Stage. By these measures of practice and thought, social time unfolds across multiple subjects at multiple speeds and modes of duration. GUILLERMO RUIZ DE TERESA is an architect and urbanist whose research focuses on the intersection of space, state, and power. Guillermo trained as an architect at the Universidad Iberoamericana and the Architectural Association in London. He received a master's in design studies at Harvard University in 2013. He is currently based in Mexico City where he works at the crossroads of governance and citizen engagement.

FFB was established in 2010 by Joar Nango, Håvard Arnhoff and Eystein Talleraas. The group is an independent platform for creative research on the field of architecture. We seek no answers, only enlightenment and cross cultural spaces in which the architecture itself suggests and insists on an enhanced cultural and material diversity within our increasingly generic, commodified and profit-oriented public domain. Through a method resembling an activist practice, FFB makes performative projects generating space for a more diversified cultural complexity, confronting the nature of our contemporary cities and communities. The starting point for each project is an inquisitive view on majorities, based on the belief that cultural advancement and superiority follows democratic and capitalistic values.

FOLDER is a design and research practice founded by Marco Ferrari and Elisa Pasqual, and based in Milan. The studio's work spans between public and private commissions—both in the cultural and commercial domain—and the investigation of autonomous research paths. These are carried on through a diverse range of outcomes which mostly encompasses data visualisation and the design of exhibitions, editorial and digital platforms. Folder's main research interest pivots around the understanding of contemporary technology and its effects on society, and the relation between cartography and politics. Marco Ferrari has been Creative Director of Domus magazine and is currently teaching at IUAV, Venice, and ISIA, Urbino. Elisa Pasqual is a PhD candidate in Design Sciences at IUAV, Venice, where she is also involved with teaching.

CORALIE GOURGUECHON is an interdisciplinary designer, with a focus on tools and systems. She is interested in the representation of technology, which she deconstructs and simplifies, both on a physical and semantic level. Her work concerning electronic and digital devices aims to bring transparency to these black boxes through making their inner-working and conceptual process more accessible. Gourguechon is currently working as an Interaction designer at Fabrica.

FEMKE HERREGRAVEN's work explores which new material base, geographies and value systems contemporary financial technologies and infrastructures carve out. Works exist in digital media and as drawings, prints, sculptures, video and installations. Recent group exhibitions include *Simon Denny: TEDxVaduz redux*, T293, Rome and online as part of the *Extinction Marathon*, Serpentine Galleries, London (all 2014); *Globale Infosphere*, ZKM, Karlsruhe; *Algorithmic Rubbish: Daring to Defy Misfortune*, SMBA; *Extension du domaine du jeu*, Centre Pompidou, Paris; *Art In The Age of… Planetary Computation*, Witte de With, *Migration Matters*, Boijmans van Beuningen, Rotterdam; *All of This Belongs to You*, V&A Museum, London; *Dark Ecology*, Norway/Russia, (all 2015); *Conversation Piece*, Transmediale, Berlin; *Neoliberal Lulz*, Carroll / Fletcher, London; *Grand New*, Future Gallery, Berlin; *Digital Abstractions*, Hek, Basel; CCS Bard / Hessel Museum, NY (all 2016).

ANDRÉS JAQUE is the founder of the Office for Political Innovation, an international architectural practice, author of awarded projects including 'Plasencia Clergy House,' 'House in Never Never Land,' 'TUPPER HOME,' 'ESCARAVOX' and 'COSMO MoMA PS1'. They have been awarded with the SILVER LION to the Best Research Project at the 14th Venice Biennale, the Dionisio Hernández Gil Award, London Design Museum's Designs of the Year, Mies van der Rohe Award (finalist) and Architectural Record's Designers of the Year. Andrés Jaque, Phd Architect (ETSAM) and Alfred Toepfer Stiftung's Tessenow Stipendiat, is Professor of Advanced Architectural Design at the Columbia University GSAPP and Visiting Professor at Princeton University SoA. His books include include *PHANTOM, Mies as Rendered Society, Different Kinds of Water Pouring into a Swimming Pool, Dulces Arenas Cotidianas* and *Everyday Politics*.

MARTTI KALLIALA is an architect whose work focuses on the intersection of technology, social innovation and built form. He recently curated and organized the symposium *Ultimate Exit* in collaboration with the Van Alen Institute in New York, conceived as a part of Kalliala's long-term research initiative on technologically enabled and spatially articulated forms of exodus, autonomy and sovereignty. Other projects in this cycle of work include the installation *ExoStead* exhibited at Home Works 7, Beirut 2015 and the six-part video piece *Exitscape* (2015), made in collaboration with artist Daniel Keller. He is the editor and co-author of *Solution 239–246, Finland: The Welfare Game* (Sternberg Press, 2011) and a regular contributor to *Harvard Design Magazine* and other journals.

KËR THIOSSANE, founded in Dakar in 2002, is a civic platform seeking to connect the development of digital art practices to other social areas such as education and training, creative industries, citizenship, ecology, and urbanism. This platform seeks to develop exchanges and collaborations with other African organizations, forging links with other continents, especially with the Global South. In 2003, with the participation of the Canadian *Foundation Daniel Langlois pour l'art, la science et les nouvelles technologies*, the association opened a "digital public space" to provide activities overcoming the consumption and fascination for the Internet fostered by the existence of many cybercafes in Senegal. In 2008, Kër Thiossane started to organize the *Afropixel Festival*, the first African Digital Art Festival to promote the use of free software in connection with civic practices in Africa.

BOUCHRA KHALILI is a Moroccan-French artist. Born in Casablanca, she later studied Film at Sorbonne Nouvelle and Visual Arts at the École Nationale Supérieure d'Arts de Paris-Cergy. She lives and works in Berlin and Oslo. Working with film, video, installation, photography, and prints, Khalili's practice articulates language, subjectivity, orality, and geographical explorations. Each of her projects investigates strategies and discourses of resistance as elaborated, developed, and narrated by individuals, often members of political minorities. Khalili's work has been internationally exhibited, including *The Mapping Journey Project*, solo exhibition, MoMa, Museum of Modern Art, New York (2016); *Foreign Office*, solo show at Palais de Tokyo, Paris (2015); "Garden Conversation," solo show at MACBA, Barcelona (2015), among many others.

DR ADRIAN LAHOUD is an architect, researcher and educator. Prior to being appointed Dean of the School of Architecture at the Royal College of Art, Adrian Lahoud was Director of the Urban Design Masters at The Bartlett School of Architecture and served as Director of the MA programme at the Centre for Research Architecture, Goldsmiths. He received his PhD from the University of Technology Sydney where taught for a number of years while running an award winning architectural practice. His dissertation titled 'The City, the Territory, the Planetary' explores the concept of scale. He has written extensively on questions of climate change, spatial politics and urban conflict with a focus on the Arab world and Africa.

L.E.FT is a New York/Beirut based architectural office, comprised of architects Makram el Kadi and Ziad Jamaleddine. The office is dedicated to examining the intersections of cultural and political productions as they relate to the built environment. The partners combine their practice with research studios they conduct at Columbia's GSAPP in New York. Lawrence Abu Hamdan is an artist, "private ear," and currently a fellow at the Vera List Center for Art and Politics at the at the New School, NYC. His works are part of collections at MoMA New York, Van AbbeMuseum Eindhoven and the Arts Council, England.

JILL MAGID is a New York-based artist and writer. She has had solo exhibitions at the South London Gallery, London, Berkeley Museum of Art, California); Tate Modern; Whitney Museum of American Art, New York; Gagosian Gallery, New York; and the Security and Intelligence Agency of the Netherlands. She is an Associate of the Art, Design and the Public Domain program at the Graduate School of Design at Harvard University, and a 2013–15 fellow at the Vera List Center for Art and Politics. Her works are included in the collections of the Whitney Museum of American Art and the Walker Art Center, among others.

ANA NAOMI DE SOUSA is a filmmaker and journalist from London (UK) who has lived and worked in Brazil, Angola and Cape Verde. She collaborates with the Forensic Architecture project based at Goldsmiths, University of London. PAULO MOREIRA is an architect based in Porto (Portugal) and a researcher at the CASS School of Architecture (London, UK). He is the co-coordinator of The Chicala Observatory, a research project based at Agostinho Neto University (Angola) [www.paulomoreira.net]. PÉTUR WALDORFF is an academic based in Reykjavík (Iceland). He holds a PhD in Social Anthropology from McGill University (2014) and is a researcher at the Nordic Africa Institute (Sweden) in the project Masters or Migrants? The New Portuguese Migration to Angola.

PA.LAC.E was co-founded by Valle Medina and Benjamin Reynolds. Medina is an architect graduated of ETH Zürich D-ARCH. Reynolds received a diploma with honours from the Architectural Association (London). They have been design fellows at the Van Eyck Academie (Maastricht) and at the Koneen Säätiö Foundation (Helsingfors). Pa.LaC.E recently won the first prize at the 50th Central Glass Award (Tokyo). Their work has been shown at the CCCB (Barcelona), the BCA (Boston), BAK (Utrecht), and the Architecture Foundation (London), amongst others. They have also contributed to printed and online publications including *EP* (Sternberg Press), the *Guardian, Ecocore* (London) and *Spéciale'Z* (Paris). Their first major monograph is slated for publication in late 2016 with Cooperative Editions (New York). Pa.LaC.E is currently based in Zürich and London.

MARTHA ROSLER is an artist based in New York. Rosler interrogates diverse issues ranging from war and security to the landscapes of everyday life, especially as they affect women. Some of her best-known works deal with the geopolitics of dispossession and entitlement, beginning with her antiwar photomontages entitled *House Beautiful: Bringing the War Home* (c. 1967–72) and her photographic work *The Bowery* in two inadequate descriptive systems (1974–75). Her project *If You Lived Here…*, a cycle of exhibitions and forums on housing, homelessness, and the built environment, was held at the Dia Art Foundation in New York in 1989. Her collected writing, *Decoys and Disruptions*, was published by October Books and MIT Press in 2004. Her most recent volume, *Culture Class* (e-flux, Sternberg Press, 2013) centers on artists and gentrification. PELIN TAN is a sociologist and art historian based in Mardin, Turkey. She is an Associate Professor of Architecture at Mardin Artuklu University, contributor to The Silent University—an educational platform for and by refugees and migrants, Visiting Associate Professor at the School of Design, Hong Kong PolyU (2016), and a fellow of the ACT Program at the School of Architecture and Urban Planning, MIT. Tan is a member of Artıkişler video collective. She is the curator of *Turkey*, part of the Actopolis project (Goethe Inst. Athens, 2015 - 2017). Lead author of "Towards New Urban Society"–IPSP (Edited by Saskia Sassen & Edgar Pieterse, 2015–2017). Tan participated at Lisbon Architecture Triennial (2013), the Montreal Biennial (2014), and the Istanbul Biennial (2007, 2015).

OMA is a leading international partnership practicing architecture, urbanism, and cultural analysis. OMA's buildings and masterplans around the world insist on intelligent forms while inventing new possibilities for content and everyday use. AMO, a research and design studio, works in areas beyond architecture that today have an increasing influence on architecture itself: media, politics, renewable energy, technology, publishing, fashion. BENGLER is an Oslo-based digital invention studio. Central to their practice is the continuous exploration of communicative and expressive affordances of technology. In their 20-year collaboration, they have worked in television, museum audio-visuals, mobile games, social media, and installation artworks.

ROTOR, founded in 2005, is a Brussels-based group working on material flows in the construction industry. On a practical level, Rotor handles the coordination of large-scale salvage operations of reusable materials, and the conception and realization of design and architectural projects. On a theoretical level, Rotor develops critical positions on design, material resources, and waste through research, exhibitions, writings and conferences. In 2015, Rotor was awarded with the Global Award for Sustainable Architecture, and the Rotterdam Maaskantprijs voor Jonge Architecten.

ESTUDIO SIC is an architectural office founded in 2004 by Esaú Acosta Pérez, Mauro Gil-Fournier Esquerra and Miguel Jaenicke Fontao. Their activity is centered on the investigation and development of questions related to the dynamics of architecture and landscape transformations. Together they also established Vivero de Iniciativas Ciudadanas, VIC, in 2007. VIC is an open-source platform, a collaborative project orientated to promote, spread, analyze and support initiatives and critic processes throughout all the civic society layers. The platform has a special incidence in the territory, the city and the public space.

SIGIL is an Arab collective based in Beirut and New York City. Through a series of specific interventions, they seek to explore the simultaneously marvelous and terrifying metamorphoses of the Arab landscape that is the stake and site of contemporary and historical struggles. Since 2014 they have been engaged in building rural architectures of resistance in Syria including water-wells and electricity generating windmills. They remain condemned to hope. In addition to multiple collaborators, the core group is comprised of Khaled Malas (architect and art historian), Salim al-Kadi (architect), Alfred Tarazi (artist) and Jana Traboulsi (designer and illustrator).

EINAR SNEVE MARTINUSSEN and JØRN KNUTSEN are designers, researchers and Associate Professors at the Oslo School of Architecture and Design (AHO), where they teach interaction design and explore culture and technology. They are also Design Directors at the Oslo based design studio Voy, specializing in interactive products, media and invention. Since 2007, Martinussen and Knutsen have been part of a network of designers exploring emerging technologies as part of the *Immaterials* project, along-side Timo Arnall, Jack Schulze and Matt Jones; they have been creating films, animations, and photographs that investigate the invisible digital world. As designers they seek to reveal the materials behind the 'seamless' technologies that make up our everyday experience, and in doing so empower others to question, critique, re-imagine and re-make.

SPUTNIKO! is a British/Japanese artist who creates machines, music and video exploring issues surrounding technology and pop culture. A graduate of London's RCA, Sputniko!'s graduation piece *Menstruation Machine—Takashi's Take* (2010), a device simulating bleeding and pain to mimic that of menstruation to allow men to understand the experience, was the first of her projects which caused ripples in the contemporary art scene and was just months later exhibited at the Museum of Contemporary Art Tokyo. Since then, Sputniko! has continued to produce playful, cross-boundary work presented internationally in museums such as New York MoMA and Museum of Contemporary Art.

SUPERSUDACA (A word combination of virtue and insult for Latin immigrants) was founded in Rotterdam in 2001. It is a collective operating worldwide in pressing themes of urban research, architecture practice and contemporary culture with branches in Buenos Aires, Lima, Curacao, Brussels, Santiago, Montevideo and Rotterdam. Supersudaca addresses subjects such as Mass Tourism in the Caribbean, China's emerging global presence, Latin American social housing experiments and direct spatial interventions amongst others. They have been recognized with the best entry award at the International Architecture Biennale of Rotterdam and were network partners of The Prince Claus Fund.

SUPERUNION ARCHITECTS is an office focusing on architectural production in a contemporary metropolitan and cultural context. The office was established in 2011 by architects Johanne Borthne and Vilhelm Christensen. In 2011 Superunion Architects won the open competition to redesign Asker Square, and in 2012 the office won the competition for Ruten in Sandnes in collaboration with Space Group. In 2014 Wallpaper Magazine named Superunion Architects among twenty of the world's best young practices in their Architects Directory. Founding partners Johanne Borthne and Vilhelm Christensen received Anders Jahre's Prize for Young Artists in 2014.

PAULO TAVARES is an architect and researcher based in Quito/São Paulo. Spanning various media and conceptual formats, his designs and visual art work has been exhibited in various venues worldwide, most recently at BAK- basis voor actuele kunst, ZMK Center for Art and Media, Haus de Kulturen der Welt, and PROA-Buenos Aires. Tavares has collaborated with many international publications and has lectured widely in different contexts and locations, including ETH-Zurich; Haus de Kulturen der Welt; São Paulo Biennale, and Ireland Biennale. He is currently a visiting scholar at the Cornell University College of Architecture, Art, and Planning, and prior to that was a visiting scholar at the School of Architecture at Princeton University. Tavares also taught at the Centre for Research Architecture at Goldsmiths, University of London, and is a fellow researcher in the project Forensic Architecture.

UNFOLD, founded in 2002 by Claire Warnier and Dries Verbruggen, is a design studio that has continuously orchestrated conversations between the fields of physical making and digital form-giving. As ad-hoc interpreters who speak neither the mother-tongue of computer code nor that of traditional craft, they create unusual scenarios of confrontation between the two in which the untranslatable, the idiomatic and the unexpected are foregrounded against a field of normative design practice. At the same time, each of their projects

also explores one of myriad tangents of the digital-analogue divide, building a line of inquiry into issues such as technical proficiency, intellectual property, and the uniqueness of the identical object.

In Residence Exhibition Participants

ILA BÊKA and LOUISE LEMOINE are artists, filmmakers, producers and publishers. They have been working together for the past 10 years mainly focusing their research on experimenting with new narratives and cinematographic forms in relation to contemporary architecture. Their films have been widely shown in some of the most prestigious international cultural institutions such as the Venice International Architecture Biennale (2008, 2010, 2014), Centre Pompidou (Paris), Palais de Tokyo (Paris), Barbican Center (London), Triennale (Milan, Italy), among others. In 2016, the Museum of Modern Art (MoMA) in New-York has acquired their entire work for its permanent collection.

JAMES BRIDLE is an artist, writer, and publisher based in London, UK. His writing on literature, culture and networks has appeared in magazines and newspapers including *Wired, Domus, Cabinet,* the *Atlantic,* the *New Statesman,* the *Guardian,* the *Observer* and many others, in print and online. His artworks have been commissioned and exhibited worldwide and on the internet. He lectures regularly at universities, conferences and other events. His formulation of the New Aesthetic research project has spurred debate and creative work across multiple disciplines. His work can be found at http://booktwo.org.

MATILDE CASSANI studied Architecture at Politecnico Di Milano and at Univesidade Tecnica de Lisboa, then Architecture and Urban culture ("Metropolis") at the CCCB (Centro de Cultura Contemporània de Barcelona) and UPC (Universidade Politecnica de Catalunya) in Barcelona/Spain (post-graduate degree). She holds a PhD in Spatial Planning and Urban Development. After her graduation Cassani worked as a consultant for the Deutsche Gesellschaft für Technische Zusammenarbeit (GTZ) (German association for technical cooperation) in Sri Lanka, where she started developing a research project on the post tsunami reconstruction. She currently teaches at Politecnico di Milano and at Domus Academy and works on a research project on "Holy Urbanism." Her practice reflects the spatial implications of cultural diversity.

ERIKSEN SKAJAA ARCHITECTS, founded by Arild Eriksen and Joakim Skajaa in 2010, is an architecture firm based in Oslo. In addition to architectural projects ranging from interiors to urban planning, the office has worked on a series of projects where public participation and social responsibility is a key element. It believes that architecture is a social act and considers the ability to create places to meet others as a most important skill. The office also runs the publishing company Pollen Forlag. Publications include the interview-based magazine *Pollen* as well as the cartoon on co-housing Tett, ikke trangt.

FIRST OFFICE was formed in downtown Los Angeles in 2011 by Anna Neimark and Andrew Atwood. Their interests bridge gaps between conceptual and practical domains of architecture and include work on representational techniques, the production of exhibition design, and the mundane realities of construction. Over the last five years, they published widely—in *Log, Perspecta, Thinkspace, Future Anterior*—and exhibited in galleries, including the Pacific Design Center and the MAK Center for Art and Architecture in Los Angeles, the Architectural League of New York, and the Graham Foundation in Chicago. In 2015, First Office published a short book of writing, titled *Nine Essays,* with Graham Foundation's Treatise Press, received the Architectural League Prize, was selected Best of 2015 Young Architects by the *Architect's Newspaper,* and became a finalist in the MoMA PS1 Young Architects Program.

HUSOS is a platform for the development of both spatial interventions and research projects in architecture and urbanism. Husos' working themes include the study of everyday life, the development of micro-community actions and their expansive power, the impact of social imaginaries and affections on the urban environment and alternative models to question anthropocentrism. Based in Madrid, Husos operates regularly between Spain and Colombia. Their work has been featured in the Biennale di Venezia, The Architecture Biennale of Rotterdam, the Fundación Tápies, and is part of the permanent collection of the FRAC Centre in France and the Historisch Museum of Rotterdam.

EMEKA OGBOH works primarily with sound and video to explore ways of understanding cities as cosmopolitan spaces with their unique characters. His work contemplates broad notions of listening and hearing as its main focus, and his sound recordings also consider the history and aural infra-structure of cities, with Lagos of Nigeria in particular. These Lagos recordings have produced a corpus of work entitled *Lagos Soundscapes,* which he has installed in different contexts. Ogboh has exhibited both in Nigeria and in several international venues. They include, The 56th Venice Biennale; The Centre for Contemporary Art, Lagos; Dak'Art Biennale, Dakar; The Louisiana Museum of Modern Art, Denmark; Seattle Art Museum, Seattle; Museum of Contemporary Arts Kiasma, Helsinki and Rauternstrauch-Joset-Museum, Cologne. Ogboh is a DAAD (Deutscher Akademischer Austauschdienst) 2014 grant recipient, and the co-founder of the Video Art Network Lagos.

AHMET ÖGÜT is a sociocultural initiator, artist, and lecturer. Working across a variety of media, Ögüt's most recent institutional solo exhibitions include *Forward!*, Van Abbemuseum, Eindhoven and *Happy Together: Collaborators Collaborating*, Chisenhale Gallery, London. Ögüt was awarded the Visible Award for the Silent University and the special prize of the Future Generation Art Prize, Pinchuk Art Centre, Ukraine among others. He co-represented Turkey at the 53rd Venice Biennale together with Banu Cennetoğlu (2009). EMILY FAHLÉN works as a mediator at Tensta Konsthall in Stockholm. With collaboration as a core value and method, she manages both local and international art projects, working in the borderland between the organizational, curatorial and pedagogical. She is also the coordinator for *The Silent University* Stockholm; an autonomous knowledge platform by refugees, asylum seekers and migrants.

THE STATE is a publishing and editorial platform based out of Dubai, interested in post-colonial vernaculars, South-South relations, alternative futurisms, Dubai, and the future weird. Its online iteration includes essays, music and more. Its publishing arm produces themed print volumes or book objects. RAHEL AIMA is a writer based in Dubai, editor-in-chief at THE STATE and a contributing editor at *The New Inquiry*. Her research interests include Internet aesthetics, non-Western futurisms, and the #gcccccc. AHMAD MAKIA is writer, researcher and editor-in-chief at THE STATE. He is currently living in Dubai. Deepak Unnikrishnan is a writer from Abu Dhabi (and now, Chicago). He is the winner of the inaugural Restless Books Prize for New Immigrant Writing. He is an editor at THE STATE.

TRANSBORDER STUDIO is a young architecture practice based in Oslo, Norway. Transborder Studio is run by Øystein Rø, Espen Røyseland and Håvard Skarstein. The office is engaged in a wide array of projects and collaborations of various scales and formats. Through the art and architecture gallery 0047, the founders of Transborder Studio have been involved in a series of projects in the Russian-Norwegian borderland and the High North.

Intervention Strategies Teams

NABIL AHMED is a researcher and educator. Recently he has participated in Cuenca Biennale (2014) and the Anthropocene Project (2013–14) at the HKW. He has written for *Third Text, Volume,* and *Forensis: The Architecture of Public Truth* and many other publications. He holds a PhD from the Centre for Research Architecture at Goldsmiths. He is a lecturer at The Cass School of Architecture at London Metropolitan University. Dámaso Randulfe is an architect, writer and designer. His research is concerned with questions of territorial and environmental conflict as mediated by material and visual narratives. His current work includes a forthcoming publication and seminar series around Aby Warburg's Mnemosyne. He is a lecturer at The Cass Faculty of Art, Architecture and Design, London Metropolitan University.

BOLLERÍA INDUSTRIAL / FACTORY-BAKED GOODS is a Madrid-based design studio established in 2012 by Ana Olmedo, Enrique Ventosa, Eugenio Fernández, and Paula Currás. They propose new critical alternatives to question the narratives that ignore social, political or collective issues. Their work focuses on design and communication for art, architecture, and diverse cultural agents.

CHER is CAITLIN BLANCHFIELD, GLEN CUMMINGS, JAFFER KOLB, FARZIN LOTFI-JAM, and LEAH MEISTERLIN. Together this New York-based group of architects, designers, planners, and writers investigate publicness, intimacy, exchange, sharing, and occasionally, over-sharing.

OPEN TRANSFORMATION are a group of two architects and a sociologist who combine their common interest in urbanism, housing and asylum issues with experience from activism, research and site specific projects. Elisabeth Søiland is currently doing a PhD on the relationship between architecture, health and well-being in the workplace. Silje Klepsvik, partner in Kaleidoscope, engages in the thematics of transformation through international projects and is trained in processing local resources through site-specific projects. Åsne Hagen has a background of activism and project work regarding asylum issues and served four years as a lay member of the Immigration Appeals Board (UNE).

RUIMTEVELDWERK (RVW), founded in 2013, is an interdisciplinary collective based in Antwerp-Leuven-Brussels that focuses on the urban environment and its users. The collective's intention is to study 'the place' of vulnerable populations in the public sphere. By approaching questions on minorities in public spaces, RVW aims to open up the boundaries of the architectural discipline and rethink the architect's role. In partnerships, we explore the interfaces between architecture, urbanism, sociology, history, art and activism. RVW's working methods consist of implementing strategies/scenarios as layers onto urban contexts — by means of architectural incentives. These activations intensify social networks and make socio-spatial frameworks negotiable.

The Embassy

THE DEMOCRATIC SELF-ADMINISTRATION OF ROJAVA is the coordinating body of the Rojava region, including its many communes and municipalities, involved in the project of self-governance known as "Stateless Democracy." The autonomous region, since its foundation, has invested in alternative cultural spaces, such as the Tev-Çand cultural centers and the Rojava Film Commune. In 2015, the Democratic Self-Administration commissioned Dutch artist Jonas Staal and his organization "New World Summit" to construct a new public parliament for the autonomous region. Construction in the city of Derîk began in August 2015, and the building will be inaugurated in late 2016.

STUDIO JONAS STAAL is the studio of artist Jonas Staal and, in addition to him, includes several members and long term collaborators: producer Younes Bouadi, programmer Renée In der Maur, architect Paul Kuipers, and designer Remco van Bladel. Since 2012, the studio has run the artistic and political organization "New World Summit" that builds alternative parliaments for stateless and blacklisted organizations from all over the world. In 2014, Studio Jonas Staal developed a first temporary embassy with Moussa Ag Assarid of the National Liberation Movement of Azawad (MNLA) — the New World Embassy: Azawad — situated in BAK, basis voor actuele kunst, in Utrecht, The Netherlands.

The Academy

THE ACADEMY is a Forum organized by the Oslo School of Architecture and Design (AHO), and lead by a team comprising: Gro Bonesmo, Professor at the Institute of Urbanism and Landscape and founder of Oslo based architectural firm Space Group; Erik Fenstad Langdalen, Professor and the Head of Institute of Form, Theory and History, and principal of the architectural firm Erik Langdalen arkitektkontor; Marianne Skjulhaug, Professor and Head of Institute of Urbanism and Landscape; and Léa-Catherine Szacka, Assistant Professor at the Institute of Form, Theory and History, and The Academy's Project Manager.

The After Belonging Conference Speakers

AMALE ANDRAOS is Dean of Columbia University's Graduate School of Architecture, Planning and Preservation (GSAPP) and co-founder of WORKac, a New York based architectural and urban practice with international reach. In addition to Columbia, Andraos has taught at universities including Princeton University School of Architecture, Harvard Graduate School of Design, University of Pennsylvania Design School, and American University in Beirut. Her publications include *Architecture and Representation: The Arab City* (April 2016), *49 Cities, Above the Pavement, the Farm!* and numerous essays. WORKac is focused on re-imagining architecture at the intersection of the urban, the rural and the natural. It has achieved international recognition and was named the 2015 AIA New York State Firm of the Year.

ATELIER BOW-WOW is a Tokyo-based firm founded by Yoshiharu Tsukamoto and Momoyo Kaijima in 1992. The pair's interest lies in diverse fields ranging from architectural design to urban research and the creation of public artworks, based on the theory called "behaviorology." The practice has designed and built houses, public and commercial buildings mainly in Tokyo, but also in Europe and the USA. Their urban research studies have led to the experimental project 'micro-public-space', a new concept of the public space, which has been exhibited across the world. Atelier Bow-Wow's works are produced from the concept "architectural behaviorology." The word "behavior" includes behaviors of natural elements such as light, air, heat, wind, and water, but also human behavior and buildings' behavior. "Architectural behaviorology" investigates the mechanism of these behaviors and aims to synthesize them in order to optimize their performance in its specific context. It focuses the repetitive, rhythmical, shareable aspects of behavior, and shifts the architectural design from individuality based to commonality based.

NEGAR AZIMI is the Senior Editor of Bidoun, an award-winning magazine on the arts and culture of the Middle East and its diaspora. Her writing has appeared in *Artforum, Frieze, Harper's, The New York Times Magazine, The New York Times Book Review, The New Yorker,* and *The Wall Street Journal Magazine* among other places. Azimi was a 2014–2015 fellow at the New York Public Library's Cullman Center for Scholars and Writers and a 2012 winner of the Andy Warhol Foundation's Arts Writers Grant. She sits on the boards of Artists Space in New York, the Beirut-based Arab Image Foundation, and Orhan Pamuk's Museum of Innocence in Istanbul. She is an advisor for the 2017 Whitney Biennial, was an advisor for the 2013 Venice Biennale, and continues to serve on Art Dubai's curatorial advisory committee. She is at work on a book, to be published by Penguin Random House, about the 1960s and 70s in Iran.

GRO BONESMO is founder of Oslo-based architectural firm Space Group, and a professor at the Oslo School of Architecture and Design. She is a graduate of NTNU, and has a Masters from GSAPP Columbia University. Bonesmo has been a guest lecturer and critic at the Royal Danish Academy of Copenhagen, KTH Stockholm, Berlage Institute, Harvard and Columbia Universities. From 1990, she worked for 8 years with OMA, finally as the Design Architect in charge of the Dutch Embassy in Berlin. Space Group has received architectural awards for works such as Varner House, Signal Media house, Aker Brygge, and won first prize in international competitions for Tromsø Ferry Terminal, Brattøra Conference Hotel and New Oslo S. At the Venice Biennale 2014 Gro Bonesmo was the co-curator and exhibition architect for the Nordic Pavilion.

GRETE BROCHMANN is professor of sociology, Department of Sociology and Human Geography at the University of Oslo. She has published several books and articles on international migration; sending and receiving country perspectives, EU policies, welfare state dilemmas as well as historical studies on immigration. She has served as a visiting scholar in Brussels, Berkeley, and Boston. In 2002 she held the Willy Brandt visiting professorship in Malmo, Sweden. Brochmann is currently head of a governmental commission on long term consequences of comprehensive immigration.

MICHEL FEHER is a philosopher who has taught at the École Nationale Supérieure, Paris, and at the University of California, Berkeley. He is the publisher and a founding editor of Zone Books, NY (in 1986) as well as the president and co-founder of Cette France-là, Paris (in 2008), a monitoring group on French immigration policy. He is the author of *Powerless by Design: The Age of the International Community* (2000) and the co-editor of *Nongovernmental Politics* (2007), with Gaëlle Krikorian and Yates McKee. He co-authored, with Cette France-là, *Xénophobie d'en haut: le choix d'une droite éhontée* and *Sanas-papiers et préfets: la culture du résultat en portraits* (2012). He most recently co-edited "Europe at a Crossroads" (with William Callison, Milad Odabaei and Aurélie Windels), the first issue of *Near Futures Online* (Zone Books, 2016).

PER HEGGENES is the CEO of IKEA Foundation, the philanthropic arm of the Swedish home furnishings company, IKEA. As CEO, Heggenes sets and drives the Foundation's funding and innovation strategies, and is a tireless advocate for children living in some of the world's poorest communities. Since becoming the Foundation's first CEO in 2009, Heggenes has presided over the Foundation's evolution into a global, grant-making philanthropy that funds programs in more than 35 countries. In 2012, Heggenes was appointed to the UN Commission on Life-Saving Commodities for Women and Children by UN Secretary-General, Ban Ki-moon, who created the commission to increase access to lifesaving medicines and health supplies for the world's most vulnerable people. Previously, Heggenes was the Global Head of Corporate Affairs for the shipping and logistics company Wallenius Wilhelmsen Logistics. Before joining WWL, he was the UK President and CEO for the global public relations firm Burson-Marsteller and Co-CEO for Europe. He also held different global roles for Burson-Marsteller based in their New York headquarters. Per served in the Norwegian Air Force and graduated from the University of Augsburg in Germany with a "Diplom Oekonom" (MBA).

JUAN HERREROS is an architect and educator, Chair Professor and Director of the Thesis Program at the Madrid School of Architecture, as well as a Professor of Architecture, Planning and Preservation at GSAPP-Columbia University in New York. Throughout the years he has held numerous lectures, courses and international seminars as well as research workshops and published a significant number of books, texts and interviews in different formats. Herreros' office estudioHerreros is conceived as a collective platform through which he pursues his professional, pedagogical and research activity. His theoretical work is focused on the re-definition of the contemporary architectural practice and its dialogue with other disciplines. His professional work has been displayed in several individual and collective exhibitions, and are widely published and awarded. estudioHerreros is currently working on projects in Spain, Norway, France, Morocco, Mexico, Uruguay, Argentina and Colombia. Juan Herreros has received the International Fellowship of the RIBA (Royal Institute of British Architects) among other distinctions.

THOMAS HYLLAND ERIKSEN is a professor of social anthropology at the University of Oslo and author of many relevant books within his field. In particular, he is known for his research on identity politics and cultural dynamics in complex societies and globalization. Currently he is leading a research project on the local reaction to global crisis. In the summer of 2016, he will publish *Overheating: An Anthropology of Accelerated Change*.

YASMEEN LARI is the first female architect and among the best-known architects of Pakistan. She graduated from Oxford School of Architecture (now Oxford Brookes University) and was elected member of the Royal Institute of British Architects (RIBA) in 1969. Lari retired from architectural practice in 2000. Her architectural works are included in the *Phaidon Books UK* (2013) publication devoted to the best examples of 20th century architecture. Lari is included among the 60 Women who have contributed the most towards UNESCO's objectives. In recognition of her services towards architectural profession, heritage safeguarding and humanitarian assistance,

the President of Pakistan awarded Lari *Sitara-i-Imtiaz* (The Star of Distinction) in 2006 and *Hilal-i-Imtiaz* (The Crescent of Distinction) in 2014. Yasmeen Lari co-founded Heritage Foundation of Pakistan in 1980 with her husband, noted historian Suhail Zaheer Lari, with the purpose of undertaking research on and safeguarding Pakistan's cultural heritage. The Heritage Foundation of Pakistan is the 2002 recipient of the UN Recognition Award for the promotion of culture and peace. Lari was elected president of the Institute of Architects Pakistan in 1978 and was the first chairperson of Pakistan Council of Architects and Town Planners in 1983. Since the 2005 earthquake in Pakistan, Lari devised several programs for post–disaster communities, which formed the basis for the World's largest zero carbon footprint shelter-program, as well as disaster-compliant low-cost initiatives, fostering pride and self-reliance among local communities.

REINHOLD MARTIN is Professor of Architecture in the Graduate School of Architecture, Planning, and Preservation at Columbia University, where he directs the Temple Hoyne Buell Center for the Study of American Architecture. At Columbia, Martin is a member of the Committee on Global Thought as well as the Institute for Comparative Literature and Society. He was also a founding co-editor of the journal *Grey Room*. Martin's research concentrates on two related areas: the material, architectural, and urban history of knowledge infrastructures, and thinking the contemporary city under globalization. He approaches architectural history as a form of media history, governed by networks, systems, technical infrastructures, and biopolitical processes. To this he brings a theoretical perspective on the city that combines aesthetics with political economy. For over a decade Martin was a partner in the firm of Martin/Baxi Architects. Martin's books include *The Organizational Complex: Architecture, Media, and Corporate Space* (MIT Press, 2003), *Utopia's Ghost: Architecture and Postmodernism, Again* (Minnesota, 2010), and *Multi-National City: Architectural Itineraries* (with Kadambari Baxi, Actar, 2007). Currently, Martin is working on a history of the nineteenth century American university as a media complex, as well as a set of theoretical essays on the contemporary city, which is forthcoming as *The Urban Apparatus: Mediapolitics and the City* (Minnesota, 2016).

KARL OTTO ELLEFSEN is Professor in Architecture and Urbanism at the Oslo School of Architecture and Design (AHO). He was heading the school from year 2000–2014 and has been taken part in the development of the OAT in different roles, exhibitor as well as head of the Board, from the start in year 2000. He is currently the president of EAAE (European Association for Architectural Education). Karl Otto Ellefsen is a practicing architect in the field of Urbanism and has produced scholarly writing within the History of Urbanism and Urban Design, Urban Strategies, Architectural Theory and Architectural Critique. He has all his professional life been doing research on Nordic urbanization. Since the 1990s he has together with PhD students done studies in East-African cities and is currently heading a research project on the transformation of Chinese Villages and the urbanization of rural China.

IPPOLITO PESTELLINI LAPARELLI is a partner at OMA since 2014, where his work has a focus on preservation, scenography, and curation. Currently Ippolito is leading the transformation design of the Fondaco dei Tedeschi in Venice, the renovation of Kaufhaus des Westens (KaDeWe) in Berlin. Recent work includes *Monditalia*, a multi-disciplinary exhibition at the 2014 Venice Architecture Biennale; scenography for the Greek theater of Syracuse in Sicily (2012); and the co-curation of *Cronocaos*, OMA's exhibition on preservation at the 2010 Venice Architectural Biennale. Through collaborations with different brands including Repossi, Galleries Lafayette, Knoll, and Prada his activity extends to research, product design, temporary installations, and publications. Since 2010, Ippolito is responsible for a range of AMO projects with Prada, including the stage design for the brand's fashion shows and special events, and the art direction of videos. He contributes to exhibition design for Fondazione Prada, with projects such as *When Attitudes Become Form: 1969/2013* and *Serial Classics* (2015). Ippolito holds a Master of Architecture from the Politecnico di Milano.

JOHN PALMESINO and ANN-SOFI RÖNNSKOG are architects and urbanists. They are the founders of Territorial Agency, an independent organization based in London that combines architecture, analysis, advocacy and action. Their work focuses on the transformations of the relation between polities and space. Projects include *The Coast of Europe* a multi-year research on the urbanisation processes of the European project, and 'North'— an investigation in contemporary forms of geopolitics, sovereignty and resource exploitation in the Arctic. Together with Armin Linke and Anselm Franke, Palmesino and Rönnskog initiated the *Anthropocene Observatory*, a documentary practice combining photography, films, interviews, spatial analysis, and exhibitions to outline the development of the Anthropocene thesis. The *Anthropocene Observatory* has been displayed over two years at the HKW Haus der Kulturen der Welt in Berlin, at BAK baasis voor actuele kunst in Utrecht and in the framework of the exhibition *Exo-Evolution* in ZKM | Karlsruhe. *Museum of Oil* is exhibited at ZKM in parallel to the exhibition *Reset Modernity!*, curated by Bruno Latour. Palmesino and Rönnskog are directors of AA Territories Think Tank, a research centre at the AA Architectural Association in London, where they also teach Diploma Unit 4. Palmesino is research fellow at Goldsmiths, Centre for Research Architecture, London, and Rönnskog at AHO, The Oslo School of Architecture and Design.

TYIN TEGNESTUE ARCHITECTS was established in 2008. The office has completed several projects in developing areas of Thailand, Burma, Haiti and Uganda. Solutions to real and fundamental an architecture where everything serves a purpose—an architecture that follows necessity. By involving the local populace actively in both the design and building of their projects, TYIN are able to establish a framework for mutual exchange of knowledge and skills. All materials used in TYIN´s projects are collected close to the sites or purchased from local merchants. TYIN is currently run by Masters of Architecture Andreas G. Gjertsen and Yashar Hanstad, and has its headquarters in the Norwegian city of Trondheim. TYIN has won several international awards and their projects have been published and exhibited worldwide.

KJETIL TRÆDAL THORSEN is a frequent lecturer internationally, and from 2004 to 2008 he was professor of architecture at the Institute of Experimental Architecture at the University of Innsbruck, Austria. Both with Snøhetta and individually he has received numerous prizes including amongst others: Mies van de Rohe Prize— for the Opera and Ballet in Oslo in 2009; Aga Khan Award for Architecture— for the Alexandria Library in 2004; Commander of The Royal Norwegian Order of St.Olav in 2008; International Fellowship Honor from the Royal Institute of British Arch-itects (RIBA); Honorary Doctor NTNU, Norway; and Honorary Member of the Norwegian Architects Association (NAL) in 2011.

EYAL WEIZMAN is an architect, professor of spatial and visual cultures and director of the Centre for Research Architecture at Goldsmiths, University of London. Since 2014 he is a global professor at Princeton University. In 2010 he set up the research agency Forensic Architecture (FA). The work of FA is documented in the exhibition and book *FORENSIS* (Sternberg, 2014). In 2007 Weizman set up, with Sandi Hilal and Alessandro Petti, the architectural collective DAAR in Beit Sahour/Palestine. This work is documented in the book *Architecture after Revolution* (Sternberg, 2014). In 2013 he designed a permanent folly in Gwangju, South Korea which was documented in the book *The Roundabout Revolution* (Sternberg, 2015). His other books include *The Conflict Shoreline* (Steidl and Cabinet, 2015), *Mengele's Skull* (Sternberg, 2012), *The Least of all Possible Evils* (Verso, 2011), *Hollow Land* (Verso, 2007), and *A Civilian Occupation* (Verso, 2003). Weizman is on the editorial board of *Third Text, Humanity, Cabinet* and *Political Concepts* and was on the advisory boards of the ICA in London and B'Tselem in Jerusalem, amongst others. He studied architecture at the Architectural Association in London and completed his PhD at the London Consortium/Birkbeck College.

EVEN WESTVANG and SIMEN SVALE SKOGSRUD are principals of the Oslo-based digital invention studio BENGLER. Central to their practice is the continuous exploration of communicative and expressive affordances of technology. In their 20-year collaboration, they have worked in television, museum audio-visuals, mobile games, social media, and installation artworks. Arguing to make more public data available, Westvang built a series of experimental data visualisations. This spawned a long-term focus on data analysis and visualization within BENGLER, and they are currently exploring the use of deep learning in describing and organizing the collections of the Norwegian National Museum. Skogsrud is the original creator of Grbl, the "industry standard" motion control system for maker-grade 3D printers, milling machines and laser cutters. BENGLER has also developed a radically simplified design for 3D printing.

# Oslo Architecture Triennale Members, Partners, and Supporters

Members

Associated Members

Public Benefactors

Acción Cultural Española, Spanish Embassy in Oslo, Norwegian Embassies in Ankara, Beijing, Copenhagen, London, Paris, Rome, Sarajevo, Seoul and Washington; Norwegian Consulates General in New York and Tel Aviv

General Partner      Main Partners

Partners

  Graham Foundation

Media Partners

Supporters

Norconsult–Arkitektur og design, LPO arkitekter, Lund Hagem Arkitekter, SJ Arkitekter, Institut français de Norvège, Vitra, Consentino, Electroniks, Bot Factory, Istituto Italiano di Cultura, Oslo

Local Partners Institutions

Danish Architecture Center, The Barents Institute | UiT, Avinor, Norwegian People's Aid and Makers Hub Oslo

*After Belonging: The Objects, Spaces, and Territories of the Ways We Stay in Transit.*

This book is the result of a two-year long research carried out by Lluís Alexandre Casanovas Blanco, Ignacio G. Galán, Carlos Mínguez Carrasco, Alejandra Navarrete Llopis, Marina Otero Verzier, Chief Curators of the Oslo Architecture Triennale 2016.

Published on the occasion of the sixth edition of the Oslo Architecture Triennale, titled *After Belonging: A Triennale In Residence, On Residence and the Ways We Stay in Transit.* September 8–November 27, 2016.

Editors: Lluís Alexandre Casanovas Blanco, Ignacio G. Galán, Carlos Mínguez Carrasco, Alejandra Navarrete Llopis, Marina Otero Verzier

Copyeditor: John Wriedt
Translator: Stig Oppedal

Graphic Design: This is our work (Megan Feehan),
with design intern Cem Eskinazi

Printing and Binding: Kösel, Altusried-Krugzell, Germany

Published by Lars Müller Publishers
Zurich, Switzerland
www.lars-mueller-publishers.com

First published September 2016
© 2016 Oslo Architecture Triennale & Lars Müller Publishers
ISBN 978-3-03778-520-1
All rights are reserved.
Printed in Germany

Distribution worldwide: Lars Müller Publishers
Printed on Amber Graphic 120gsm, MultiArt Silk 135gsm, and Munken Print White 90gsm.
Typeset in Neue Haas (using all the diacritical marks available in the extended set), Univers Std., and Atlas Grotesk Typewriter.

Special thanks to Elise Jaffe and Jeffrey Brown for their generous support for this publication.

_____

*After Belonging: A Triennale In Residence, On Residence and the Ways We Stay in Transit.*

Chief Curators and Exhibition Designers : Lluís Alexandre Casanovas Blanco, Ignacio G. Galán, Carlos Mínguez Carrasco, Alejandra Navarrete Llopis, Marina Otero Verzier

Graphic Design: This is our work (Megan Feehan)

Design and Production Associates: Juan Ruiz Antón and Paola Simone García

Design Assistant: Kamilla Csegzi
Research Associate: Jess Ngan
Assistant: Nick Oelrich

OAT Team: Hanna Dencik Petersson, Alexandra Cruz, Kaia Hødnebø Nelson, Ingrid Dobloug Roede, Christina Holter Endresen, Elisabeth Cavallini Fevik, Bjørg Borgenheim, Hege Maria Eriksson

OAT members of the board: Nina Berre, Ole Gustavsen, Pål Stephensen, Caroline Støvring, Trude Gomnæs Ugelstad, Fredrik Winther.

Thanks to all members, partners, collaborators, supporters and all the staff at OAT's member organisations without whom the Oslo Architecture Triennale 2016 could not have taken place. Thanks also to the local partner institutions for the Intervention Sites: Danish Architecture Center, The Barents Institute | UiT, Avinor, Norwegian People's Aid and Makers Hub Oslo.

Thanks to Thomas Keenan, Jesse M. Keenan, Reinhold Martin, Felicity D. Scott, Mark Wasiuta, and Mabel O. Wilson for their feedback on the project from its inception, as well as to Nabil Ahmed and Dámaso Randulfe, Morgen Alexandre Ip, Agnès Arquez-Roth, David Basulto, Gro Bonesmo, Anna Maria Bogadottir, Shumi Bose, Lindsay Bremner, Luis Callejas, Arild Eriksen, Emily Fahlén, Eva Franch i Gilabert, Bjarki Gunnar Halldórsson, Homa Hasan, Tor Inge Hjemdal, Tom Hjertholm, Juulia Kauste, Erik Fenstad Langdalen, Katya Larina, Giulia Maci, Thomas Mcquillan, Leah Meisterlin, Henrik der Minassian, Eva Moksnes Vincent, María Nicanor, John Palmesino and Ann-Sofi Rönnsko, Øystein Rø, Julian Rose, Joakim Skajaa, Søren Smidt-Jensen, Brett Steele, Léa-Catherine Szacka, James Taylor-Foster, Ragne Thorshaug, Füsun Türetken, Sigurd Tvete, Manijeh Verghese, Karin Åberg Waern, Christine Wergeland Sørbye, Mark Wigley, Nafisa Yeasmin for their support and feedback in the public discussions organized in preparation for the Triennale. Thanks also to Amale Andraos, Lucia Allais, Shahdeh Ammadi, Siri Aronsen, Andrés Asturias, Ethel Baraona and César Reyes, Barry Bergdoll, Guus Beumer, Brett Beyer, Damon Casarez, Beatriz Colomina, Alastair Donald, Luis Fernández-Galiano, Mathis Herbert, Juan Herreros, Adrian Lahoud, Ivan López Munuera, Matti Ostling, Spyros Papapetros, Javad Parsa, Christopher Pierce, Luis Rojo, Enrique Walker. Warm thanks to our family, partners, and friends, including Rafael Baena, Maria Luisa Blanco, Meritxell Casanovas, Jaume Casanovas, Rafaela Carrasco, Inés Galán, Armando García, José Ignacio González, Begoña and Blanca González, Sebastian Langham, Scott Langham, Patricia Llopis, Albert Luong, Roberto Mínguez, Begoña Mínguez, Alberto Mínguez, Leo Mínguez-Navarrete, Salvador Navarrete A., Salvador Navarrete Ll., César Otero, Brenda Otero, Javier and Paula Ruiz-Castillo, and Isabel Verzier.